A CONCORDANCE-DICTIONARY

TO

THE YOGA-SUTRA-S OF PATANJALI

AND

THE BHASHYA OF VYASA

Owing to the antiquity and rarity of this book, certain pages are regrettably absent, and readability is compromised due to the blurring of the original text. If you possess any insights regarding the availability of these missing sections, kindly inform us. Your assistance is crucial in ensuring the completion of this significant work for the benefit of future generations.

A CONCORDANCE-DICTIONARY
TO
THE YOGA-SUTRA-S OF PATANJALI
AND
THE BHASHYA OF VYASA

BY

BHAGAVAN DAS

GYAN

Published by

Gyan Publishing House
5, Ansari Road
Daryaganj, New Delhi-110002
Phone: 011-47034999, 9811692060
E-mail: books@gyanbooks.com

Distribution Network
gyanbooks.com
India, USA, Canada, UK, Australia

ISBN: 978-93-6208-711-9 (PB)
First Published, 1938

2nd Impression 2024

Printed at: Gyan Press, Delhi.

A CONCORDANCE-DICTIONARY TO THE YOGA-SUTRA-S OF PATANJALI AND THE BHASHYA OF VYASA

Author: BHAGAVAN DAS

योग-सूत्र-भाष्य-कोषः

A CONCORDANCE-DICTIONARY

TO

THE YOGA-SŪTRAS OF PAṬANJALI

AND

THE BHĀSHYA OF VYĀSA

OTHER WORKS BY DR. BHAGAVAN DAS

THE SCIENCE OF THE EMOTIONS, 3rd. edition.

THE SCIENCE OF SOCIAL ORGANISATION, OR THE LAWS OF MANU, 2nd. edn., Vols. I & II; (Vol. III *in preparation*).

THE SCIENCE OF THE SACRED WORD, OR THE PRAṆAVA-VĀḌA OF GĀRGYĀYAṆA, 3 Vols.

THE SCIENCE OF RELIGION, OR THE PRINCIPLES OF SANĀṬANA VAIḌIKA ḌHARMA.

KṚṢHNA, A STUDY IN THE THEORY OF AVAṬĀRAS.

MYSTIC EXPERIENCES, OR TALES FROM THE YOGA VĀSISHTHA.

ANCIENT *versus* MODERN SCIENTIFIC SOCIALISM.

THE ESSENTIAL UNITY OF ALL RELIGIONS.

THE SCIENCE OF THE SELF, OR THE PRINCIPLES OF VEDANTA-YOGA.

ANCIENT PSYCHO-SYNTHESIS *versus* MODERN PSYCHO-ANALYSIS, (*in preparation*).

ANNIE BESANT AND THE CHANGING WORLD.

COMMUNALISM; ITS CAUSE AND CURE.

ANCIENT SOLUTIONS OF MODERN PROBLEMS.

THE ETHICO-PSYCHOLOGICAL CRUX IN POLITICAL SCIENCE AND ART.

THE PSYCHOLOGY OF CONVERSION.

SAMANVAYA *(in Hindi)*.

PURUSHĀRTHA („ ; *in preparation)*.

PRAYOJANA („ ; „).

Etc.

To be had of the Theosophical Publishing House, Adyar, Madras; or, The Indian Book Shop, Benares.

ॐ

योग-सूत्र-भाष्य-कोषः

A CONCORDANCE-DICTIONARY

TO

THE YOGA-SŪṬRA-S OF PAṬANJALI

AND

THE BHĀSHYA OF VYĀSA

BY

BHAGAVAN DAS

(M. A., Calcutta University; D. Litt., hon. cau.,
Benares University; D. Litt., hon. cau.,
Allahabad University).

THE KĀSHĪ VIDYĀ-PĪTHA

BENARES.

1938.

FOREWORD

Some thirty-five years ago, the wish came to me to study the *Yoga-Sutra-s of* Patanjali, and the *Bhashya* thereon of Vyasa, in the original Samskrt.

But I was very busy, in those years, with the work of the Central Hindu College of Benares; which had been founded in 1898, by Mrs. Annie Besant and Indian colleagues, to form a centre for the rationalisation, liberalisation, and solidarisation of what is now called 'Hinduism'.

This 'Hinduism' is obviously something very degenerate now. Formerly it was Vaidika Dharma, 'the Religion of Knowledge, of Spiritual and Material Science', 'Scientific Religion'; Arya Dharma, 'the Noble Religion', 'the Religion of the Philanthropic and Noble-minded'; Sanatana Dharma, 'the Eternal Religion', 'the Religion of the Eternal Spirit, the Supreme Universal Self'; Bauddha Dharma, 'the Religion of Buddhi, Rational Intelligence', 'Rational Religion'; Manava Dharma, 'the Religion of Man, the child of Manu the Thinker', 'the Human and Humane and 'Humanist Religion'. It was a spirituo-material, psycho-physical, scientific, far-sighted, comprehensive Code of Individuo-Social and Socio-Individual Life; a scheme of a fourfold Educational-Political-Economic-Industrial Organisation of the whole Human Race, calculated to secure, for that Race, the maximum happiness possible, individual and social, this-worldly and other-wordly, here and hereafter. But for some centuries now it has been, and is today, an unsightly heap of conflicting superstitions, a dazing turmoil of hundreds of struggling sects, mostly senseless, some foul also (as, indeed, unhappily, are the other great living religions too, though in a lesser degree); its followers, an amazing jumble, a jostling welter, of between two and three thousand mutually 'touch-me-not', mutually exclusive, mutually abusive, petty castes, sub-castes, and yet further sub-divisions, to the fifth or sixth degree, all utterly disorganised.

The honorary secretary-ship of the Board of Trustees and the Managing Committee of the institution was placed upon my shoulders. We were all working hard, Mrs. Besant hardest of all, to build up the college and make it a fit instrument for realising our ideal, viz., gradually restoring the old 'order' in place of this disorder, of re-organising the disorganised.

The hundreds of branches of the Theosophical Society, dotted all over India, in the large and small towns, became committees for collecting funds. This was one main cause of such success as was achieved. Part of my duties was to go round, in the winters, with the President of the College, Mrs. Besant, on the tours she made to enlist sympathy and secure financial aid.

In such conditions, I was not master of my time. I could not arrange to study the original Aphorisms and Commentary systematically, day after day, with a Pandit acquainted with the 'traditional' meanings.

Also, the subject has fallen into neglect among the Pandit-scholars of Benares, because of lack of the requisite earnest inclination for such a difficult thing as 'Yoga'; which, moreover, is a matter, not only of theoretical discussion and intellectual argumentation, but of heart-discipline, mind-control, persistent introspection, and 'practical exercises' of other kinds as well. And, even as regards the theoretical part, the *Bhashya* of Vyasa, in particular, has been largely avoided by the Pandits, for centuries perhaps, because of its often peculiar syntax and strange and obscure diction. I am told by a friend who has specialised in Buddhist literature, that it has points in common, with the earlier Buddhist works in Samskrt. This is not surprising when we remember that Buddha studied Sankhya and Yoga with Alara Kalama and Rudraka Rama-putra, in the course of his strenuous search for Truth. Buddhist writings have practically not been touched for six or seven centuries now by the orthodox Pandits. It is no wonder then that they should find the style of the *Bhashya* not easy to follow; Samskrt style having taken a rather different direction after the disappearance of Buddhism from India, some time about the 12th century A.C.

A reliable teacher of even the theory, very much more the practice, was not easily available therefore, in the town of Benares; and I had neither the needed reckless courage of passionate seeking, nor the opportunity, to wander forth asearch in the jungles and the mountains for such a true teacher; though the air of even present-day India is full of rumours that such 'mystic persons' are to be found, not only in the distant and less accessible places, but even in the busy haunts of men, now and then, in disguises not easy to penetrate for the half-hearted seeker !

But though, unfortunately, I was not much more than half-hearted, nor gifted with any special mental capacity, yet my interest in the deep ultimate problems of philosophy and psychology was and is constitutional, unabateable, ever since I can remember. Life, without a 'philosophy of life', individual and social, has always appeared to me unsatisfying, ever since I have been able to think, at first semi-consciously, then more and more clearly, with the passing of the years. Right administration of human affairs, individual or social, planning out of the single life, organisation of the collective life, is impossible without right knowledge of the fundamentals of human nature, and of the origin, nature, meaning, purpose, and end of life. Sound practice is not possible without sound theory. So my studies in the whole subject, and my craving to know something of the theory, and if possible, a touch of the practice also, of the Yoga-system, as important part of the whole subject, persisted side by side with the need to attend to the executive work entrusted to me.

I decided to be content with an endeavour to learn, by myself, something of the Yoga-theory, from the recognised current main text-book, however obscure; and to do this by reading it over and over again, (it is a small book), in the intervals between the spells of other unavoidable work. I soon found that the technical terms, the peculiar Samskrt, the use of common words in uncommon ways and senses, created extra-ordinary difficulties in addition to those inherent in the subject. But it is well known that to see or hear an even wholly unknown word, written or spoken by others, in a number of varying contexts and situations, lightens up its meaning and makes it even familiar. That, indeed, is how we all learn our mother-tongues. I resolved to make a Concordance. This kind of work did not require continuous uninterrupted day by day application.

In the course of three to four years, by the end of 1907 or 1908 (—my memory is not clear now—), the manuscript was completed. It was full of defects. Bye and bye, I made a fair copy.

Then the work was put aside. Other work occupied me. Twenty years and more passed. The Central Hindu College had grown into the Benares Hindu University, (which was formally founded on 4th February, 1916, when the Great War was at its height), and had long passed into other management. Astonishing speed had been put on by human history all over the world. Its march had become an overwhelming rush. Extraordinary, undreamt of, events had actually occurred on gigantic scales. The World-War had been fought; empires had toppled over and been replaced by republics; an epidemic had killed more human beings in four months of 1918-1919 in India, than the Great War had in four years in Europe; leviathan Communism and titan Fascism-Nazism were glaring at each other and preparing to grapple in a greater World-War; diplomatic imperialistic Democratism was sitting on the fence, trying to play off the two against each other, primarily for its own self-defence, but always keeping one eye 'on the main chance' also. India too had been struggling more strenuously for politico-economic emancipation from subjection. The Civil Disobedience Movement was raging throughout the country in 1930 and again in 1932. My elder son had gone to prison for the second time, in the latter year, together with other members of the Kashi Vidya Pitha. This wholly non-official educational institution, of which I was President, then, (and which is now publishing this work), had been closed by, and was, then, in the custody of, the Police.

But the small private lives of individuals had to be lived and were being lived; small personal interests had to be looked after and were being looked after, when not directly made impossible to attend to; even while enormous events were shaking the human world like vast earthquakes; though to Mother-Nature, the destruction of some millions of human beings, or of a whole continent, or a whole planet or solar system, must be the same as the destruction of an ant-hill. India was fortunate, in this that here the violence was confined to the side of the Government only; and that too was perforce reduced to a minimum, because of the non-violence of the people. But on the other hand, there was a violent outbreak of engineered communal riots, accompanied with much murder, bloodshed, and destruction of property, in many towns, including Benares, especiallyin 1931.

To keep my mind occupied in some mind-resting work in the intervals between distractions and alarms of various kinds, I began, in 1932, to take the long-sleeping Concordance through the press.

It was not merely a Concordance. It was a lexicon also. I had endeavoured to explain each complete word, simple or compound, in English; very doubtful though I frequently was, of the accuracy of my explanations.

But, for various reasons, the work was interrupted after only 56 pages had been printed. I could not take it up again until this year, 1938; though the Civil Disobedience Movement was suspended by its leaders in 1934, and it was decided that the Indian National Congress should send members into the Legislature under the changing Constitution. I had to attend to some other more urgent literary work. I had also been forced into the Central Legislative Assembly of India by kind friends, from the beginning of 1935. Hence the interruption. I have been allowed by them to resign only now, barely in time. I am very near the completion of my seventieth year, ailments increasing, all mental and physical powers decreasing. Study of Vedanta and Yoga is specially appropriate for the last years of life; though, if the principles thereof were studied early in life, particularly by statesmen and rulers, and *applied* by them to the administration of affairs, as in ancient India (—as I have endeavoured to explain in my other books, most recently in *The Science of the Self, or the Principles of Vedanta-Yoga)*, they would be found exceedingly useful for all, would appease and allay the raging passions of nations, point out the way of rational social organisation, minimise jealousies, hatreds, competitions, maximise co-operation, between all peoples, and save them from the horrors of war, and the scarcely lesser horrors of perpetual preparation for war, and hairbreadth escapes from outbreak of universal war, such as the world has experienced on the 30th September, 1938—an escape secured, for the moment, by the disruption of Czecho-slovakia.

I have now managed to take the rest of the work through the Press, in the belief that it may perhaps be of some use to cognate souls feeling difficulties similar to mine. Naturally, I have been in somewhat of a hurry to 'wind up affairs', at this time of my life, and have not been able to give it as thorough a revision as I should have liked to. The work therefore remains full of all sorts of defects, omissions, wrong figures of reference, superfluous entries, erroneous interpretations. One merit only it can claim—that of a Concordance. The student of Yoga-Darshana has now, what was not available so far, the means (1) to readily find out all the places in which any word, whose uses he wishes to trace, has been used, (2) to compare the several uses, and (3) to decide the meaning for himself.

I should acknowledge the help received. Shri Hari Govinda Borvankar, then a student of the Kashi Vidya Pitha (founded by Shri Shiva Prasad Gupta), prepared another fair copy for the press, from the one made by me. I have made many revisionary changes in the English explanations in this last copy, and more in the proofs. Shri Mukundi Lal (to some extent), and again Shri Gopal Shastri (to a greater), both then belonging to the staff of the Kashi Vidya Pitha, tested this copy and detected some mistakes and omissions, in the entries and reference numberings, here and there, before I began revision. Maha-maho-padhyaya Pandit Gopinath Kaviraj, M. A, retired Principal of the Government Samskrt College of Benares, kindly consented to look through one proof and suggest modifications of the English explanations where they seemed desirable. It would have converted my diffidence into confidence, in offering the work to the student-public, if this arrangement could have been carried out. Unfortunately for the book, he was not able to scrutinise the proofs of more than one or two eight-page forms. He had to leave Benares repeatedly on distant journeys; and I could not keep the work pending. A promising young student of the Kashi Vidya Pitha, Shri Kumara-pala (alias Kanwar Lal) B.A., has helped me in the correction of proofs, with his younger and keener eyes. I offer gratitude to all these friends, in the due degrees.

I should mention, in conclusion, another effort which I made to ensure greater accuracy in the explanations. Shortly after he retired from the Vice-Chancellorship of the Allahabad University, some six years ago, I asked my dear old friend Maha-maho-padhyaya Dr. Ganganath Jha, M. A., D. Litt., to revise my Ms., After some correspondence, I even sent it on to him at Allahabad. But, as ill-luck would have it, he had a bad attack of influenza, shortly after, and returned the Ms. to me. Fortunately, he recovered, and was able to bring out a revised, or rather re-written, edition, in 1934, of his own English translation of the *Yoga Sutra* and *Bhashya.* I have made use of this to check my interpretations, where necessary; but, where left in doubt by it, have not hesitated to follow my own conjectures. Dr. Ganganath, at the end of the Preface to the new edition of his work, has encouraged me, and indirectly and affectionately put pressure upon me, to make haste with this Concordance, by speaking of it as "an important and instructive glossary-index of the terms used in the text of the *Yoga Bhashya*" which "is being put into shape and should, before long, appear as a companion-volume to this translation."

Many English renderings have been made of the *Yoga Sutras:* some, of the short and easy *Vrtti* or gloss upon them by Bhoja; three, that I have seen, of Vyasa's *Bhashya*, viz., by Dr. Ganganath Jha, by Pt. Ram Prasad, and by Mr. Woods. There are also a number of independent brief comments or running expositions of their purport; e.g. by Johnston, and by W. Q. Judge.; and a long one by Mrs. Alice Ann Bailey; all these are done more or less from what may be called the 'mystical' standpoint, which keeps superphysical super-human experiences in view, especially the one by Mrs. Bailey, which is often very suggestive. A recent one is by Miss G. Coster, which is incorporated in her book, *Yoga and Western Psychology, a Comparison,* (published in 1934, by the Oxford University Press, London). The title indicates the standpoint; the western psychology dealt with is the 'new psychology' of the several schools of psycho-analysis. A work of mine, *The Science of the Emotions*, is referred to in her chapter on "Patanjali's philosophy"; that book of mine may indeed be regarded as an extended commentary on a few of the Sutra-s, viz , ii, 3—9, 33; as two other books of mine, viz., *The Science of Peace* and *Pranava-Vada or The Science of the Sacred Word*, are attempts to work out i, 27—28.

In my interpretations, here, I have endeavoured to maintain the simple human psychological point of view, but without losing sight

(1) of the fact that nothing 'unfamiliar', 'ab-normal', 'super-physical', is or can be more wonderful than our familiar psycho-physical experiences of every day; and (2) of the maxim or axiom, that the Law of Analogy reigns supreme throughout Nature, that "as the small, so the large", "as the microcosm, the Kshudra-virat, so the macrocosm, the Maha-virat". Reasons for such views I have expounded in my other writings, mainly *The Science of Peace.*

That the subject of Yoga, (Suluk, in the language of Sufism; see my book on *The Essential Unity of All Religions*), in its different aspects, is beginning to 'occupy' even the 'professorial' or 'officially scientific' mind, as something serious and worth investigation, and not as merely 'juggling' and 'sleight-of-hand', (though, unhappily, most of its 'professional' exponents in India are undoubtedly frauds), is shown by works like Miss Coster's above-mentioned, and by passages like the following which occurs in Dr. Joad's *Guide to Modern Thought* (pub. 1933), ch. vii, 'Abnormal Psychic Phenomena': "To one and another, here and there, access may be permitted to the full *hidden powers of his own being.* Some may even have found a way of access for themselves, and by *discipline and meditation*, have learned to tap the *sealed store* of their innate vital endowment. It is in this direction that we may look for an explanation of the powers of the yogi and the mystic; and the humbler faculties of the crystal-gazer and the clairvoyant may be traced to the same source......Most reported cases of telepathic communication occur in times of *great mental stress*"; pp. 189-190.

Yoga may, not inappropriately, be defined as the Science and Art of intense Attention, *mental stressing,* of 'inhibiting', all distractions, and 'exhibiting' the mind, turning it towards, some one object, so exclusively that that object is necessarily reflected, imaged, in the mind, as a thing is in a mirror, or an object on the retina, when there is no veil between, and no disturbance or clouding or ruffling of the surface of the mirror or the retina. Yoga, (Skt. *yuj*, Lat. *jugare,* to 'join', to 'yoke', the mind to an object), is thus the essential of *all* educational work, simplest to most complex—'Attend !', 'Concentrate!'. Animal, 'freezing' to escape detection by hunting predacean, or crouching moveless to intensely watch prey before pouncing upon it; burglar, financier, diplomat, commander, *planning* a coup, or detective tracing a crime, sign by sign, in mind; child mastering its a, b, c; artist absorbed in painting or sculpting from morn till eve; scientific genius forgetting food and drink while intent on making great discovery; philosopher lost in thought for days and nights, determined to solve a problem; Rshi or Nabi or 'Son of God' seeing with opened 'inner eye' the happenings of distant past, present, future, even as the owner of a good radiophone can catch music or speech broadcast from any quarter of the globe, by 'tuning' the instrument properly:-all these are performing 'yoga'; only the objects, the purposes, the degrees of developement of intelligences and content of consciousness differ.

It has been well observed by E. Kapp, quoted by Maeterlinck in his *Life of the White Ant*, (p. 183), that "all our machines are merely organic projections, i. e. uncouscious imitations of models supplied by nature", in the organs of living animals, which serve the same purposes for the animals as the machines for man. Yoga-discipline, Yoga-training, Yoga-education, is intended to develope the powers latent, hidden, in seed, in man. If he succeeds in unfolding and exfoliating them, he may become largely independent of machines, may become Self-dependent and put aside sordid diplomacies and brutal wars, and achieve Spiritiual Fraternity and Equality, Social and Economic Equitability, Political Liberty.

Some friends ask, "Why have you tried to explain the Samskrt words in English, rather than Hindi, far more widely known in India, and your own mother-tongue ?". I have partly answered such censure' of my dear and patriotic Indian friends, at the close of the preface to my book on *The Science of the Emotions* (3rd. edn.). I may add a few words here.

When I first began literary work, over forty years ago, I felt sub-consciously, and since then have realised more and more clearly, that the Indian People have largely forgotten the true, liberal, far-reaching, and most helpful meanings of the most significant and most valuable words and phrases of Samskrt, and have put in narrow and misleading ones instead; and that these true meanings can be restored, sometimes directly, often indirectly, by study of modern western thought, through some one of the three or four most highly developed European languages, of which English is the nearest and most easily and fully available to Indians at present. The hereditary treasure-house of gems and jewels of spiritual and psychical science is ours; and the eyes are ours. But the eyes are blinded by the thick darkness of petty selfishness, narrow-mindedness, and fissiparous separatism; the gems and jewels are covered deep with dust and dirt, and the storehouse is filled with cobwebs, all created by what the *Yoga-Sutras* describe as the "five-jointed, evil-bearing, sorrow-laden, misery-bringing, 'original sin' of Primal Error and Untruth, Egoism, Lust, Hate, and Infatuate Clinging to the things of sense". To clear away the thick deposit of dust, dirt, and cobwebs, the strokes of the strong-sweeping brooms of western critical habit are needed; and to light up the darkness, the lamps and lanterns of modern extensive and intensive science, and of research in, and record of, History in the broadest sense (of the Purana-Itihasa), cosmogonic, biological, anthropological, sociological, economical, political, religious, is necessary. But we must not forget that these are only means; the eyes that will ultimately see, are and must be our own; and the gems and jewels of spiritual and psychological science are and will continue to be those left by the ancient seers and sages of Bharata-varsha; and left for the use of not only the Indian People, but of all mankind; for they were not motivated by any narrow nationalism but by Humanism; to them, all the branches of the Aryan Root-stock were equally their own descendants.

Perhaps that is why the Ultimate Mystery, which those Sages and Seers beheld with the 'vision-ary' inner 'third' eye of true Vision; which, in their records of Vedanta they have called Brahma and Param-Atma, "the infinite and Supreme Self"; and in the teachings of Yoga have named the Kevala Drashta and Chiti-Shaktih, "the One Seer of all, the Omni-scient, Omni-potent, Omnni-present Store-holder of all experiences, past, present, and future, the Principle of Universal Life and Consciousness";—that is why that Mystery has sent the western peoples, latest and most vigorous offshoots of the ancient Indo-Aryan Root-Race, back to the east generally and to India specially; so that both the eastern and the western latest descendants of that Root-Race may ultimately benefit by the contact and 're-union', after long partition and separation; however rough, unpleasant, painful in the beginning, however full of trials and tribulations, that re-union may have been. The vast amount of admirable industry and research that has been bestowed upon the Samskrt language and literature by the scholars of Britain, France, Germany, U. S. A., Russia; the permeation of cultured western thought by some of the deepest spirituo-psychical ideas and beliefs of the east; and the rapid corresponding absorption of western physical science and of the ways of living of the west by the intelligentsia of the east; these are proofs of the inherent affinity and attraction between the 'cousins' descended from the same Root-'ancestors'. Some persons talk of the difference between east and west. But it is even patent that each and every country is both east and west. America is east to Asia; Asia is east to Europe and Africa; Europe and Africa are east to America; Asia is west to America; Europe and Africa are west to Asia; America is west to Europe and Africa. The One Sun illuminates them all, turn by turn. The only difference, if any, is that of earlier and later, before and after, old and young. All lovers and well-wishers of Humânity cannot but wish and pray that there may be ever less and less antagonism and ever more and more sincere fraternisation between east and west.

I pray that this Concordance may be of greater service to those who consult it for help in understanding the ancient doctrines of Yoga, than the labor of compiling it has been to me, and I sincerely offer all good wishes to them.

Benares, 4-10-1938, A. C.
Vijayā Dashami,
18, Ashvina, 1995, Solar, A. Vikrama. BHAGAVAN DAS.

निवेदन

आलोचक सज्जन !

पतंजलि के बनाये योगसूत्र और व्यास नाम के विद्वान् के लिखे भाष्य के सब शब्दों की, वर्णमाला के क्रम से इस अनुक्रमणी और उन शब्दों की अंग्रेज़ी मे व्याख्या का, क्यों, कब, किस प्रकार से संकलन किया गया, इस की कथा अंग्रेज़ी मे लिखे 'निवेदन' मे कही है। थोड़े मे यह कि, इसमें, सूत्र और भाष्य का प्रत्येक शब्द जिस जिस स्थान मे आया है, उसका अंकन यहां कर दिया हैं; विविध सम्बन्धों मे अज्ञात शब्द का प्रयोग सुनने देखने से उसका अर्थ ज्ञात हो जाता है; सब मनुष्य अपनी अपनी मातृभाषा इसी प्रकार से सीखते हैं; योग के कठिन अप्रसिद्ध संशयितार्थ शब्दों के अर्थों का निर्णय इसी प्रकार से हो सकता है।

अपने हिन्दी-प्रेमी 'हिन्द-वासी' 'हिन्दी' भाइयों के लिये उसके कुछ अंश का रूपांतर हिन्दी शब्दों मे लिखता हूँ; विशेष कर इस हेतु से कि ऐसे कई प्रिय मित्रों ने मुझ से पर्यनुयोग (अभियोग, शिकायत) किया है कि तू अंग्रेज़ी मे क्यों लिखता है, हिन्दी मे क्यों नहीं।

उत्तर थोड़े मे यह है, कि भारत जनता को, अपने पूर्वजों के दोष से, और अपने पूर्व जन्म की भूलों से, 'चौदह वर्ष वनवास' के विविध दुःखों को भोग कर के ही, नये अनुभवों को प्राप्त कर के ही, प्राचीन ज्ञान का जीर्णोद्धार और प्र-णवी-करण साध कर के ही, 'राम-राज्य' प्राप्त हो सकेगा—ऐसी 'वासना वासुदेवस्य' जान पड़ती है। उसी 'वासना' ने पाश्चात्यों को पूर्व देशों मे, विशेष रूप से भारत मे, भेजा होगा; और इसी शुभेच्छा अनुग्रहेच्छा से, कि परस्पर गुण-ग्रहण, परस्पर दोष-मार्जन करें। दुर्भाग्यवश, अविद्यावश, दोनों के उत्कट दोषों के कारण, अब तक ऐसा कम हुआ, परस्पर दोष-ग्रहण बहुत हुआ। पर सर्वथा दोष-ग्रहण ही नहीं हुआ, गुण-ग्रहण भी कुछ हुआ। पाश्चात्य जातियां भी, अंग्रेज़, फ़रासीसी, जर्मन, रूसी, अमेरिकन, सब मूल आर्य जाति की ही शाखा प्रशाखा हैं; उनके विद्वानों को, आर्य जाति की मूल भाषा संस्कृत और उसके लौकिक वैदिक साहित्य की ओर, भारी आकर्षण स्वभावतः हुआ; "व्यतिषजति पदार्थानान्तरः कोऽपि हेतुः"; और जैसा परिश्रम उस पर, और उसके जीर्णोद्धार पर, और लुप्त ग्रन्थों के छपाने पर, उन्होंने किया, वैसा भारत मे, सायण-माधव के पीछे, चार सौ वर्ष से, नहीं हुआ, और अब उनके अनुकरण से ही होने लगा है। तथा, उपनिषदों के, गीता के, आध्यात्मिक भाव, पश्चिम के शिक्षितों मे फैले; और पुनर्जन्म, कर्म, इत्यादि के विचार वहां बहुतों ने अपना लिया। एवं, भारत मे, पाश्चात्य आधिभौतिक विज्ञान अपनाया गया है, अन्ध-श्रद्धा कम हुई है, नई नई गवेषणा करने की, परीक्षा करके विश्वास करने की, "पुराणमित्येव न साधु सर्वं" की, बुद्धि बढ़ी है। दार्शनिक ग्रंथों के, तथा इतिहास-पुराण, स्मृति, आदि ग्रंथों के, एवं वेदों के भी, प्रचलित अर्थों की इसी परीक्षा-बुद्धि से बड़ी जांच करने की आवश्यकता है; और पाश्चात्य वैज्ञानिक बल से, ऐसी जांच में सहायता देने वाली सामग्री भी बहुत एकत्र हो गई है, जो सायण-माधवादि के समय मे उपलब्ध नहीं थी। उनके शब्दों के मार्मिक, गूढ़, अर्थों का पता, बिना ऐसी जांच किये, नहीं चल सकता। पुराणों मे, वेदों मे, अर्थवाद और रूपक भरे पड़े हैं; उनके शब्दों का अब अक्षरार्थ ही कर लिया जाता है, और प्रश्न अथवा शंका करने पर

'नास्तिकता' का निश्शंक अध्यारोप किया जाता है। इनका तात्त्विक अर्थ समझने के लिये इधर उधर पुराणों मे, वेदों मे, निरुक्त में, ही, संकेत रख दिये हैं; पर उनकी ओर ध्यान नहीं दिया जाता; बिना बहुश्रुतता के इन संकेतों का पता नहीं लगता, और अर्थ का अनर्थ ही किया जा रहा है। "बिभेत्यल्पश्रुताद् वेदो मामयं प्रतरिष्यति"। वेद की, पुराण की, वंचना प्रतारणा हो रही है। यह 'बहुश्रुतता', विविध ज्ञान विज्ञान के शास्त्रों की जानकारी, इस काल मे, भारतीय को, बिना पाश्चात्य अंग्रेज़ी, फ़रासीसी, या जर्मन भाषा के ज्ञान के नहीं हो सकती।

निष्कर्ष यह, कि आंखें हमारी ही हैं, पूर्वजों के संचित परम्परागत रत्न भी हमारे ही हैं; पर आंखों पर क्षुद्रस्वार्थपरायणता, शीलाभाव, परस्पर भेदभाव का अंधकार छाया हुआ है; रत्नकोष रजस् तमस् की धूलिं के नीचे दबा, मलाच्छन्न, अदृश्य हो रहा है; रत्नागार में 'अविद्या-अस्मिता-राग-द्वेष-अभिनिवेश' की मकड़ियों के झाले भर रहे हैं। बिना पश्चिम से मार्जनी और दीपक मंगनी लिये, और उनसे अभी कई दशाब्दियों तक काम लिये, यहां का भेदभाव, ईर्ष्या, मत्सर, अहंकार का अंधकार, और यह क्षुद्रस्वार्थपरता दुःशीलता रूपिणी लूता का सर्वाच्छादक तन्तु, दूर नहीं होता देख पड़ता। पर, इसके दूर होने पर, अपनी ही आंखों से देखना होगा, अपने ही रत्न पहिचानने होंगे।

अंतःप्रेरणया, ऐसे भावों से, पहिले अनुद्बुद्ध अस्पष्ट अव्यक्त 'प्रसुप्त-तनु-विच्छिन्न' रूप से, और पीछे अधिकाधिक बुद्धिपूर्वक व्यक्त रूप से, भावित होकर, चालीस वर्ष से, संस्कृत भावों का, आंग्ल भाषा के द्वारा, जीर्णोद्धार करने का, अपनी अति क्षुद्र शक्ति और अत्यल्प बुद्धि के अनुसार, प्राचीन महाकारुणिक महावत्सल मन्वादि महर्षियों का हृदय से आवाहन शुश्रूषण करता हुआ, यत्न कर रहा हूँ। खेद सदा यह बना रहता है कि अपना ऐसा पुण्य नहीं, भाग्य नहीं, तपस् नहीं, शौच नहीं, हृदय मे शुद्धि और बल नहीं, ठीक ठीक स्वाध्याय भी नहीं, कि साक्षात् 'सिद्ध-दर्शन' प्राप्त हो जाता, और अधिक निश्चय के साथ इस कार्य को कर सकता। योग शास्त्र के विषय पर कुछ लिखना तो नितराम् धृष्टता ही है, मेरे ऐसे जीव के लिये, जो उसके किसी भी रहस्यांश को प्रत्यक्ष नहीं कर पाया है। प्रस्तुत प्रयत्न के लिये अपना आश्वासन इतने से ही कर लेता हूँ कि, स्वयं भाष्यकार ने लिखा है, "योगः समाधिः, स च सार्वभौमः चित्तस्य धर्मः"; क, ख, सीखते हुए बच्चे भी 'मनी-योग' करते हैं, और उनके शिक्षक उनसे समय समय पर कहते हैं कि 'ध्यान दो', 'मनो-योग' करो; इसी भाव से मैंने योग शास्त्र की ऊपरी बातों के आरम्भिक 'क', 'ख' को आप सीखने का प्रयत्न किया है; छापने का विचार इस लिये किया कि स्यात् मेरी ऐसी दशा में पड़े हुए अन्य किन्ही सज्जनों की इससे कुछ सेवा हो जाय।

संस्कृत भाषा सभी आर्य भाषाओं की प्रपितामही है। पर अति वृद्ध हो जाने के कारण निष्प्राण सी हो रही है। उसकी सन्तति रूप भाषाओं मे अभी वह सब 'संस्कार', 'परिष्कार', एक एक शब्द मे अर्थपूर्णता, आध्यात्मिकता, नहीं सम्पन्न हुई है जो 'संस्कृत' मे है; किन्तु नये शरीर मे प्राण अधिक है। वृद्ध प्रपितामही को अभी बहुत शताब्दियों तक आर्य कुटुम्ब की आदि-जननी के रूप से, मूर्त्तिमान् आशीर्वाद और वात्सल्य के रूप से, सादर, सस्नेह, उच्च स्थान पर बैठाये रहना और उससे उपदेश लेते रहना आवश्यक है; किन्तु नई पुत्रियों मे, जिनका प्राण वर्द्धमान है, सर्वांगीण सौष्ठव का सम्पादन, और उनका अलंकरण संस्करण

अधिकाधिक करते रहना भी आवश्यक है। 'अंग्रेज़ी' से 'हिन्दी' को इस कार्य मे सहायता मिल सकती है, मिली है, और कुछ काल तक मिलती रहेगी; उस सहायता को लेने से मुंह फेरना, बड़ी भूल होगी। मेरा निजी अनुभव है कि मुझ को कितने ही दर्शन, स्मृति, पुराण के प्राचीन संस्कृत शब्दों और वाक्यों के उन उदार भावों के पहिचानने में, जिनके स्थान पर अब अति संकुचित संकीर्ण अर्थ ही प्रसिद्ध हो रहे हैं, अंग्रेज़ी दर्शन, अंतःकरण शास्त्र, राज शास्त्र, समाज शास्त्र, इतिहास, विज्ञान आदि के ग्रन्थों से बहुत सहायता मिली, और यह भान हुआ कि, यद्यपि आधिभौतिक विज्ञान मे हमारे पाश्चात्य भ्रातृव्य बहुत आगे बढ़ गये हैं, परंतु उनसे अधिक आध्यात्मिक और समाजव्यवस्था संबंधी प्रज्ञान हमारी परम्परागत मंजूषाओं मे पड़ा है, यदि हमसे वह खोलते बनें। उनकी कुंजी बनाने मे हमको पच्छिम के विज्ञान से, और स्यात् उसी से, अन्यथा नहीं, सहायता मिल सकती है। तथा उनको भी, हमारी पुरानी मंजूषाओं मे से निकले प्रज्ञान से, प्रवर्त्तमान और प्रवर्धमान घोर राग-द्वेष के महा तमस् के महा भय से छूटने मे सहायता मिल सकती है। स्यात् इसी लिये 'वासना वासुदेवस्य' ने पूर्व और पश्चिम का भारत मे 'योग' किया है।

भवद्दासः

भगवद्दासः

काशी, विजयादशमी,
आश्विन, १९९५, वि०

NOTE

Of the Rules followed in Printing.

1. The words of the Aphorisms are printed in larger type.

2. Words, which are parts of compound words, are printed with dashes, before, or after, or on both sides, of them, according to their position in the compound. They are not explained in English, except rarely; the explanation will be found under the complete compound word, which may be traced by the figures of reference given.

3. The figures are for the chapter and the aphorism, or corresponding commentary.

4. Sometimes a word occurs repeatedly in the commentary on an aphorism; it is given only once in the Concordance.

5. Simple words of very frequent occurrence, like pronouns, conjunctions, indeclinables, which have no technical meaning, are not indexed completely; only one reference, for each of the four chapters of the work, is given.

6. English equivalents are usually not given for the declensional variants of the principal word, when its nominative singular has been explained.

7. Inverted single commas are used now and then to draw attention to the literal significance or the etymological identity; thus योग, *yoga*, Skt. *yuj*, Lat. *iugare*, to 'yoke' to 'join'; or स्नायु, *snayu* 'sinew'. Important words are begun with capitals.

ADDENDA ET CORRIGENDA

28. After "अविध्यत्, add "अविनाशिनाम्, iii. 13 Of the unperishing."

87. To explanation of "आभोगः", add " engagement; occupation. "

39. Below"—आलोचितः", insert "आवव्यः, आवव्यम् iii, 18".

39. After "—आशयः iv. 6", add "(आ + शी, to sleep). 'Sleeping' instinct; 'dormant' propensity; tendency; disposition; inclination; proclivity; bent; thought-root; wish-seed; embryonic idea; rudimentary desire; that which is meant (as in the English expression 'What do you mean ?', i. e., 'What is your real purpose ?'). (See IV. 9, *Bhashya* संस्काराः वासनाः आशयाः इत्यर्थः; and the separate words in this *Concordance*).

49. After "उपावर्त्तते", add " turns away; is finished; is satisfied. "

56. After "कर्म", add "desert, deservingness of reward or punishment earned by good or bad deeds respectively; also, in grammar, the object of an action, the accusative."

59. After "कल्पिता iii. 43," add " —कल्पितानाम् ii. 4. (Some editions read विकल्पानाम्, which seems erroneous).

62. After "कालः", for "iii 52", read "iii. 26, 52".

68. After "क्लिष्टाः", add "leading to pain; pregnant with misery; big with sorrow and suffering; hence 'sinful', 'erring from the right path."

74. To the explanations of "गुणाः", add "(See ख्याति, प्रकाश, प्रख्या, प्रवृत्ति, क्रिया, स्थिति ॥ गुणयंति, आमंत्रयति, आम्रेडयंति, आवृण्वंति, प्रलोभयन्ति, बहुलीकुर्वन्ति, पंचक्लेशात्मिकाभिः वासनाभिः जीवं वेष्टयंति, बध्नन्ति, इति गुणाः। Because they tempt and invite with their attractive qualities, over and over again, and create variety and multiplicity in place of unity and simplicity, and twine round the soul, the ego, and bind it in the chains of the five-fold, sin-bearing, misery-causing, desires, appetites, instincts, therefore are they called 'guṇa-s'. The verb-root गुण्, in Skt., has this threefold meaning, to tempt and invite, to repeat and multiply, and to twine round and enwrap).

79. To the explanation of "घोरम्", add "(This quality is connected with rajas).

79. After "चतुर्विधकल्पितानाम्", add "(Some editions read चतुर्विधविकल्पानाम्, which is not satisfactory).

80. After "चितिः", add "awareness; pure sentience; pure percipience; appercipience".

82. After "चित्तस्य", add, (Some editions omit this word in iv. 10).

96. After "—तर्क—", for "iii. 39", read "iii. 26, 39".

107. After "देशलक्षणभेदः", for "charactering works" read "characterising marks."

109. After "द्वीपेषु", "for contiments" read "continents."

111. After "धर्ममेधः", add (धर्मान् मेहति).

118. After "निमज्जति", for "iii.54" read "iii.45".

,, . Below "निमज्जति", insert "—निमंत्रणे iii.51".

123. After "—निर्भासः", add "iii. 17".

123. After "निर्विचारा", add "(सविचारा seems to mean meditation about an abstract concept, but in connection with some concrete embodiment, as, e.g., looking at a particular triangle drawn on paper, we may think about the properties of all triangles generally, i.e. of the abstract triangle. If so, then निर्विचारा may mean meditation about an abstract concept, without reference to any particular concrete embodiment of it, and covering all possible concrete forms of it, past, present, future. See also वितर्क...रूपानुगमात्)."

124. After "निर्वितर्का", add "(See also वितर्क...रूपानुगमात्)."

126. Above " पण्डिताः", insert "पण्डकः ii.24 (See षण्डकः)"; and "पण्डकोपाख्यानेन). ii. 24 (See षण्डकोपाख्यानेन)."

147-148. Strike out the explanation given of "प्रत्ययविवेकनिम्नस्य", and read instead, "of (the mind) inclining towards discrimination, of (itself as the locus of) cognitions or ideas, (from the apperceiving self; and no longer indiscriminately and deeply interested in worldly things)."

156. After "प्रातिभम्", add "(प्रति+भा, to shine out, to appear in a flash)."

175. After "मूढः", add "(This quality is connected with ṭamas)."

196. Col. 1, l. 20, for "p. 68", read "p. 35, 68."

198. For "—विनाशि", read "विनाशि."

236. After "सद्लक्षणभेदात्", "for ii. 53" read "iii. 53."

योगभाष्य-कोष।

अ

अंशः iii. 54 Part; portion.

अकरणं iii. 51

—अकरणात् ii. 23

अकर्त्तरि ii. 18 In the non-doer.

अकर्मण्यता i. 30 Unfitness for work. [real.

अकल्पिता iii. 43 Unimaginary;

अकस्मात् iii. 22 Without (perceptible) cause; 'why-less', without a why; suddenly.

अकार्ये ii. 52 In non-work, ill-work, sin.

अकुर्वतः iii. 51 Of the not-doing; of him who abstains.

—अकुशलयोः ii. 9

अकुशलानि i, 24 Un-skilful; unwell; non-good; evil.

—अकुशलाः iv. 30

अकुसीदस्य iv. 29 Of one who has no interest left.

अकृतभवनन्यासाः iii, 26 Who do not 'lay down' (ideate, mentally create) abodes.

अकृतार्थम् ii. 22 With its work not done, duty undischarged, purpose not achieved.

अकृत्वा iii. 51 Having not-made; having avoided.

—अकृष्णम् iv. 7

अक्रमम् iii. 54 Successionless; simultaneous; timeless; "Eternal Now."

अक्रमम् iii• 17

अक्रमोपारूढम् iii. 49 Not "mounted on", entered upon, succession; non-successive; synchronous; timeless.

अक्लिष्टच्छिद्रेषु i. 5 In the interstices or intervals between the sorrowless, sinless, (or emancipating moods of mind).

—अक्लिष्टाः i. 5

अक्षयम् iii. 51 Unperishing.

अक्षिपात्रकल्पम् ii. 15, 16 } Like the eye-socket.
अक्षिपात्रकल्पः ii. 15 }

अक्षिपात्रे ii. 15 In the eye-socket.

—अक्षी ii. 5

अगतिः i. 7 Motionless.

अगस्त्यवत् iv. 10 like the ṛshi Agastya.

अगृहीतस्वभावकम् iv. 16 Of unapprehended nature.

अगृहीता ii. 20 Un-apprehended.

अगोष्पदम् ii. 5 No-cow-hoof-puddle; no trifle (but a large space).

—अग्नि— ii. 19; iii. 17

अग्निः ii. 28; iii. 45; iv. 19 (**अग्रे नयति**, He who leads on in front) Fire.

अग्निवत् iv. 19 Like fire.
—अग्निना ii. 2; iv. 28
अग्निज्ञानस्य ii. 28 Of the knowledge of fire.
अग्निष्वात्ताः iii. 26 A race of ḍevas; (in the Purāṇas, a class of piṭṛs).
—अग्रहणात् i. 2
अग्रहणे iv. 19 In (the state of) or on non-apprehension.
अग्राह्यम् iv. 19 Inapprehensible.
अग्रीवः iv. 31 Throatless; without a neck,
—अग्रे i. 35; iii. 1; iv. 16
—अग्रेण iii. 45
—अङ्कुरस्य iv. 25
—अङ्ग—ii. 28, 40
—अङ्गम् iii. 7, 8
—अङ्ग—ii. 18
अङ्गमेजयः ii. 47 Body-tremor; restlessness of body generally, or of any limb.
—अङ्गमेजयत्व—i. 31
अङ्गमेजयत्वम् i. 31 Shaking of the body.
अङ्गानि ii. 29 (अङ्ग्, to go; to mark; अञ्ज्, to mark, to demarcate, define, depict, delineate, bring into relief. "The body is the soul made visible" See अञ्जन, and व्यञ्जक) Limbs; organs.
अङ्गानि i. 31
—अङ्गानि ii. 28; 29; iii. 1
—अङ्गारेषु ii. 33; iii. 51
—अङ्गित्वे ii. 18
—अङ्गुलिः iv. 31
अङ्गुल्यग्रेण iii. 45 With the finger-tip.
—अङ्गे ii. 40
—अचेतन—ii. 15; iv. 23
—अचेतनेषु ii. 5
अचेतनम् ii. 34; iv. 23 Unconscious.
अचेतना ii. 20 Unconscious,
अच्युताः iii. 26 One of the highest orders of gods; the "unfallen," the "un-procreating".
अजरम् iii. 51 Unaging.
अजापयः iii. 17 Goat's milk; (and also) "thou causedst to be conquered, or to be repeatedly recited." (A play upon a word).
अजिताधरभूमिः iii 6 One who has not conquered the lower stage.
अजिह्वः iv. 31 Tongueless.
अज्ञातः ii. 20; iv. 17 Unknown.
—अज्ञात—ii. 20
—अज्ञातम् iv. 17
—अज्ञान—i. 2; ii. 34
—अज्ञान—ii. 34
अज्ञाननिम्नम् iv. 26 Sloping to, inclining to, heading towards, Error.
अज्ञानम् ii. 34 Non-knowledge; igno-rance; wrong or false knowledge; ne-science; Error (due to misleading Desire, hence), Root-Desire.
—अञ्जन—iv. 9
—अञ्जनः i. 11, 43
—अञ्जनता—i. 41 (See अङ्गानि)

—अञ्जनस्य iii. 13

अञ्जनाभाः iii. 26 A race of high devas.

—अञ्जनेन ii. 4

—अणिमा—iv. 1

अणिमादिप्रादुर्भावः iii. 45 The appearance of 'atomicity' etc.; the development of the mystic power of becoming small as an atom.

अणिमाद्या ii. 43 Atomicity etc.

अणिमाद्यैश्वर्योपपन्नाः iii. 26 Possessed of the sovereign powers of assuming atomic size etc.

अणीयान् i. 43 Atomic; smaller; very small; infinitesimal.

—अणु— i. 40

—अणुः iii. 44; iv. 14

अणुः iii. 26, 45 Atom; small; minute.

अणुप्रचयविशेषात्मा i. 43 Of the nature of a special or peculiar agglomeration, grouping, combination, accumulation, of atoms. (Compare isomerism, isomorphism, allotropism).

—अणुभ्यः iii. 42

अणुमात्रम् i. 36 Only an atom.

अणोः iii. 26 Of an atom.

अण्डम् iii. 26 Egg; world-egg; world-system; orb; globe.

अण्डमध्ये iii. 26 In the middle of the world-egg or sphere.

अतदात्मा ii. 20 Not-that-natured; not having that nature.

अतद्रूपप्रतिष्ठम् i. 8 Established on, resting on, attached to, what is not the true form of that (viz., the object of knowledge) i. e., an erroneous belief or notion.

अतद्रूपप्रतिष्ठम् i. 43

अतपस्विनः ii. 1 Of the non-ascetic.

—अतल—iii. 26

अतः i 2; ii. 4, 20; iii. 23, 53; iv. 6, 9 etc. Hence.

—अतिक्रमात् iii. 13

अतिक्रान्तभावनीयः iii 51 Name of the Yogi of the fourth stage, who has passed beyond desires and meditations.

अतिक्रान्तसर्गादिषु i. 26 In past or previous manifestations, emanations, creations, cycles, etc.

—अतिक्रान्तं, न्तः, न्ताः iii. 13

अतिक्रामन्ति ii. 4 Overpass, pass beyond, avoid, escape; transcend.

अतिदीप्तेन ii. 33 By the very blazing, raging, rampant, furious.

अतिप्रसङ्गः iv. 21 Too much attachment; excessive addiction, ("too much of a good thing", proving too much, reductio ad absurdum).

अतिरिक्तम् ii. 18 Other than; going beyond; reaching beyond.

अतिवाहयन्ति i. 19 Pass; pass across; carry over; carry on.

अतिवाहितम् ii. 16 Carried through, tided over; exhausted.

—अतिवृत्तेः ii. 19

—अतिशय—i. 24

—**अतिशयम्** i. 25

—अतिशयः i. 50

अतिशयबलः iii. 46 Possessed of exceedingly great strength.

—अतिशयाः ii. 15; iii. 13

अतिशयैः ii. 15; iii. 13 (अति, much, more + शी, to sleep, to rest; "to rest or stand above another"). By or with excesses; by or with excellences.

अतिशय्यते i. 24 Is excelled, surpassed.

अतिशय्येते iv. 10 (Two) are surpassed.

अतिशायि i. 24 Excelling supremely.

अतीत—i. 25; ii. 19; iii. 13

—अतीत—iii. 36

अतीतम् ii. 16 (अति + इ to go) "Much-gone"; past; crossed beyond; transcending.

—अतीतः ii. 27

अतीतः iii. 13 Past

—अतीतत्वात् ii. 27

अतीतभावक्रमः iii. 15 The order, succession, *into* pastness, (क्रम = moving, proceeding, passing, into change). (The expression is obscure; some editions read अतीतभावः क्रमः)

अतीतलक्षणम् iii. 13 The quality of pastness, or having the quality of the past.

अतीतलक्षणयुक्तः iii. 13 Possessed of the characteristic of pastness.

अतीतस्य iii. 14, 15 Of the past.

अतीताः iii. 14 The past (pl:)

अतीतानागतम् iv. 12 The past and the "not-yet-come", i. e. the future.

अतीतानागतज्ञानम् iii. 16 Knowledge of the past and the future.

अतीतानागतप्रत्युत्पन्नम् iii. 54 Past, future, and present.

अतीतानागतवर्तमानेषु iii. 13 In the past, the future, and the present.

अतीतानागताः iv. 13 Past and future (pl.).

अतीतानागताभ्याम् iii. 13 By the past and the future.

अतीतान् iii. 22 The past; the departed.

—अतीताभ्याम् iii. 13

—अतीन्द्रिय—i. 25

—अतुल्य—ii. 18

अत्यन्तम् ii. 20, 40 Extremely, finally, wholly, entirely.

अत्यन्तभिन्नेषु i. 32 In the extermely different.

अत्यन्तमूढेषु ii. 9 In the utterly dull, inert.

अत्यन्तविधर्मा iii. 35 Of very different property or nature.

अत्यन्तविभक्तयोः ii. 6 Of (two) entirely separate or different.

अत्यन्तविरोधात् iv. 3 Because of extreme opposition.

अत्यन्तासंकीर्णयोः iii. 35 Of the

(two) extremely unallied, wholly unmixable.

अत्यंतासंकीर्णयोः ii. 6

—अत्यये ii. 34

अत्र i. 9; ii. 24; iii. 6; iv. 3, 19 Here.

अथ i. 1 Now; henceforth; herewith; hereafter.(Also 'but if').

अथ i. 12, 17, 18, 23, 24, 27; iii. 9, 44; iv. 4, 32

अदग्धबीजभावाः ii. 13 With their seed-nature unburnt, germinating capacity or seed-quality undestroyed.

अदर्शनम् ii. 23, 24; iii. 55 Non-vision; disappearance; non-cognition (of the Final Truth).

अदर्शनस्य ii. 23, 25

अदर्शनकारणाभावात् ii. 24 From absence of cause of non-vision (of truth).

—अदर्शना ii. 24

अदर्शनात् ii. 4 By or from or because of non-seeing, non-appearance.

अदर्शनाभावात् ii. 23 From absence of non-vision, disappearance of ignorance.

—अदिव्य—i. 15

अदृश्यः iii. 45 Invisible.

—अदृष्ट—ii. 12

अदृष्टजन्मवेदनीयम् ii. 13

अदृष्टजन्मवेदनीयः ii. 12, 13 To be experienced, to bear fruit, in some (future) birth now unknown.

अदृष्टजन्मवेदनीयस्य ii. 13

अदोषः iii. 13; iv. 33 "No-fault"; not-defective; faultless.

अद्राक्षम् i. 32 I saw; I have seen.

—अधर— iii. 6

अधरभूमिषु iii. 6 In the lower levels, planes, stages, grounds.

अधर्म—i. 2

—अधर्म—iii. 18

अधर्मम् iv. 3

अधर्मः iv. 3 Not-ḍharma; opposite of ḍharma or duty; sin.

अधर्मात् iv. 11

अधर्मापेक्षम् iv. 15 Looking to, depending on, in consequence of, due to, sin.

—अधर्मौ ii. 15

अधः iii. 31 Below.

अधस्तात् iii. 30 Below.

अधिकम् iii. 18 Greater; more.

—अधिकः iii. 13

अधिकस्य ii. 32

—अधिकार—i. 5; iv. 28, 34

—अधिकारम् i. 5, 50, 51; ii. 3; iii. 55; iv. 11.

अधिकारः ii. 23 (अधि, अधिकम्, more or specially + कृ, to do; more specific work). Title, right; function, office, province; appointed work, fixed duty; power, authority; urge, momentum; course.

अधिकारवशात् i. 19 By compulsion of function or urge.

अधिकारविरोधिनः i. 51 Hostile to functioning.

अधिकारविशिष्टम् i. 50 Function-defined; marked or characterised by a specific function.

—अधिकारा ii. 2, 24, 27

—अधिकाराः iii. 55

अधिकारार्थः i. 1 Having the purpose or significance of, being indicative of, the subject which is in hand (or is in possession of, or has the right and title to engage, attention).

—अधिकारे i. 19; ii. 10; iv. 11

अधिकृतम् i. 1 Taken up (as subject of treatment); installed, put in charge; put in office; placed on duty.

अधिकृत्य iv. 33 Having regard to; 'making' comparison with.

अधिक्रियेत iii. 14 May become entitled or subject to.

अधिगच्छति i. 29; iii. 25 (अधि + गम्, to go) Finds; approaches; reaches; goes up to; perceives; understands.

अधिगतः iv. 23 Understood, perceived, found,

—अधिगमः i. 29

—अधिगमः ii. 32; iii. 36

अधिगम्यते ii. 41 Is obtained; is understood.

अधिगम्यन्ते iii. 48 Are obtained; are achieved.

अधिमात्र;—अधिमात्र—i. 21, 22

अधिमात्रतीव्रः i. 22; ii. 34 Of exceeding intensity.

अधिमात्रतीव्रसंवेगस्य i. 22 Of him who possesses keen intensity of urge in the fullest degree.

—अधिमात्रत्वात् i. 22

—अधिमात्राः ii. 34

—अधिमात्राः ii. 34

अधिमात्रोपायः i. 21 Possessing means in excessive or fullest degree.

अधिमात्रोपायस्य i. 22

अधिमात्रोपायानां i. 21

—अधिष्ठातृत्वम् iii. 49

अधिष्ठानम् ii. 17 (अधि + स्था to stand) Standing upon or above; occupying.

—अधिष्ठाने ii. 5

अधिष्ठाय i. 25 Having occupied; presiding over; sitting on or above; inspiring.

अधीते iii. 17 (अधि + ई, to go, to approach) Studies.

—अधीनम् iv. 10

—अधीनः i. 12; ii. 15

—अधीना iv. 7

—अध्ययनम् ii. 1

अध्ययनम् ii. 32 "Going specially or more near"; approaching; understanding; close study.

—अध्यवसायकत्वात् ii. 20

अध्यात्मप्रसादः i. 47 The placidity of the 'subjective element'; the dawning of the inner light and joy which illuminates all; lucidity of mind.

अध्यारोपितसद्भावाः ii. 18 Assumed to have existence; having existence falsely imposed upon them; falsely imputed.

—अध्यास—iii. 17

—अध्यासात् iii. 17 (अधि + अस् to throw, to cast repeatedly, to superimpose).

अध्वनः iii. 13; iv. 12

अध्वभिः iii. 13

अध्वभेदात् iv. 12 Because of difference of way or path.

अध्वसु iii. 13

अध्वसंकरः iii. 13 Confusion or adulteration of paths.

अध्वा iii. 13 Path; way; road.

—अध्वानः iii. 13; iv. 13

अध्वानम् iii. 13

अनंगुलिः iv. 31 Fingerless.

अनतिक्रमात् iii. 13 Because of not over-leaping, not getting beyond.

अनतिक्रान्तम् iii. 13 Not crossed or passed beyond.

अनतिक्रान्तः iii. 13

अनतिक्रान्ताः iii. 13

—अनतिवृत्तेः ii. 19

—अनधिष्ठानम् ii. 17

अननुभूतक्रमक्षणा iv. 33 Without experience of the succession of moments, or without passing through sequential moments.

अननुभूतमरणधर्मकस्य ii, 9; iv, 10 Of him who has not experienced the function of dying.

—अननुरोधी i. 47

—अनन्त—ii. 47

अनन्तम् i. 36 End-less.

अनन्तः iv. 33 Un-ending.

अनन्ता i. 2 Endless; infinite.

अनन्तफलम् ii. 34 Endless fruit; unending consequence. (Some editions read अनन्तं फलं)

—अनन्तफलाः ii. 34

अनन्तरभूमिम् iii. 6 The next or immediately succeeding stage.

अनन्तरा iii. 6, 14 Im-mediate; next after.

—अनन्तरेण iv. 21

अनन्ते ii. 47 In the Infinite.

अनन्विताः i. 32 अन्, not + अनु, after + इ to go) Unfollowed; unaccompanied.

—अनभिघातः ii. 48; iii. 45 (अन् + अभि, from all sides, + हन्, to strike, to slay).

—अनभिघातात् iv. 33

अनभिद्रोहः ii. 30 Non-hate.

अनभिभूतः i. 47 (अन् + अभि + इ, to be; to be over another, to overpower). Un-overpowered.

अनभिभूतबुद्धिसत्त्वेन iii. 18 With undefeated cognitive intelligence; with invincible power of cognition; with irresistible insight.

अनभिभूतविषयः i. 14 The object of which is not over-powered.

—अनभिष्वङ्गी ii. 40

—अनभिसम्बन्धात् iv. 34

—अनभ्यधिकः iii. 13

—अनभ्युपगमात् iii. 13

अनया iii, 51; iv. 14 By this (fem:)

अनयोः iv. 15 Of these two.

अनर्थे ii. 5 In the 'undesirable'.

—अनल—iii. 26

—अनवच्छिन्नाः ii. 31

अनवच्छिन्नाः ii. 31 (अन् + अव् + छिद्, to cut off, to limit) Unlimited, unconditioned.

—अनवच्छिन्नेषु i. 44

अनवच्छेदात् i. 26 By non-limitation.

—अनवच्छेदात् iii. 53

—अनवधारणम् iv. 20

—अनवधारणम् iv. 21 Non-establishment; non-indication; non-discrimination; non-determination.

अनवस्थितम् i. 10 Unsteady; unfixed; unsettled; distracted; restless; fluctuating.

अनवस्थितत्वम् i. 30 Restlessness; unsteadiness.

—अनवस्थितत्वानि i. 30

अनष्टम् ii. 22 Undestroyed; unabolished.

अनाकुलम् i. 20 Undisturbed; without excitement, agitation, confusion, perplexity,

—अनागत—iii. 16

—अनागत—i. 25; ii. 19; iii, 13, 16, 36, 54.

अनागतम् ii. 16 Un-arrived; future; yet to come.

—अनागतम् iv. 12

अनागतम् iii. 13; ii. 16.

अनागतभावात् iii. 15 From the state of futurity.

अनागतलक्षणम् iii. 13 The mark of the 'not-come', the future; the character of futurity; the quality of being yet in the future.

अनागतलक्षणयुक्तः iii. 13 Possessed of the character of futurity.

अनागतवर्त्तमानयोः iii. 14 Of the future and the present.

अनागतवर्त्तमानाभ्याम् iii. 13

अनागतः iii. 13

अनागतस्य iii. 14

—अनागताभ्याम् iii. 13

—अनागताः iv. 13

अनात्मनि ii. 5 In the not-Self.

—अनात्मसु ii. 5

अनादि ii. 15

अनादिः i. 24; ii 17, 22 Beginningless.

अनादिकर्मक्लेशवासनाचित्रा ii. 1 Variegated (diversified, multiform, complex) with, compounded of, beginningless desire-germs of (propensities, tendencies, inclinations, dispositions to) activity and (of or to) "sins", "miseries", "hindrances".

अनादिकालप्रचितस्य ii. 13 Of (karma) accumulated through beginningless (past) time.

अनादिकालसंमूर्छितम् ii. 13 "Thrown into a swoon", overpowered, held, gripped, obsessed, pervaded, clouded, com-pounded, for beginningless time.

अनादिकालीनाः ii. 13 Belonging to, coming down for, beginningless time.

अनादित्वम् iv. 10 Beginninglessness.

अनादिदुःखस्रोतसा ii. 15 By the beginningless stream or current of pain.

अनादिवाग्व्यवहारवासनानुविद्धया iii. 17 By (the people's mind) permeated with the beginningless propensity to vocal activity i.e., speaking.

अनादिवासनानुविद्धम् iv. 10 Permeated with beginningless instincts, inclinations, dispositions.

अनादिवासनाविचित्रया ii. 15 By (mind functioning) complicated with beginningless instincts.

अनादिसंबंधः i. 4 Beginningless relation or connection.

अनादिसंयोगात् ii. 22 By, from, because of, beginningless conjunction.

अनाभोगात्मिका i. 15 Of the nature of non-enjoyment, non-inclination, non-tasting.

अनालोचितः iii. 47 Unperceived, unsensed.

अनावरणदर्शनात् iii. 41 By from, because of, (the fact, of our) seeing (that the formless does not cause and has) no limit or veil.

अनावरणम् iii. 41 Unveiling; non-hiding; not screening or covering.

अनावरणात्मके iii. 45 In (ākāsha or space) of the nature of the veilless or non-screening.

अनावृतज्ञानविषयाः iii. 26 With all objects of knowledge (lying) unveiled (before them).

अनाशयम् iv. 6 Germless; free or devoid of desire-germs; (which is not born of, and does not create, any germ or seed).

अनाश्वासः ii. 13 Lack of assurance; "want of free and peaceful breathing".

अनित्य —ii 5

अनित्यः i. 43 Non-permanent.

अनित्या ii. 19, Fleeting, passing, transitory.

अनित्ये ii. 5

अनियतविपाकम् ii. 13

अनियतविपाकः ii. 13 With or of uncertain maturation or fruition.

अनियतविपाकस्य ii. 13

अनियतासु i. 35 Amongst the unfixed, unsettled, unrestrained, uncontrolled, random.

—अनियमात् ii. 13

—अनिल—iii. 26

अनिवृत्तमिथ्याज्ञाना ii. 26 With false or illusory knowledge unwithdrawn, unabolished.

अनिशम् i. 5 (= अहर्निशम्) Day and night; incessantly, perpetually.

—अनिष्ट—ii. 18

अनिष्टम् ii. 34 Undesirable; undesired; unhappy; unpleasant.

अनिष्टः ii. 13 Unacceptable.

अनिष्टप्रसंगात् iii. 51 From, because of, re-addiction or re-attachment to, revival or resurgence of, the undesirable, the evil.

अनिष्टप्रसंगः iii. 51

अनीश्वरस्य iii. 55 Of the non-sovereign, the powerless.

अनु—, —अनु—i. 1. 7, 9, 11, 17, 49; ii. 7, 8, 20, 28, 34, 54; iii. 14; iv. 8.

अनु—ii. 4, 13

अनु ii. 4, 54; iii. 38; After; following; behind; in the train or wake of; together with; close upon.

अनुकम्पनीयाः iv. 23 (अनु + कम्प्, to tremble; to shake, shiver, vibrate, tremble in company with; to sym-pathise with). To be pitied; pitiable (pl:)

—अनुकारः ii. 54

अनुकारमात्रतया ii. 20 By mere imitation or reflexion.

अनुकारिमात्रतया iv. 22 By pure imitativeness.

—अनुकूलम् iii. 18

अनुकूला iii. 51 Favourable; agreeable; kind; sympathetic; propitious; "following or going along the bank".

—अनुकूलाभिः iii. 26

—अनुगतः i. 1, 17; iii. 44,47

अनुगतम् ii. 34; iii. 11, 12 Accompanying; accompanied; going or running through or after; following; persisting; threading; continuing.

—अनुगमात् i. 17

—अनुगुणानाम् iv. 8

अनुगृह्णन्ति iv. 2 "Accompany in catching, holding, supporting"; "hold along with"; pity; favour (pl:)

अनुगृह्णाति i. 23; ii. 15; iv. 11 Favours; helps (sing:)

—अनुग्रह—i. 25; ii. 3, 15; iii. 17; iv. 7, 10.

—अनुग्रहणम् iv. 12

अनुग्रहाय i. 1 For benefitting, helping.

—अनुच्छेदेन iii. 14

अनुज्ञायते ii. 13 Is "after-known", inferred, concluded; is permitted, assented or agreed to.

अनुतप्यते ii. 17 Is "after-heated"; is distressed sym-path-etically.

अनुत्तम—ii. 42

अनुत्तमम् iii. 18 Unsurpassed.

अनुत्तमः iii. 48 Unexcelled.

अनुत्तमसुखलाभः ii. 42 Gain of unsurpassed happiness.

अनुत्पत्तिधर्मा i. 9 Having the attribute of birthlessness.

अनुत्पादः ii. 23 "Non-birth"; non-development.

अनुत्पादाय iv. 21 For non-rebirth.

—अनुत्पादे ii. 27

अनुधावतः i. 40 Of the (yogi's mind) running after.

अनुनिविशन्ते iii. 38 Settle down after or in company with.

अनुपतति ii. 20; iv. 22 Follows.

अनुपतन्ति iii. 38 "Fall after"; follow (pl.)

अनुपतित iii. 13 Following; fallen into; undergoing.

— अनुपपत्तिः i. 32; iii. 53

अनुपलब्धिः iii. 13 (अन् + उप + लभ्, to gain). Non-apprehension; "non-finding".

अनुपलभ्यम् i. 43 Undiscoverable; impossible to find; unknowable.

अनुपशान्तिः ii. 15 Not-peace; dissatisfaction; peacelessness; restlessness.

—अनुपश्यः ii. 20

— अनुपश्यः ii. 20

अनुपश्यतः iii. 18 Of the beholding, mirroring, apperceiving,

अनुपश्यति i. 47; ii. 20 (अनु + दृश् = पश्य, to see; to see along with; to see consciously, as a witness; "I know and I know that I know"). Beholds (as a spectator); apperceives, witnesses.

अनुपश्यन् ii. 18, 20, 27 Observing; mirroring; witnessing; apperceiving.

अनुपश्यन्तः iii. 51

अनुपसर्गः i. 29 (अन्, not + उप, near + सृज्, to surge, to emanate, to create). Without (troublesome) secondary consequences; having no bye-products or excrescences; (not beset with, oppressed by, liable to, consequences, viz. birth, life-term, and pleasant and painful experience).

अनुपस्थाप्य iii. 17 Not having established, constituted, composed.

अनुपस्थिताः iv. 16 Non-present.

अनुपहत्य ii 15 Without slaying.

—अनुपातिनम् ii. 15

—अनुपातिनः ii. 18, 19; iii. 44

—अनुपातिना iii. 15

—अनुपातिषु i. 44

—अनुपाती i. 9; iii. 14

अनुपाती iii. 14 "Falling after"; following.

अनुपादानात् iv. 7 Because of non-taking, not-doing.

अनुपादित्सा ii. 32 Non-wish-to-acquire; absence of desire to obtain.

अनुपायः ii. 15 Not (the right) means.

अनुप्रविशति iii. 45 Enters with or after. (Some editions read अनुविशति).

अनुप्रविशन्ति iv. 3

अनुप्रवेशयितुम् iv. 3 In order to cause to enter.

—अनुप्रवेशात् iv. 2

अनुप्लवन्ते ii. 15 "Jump after"; "float, swim after"; pursue.

—अनुभव—i. 32, 44; ii. 13
—अनुभवः ii. 9, 15
अनुभवकर्मविषयताम् ii. 17 The state of being the object of the act of experiencing.
अनुभवति ii. 28, 34; iii. 52 (अनु after + भू to be) "Becomes like"; experiences.
अनुभवन् iii. 13, 14 Experiencing.
अनुभवन्तः i. 19
अनुभवन्ति i. 19; ii. 19
अनुभवात् i. 11 From experience.
—अनुभवात् ii. 9, 15
अनुभवाः iv. 9, 21 Experiences.
—अनुभवे i. 10
—अनुभवैः iii. 18
—अनुभावानाम् ii. 12
—अनुभावेषु ii. 12
—अनुभूत—ii. 9; iv. 9; 10, 33
—अनुभूतम् ii. 9; iii. 18
अनुभूतविषयासम्प्रमोषः i. 11 The not letting go of an object (which has been) experienced.
अनुभूतव्यक्तिकम् iv. 12 Of which the "manifestation", "individuation", has (taken place and) been experienced in the past.
अनुभूयते iv. 33 Is experienced.
अनुभूयमाने ii. 15 Being experienced.
—अनुमान—i. 7, 49
—अनुमान—i. 35, 43; ii. 9
अनुमानम् i. 7, 49 (अनु after, behind + मा to measure), "After-measuring"; measuring in accordance with a standard (premiss); inference.
अनुमानेन i. 48, 49; iii. 15 By inference.
अनुमापयति ii. 9, iv. 18 Causes to be inferred; leads to the inference.
—अनुमित—i. 7; ii. 18; iii. 14
अनुमितम् ii. 30 Inferred.
—अनुमितम् iii. 41 (Some editions read निमित्त)
अनुमितः i. 7, 43 Inferred.
अनुमीयते iv. 25 Is inferred.
अनुमेयम् i. 51 Inferrible.
अनुमेयस्य i. 7 Of the deducible.
—अनुमोदिताः ii. 34
अनुमोदिता ii. 34 (अनु after + मुद् to rejoice or to mix) Approved; abetted.
—अनुरागात् iii. 26
—अनुरूपाः iv. 9
—अनुरोधिनः iii. 17
—अनुरोधिनी ii. 28
—अनुरोधी i. 47; ii. 17
अनुवर्त्तते i. 36 (अनु after + वृत् to exist). Persists; continues.
अनुवर्त्तमानाः ii. 18 Following; accompanying; pursuing; persisting.
अनुवादः iii. 17 "After-statement"; re-statement; re- production; rendering; translation; particular mention.
—अनुवासितः ii, 15
अनुविद्धम् i. 2; ii. 15; iv. 10 Pierced through, penetrated;

pervaded, permeated; streaked, stained, colored, affected, tinged.

—अनुविद्धः i. 42; ii. 15

—अनुविद्धया iii. 17

अनुविद्य i. 36, Having known, recognised.

अनुविधायिन्यः iii. 44 Carriers out of (his) command; obeyers of (his) law; followers of (his) mood.

अनुविधीयन्ते iii. 38 Accompany; follow obediently.

अनुविवर्द्धन्ते ii. 15 Increase with, in the wake of, in consequence of.

अनुवृत्तः i. 7 "Existing through or after"; continuous; persisting (like a thread through beads).

अनुव्यवसीयेत iii. 47 Be consciously ascertained, be apperceived.

—अनुशयी i. 11

—अनुशयी ii. 7, 8

—अनुशासनम् i. 1 (अनु + शास्, to command, instruct, direct, teach). Expounding; explaining; repeating (ancient teaching freshly).

—अनुशासनम् i. 1; iv. 13

अनुशेरते ii. 4; iv. 8, 28 (अनु + शी to sleep). "Sleep after or with"; follow; accompany; become mixed up with (pl:)

—अनुषङ्गः ii. 13

—अनुष्ठानम् i. 13; ii. 28 iv. 12

अनुष्ठानम् ii. 29 (अनु + स्था to stand) Practising, following, performing; observance; resolve; "standing up".

—अनुष्ठानात् ii. 28

अनुष्ठानात् ii. 28

अनुष्ठीयन्ते ii. 28 Are practised.

—अनुसंहार—iii. 17

अनुसंहारः iii. 17 Summation of a series; the sum, the net result, the resultant; (concomitant dissolution or disintegration, as of molecules in physiological functioning, while producing a result).

—अनुसारिण्यः iii. 44

—अनुस्मृति—ii. 7, 8; iv. 10

अनूत्पतन्ति iii. 38 Fly after.

अनृतम् ii. 33 Untruth.

अनृतादिषु ii. 34 In untruth etc.

अनेकम् ii. 13 Not-one; many; manifold.

अनेकचित्तपरिकल्पितम् iv. 15 Formulated, imagined, ideated by many minds.

अनेकधर्मस्वभावः iv. 12 Having the nature of possessing many functions, attributes.

अनेकधा i. 1 In many ways.

अनेकभवपूर्विका ii. 13 Preceding or preceded by (engendering or engendered by) many births.

अनेकमनस्काः iv. 4 Many-minded; having separate minds.

अनेकस्य ii. 13 Of not-one; of many; of manifold.

अनेकार्थम् i. 32 Having many meanings, interests, objects, purposes.

अनेकेषाम् iv. 5 Of many.

अनेकेषु ii, 13

अनेन i. 24; ii. 1; iii. 22; iv. 23 By this.

—अनैश्वर्य— i. 2

अनौपदेशिकम् iii. 54 Untaught.

—अन्त—ii. 39

—अन्त—iii. 22; iv. 33

—अन्तम् iv. 3

—अन्तः i. 40

—अन्तर्—ii. 18; iii. 51

अन्तरङ्गम् iii. 7 (अन्तः + अङ्गम्) "Inner-organ"; internal part; internal; inner.

अन्तरङ्गम् iii. 7, 8

—अन्तर—iv. 2, 21

—अन्तर—i. 7, 43; ii. 19, 27; iii. 13, 17

—अन्तरम् ii. 5, 19, 28, 54, 55; iv. 3

—अन्तराणि iv. 27

—अन्तराणि iv. 29

अन्तराभावः iv. 10 Existence in the interval, (between two births).

अन्तराय— i. 29

अन्तराय— ii. 32

अन्तरायाः i. 29

अन्तरायाः i. 30 Obstructions; obstacles; hindrances; interruptions.

—अन्तरायाः i. 30

अन्तरायाभावः i. 29 "Non-being" of interruption; absence of hindrances or obstacles.

अन्तरालचारिणाम् iii. 32 Of movers in the interspace.

अन्तरिक्षलोकः iii. 26 The "interspace" world; Bhuvaḥ; astral world.

—अन्तरिता iv. 1

अन्तरीयकम् i. 16 Separated by an interval.

—अन्तरे ii. 4, 13, 16, 45

अन्तरेण ii. 1, 18, 28 With-out; by an interval from; with omission of or separation from.

—अन्तरेण iii. 2; iv. 21

—अन्तरेभ्यः iii. 14

—अन्तरेषु ii. 23, 33; iii. 38; iv. 14

अन्तर्धानम् iii. 21 (अन्तः in + धा to do, to place), "Going inwards"; disappearance; invisibility.

अन्तवान् iv. 33 "With-end"; ending; having a final end without renewal.

अन्तश्छिद्रम् iii. 32 Within a hollow.

—अन्तस्य ii. 9

अन्तिके iv. 21 Near.

अन्ते iv. 33 At the fringe or end.

अन्त्यवर्ण-प्रत्यय-व्यापारोपस्थापितम् iii. 17 Established by the operation of the idea of the final letter-sound.

अन्त्याः iii. 53 Final; last.

अन्धः iv. 31 Blind.

अन्धकारं iv. 22 Darkness.

—अन्धकारे iii. 51

अन्धतामिस्रः i. 8 "Blind darkness"; blind clinging; obstinate purblind tenacity.

अन्धतामिस्रा iii. 26 (Name of a class of hells).

अन्नपानम् i. 15 Food and drink.

अन्य—i. 49. 50; ii. 22

अन्यः i. 18 Another.

अन्यः i. 23, 32; iii. 14, 35, 50; iv. 17, 23.

अन्यचित्तपरिकल्पितेन iv. 15 By (a thing) framed, fashioned, ideated, imagined, created, by another mind.

अन्यजातीयपरिणतानाम् iv. 2 Of (a body and senses) evolved into, belonging to, another type or genus.

अन्यतरावधारणे iv. 33 In deciding or answering for one of the two.

अन्यत् ii. 5, 13, 18; iii. 14 Another (neu:)

अन्यतः iii. 6 From elsewhere, from another.

अन्यतर--iii. 13

—अन्यता—iii. 49

—अन्यता—ii. 2, iii. 35, 49;. iv. 27

—अन्यता i. 2

अन्यतानवच्छेदात् iii. 53 Because of difference, otherness, separateness not being marked out, defined sharply, made clear.

अन्यताप्रत्ययं iii. 53 Recognition, awareness, belief, of difference.

अन्यताप्रत्ययमात्राधिकारम् iii. 55 Having only the office or function of recognising (the) difference (of Purusha and Prakṛti).

—अन्यत्व – ii. 28

—अन्यत्वम् iii. 15

अन्यत्वकरम् iii. 53 Differentiater.

अन्यत्वकरः iii. 53

अन्यत्वकारणम् ii. 28 Cause of otherness, change, or transformation.

अन्यत्वप्रत्ययः iii. 53 (See अन्यताप्रत्ययं)

—अन्यत्वे iii. 15

अन्यत्वे i. 32 In or on otherness.

अन्यत्वेन iii. 13

अन्यत्र i. 39; ii. 4, 31; iii. 13, 26; Elsewhere.

अन्यथा ii. 23, 28, 31; iii. 13, 17; iv. 26 Otherwise.

—अन्यथात्वम् iii. 9, 13, 14

अन्यदृष्टस्य iii. 14 Of (something) seen by another.

अन्यदेशक्षणानुभवः iii. 53 Experience of another place and moment; experience of the moment corresponding to another space (i.e. another point, position, place in space).

अन्यधर्मस्वरूपापेक्षया iii. 15 With reference or in relation to the own-form of another property or function.

अन्यपुरुषसाधारणत्वात् ii. 22 Because of being common to other egos, souls, purushas.

अन्यप्रत्ययदृष्टस्य i. 32 Of what has been seen by another idea, pratyaya, state of consciousness.

अन्यप्रत्ययोपचितस्य i. 32 Of what has been developed by or in another idea or state of consciousness.

अन्यया iv. 21 By another (fem:).

अन्यविषया i. 49 Having another object or content.

अन्यव्यग्रस्य iii. 53 Of (an observer) engaged with another.

अन्यसंस्कारप्रतिबन्धी i. 50 Preventor or obstructor of other tendencies, proclivities, propensities, impressed or acquired tendencies.

अन्यसाधारणत्वात् ii. 22 Because of being common to others.

अन्यस्य iii. 14, 45; iv. 15, 16 Of another.

अन्यस्वरूपेण ii. 17 By or through another form or the form of another.

अन्यान् iv. 21

अन्याय्यम् iv. 14 (अ not + नी, to lead, to guide rightly). Illogical; unjust; untrue; improper.

अन्यासु ii. 4 In or among others (fem:)

अन्ये i. 42; ii. 55 (Plu: of अन्यः).

अन्येन iii. 14 By another.

अन्येषाम् iii. 45 of others.

अन्येषु ii. 15 In or among others (mas:)

—अन्वय—iii. 44, 47

—अन्वयम् iii. 14

—अन्वयः iii. 9

अन्वयशब्देन iii. 44 By the word anvaya, (meaning, "con-comitance" "connection," "per-vasion").

अन्वयिकारणम् i. 45 Material cause.

अन्वयिनी iii. 44 (अनु + इ, to go) Going through, con-comitant (fem:)

—अन्वयिनीभिः ii. 19

अन्वयी iii. 13, 14 Threading, pervading (mas:)

अन्वर्था i. 48 Following the meaning; true to the sense (of the name).

—अन्वागतः iii. 13, 14

—अन्विताः iii. 52

—अन्वितानाम् iii. 44

अन्वेति iii. 9 Follows; goes with.

अपकर्षम् ii. 13 (अप away, down + कृष् to drag). (To) degradation, descent, falling.

अपकर्षति iv. 3 Draws; drags; carries.

अपकर्षपर्यन्तम् iii. 52 Down to extreme involution, descent, division, separation.

अपकर्षाय ii. 13 For 'degradation', nullification.

अपकारः ii. 12 Evil doing; ill-deed; injury.

अपकारिणम् ii. 33 To the harm-doer, the injuror.

अपकृतम् ii. 34 Acted injuriously.

अपकृष्टेषु iv. 3 Being pulled away, weeded out.

अपक्वस्य ii. 13 Of the unripe. (Some editions read अविपक्वस्य)

अपगतमलम् iv. 31 Free of impurity.

अपगता ii. 34 Gone, removed, counteracted, neutralised.

—अपगमात् ii. 27, 43; iii. 18

—अपघाताय i. 31 (some editions read उपघाताय).

अपत्यम् ii. 24 Progeny.

अपत्यवती ii. 24 Having children (fem:)

—अपत्स्यत iv. 12

अपदस्वरूपाः iii. 17 Not of the form of a word; not being words.

अपनयनात् iii. 39 From or because of carrying away.

अपनीतक्लेशः ii. 13 With (the causes of) misery or affliction removed; freed from (the) miseries (of sin).

अपनीततुषाः ii. 13 With husk removed.

अपनीयते ii. 11 Is carried off or away; is removed.

—अपर—ii. 9

अपरः iii. 13 Another.

—अपरा—iii. 13

—अपरान्त –iv. 33

अपरान्तज्ञानम् iii. 22 Knowledge of the other or final end i.e. death.

अपरान्तम् iii. 22 Death; the other or final end.

अपरान्तस्य iii. 22

—अपरान्तस्य ii. 9

अपरान्तेन iv. 33

अपरामृष्टम् iv. 16

अपरामृष्टः i. 24 Untouched.

अपरामृष्टः i. 24, iii. 2

अपरामृष्टा ii. 2

—अपरामृष्टा ii. 20

अपरिग्रह—ii. 9

अपरिग्रहः ii. 30 (अ + परि, from all sides + ग्रह्, to seize) Non-acquisitiveness; non-holding, non-possession, of property; renunciation of property or possessions.

अपरिग्रहस्थैर्ये ii. 39 On the establishment or confirmation of non-acquisitiveness.

—अपरिग्रहाः ii. 30

अपरिदृष्टाः iii. 15, 18 Unseen; imperceptible.

अपरिनिर्मितवशवर्त्तिनः iii. 26 (A race of devas).

अपरिणामित्वम् ii. 20 Unchangingness; changelessness

अपरिणामित्वात् iv. 18 (अ, not + परि, all round + नम्, to bend) Because of changelessness.

अपरिणामिनि ii. 17 In the unchanging.

अपरिणामिनी i. 2; iv. 22 Unchanging. (fem:)

अपरिणामी iii. 50 Unchanging. (mas:).

अपरिसङ्ख्येयत्वात् ii. 34 Because of uncountability or countlessness.

—अपरिसमाप्तिः ii. 18

अपरे iii. 53; iv. 10, 23 Others.

अपलपद्भिः iv. 21 By those who contradict or repudiate.

अपलपन्तः iv. 14 Those who traverse, reject, refute, oppose, discard.

—अपवर्ग—ii. 18

—अपवर्ग—ii. 21; iii. 44; iv. 24

अपवर्गभागीयम् iv 25. Having a share in, belonging to the division of, destined for, salvation.

अपवर्गभागीयस्य iv. 12

अपवर्गः ii. 18, 23 (अप, away + वृज्, to shun, abandon, renounce, prohibit, cut off). Renunciation; ab-solu-tion; liberation; salvation.

—अपवर्गाणाम् iv. 34

अपवर्गात् i. 35

अपवर्गादिषु i. 35 In Mokṣha etc.

—अपवर्गाः iv. 32

—अपवर्गौ ii. 18

अपवादात् ii. 13 (अप away from + वद् to speak) Because of (contradiction, refutation, repudiation, negation) exception, (calumny).

अपश्यन् ii. 6, 40 Not-seeing.

—अपस्मारक—iii. 26

अपहन्ति ii. 13 Destroys.

—अपह्नवः i. 32

अपह्नुवते iv. 14, 16, 21 (They) traverse, deny (pl:).

अपानः iii. 39 The vital force or nerve-current known as apāna; in-breathing. (Some regard it as out-breathing.).

अपाम् iv. 3 Of waters.

—अपाय—ii. 19

—अपाये iv. 2

अपायोपजननयोः iii. 11 Through or in removal and production (of two states, respectively).

अपि i. 22, 26, 29, 51; ii. 9, 20. 22; iii. 8, 50; iv. 9, 24, 29

अपि i. 2; ii. 1; iii. 8; iv. 3 etc.

—अपुण्य—i. 33; ii. 14

—अपुण्य—ii. 12, 13

अपुण्यहेतुकाः ii. 14 Caused by sin.

अपुण्यात्मकेषु i. 33 Towards the sinful. (Some editions read अपुण्यशीलेषु)

अपुण्ये ii. 5 In sin.

—अपूजयत् iv. 31

अपूर्वम् iv. 12 Not (experienced) before; altogether new; original.

अपूर्वावयवानुप्रवेशात् iv. 2 Because of the coming in of new parts or factors.

अपूर्वोपजनः iv. 11 The creation, invention, origination of something new, not seen before.

अपूर्वोपजनने iv. 12 In or for the production of the new.

अपेक्षते i. 40 (अप्, away, sidewise + ईक्ष्, to look). Expects, looks for.

अपेक्षन्ते ii. 54, 55 (pl:)

—**अपेक्षम्** ii. 23; iv. 10, 15

अपेक्षमाणाः iv. 2 Expecting, depending on, looking to.

—**अपेक्षया** iii. 15, 18

—**अपेक्षः** iii. 48

अपेक्षा iii. 55 Looking to; expectation; dependence; need.

—**अपेक्षा** iii. 10, 43

—**अपेक्षित्वात्** iv. 17

अपेतम् iii. 13 Gone away; vanished.

—**अपेतम्** i. 2

—**अपेतस्य** i. 47;

—**अपेतस्य** iv. 31

अपैति iii. 13 Goes away; disappears.

—**अपोह**—ii. 18

—**अप्यय**—iii. 45

अप्रकाशम् iv. 19 Non-luminous; unperceived; hidden.

अप्रतिघातः i. 40 Non-defeat; non-frustration; 'non-counter-stroke'; irresistibility; resistlessness.

अप्रतिघान् ii. 38 Indefeasible, irresistible.

अप्रतिपत्तिः ii. 55 Non-perception.

अप्रतिबन्धेन i. 35 (अ, not + प्रति, opposite + बन्ध् to bind). Without hindrance.

अप्रतिबुद्धः ii. 5 Un-enlightened.

अप्रतिसङ्क्रमा i. 2; ii. 20; iv. 22 (अ + प्रति + सं + क्रम्, to move or pass from place to place) Un-passing; intransmissible; not-passing from one to another.

अप्रतिसङ्क्रमायाः iv. 22

अप्रतिष्ठस्य iii. 38 Of the unstable.

अप्रतिष्ठा i. 30 Non-establishment; non-fixity. unsettledness; unsteadiness.

अप्रतिहतज्ञानाः iii. 26 With undefeated knowledge, unbaffled unthwarted or irresistible insight.

अप्रधानम् ii. 23 Non-praḍhāna; not the primary or principal cause.

अप्रमत्तः iii. 6 (अ + प्र + मद् to be glad, over-glad, mad, intoxicated). Uncareless; unintoxicated; careful; vigilant; alert.

—**अप्रमाणकम्** iv. 16

अप्रमाणस्य i. 8 Of the 'non-fact,' the unproved, the unreliable.

अप्रमाणात्मकेन iv. 14 By the incredible, the unproveable.

अप्रयतैः ii. 40 By the "unrestrained", unwatchful, uncontrolled; by the unclean, the impure.

अप्रयोजकम् iv. 3 non-moving, non-energising; not (directly) causing (stimulating, instigating, innate or inherent tendencies) to act.

अप्रयोजनम् ii. 18 Without motive.

अप्ररोहः ii. 4 Non-germination; non-growth.

अप्रवृत्तिः i. 30 (अ + प्र + वृत्, to exist; to turn round and round; cf. Lat. vertere) Non-engagement (in work), non-inclination (for work); inactivity; languor.

अप्रसवधर्माणः ii. 35 Not having the property of progenition, reproduction, multiplication.

अप्रसवधर्मिणः ii. 2 Do: (accusative).

अप्रसवः ii. 26 Non-reproduction.

अप्रसवसमर्थानि iii. 50 Incapable of germination, reproduction.

अप्रसाध्यम् iii. 13 Not required to be proved, accomplished.

अप्राप्तविवेकजज्ञानस्य iii. 54 Of one who has not attained the discriminative-knowledge.

अप्राप्तिः i. 7, 49 Unreaching; non-arrival (at another place).

अप्रामाणिकस्य (or **अप्रमाणकस्य**) i. 49 Of the unproved or untrustworthy.

—**अप्सरः**— iii. 26

अप्सरसः iii. 51 Fairies; nymphs.

अप्सरोभिः iii. 26 By fairies.

—**अबधिरयोः** iii. 41 Of the (two) non-deaf.

अबन्ध्यवीर्याणि iii. 23 Un-sterile seeded; resistless; efficient.

अबहिःसाधनाधीना iv. 7 Not dependent on external means.

अबाध्यम् iii. 18 Indefeasible.

अबाधमानम् ii. 1 Not oppressing; not conflicting with or going against or neutralising or destroying.

—**अभय**—ii. 33

अभविष्यत् iv. 12 If it were; it would be.

अभागम् iii. 17 Partless.

अभाव—i. 10.

—**अभावः** i 29, ii. 25; iv. 11

—**अभावः** ii. 5, 13. 23, 32, 49, 50, 51; iii. 14, 55;

अभावः i. 49; ii. 50; iii. 13 Non-being; non-existence; absence.

अभावनम् i. 30 Non-realisation; "not bringing into being."

अभावप्रत्ययालम्बना i. 10 Depending on, resting on, holding on to, the notion of non-being, no-thing; having the notion or concept of "no-thing", "non-being", for its object.

अभावप्राप्तम् i. 18 Arrived at the condition of, attained to, non-being.

अभावमात्रम् i. 9 Only non-being; mere absence.

अभावहेतुः ii. 15 Cause of non-being; means of abolition or annihilation.

—**अभावात्** ii. 25

—**अभावात्** i. 43; ii. 23, 24, 27; iii. 23.

अभावात् iv. 25 Because of absences.

अभावितस्मर्त्तव्या i. 11 That wherein the object remembered is not realised or recognised as now present and real (yet is also known to be not wholly imaginary, but as something which has been actually experienced before).

अभावे iv. 11 In absence.

अभावे i. 30

—अभावे i. 25; ii. 54, 55; iii. 8

आभास्वराः—iii. 26 A race of very high gods.

—अभिघातः ii. 48; iii. 45

—अभिघातः iii. 45

—अभिघातात् iv. 33

—अभिघातात् i. 31 (some editions read -विघातात्).

अभिजातमणिकल्पस्य i. 41 Of (a mind) like to a highly polished gem.

अभिजातस्य i. 41 Of the well-born, high-born; well-polished and refined; transparent.

—अभिज्ञस्य ii. 7, 8

—अभिज्ञानात् iii. 14

—अभिज्ञायते iii. 14

अभिदधति ii. 23 (अभि + धा, to do; to posit; to name). (They) declare, say, hold.

अभिधातुम् i. 49 To declare.

—अभिधान—iii. 17

अभिधायिष्यमाणानि ii. 28 The (factors of yoga) now to be declared.

अभिधास्यन्ते i. 8 Will be declared or explained.

—अभिधित्सया i. 1

अभिधीयते ii. 13, 15, 24; iii. 15, 44. Is declared; is said to be.

अभिधीयन्ते i. 30

अभिधीयमानः iii. 51 Being addressed.

अभिधीयमाना ii. 30 Being spoken.

अभिधीयमानैः iii. 17

—अभिधेयस्य i. 28

अभिध्यानमात्रेण i. 23 (अभि + ध्यै, to think). By mere well-wishing.

—अभिध्यानात् i. 23

अभिनयति i. 27 (अभि + नी, to lead, to carry). Carries out,; enacts, shows forth.

अभिनवस्य iii. 15 Of the new.

अभिनिर्वर्त्तयन्ति iv. 10 Bring about; bring into being; produce; accumulate; store up.

—अभिनिर्वर्त्तितम् iv. 25

अभिनिर्हरन्ति ii. 3 Bring about; achieve.

अभिनिवेशः ii. 9 (अभि + नि + विश्, to enter; to sit down) 'Permeation', 'close penetration', 'pervasion', 'thorough infiltration'; insistent notion; stubborn idea; pertinacity; tenacity; clinging.

अभिनिवेशः ii. 9 Obstinate notion.

—अभिनिवेशाः ii. 3

—अभिनिवेशः i. 8; ii. 18

अभिप्रतीत्य ii. 5 Believing, having understood.

—अभिप्राय—iv. 5 Purpose, intention.

अभिप्रेतदेशकालविषयापेक्षः iii. 48 Apprehending at will any object belonging to any place or time.

अभिप्लवते ii. 4; iii. 13 'Floats', 'comes to the top', 'appears on the surface'; is patent; 'flows' or runs through.

अभिभवप्रादुर्भावौ iii. 9 'Suppression or defeat, and upcoming or appearance'; latence and patence.

अभिभवप्रादुर्भावौ iii. 13

अभिभूतम् ii. 13; iv. 31 Repressed.

—अभिभूतः i. 47

अभिभूतस्य ii. 13

अभिभूयते i. 32; ii. 48; iii. 10 Is overpowered.

—अभिमत—i. 39

अभिमतम् i. 39 Agreeable, acceptable, 'thought (well of)'.

अभिमुखम् i. 1 Face to face; inclined.

—अभिमुखम् ii. 13

—अभिमुखाः ii. 27

अभिमुखीभविष्यति iii. 51 Will come to the front, face to face.

अभिमुखीभूतम् iv. 11

—अभिवादन—iv. 10

अभिव्यक्तधर्मकेषु. i. 44 Amongst (subtle elements) whose products or attributes are manifest.

अभिव्यक्तः ii. 4 Manifest.

—अभिव्यक्तः ii. 13; iv. 9

अभिव्यक्तानभिव्यक्तेषु iii. 14 Amongst the manifest and the unmanifest.

अभिव्यक्तानाम् iii. 50 Of the manifested.

—अभिव्यक्ति—ii. 28

अभिव्यक्तिकारणम् ii. 13, 28 Cause of manifestation.

अभिव्यक्तिः ii. 28; iii. 13, 14; iv. 8 (अभि + वि + अञ्ज्. to limn, to delineate, color, stain, tinge, paint, make plainly visible) Manifestation; (shaping out as a concrete individual); definition.

अभिव्यक्तिः iv. 8

—अभिव्यक्तिः ii. 23; iii. 17

—अभिव्यक्तौ iii. 13

अभिव्यज्यमाना iii. 15 Being manifested.

—अभिव्यञ्जकम् ii. 13; iv. 9 Manifestor.

—अभिष्वङ्गी ii. 40

अभिसम्बद्धम् iv. 23 Connected; 'bound up'.

अभिसम्बध्य iv. 17 Having brought into relationship. (Some editions read अभिसंबन्ध्य).

अभिसम्बध्यते iv. 15 Is bound up.

अभिसम्बन्धः ii. 5 Connection, relevancy, pertinency.

—अभिसम्बन्धः iv. 6

अभिसम्बन्धात् iii. 17

—अभिसम्बन्धात् iv. 34
—अभिसंस्कृता iv. 9
अभिहताः i. 31 Struck, oppressed.
अभूत्वा iv. 12 Not having been.
—अभेद—iii. 44
अभेदात्मा i. 32 Of the nature of non-difference.
अभेदेन i. 32 By non-difference; as identical.
अभेदोपचारः iii. 15 Treatment as non-separate.
—अभ्यधिकः iii. 13
अभ्यपूजयत् iv. 31 Praised, honored.
—अभ्यवहरणादि ii. 32
अभ्यसेत् i. 32; iii. 26 May or should practise.
अभ्यस्तः ii. 50 Practised.
अभ्यस्यतः ii. 52 Of the practising.
—अभ्यास—i. 18
—अभ्यास—i. 18, 48; iii. 10
अभ्यासकृतम् i. 40 Made or created by practice.
—अभ्यासम् ii. 15
अभ्यासवैराग्याभ्याम् i. 12 By perseverent practice or 'approach' and revulsion.
अभ्यासवैराग्याभ्याम् i. 32
—अभ्यासः i. 32
—अभ्यासः ii. 15
अभ्यासः i. 13 (अभि = all round, near + आस् to sit or अस् to throw) Practice.
अभ्यासः i. 18
अभ्यासस्य i. 32 Of practice.
—अभ्यासात् i. 16; ii. 52, 53
अभ्यासी iii. 51 Practiser.
—अभ्यासेन i. 12; ii. 15
अभ्युपगतः iii. 14 Come to; arrived at; postulated.
अभ्युपगम्यते iv. 23 Is found, admitted, accepted, understood.
अभ्युपगमः iv. 20 Hypothesis.
—अभ्युपगमात् iii. 13
अमरस्थानम् iii. 51 The place or abode of the immortals.
अमराः iii. 26 Immortals.
अमलः ii. 27; iii. 55 Dirtless; refuseless; dustless; taintless.
अमित्रः ii. 5 Non-friend; unfriendly; inimical.
अमित्रागोष्पदवत् ii. 5 Like 'unfriendly', 'un-cow-hoof' (i.e., untrivial) etc; (like the words 'unfriendly', 'no-joke').
अमिश्रीभावः ii. 25 Un-mixed-ness.
अमी ii. 4, 34; iii. 18, 51, 52; iv. 13 These.
—अमुञ्चत् iv. 31
अमुत्र iv. 19 Here; there; in the svarga-world.
अमुम् ii. 34 To this one.
अमुष्मिन् iii. 20 In this one.
अमून् iii. 13 To these.
अमूर्त्तस्य iii. 41 Of the form-less.
—अमृत—ii. 5 Nectar (of immortality).
अमृतभोगभागी ii. 32 Sharer of the bliss of immortality.
अमृताः ii. 5 'Un-dead', immortals.
अमोघा ii. 36 Not-vain; un-failing.

—अम्बरीष—iii. 26 (Name of a purgatory).

अयन्ते ii. 19 Go.

अयम् i. 1, 10; ii. 9; iii. 12; iv. 19 This.

अयस्कान्तमणिकल्पम् i. 4; ii. 17 Like to the 'iron-loved' crystal; lodestone; magnet.

अयस्कान्तमणिकल्पाः ii. 18; iv. 17

अयःसधर्मकम् iv. 17 Having the same property as iron.

अयुतसिद्धावयवभेदानुगतः iii. 44, 47 Accompanied by, made up of, different parts which are not self-complete or independent.

अयुतसिद्धावयवः iii. 44 Not accomplished by mere juxtaposition or collection of parts; composed of organically interdependent parts; not a mere mixture; an orga-compound.

—अरण्यम् iv. 10

—अरम् iv. 11

अरिष्टम् iii. 22 Omen.

अरिष्टेभ्यः iii. 22 From omens, portents, malefic signs or influences.

अरिष्टेभ्यः iii. 22

अरुचिः iv. 25 Disinclination, distaste, indisposition.

अरे iii. 35 O thou!

अर्जन—ii. 30 Earning.

—अर्जित—ii. 18; iii. 26

—अर्जितम् iii. 51

—अर्थ—i. 28, 42; iii. 17, 35; iv. 34

—अर्थ—i. 8, 9, 47; ii. 18, 20, 21; iii. 16, 17.

अर्थकृतः ii. 17 Caused by mutual need or interest.

अर्थतत्त्वम् i. 35 The essence or substance of the meaning.

—अर्थतः iv. 13

—अर्थता iii. 11

—अर्थता ii. 19, iii. 44

—अर्थतानाम् ii. 21

—अर्थत्वात् ii. 17

—अर्थत्वात् i. 49; iii. 35

अर्थधर्माः i. 42 The properties of objects, 'meanings', things meant.

अर्थप्रत्ययः ii. 5 The belief, feeling, or idea of (a thing being 'desired',i.e.,) desirability.

—अर्थम् i. 32; ii. 18, 22; iv. 23, 24.

—अर्थम् ii. 19, 20, 22, 23, 24, 30; iv. 31.

अर्थम् i. 1, 27; iii. 17, 25

अर्थमात्रनिर्भासम् iii. 3 Only the meaning, the thing desired or contemplated, the 'object' shining, appearing, therein.

अर्थमात्रनिर्भासा i. 43 Appearing as only, or becoming wholly identified with, the object.

अर्थमात्रा i. 44 Only the object.

— अर्थयते iv. 29 Desires.

अर्थवती iii. 17 Possessed of a meaning.

अर्थवत् iii. 44 Purposeful.

अर्थवत्ता ii. 23 Significance; possession of significance; importfulness; purposiveness; interest-ful-ness; indefeasibility; indestructibility; effectiveness; efficiency.

— अर्थवत्त्व —iii. 44, 47

—अर्थवत्त्वम् iii. 44

अर्थवान् iv. 24 Interested.

अर्थविसहचरम् iv. 14 Parted from sense; devoid of, 'not accompanying or accompanied by' (a real) object.

अर्थशून्यः i. 18 Empty of sense or object.

—अर्थः ii. 2, 21

—अर्थ: i. 1, 7; ii. 19, 21

अर्थसङ्केतेन iii. 17 By a convention as to sense or meaning.

—अर्थस्य iii. 6

अर्थस्य i. 7 iii. 17

अर्थः i. 7, 42. 43; ii. 3, 17, 19, 20, 21, 25; iii. 11, 17, 38, 49; iv. 14. 16 Import; intention; meaning; sake; object; object desired or intended or prayed for; sense; significance; fact; purpose; purport; interest.

—अर्था ii. 20, 23

अर्थात्मा i. 43 Of the nature of the object.

—अर्थानाम् iv. 32

—अर्थाः iv. 28

—अर्थे i. 5, 30, 31

अर्थे i. 24, 32, 46; ii. 20; iii. 25; iv. 22.

—अर्थेन i. 26; ii. 34; iv. 24

अर्थेन iv. 15, 23,

अर्थेषु i. 35

अर्पणम् ii. 1, Offering up.

— अर्पणम् ii. 32

—अर्पित—ii. 45

अर्हतः ii. 42 (The two) deserve.

अर्हति ii. 15 Deserves; is worthy of.

अलक्षिताः iii. 13 Un-noticed, unobserved.

अलब्धपर्यवसानः iv. 33 Not having found finality.

—अलब्धभूमिकत्व—i. 30

अलब्धभूमिकत्वम् i. 30 'Not finding ground'; the state of not having found a firm footing); nonachievement of (a preliminary) stage.

अलम् ii. 13 Enough.

अलसम् i. 10 "Lazy", languid, indolent, dull.

अलाभः i. 30 Non-gain, non-attainment.

अलिङ्गपरिणामः ii. 19 Transformation or change into the 'markless', the indefinable.

अलिङ्गपर्यवसानम् i. 45 Ending with, extending up to, the 'markless', the 'undefined'.

अलिङ्गम् i. 45; ii. 19 Without mark, sign, differentiating characteristic.

अलिङ्गस्य i. 45; ii. 19

अलिङ्गात् i. 45

—अलिङ्गानि ii. 19

अलिङ्गावस्थायाम् ii. 19 In the condition of the indefinite.

अल्पम् iv. 31 Small, little.

अल्पम i. 25; ii. 13

अल्पायुः ii. 34 Short-lived.

अवकाशदानात् iii. 42 From or because of yielding place, space, room.

—अवकाशदानानि iv. 14

अवगतत्वात् iii. 6 Because of being understood.

अवगतम् i. 35 Understood.

अवगम्यते i. 9 (अव, near + गम्, to go) Is understood; 'gone to', 'approached (in mind)'.

अवचनीयम् iv. 33 Unanswerable; nor worthy of answer; not to be said; unspeakable.

अवचनीयः iv. 33 Indescribable.

अवच्छिद्यते i. 43 (अव + छिद्, to cut) Is marked off, 'cut off', determined, de-fined, delimited, demarcated, specified.

अवच्छिन्नानाम् iii. 17

—अवच्छिन्नाः ii. 31; iii. 14

अवच्छिन्नाः ii. 50 Delimited.

अवच्छिन्नानाम् iii. 17

—अवच्छिन्नेषु i. 44

—अवच्छेदात् i. 26; iii. 53

अवच्छेदार्थेन i. 26 For the purpose, or in the way or nature or with the effect, of de-limitation.

अवच्छेद्यन्ते i. 26 Are delimited.

—अवतंस— iii. 16

अवतिष्ठते iii. 13 Stands still; stops; rests.

—अवदात—ii. 30

अवदातरूपाम् ii. 30 Of perfected, refined, form.

—अवद्य—ii. 40

अवद्योत्यते i. 27 Is 'lighted up', shown forth.

—अवधारण—i. 7; ii. 19, 20

—अवधारणम् (अव, away, down + धृ, to hold) 'Hold down' in mind; cognise clearly; ideate definitely) iv. 20.

—अवधारणम् ii. 18; iv. 20, 21

—अवधारणात् ii. 51

—अवधारणे iv. 33

— अवधारणेन ii. 50

अवधार्यते iv. 23, 34 Is ideated, defined clearly.

अवधार्यन्ते ii. 29 Are ideated.

अवधार्येत iv. 23 May be cognised distinctly.

—अवनद्धः ii. 13

—अवनद्धाः ii. 13

—अवभासते ii. 20

अवभासते ii. 23; iii. 52 (अव + भास्, to shine, to appear) Shines out; appears.

अवभासन्ते ii. 19

—अवयव—ii. 5; iii. 44, 47; iv. 2.

—अवयवः iii. 44; iv. 14

अवयवः iii. 26 (अव + यु to mix; and also to separate) An organ, a factor, a constituent.

अवयवित्वेन i. 43 By reason of being अवयवी.

अवयविना i. 43 By अवयवी.

अवयवी i. 43 Organism; the possessor of parts, limbs, organs, constituents, factors.

—अवयवेषु ii. 15

अवयवेषु iii. 22

अवयव्यभावात् i. 43 From absence of अवयवी.

अवर्णम् iii. 17 Without varṇa or (alphabetical) letter-sound.

—अवलम्बन—iv. 15

—अवलम्बनम् i. 32

—अवलम्बी iii. 52

—अवलेही ii. 33

—अवलोकी ii. 40

अवशिष्टकर्मणः ii. 13 Of the remaining karma.

अवशिष्टस्य ii. 13 Of the remainder.

अवश्यम् i. 35 Uncontrollably, helplessly, irresistibly.

अवश्यः iii. 45 (अ+वश्, to wish) That which is beyond desire, reach, power; uncontrollable.

अवष्टब्धे iii. 22 (अव+स्तम्भ्, to stiffen up, to hold up as a column) Being pressed, stiffened.

अवसादयन्ति i. 50 Degrade; lower; make feeble.

—अवसानम् i. 50

—अवसानः ii. 23

अवसानेन iv. 33 (अव+सो, to finish) By end, finish, completion.

—अवसायित्वम्,—यिनः iii. 45

अवसिताधिकारम् i. 5, 51 With its momentum exhausted, its course run, its office expired.

अवसिताधिकारे iv. 11 Its functioning finished.

अवस्तुकः i. 43 Substanceless; un-substantial; unreal.

—अवस्था—iii. 13

—अवस्था—ii. 19; iii. 13

अवस्था ii. 4; iii. 13 (अव+स्था, to stand) State; condition.

अवस्थातुम् iv. 32 To stay.

अवस्थानम् i. 32 Standing; resting; the condition of standing.

अवस्थानम् ii. 13; iii. 45, iv. 34

अवस्थानाम् iii. 13;

—अवस्थानाः ii. 27

अवस्थान्तरतः iii. 13 Because of difference of condition.

अवस्थापयन्ति ii. 3 (They) establish, confirm, set up strongly.

अवस्थापरिणामक्रमः iii. 15 Succession of अवस्थापरिणामः

—अवस्थापरिणामाः iii. 13

अवस्थापरिणामम् iii. 13

अवस्थापरिणामः iii. 13 Change, transformation, of the conditions.

—अवस्थापरिणामाः ii. 19

अवस्थापरिणामे iii. 13

—अवस्थापरिणामैः iii. 13

अवस्थापितः iii. 17 Placed; fixed.

अवस्थाभिः iii. 13, 17

अवस्थाम् iii. 13

अवस्थाय ii. 19 Having stood.

—अवस्थायाम् ii. 15. 19

अवस्थायाम् ii. 27; iii. 55 In the state.

—अवस्थारूपेण iii. 13

अवस्थाविशेषाणाम् ii. 19 Of special states.

अवस्थितम् i. 27, 30, 32

अवस्थितः i. 27, 43; ii. 13 Stayed; steady; fixed; standing.

अवस्थितस्य iii. 13

अवस्थितायाम् i. 51 In (the condition of) being fixed, steadied.

—अवस्थिताः iv. 12

—अवस्थे i. 3

अविकल्पस्य i. 43 Of him (or that) who (or which) is free from uncertainty.

अविच्छेदः iii. 52 Non-severance.

अविच्छेदात् i. 16

अवितथम् ii. 45 (अ, not + वि, not + तथा, like that; not unlike the fact) Not-falsely; exactly; precisely; accurately; not otherwise than true.

अविदितव्यभिचाराः ii. 31 Not knowing variation or straying.

अविद्यया ii. 4, 15

अविद्या (अ + विद्, to know, wit) i. 8, 11; ii. 4, 5, 15, 23, 28; iv. 11 "Non-knowledge"; the opposite of true knowledge; positive error.

अविद्या ii. 4, 5, 24 Error; nescience; mistake; false knowledge; illusion; delusion.

अविद्या— ii. 3

अविद्यादयः i. 24; iv. 30 Error etc.

अविद्यापेक्षम् iv. 15 Dependent on Error.

अविद्याभेदाः ii. 4 Varieties, subdivisions, of Error.

अविद्याम् ii. 4

अविद्यायाम् iv. 25

अविध्यत् iv. 31 Pierced.

अविपक्वस्य ii. 13 Of the un-matured, the un-fruited, the unripe.

अविप्लवा ii. 26 'Un-float-ing'; unwavering, un-swerving, unfluctuating; unbroken; incessant; unremitting.

अविभागप्राप्तौ ii. 6 On the attainment of non-separateness.

अविभागापन्नम् ii. 18 Arrived at identity.

अविभागेन i. 42 Without separating or distinguishing.

अवियुक्तः iii. 13 Undisjoined; unseparated.

—अविरति—i. 30

अविरतिः i. 30 Non-cessation (from the pursuit of sense objects); non-surfeit.

अविरुद्धा ii. 55 Unopposed.

अविवेकविषयनिम्ना i. 12 Sloping towards, running or inclining in the direction of, the domain or the objects of error.

अविशिष्टः i. 7 Non-different.

—अविशिष्टा ii. 20; iv. 22

अविशिष्टाम् iv. 22 Unspecific; undifferentiated; differenceless.

—अविशेष—ii. 19

—अविशेषः iii. 35

—अविशेष—iv. 13

अविशेषपरिणामाः ii. 19 Transformations of the indefinite, the generic.

अविशेषः ii. 19 Non-specific; non-discrete; non-particular; in. definite.

अविशेषस्य ii. 19

अविशेषाणाम् ii. 19

अविशेषाः ii. 19

अविशेषेभ्यः ii. 19

अविशेषेषु ii. 19

अविषयात्मकम् iv. 23 Not of the nature of object.

अविषयीभूतत्वात् iii. 20 Because of its not being the object.

अविषयीभूतम् iii. 54; iv. 16 Un-objectified; not-cognised.

अवीचेः iii. 26 From a-vīchi, the 'waveless'.

अवृत्तिकस्य i. 13 Of the mode-less.

—अवैराग्य—i. 2

—अव्यक्त—i. 16

अव्यक्तम् ii. 5 (see अज्ञानि and अभिव्यक्तिः) Un-manifest; indistinct; indefinite.

अव्यपदेश्येभ्यः iii. 14

—अव्यपदेश्य—iii. 14

—अव्यपदेश्य—i. 44; iii. 49

अव्यपदेश्याः iii. 14 (अ + वि + अप + दिश्, to point out) Indescribable; as yet in the future.

अव्यसनम् ii. 55 Non-addiction.

अव्यात् i. 1 May (he) guard and protect.

अशास्त्रपूर्वकम् ii. 30 Not-preceded, not-guided,-by Science; against rule and law; contrary to science.

—अशीति ii. 34

अशुक्लम् iv. 7 Not-white; black; evil.

अशुक्लाकृष्णम् iv. 7 Non-white and non-black; neither good nor evil.

—अशुचि— ii. 5

अशुचिम् ii. 5 Impure.

अशुचौ ii. 5

अशुद्धिक्षयात् ii. 43 From or by the 'consumption', decay, abolition, removal, of impurity.

अशुद्धिक्षये ii. 28 On the clearing away of impurity.

अशुद्धिपरिणामः iv. 3 The product or result of impurity.

अशुद्धिरूपस्य ii. 28 Of (error of) the nature of impurity.

अशुद्धिः ii. 1, 28 Im-purity; error; inaccuracy; wrong.

अशुद्ध्यावरणमलम् ii. 43 Dirty envelope of impurity.

अशुद्ध्यावरणमलापगमात् ii. 27 By the removal of the dirt of the veil of impurity.

अशुद्ध्यावरणमलापेतस्य i. 47 Of the intelligence freed from the dirty envelope of impurity.

अशुद्धेः ii. 28

—अशुद्धयोः iv. 3

अशेषदृश्यात्मत्वेन iii. 49 By way of, in the nature of, all the Seen.

अशोच्यः i. 47 Unlamentable; not to be grieved for or over.

अश्रद्धेयार्थः i. 7. Whose intention, meaning, (statement), is unbelievable, unreliable, incredible, untrustworthy.

—अश्रु—iv. 25

अश्वः iii. 17 'Horse'; 'thou wentest'; and 'not-tomorrow'. (The word has three meanings, two as a noun, and one as a verb. A play upon words is illustrated).

अष्टमो iii. 26 Eighth.

अष्टौ ii. 29 Eight.

अष्टौ ii. 28; iii.45

असंयोगः ii. 25 Non-conjunction.

असंसर्गः ii. 40 Non-contact.

असंस्पृश्य iii. 17 Not having touched.

असङ्करः iii. 13 Non-mixture.

असङ्कीर्णम् i. 43 Unmixed, unalloyed; uncrowded; not 'flung-together'; not confused.

—असङ्कीर्णयोः iii. 35

—असङ्कीर्णयोः ii. 6

असङ्ख्येयवासनाभिः iv. 24 By countless tendencies, desires, indwelling propensities.

असङ्ख्येयस्य ii. 13 Of the uncountable, innumerable.

असङ्ख्येया ii. 34 Uncountable (fem:)

असङ्ख्येयाभिः iv. 24

असङ्गः iii. 39 Non-attachment.

—असत् ii. 19

असतः iv. 12 Of the non-existent.

असति i. 10 In case of (its) not-being; if there were not.

—असत्तम् ii. 19

असत्याम् iv. 25 (fem: of असति)

असन्दिग्धेन iii. 53 (अ + सं + दिह्, to anoint; to plaster and so make vague) By the non-uncertain; by the sure, the certain, the un-doubted.

असमुदाचारात् iii. 13 (अ + सं + उत् + आ + चर्, to move) Because of non-up-moving, non-manifestation.

असम्प्रज्ञातः i. (अ + सं + प्र + ज्ञा, to know) 1, 2, 11, 18, 20 Unconscious; that wherein nothing particular and definite is known and which itself is not known.

असम्प्रज्ञातसमाधिः i. 18 Unconscious trance. (Many editions read असंप्रज्ञातः समाधिः)

—असम्प्रमोषः i. 11 (अ + सम् + प्र + मुष् to steal) Not letting go; non-abandonment; non-forgetfulness.

—असम्प्रयोगे ii. 54, iii. 21 (अ + सं + प्र + युज, to join).

असम्भवात् iii. 52 Because of impossibility.

असम्भावितः ii. 9 Not made possible, realisable, conceivable, imaginable.

असम्भिन्नशक्तिप्रविभागाः ii. 18 With the distinctions of their several powers, forces, functions, unconfused, unobliterated, not mixed up together; possessed of distinct functions.

असाधना iii. 17 Meansless; without means.

असाध्यं iii. 13

असुर—iii. 26; iv. 1 A kind of spirits or jīvas (titans as opposed to suras, gods).

असुरभवनेषु iv. 1 In the mansions of the asuras.

असौ i. 24, 43; ii. 4; iii. 13; iv. 24 This one.

—**अस्त**—i. 41

—**अस्तम्**—iii. 44

—**अस्तम्** ii. 19

अस्तम् ii. 10, 27 (**अस्** to throw) Setting; 'flung-away-ness', mergence; disappearance.

अस्ति iv. 12 Is; ex-ists.

अस्ति i. 9, 24; ii. 4, 13, 14; iii. 13; iv. 6, 12, 33 etc.

अस्तिक्रियाम् iv. 33 The action of existing.

—**अस्तिता** iv. 33

—**अस्तिताः** ii. 18

—**अस्तित्वम्** i. 51

अस्तु i. 24; ii. 20 Let be; may be; may exist; let it be so; may it be so.

—**अस्तेय**—ii. 30

अस्तेयप्रतिष्ठायाम् ii. 37 On confirmation of or in, or on full establishment of or in, non-misappropriativeness.

अस्तेयम् ii. 30 Non-theft; honesty.

अस्थाने ii. 24 In the 'non-place', the wrong place; baseless; causeless; groundless.

—**अस्थि**—iii. 29 Bone.

अस्पृहारूपम् ii. 30 Of the form of non-coveting.

अस्प्राक्षम् i. 32 I have touched.

अस्मि i. 36; iv. 27 Am.

—**अस्मिता**—i. 17; ii. 3; iii. 47; [iv. 4

—**अस्मिता**—i. 8

अस्मिता ii. 6 'I-am-ness'; egoism; (sense of personality, individuality, separate individual existence as one among and distinct from others).

अस्मिता i. 17 (**एकात्मिका संवित्**) (The feel or consciousness of individual separate uni-queness; '*I am one*').

अस्मिताक्लेशः ii. 6 The misery or 'sin' of egoism.

अस्मितादीनाम् ii. 4 Of **अस्मिता** etc.

अस्मिताऽनुगतः i. 1 Accompanied by 'am-ness' i.e. the sense of separate individual existence.

अस्मितामात्रध्यानसुखाः iii. 26 Rejoicing in the contemplation of mere 'am-ness', in the mere voluminous feel of being.

अस्मितामात्रम् i. 36; iv. 4 Mere 'I-am-ness'.

अस्मितामात्रः i. 17; ii. 19

अस्मितामात्रा i. 36 (Fem:)

अस्मितामात्रात् iv. 4 From or out of I-am-ness only.

अस्मितायाम् i. 36 In egoism.

अस्मितालक्षणः iii. 47 Having the nature or character of egoism.

अस्मितालक्षणस्य ii. 19

अस्मिन् iii. 34 In this.

अस्य i. 40 Of this.

अस्य i. 23, 33; ii. 5; iii. 4, 13; iv. 8, 11, 16. 33 etc. Of this one (mas:)

अस्याः i. 43; iii. 6 Of this one (fem:)

अस्वाप्सम् i. 10 I have slept.

अस्वीकरणम् ii. 30 (अ+स्व, self, own+कृ, to make; making a thing one's own) Non-appropriation, non-acceptance, non-accumulation.

अहङ्कारममकारानुपातिनम् ii. 15 Following or 'running after' 'I-ness' and 'mine-ness' (i.e., attaching his egoism and proprietary feeling to the objects of the senses).

अहङ्कारः i. 45; iii. 47 I-ness ('I-making'; self-assertion; egoism.

अहनि ii. 31 In or on the day.

अहम् i. 10, 32; ii. 24, 33, 39; iii. 51; iv. 19, 25 I (अ is the first and ह the last letter of the Samskṛt alphabet; between the two are contained all verbal expressions of all the moods, modes, experiences of the self; therefore the individual, manifest, self is named **अहम्** ; म् being the primal nasal intonation which may be said to be the matrix of all articulate letter-sounds from and into which they emerge and merge. As ॐ (अउम्) denominates the Universal Self, so **अहम्** the individual self.

अहिंसा—ii. 30

अहिंसा ii. 30, 31 (अ + हिंस्, to kill) Non-slaying; non-violence; non-injury; harmlessness.

अहिंसादयः ii. 31 Harmlessness etc.

अहिंसाप्रतिष्ठायाम् ii. 35 On establishment of or in harmlessness.

अहीशः i. 1 The lord of ahis, serpents (the wise ones .

आ

आ ii. 28 Up to; till.

आ i. 35; iii. 42

—आकार—iv. 22

—आकार—i. 11, 42; ii. 6, 17, 32; iii. 3, 14; iv. 10, 23.

—आकारम् i. 38; iii. 47

—आकारः iii. 17

आकारशीलविद्यादिभिः ii. 6 By form or features, manners, or character, and learning etc. (Here, with reference to the Ego, 'by purity of formlessness, by characteristic of desirelessness, and by consciousnes of the nature of pure awareness).

—आकारा iii. 31

आकारादिभिः iii. 44 By form or appearance etc.

—आकारेण i. 41

आकार्यते ii. 4 Is called up; is called up before the mind, formulated, supposed, imposed, postulated.

—आकाश— iii. 26

आकाशम् iv. 19 Space.

आकाशः iii. 44 (कश्, to sound; काश्, to shine) Space; vacuum; the ākāsha tattva, the substratum of sound; the luminiferous ether.

आकाशकल्पम् i. 36 Of the form of, like, similar to, almost as, space.

आकाशगतिः iii. 42 Movement in space; the power of movement in space, air, ether, sky, heaven.

आकाशगमनम् iii. 42 Going in space, sky, air.

आकाशगमनाणिमादिलाभः iv. 1 The gain of (the occult powers) of flying in the sky, and of minimising oneself to an atom etc.

—आकाशयोः iii. 41, 42

आकाशवाय्वग्न्युदकभूमयः ii. 19 Ether, air, fire, water, earth.

आकाशस्य i. 45

आकाशे iii. 26, 45; iv. 31

—आकृतिना iii. 26

—आकृतयः iii. 26

आक्षालनम् ii. 32 (The act of). washing.

आक्षालयन् ii. 40 Washing.

आक्षिपति i. 32; ii. 13, 34; (आ + क्षिप् to throw) Drags in; flings at or away; beats down; scorns; runs to; strikes at or down; surpasses; excels; includes; covers; extends to or over; transcends; attacks; contracts.

—आक्षिप्तम् iii. 17

आक्षिप्तः ii. 51 Contracted or transcended.

आक्षिप्य iii. 26 Having dragged in, acquired, earned.

—आक्षेप—ii. 51

आक्षेपः iii. 17 A fling at; a contacting of; a dragging or bringing in.

—आक्षेपात् ii. 34

—आक्षेपी ii. 51

—आख्यम् ii. 25

—आख्यात—iii. 17 (Verbs, which 'make clear', 'declare' by action; action throws ex-istence into relief, brings it out, proclaims it; आ + ख्या, to declare.)

—आख्यातम् ii. 20

आख्यानम् iii. 18 Narrative; story.

—आख्यानि iii. 26 (Names, because the characteristic activity fixes the name).

आख्यायते i. 1, 2; ii. 19, 20, 27; iv. 22 Is called, declared, designated, proclaimed, explained.

—आख्यायिष्यन्ते ii. 19

—आगतम् iv. 12

—आगतः iii. 13, 14

आगमः i. 7 'Coming;' that which has come down from the past and from those who knew; coming into the mind; communi-cation; revelation; tradition'). (All scriptures generally, including Veḍas, Smṛṭis, Purāṇas and Iṭihāsas, are called Āgama; the Veḍas by themselves are called Nigama).

आगमतः i. 25 From Āgama, the scriptures, the Testimony of the wise, the seers, the ṛṣhis.

—आगमवतीभिः ii. 19

आगमविज्ञानम् i. 49 Knowledge based on Testimony; knowledge based on Scripture.

—आगमाः i. 7

आगमिनः i. 27 Those versed in the Āgama,

आगमेन i. 48, 49

—आगमैः ii. 9

आघ्रातम् i. 43 (or आम्नातम) 'Smelt'; smelling of; (or cognised or thought of as).

आचक्षते i. 2; ii. 52; iii. 52 (आ + चक्ष् to declare) (They) declare.

आचमनम् ii. 49 Drinking; sipping.

आचामति i. 31 (आ + चम् to drink). Drinks in.

—आचार्य—i. 35

आचार्यः iv. 10 (आ + चर्, to go, to act; one who teaches by action, by example) Preceptor.

आचार्यदेशीयः ii. 24 One in the place of an āchārya; one almost as venerable as an āchārya; not fully qualified but nearly so.

आततम् ii. 13 (आ + तन्, to spread Bespread; overspread.

—आत्म—i. 30; iii. 11

—आत्मकम् ii. 18

—आत्मकम् i. 43; ii. 14, 17, 18, 21; iii. 14; iv. 23.

—आत्मकः ii. 20; iii. 17

—आत्मकत्वात् ii. 15

आत्मकल्पेन i. 5 By form like that of the Self, the Ego; by similarity to the Self; as if it were the Self.

—आत्मकाः iii. 9, 15, 49

—आत्मकानाम् iv. 14

—आत्मके iii. 44

—आत्मकेन iii. 3

—आत्मकेषु i. 33, 43

—आत्मख्यातिः ii. 5 Awareness, recognition, knowledge, belief of (i.e. that it is) the Self.

आत्मख्यापनार्था ii. 23 For the sake of self-declaration; for the sake of making itself known.

—आत्मता ii. 6

—आत्मत्वेन iii. 49

आत्मत्वेन ii. 5 By selfness; in the way of selfness; as if it were oneself.

—आत्मदर्शनयोग्यत्वानि ii. 41

आत्मदर्शनयोग्यत्वं ii. 41 Fitness for vision of the Self.

—आत्मनः i. 47; iii. 43

आत्मनः ii. 19 (महतः) Of Mahat, the 'large' Self, the Universal Mind.

—आत्मना iii. 35

आत्मना ii. 4; iv. 15 By (that) nature; by (that) self (-characteristic).

—आत्मनाम् iv. 7, 34

आत्मनाम् iii. 14 (भावानां) Of special forms of being; of beings, things.

आत्मनि ii. 19 (महति)

आत्मबुद्धिम् ii. 6 Belief of selfness; the belief, the feeling, that 'I am this mind'.

आत्मभावजिज्ञासा ii. 39 Wish to know the way of existence of oneself.

आत्मभावभावनाविनिवृत्तिः iv. 25 Remission or cessation of reflection on the nature of the Self.

आत्मभूतः i. 43 'Become the self'; which is its very soul, its very nature; its constituenr characteristic; natural.

आत्मरूपम् ii. 22 Its own form; its (continued) existence.

आत्मव्यापदम् ii. 5 The misfortune of oneself.

आत्मसम्पदम् ii. 5 The prosperity of oneself.

आत्मस्वरूपम् iv. 19 Self-form; its own form.

—आत्मा—i. 32.

—आत्मा i. 43; ii. 20; iii. 14, 17, 44, 47, 52; iv. 33.

आत्मा ii. 21 Being; Self; Nature; essence.

आत्मानम् i. 36; ii. 15; iii. 51

—आत्मानः iv. 13

—आत्मानः iii. 17, 26, 49; iv. 10

आत्मानुग्रहाभावे i. 25 'In the absence of self-compassion'; in the absence of all wish to benefit himself.

आत्माशीः ii. 9; iv. 10 (आ + शास् to wish) Self-blessing; the instinct of self-preservation.

—आत्मिक—ii. 15.

—आत्मिकम् i. 31; iv. 10

आत्मीयया iv. 23 By its own.

आत्यन्तिकः ii. 17, 25; iii. 50 Final; ultimate; absolute; complete; supreme; extreme; conclusive.

आत्यन्तिकी ii. 15 Final etc. (fem.)

आददानः ii. 33 Taking up.

—आदयः ii. 34

—आदयः ii. 19, 31, 33

—आदर्श— iii. 36

आदर्शात् iii. 36 By 'comprehensive vision', clear-vision, clairvoyance.

—आदानात् iv. 7

—आदाय iv. 33

—आदि—iii. 45; iv. 10

—आदि—i. 43; ii. 1; iii. 7

आदि ii. 33; iv. 1 Beginning with; etc.

—आदिः ii. 20

आदिः iv. 14 Beginning; origin.

—आदित्य—i. 35 The sun (the son of A-ḍiṭi.)

—आदित्वम् ii. 4

—आदिना ii. 18

आदिमत् iii. 13 Having a beginning.

आदिविद्वान् i. 25 The Primal Sage.

—आदिषु iii. 23, 39

—आदिषु i. 35; iii. 6

आदिषु iii. 1

—आदीनाम् ii. 4; iii. 13

—आदीनि iii. 24

आदीनि ii. 46

आदौ i. 26; ii. 19 In the beginning.

आद्यम् i. Original; primal.

आधातुम् ii. 38 To implant.

आधिदैविकम् i. 31; iii. 22 Pertaining to the ḍevas, gods, nature-forces; caused by the action of superphysical agents.

आधिभौतिकम् i. 31; iii. 22 Pertaining to the elements; external, extraneous.

आधीयन्ते iii. 9 (आ + धा to do, to put). Are put on or in; are implanted, nourished, fostered; thrive.

—आधेयः iv. 14

आधेयशौचत्वात् ii. 5 Because of requiring artificial cleansing.

—आध्यात्मिक—ii. 15

आध्यात्मिकम् i. 31; iii. 22; iv. 10 Connected with, pertaining or referring to the self, the subject; self-referring; subjective; internal; mental and bodily i.e. connected with mind-and-body as constituting a living, embodied, individual self.

—आनन्तर्य—iii. 52; iv. 33

आनन्तर्यम् iv. 9 Im-mediacy; immediate succession.

आनन्त्यात् iv. 31 Because of endlessness.

—आनन्द—i. 17

आनन्दः i. 17 Rejoicing; bliss; joy.

आनन्दमात्रध्यानसुखाः iii. 26 Rejoicing in the contemplation or feeling of a voluminous bliss.

आनन्दानुगतः i. 1 Accompanied or pervaded by the sense or feeling of happiness or bliss.

आनाभिवृत्तिः iii. 39 Functioning up to the navel.

—आनुश्रविक—i. 15

—आनुश्रविक—i. 15, 16

आनुश्रविकविषये i. 15 (अनु+श्रु to hear) In matters heard or revealed, matters pertaining to the life hereafter.

आपः iii. 45; iv. 3 Waters.

—आपत्ति—ii. 47

—आपत्तिः i. 41; ii. 6

—आपत्तौ iv. 22 On the happening, accomplishment.

आपद्यते ii. 1, 16, 28, 50; iii. 15 (आ+पद् to become). Becomes; arrives at the condition of; approaches; becomes transformed into; falls into.

—आपन्नम् ii. 18, 47; iv 12, 23

आपन्नम् ii. 17, 21 22; iii. 55 Fallen into; brought to; arrived at.

—आपन्नः i. 43

आपन्नः iii. 17 Come to; reduced to; befallen.

—आपन्ना i. 43

—आपन्नेषु i. 33

आपादतलवृत्तिः iii. 39 Functioning, existing, working, down to the sole of the foot.

—आपूरात् iv. 2

आपूरेण iv. 2 By overflow; by flood.

—आप्त—iv. 22

—आप्तम् iv. 13

—आप्तयः ii. 28

—आप्तिः iv. 32

आप्तेन i. 7 By one who has 'arrived at or found'; one who has found and been espoused by the Truth; one who knows the Truth and is trustworthy.

—आप्नुवन्ति iv. 21

आप्नोति ii. 17 (आप् to gain, to find) Obtains, gains, attains, finds, undergoes, suffers.

आप्यस्य i. 45 Of the aqueous.

—आप्यायित—i. 16 (Watered, nourished, fostered).

आप्लावयन्ति iv. 3 Flood; inundate; fill with water; irrigate.

—आभासम् iv. 19

—आभासम् i. 41

आभास्वराः iii. 26 A class of gods.

—आभोग—i. 15

आभोगः i. 17 (आ+भुज् to taste, eat, experience) Extent; expanse, magnitude; enjoyment, appreciation, experience.

—आभ्यन्तर—ii. 50, 51

आभ्यन्तरम् ii. 32 Internal (neuter).

आभ्यन्तरः ii. 50 Internal (masc.).

आभ्यन्तरविषयः ii. 51 Pertaining to, having for object, or being the object of, the internal.

आमलकयोः iii. 53 Of two myrobolan fruits.

—आमृष्टा ii. 20

—आम्नायः ii. 27

आम्रवणम् iii. 44 A forest of mango trees.

आम्राणाम् iii. 44 Of mangoes.

—आयत—ii. 5 drawn-out, stretched out; pulled straight; extended, extensive, large.

आयतत्वात् iv. 7 (आ+यम् to rule, to place under compulsion) Because of being bespread, drawn out, extended, controlled.

—आयामः—iii. 26
आयुषि ii. 13 In the life-term.
—आयुष्कम् ii. 13
आयुष्करम् iii. 22 Determinative of the life-term.
आयुष्मतः iii. 18 Of the long-lived.
आयुष्मता iii. 51 By the blessed.
—आयुः—ii. 14
—आयुः ii. 13
—आयुः ii. 34
आयुः ii. 13; iii. 22, 26 Life-term; life-time; life-period.
आयुर्भोगहेतुत्वात् ii. 13 Because of being the cause of experience and of life-term.
आयुर्विपाकम् iii. 22 That which produces, results in, determines the extent or term of, the life-time, the term or period of life; that which governs, fixes, the limits of the life.
—आयुषः iii. 26
—आरब्धः ii. 51
आरभते i. 11 Begins, initiates, commences, sets up.
आरभन्ते ii. 15 (Plural).
आरभमाणः ii. 17, 40 Commencing.
आरभ्य iii. 26 Having begun; beginning with.
आरभ्यते ii. 1, 19, 20, 28 Is commenced.
—आरम्भी ii. 13
आराधनात् ii. 12 By propitiation.
आरुह्य i. 47 Having ascended or mounted to or on.
—आरूढम् ii. 16; iii. 49
आरोग्यम् ii. 15 Absence of disease; good health.
आर्द्रवस्त्रम् iii. 22 Wet cloth.
आर्यपुत्र ii. 24 Son of the elder; husband.
—आलम्बन— i. 37, 41
—आलम्बनम् i. 38; iii. 20
आलम्बनम् iii. 20; iv. 11 Support; rest; that from or on which a thing 'lengthens' out, pends, hangs, depends.
—आलम्बनः i. 18
—आलम्बनस्य iii. 2
—आलम्बना i. 10
—आलम्बनाः i. 17
आलम्बनीकृतम् iii. 20 Made a support; made object (of attention).
आलम्बनीक्रियते i. 18 Is made a support, a rest; is rested on.
आलम्बनीभूतम् i. 44; iii. 20 Become or acting as the support.
आलम्बनीभूतः iii. 17
आलम्बनीभूतत्वात् iv. 23 Because of being the support.
आलम्बने i. 17; ii. 4; iii. 20
—आलम्बनैः iv. 11
—आलस्य— i. 30
आलस्यम् i. 30 Laziness; lassitude.
—आलोक—iii. 25
—आलोकः iii. 5
—आलोकः iii. 6, 51
आलोकः i. 47; iii. 5, 25 (आ + लुक् to look) Light; luminosity; what makes visible.

—आलोचितः iii. 47

आवयत् iv. 31 (आ + वि to weave) wove, strung.

आवरकेण iv. 31 By that which veils.

—आवरण—iii. 43; iv. 31

—आवरण—i. 47; ii. 27, 43; iii. 45

—आवरणम् ii. 52

—आवरणम् i. 20; iii. 41

आवरणम् iii. 43; iv. 3 (आ + वृ to wrap) That which wraps, envelopes, covers up, screens, hides, veils, conceals, distorts, makes hazy; also a barrier, ridge, hedge.

—आवरणीयम् ii. 52

आवर्जितः i. 23 (आ not, the reverse of + वृज्, to shun, to forbid, to exclude) Won over; inclined; made to incline; propitiated.

आवर्त्तते i. 5, 19; ii. 24 'Exists on all sides'; rotates; comes back; revolves round and round.

आवर्त्तमानस्य iv. 11 Of the whirling, revolving, turning.

आवापम् ii. 13 (आ + वप् to sow, to put into the ground) Immersion, sheathing.

आवापगमनम् ii. 13 'Going into sheath'; mergence; disappearance; absorption; neutralisation.

आविर्भावः iii. 11 Becoming apparent; manifestation; outcoming; appearing; coming forth.

आविर्भूताः iii. 17 Manifested; externalised.

आविशन्ति iii. 43 (आ + विश् to enter) Enter.

आवृतम् iv. 31 Covered up.

आवृतकायः iii. 45 With body hidden.

आवृत्य ii. 52 Covering up; enveloping; wrapping.

—आवेशः iii. 38

आशङ्का iv. 19 Doubt; objection.

—आशय— i. 5; ii. 13, 15; iii. 38; iv. 7, 9.

—आशयम् iv. 6

—आशयम् i. 50; iv. 6

—आशयः ii. 12

—आशयः ii. 12, 13, 15

आशयः iv. 6

—आशयस्य ii. 5

—आशयाः iv. 30

आशयाः i. 24 (आ + शी to sleep) sleeping-places; seed-germs of desires, wherein desires sleep, lie latent; vessels; receptacles; capsules; glands; also intentions (which 'sleep' in the mind and in words).

— आशयैः i. 24

आशिरोवृत्तिः iii. 39 Functioning or existing up to the head.

आशिषः iv. 10 (अश् to eat) Of the blessing.

—आशीः ii. 9; iv. 10

आशीविषेण ii. 15 By a serpent.

—आश्रय—iv. 11

—आश्रयत्वम् ii. 36

आश्रयः iv. 11 Substratum; support

—आश्रयेण ii. 15, 18

आश्रयेत् i. 32 May rest in or lean on

—आश्रिताः i. 10

—आश्वासः ii. 13

आश्वासयन्ती ii. 5 'Giving breath'; giving life; filling with life; vitalising; assuring; encouraging.

आसते i. 28 (They) 'sit near', practise.

—आसन—ii. 29

आसनम् ii. 46 (आस् to sit) Posture; seat.

—आसनम् ii. 46

आसनम् ii. 47

आसनजयात् ii. 48 From conquest or mastery of posture.

आसनजये ii. 49 In winning, achieving, the (firm) seat.

आसनादीनि ii. 46 Posture etc.

—आसने ii. 32

—आसन्नम् ii. 19

आसन्नः i. 21 (सद् to sit) 'Sitting near'; close by; near at hand; imminent.

आसन्नः i. 22

आसन्नतरः i. 22, 23 Nearer.

आसन्नतमः i. 22 Nearest.

आसम् ii. 39; iv. 25 I was.

आसादितः iii. 51 'Caused to sit', 'brought to a stand'; found.

आसाम् i. 11, 12; iv. 3, 9 Of these (fem.).

आसीत् iv. 26 Was.

आसीत i. 28 Let him 'sit near', practise.

आसुरये i. 25 To the ṛshi Āsuri.

—आसेवितः i. 14 (आ + सेव् to serve.) Served; practised; followed; observed.

आसेव्यम् ii. 1 To be served or observed.

आसेव्यमानः ii. 2 Being observed, practised.

—आस्वाद—iii. 36

आस्वादात् iii. 36 From superphysical-taste.

आह i. 32; ii. 24, 28; iii. 13 Says.

—आहरेत् iv. 24

आहारः ii. 28 Food.

—आहार्याः iv. 3

आहुः iv. 14, 15, 23 They say.

आहृदयवृत्तिः iii. 39 Functioning, working, up to the heart.

आहोस्वित् i. 11, 24; ii. 23 Or; perhaps; or is it that?

—इ—

इक्षुरस—iii. 26 Sugar-cane-juice.

इच्छन् ii. 34 Desiring; wishing.

—इच्छया ii. 55

इच्छस्व ii. 13 Do thou desire.

इच्छानभिघातः iii. 45 Non-defeat of desire; success of will.

इच्छाभिघातात् i. 31 Because of frustration of desire.

—इत—i. 41; iii. 44; iv. 12, 13, 33 See प्रत्यस्तमित, अतीत, अपेत उपेत, उदित.

— इत—iv. 12

—इतम् i. 2; iii. 13

इतरम् ii. 15, 16 To another.

इतरः iv. 33 Another.

इतरत्र i. 4 Other-where; elsewhere; in other states, circumstances, or conditions; on other occasions.

इतरप्रत्ययवत् i. 10 Like other apprehensions, aware-nesses, cognitions, moods, modes, notions.

इतरस्य i. 24; iii 55 Of another.

इतराणि iv. 19 Others.

इतरेतरसहगतः iii. 17 Accompanied by or accompanying each other.

इतरेतराध्यासरूपः iii. 17 Of the form or nature of mutual reflexion, imitation.

इतरेतराध्यासात् iii. 17 Because of reflexion, superimposition, imitation, in, on, of, each other.

इतरेतराश्रयेण ii. 15 By mutual support.

इतरेतरोपाश्रयेण ii. 18 By support of each other.

इतरेन्द्रियजयवत् ii. 54, 55 Like the conquest, subjugation, of any other organ (separately, one by one).

इतरेषाम् i. 20; iv. 7 Of others.

इतरेषाम् iv. 6, 7

इति ii. 34; iii. 54, 55; iv. 34 Finis; thus; so; this.

इति i. 1; ii. 1; iii. 1; iv. 1; etc.

इत्थम् iii. 18 Thus.

इदम् i. 2; ii. 13; iii. 9, 53; iv. 11; etc. This.

इदानीं iii. 44 Now; at present.

—इन्दु—i. 36 The moon.

इन्द्रः ii. 12 Inḍra, the sovereign of the gods.

इन्द्रजालेन ii. 52 By jugglery, sorcery, magic; phantasmagoria; ('the network' of phantasms spread by Inḍra the king of the gods; इन्दति, shines and reigns supremely.

—इन्द्रिय— ii. 18, 41, 43

—इन्द्रिय— i. 41; ii. 54, 55; iii. 39, 51

इन्द्रियम् iv. 14 (इदं द्रवति = इदंद्रः = इंद्रः, the Self, which pervades the 'This'; इंद्रः ईयते अनुमीयते अनेन इति इंद्रियम्, that by which the Self is indicated). A sensor or motor organ.

—इन्द्रियजय—ii. 41

इन्द्रियजयः iii. 47 Conquest, subjugation, control of the organs.

इन्द्रियजयः ii. 41, 55

इन्द्रियप्रणालिकया i. 7 By the channel of the organs.

इन्द्रियभावेन ii. 18 By or in the form or shape or being of an organ or organs.

इन्द्रियरूपेषु iii. 47 On the aspects of the organs,

इन्द्रियसिद्धिः ii. 43 Accomplishment or perfection of organ.

—इन्द्रियाणाम iv. 1

इन्द्रियाणाम् ii. 54, 55 Of the organs.

इन्द्रियाणाम् iii. 47, 48

—इन्द्रियाणि ii. 19

इन्द्रियाणि ii. 54, 55 ; iii. 38; iv. 19 Organs.

—इन्द्रियेषु iii. 13

इन्द्रियेषु ii. 14, 28

—इन्द्रियेषु iii. 13

इन्धनीकुर्याम् iii. 51 May I make fuel.

इयत्तावधारणेन ii. 50 By ideation of 'so-much-ness'; by the notion of quantity; by regulation or determination of the length or number.

इयन्तः iii. 17 So many.

इयम् i. 2; ii. 5; iii. 6, 17; iv. 7; etc. This (fem:)

इयान् ii. 50 So much.

इलावृतम् iii. 26 The Purāṇic name of a continent; Ilāvṛtam.

इव i. 41, 43; ii. 6, 54; iii. 3 As if; like.

इव i. 10; iv. 13; etc.

—इष्ट—iii. 51

—इष्ट – iii. 51

इष्टम् iii. 42 Desired.

इष्टदेवतासम्प्रयोगः ii. 44 Union or association with, finding or vision of, coming into touch with, inspiration or stimulation by, the wished for deity.

इष्टानिष्टगुणस्वरूपावधारणम् ii. 18 The 'holding (before the mind)', 'assuming', 'postulating', 'putting on', 'imagining', 'ideating', 'conceiving', being conscious of, the pleasant and painful forms of (the primal trinity of) attributes.

इह ii. 5, 13 ; iii. 51 Here.

ई

ईक्षमाणः ii. 32 Beholding; patiently watching and awaiting.

—ईक्षित्वात् iv. 17

ईप्सितम् ii. 45 (आप् to obtain) Desired to be ob-tained.

ईशितृत्वम् iii. 45 Lordship; lordliness; sovereignty; ruling might.

—ईश्वर—ii. 1, 32

—ईश्वर—iv. 3

ईश्वर—i. 23; ii. 45

ईश्वर—i. 24; ii. 1, 12, 32, 45; iii. 6.

ईश्वरः i. 24 (ईश् to rule) Supreme; Lord; Sovereign; Omnipotent; Ruler.

ईश्वरः i. 23, 24, 27, 29

ईश्वरप्रणिधानम् ii. 1, 32

ईश्वरप्रणिधानात् i. 23; ii. 45 By 'placing oneself in' God,

(abiding in the Lord); by submission, surrender, resignation to the will of, God; by contemplation of God; by placing God in one's own consciousness.

ईश्वरप्रसादात् iii. 6 By the grace of God.

ईश्वरसत्त्वे i. 24 In the sattva, that 'finest' or that particular factor or attribute of Prakṛti which, predominantly cognitive, constitutes the garment, the veil, the body, the consciousness or knowledge, of Īshwara.

ईश्वरस्य i. 24, 27, 28; iii. 53, 55 Of Īshwara.

—ईश्वरस्य iii. 55

ईश्वरार्पितसर्वभावस्य ii. 45 Of him who has offered up, deposited, placed, assigned, all (his own) moods, conditions, impulses, in and to Īshwara; who regards all his moods and acts as ordained by God.

ईष्टे iii. 45 Prevails; rules; governs; exercises sovereignty.

उ

उक्तम् iv. 28

उक्तम् i. 25, 36; ii. 5, 25; iii. 6, 13; iv. 10, 25, 31, 34 Said; declared; has been said (neuter).

उक्तः ii. 13; iii. 13 (Mas:)

उक्ता ii. 4; iii. 25 (Fem:)

उक्ताः ii. 46

उक्तानि iii. 1

उक्ते iii. 17

—उक्तेन iii. 13

उक्त्वा iv. 21 Having said.

उच्छिन्नक्लेशमूलः ii. 13 That of which the sin, the misery-root, the root-misery, has been severed, torn out, destroyed.

उच्छेददृष्ट्यात्मकः ii. 9 Of the nature of a prospect, apprehension, of annihilation.

उच्छेदवादप्रसङ्गः ii. 15 The ensuing or entailment of the doctrine of annihilation.

उच्छ्वसिति ii. 34 Sighs; upbreathes; breathes with difficulty; sobs.

उच्यते i. 17, 36, 41, 48, 49; ii. 4, 42; iii. 3, 4; iv. 23 Is said; is declared.

उच्यन्ते iii. 17, 48 Are said.

उत्कर्षः i. 24 Uplift; elevation; progress; evolution.

उत्कर्षयति ii. 38 Uplifts; developes; elevates; enhances.

उत्क्रान्तिः iii. 39 Up-springing: up-going; ascension, ascent.

उत्क्रान्तिः iii. 39

—उत्तम—ii. 42

उत्तमम् i. 48 Highest; best; most excellent.

—उत्तमः iii. 48

उत्तमाः iii. 51

उत्तमानुकूलाभिः iii. 26 By excellent and favourable, sympathetic, affectionate (nymphs).

उत्तम्भयिष्यति iii. 51 Will uphold, re-arouse, upraise, foster.

—उत्तर—iii. 6, 26

उत्तरम् i. 16; iii. 53 'More upwards'; next, second, later in order (neu:); what comes after (the query); answer; (the north).

उत्तरः iii. 12, 17, 26 (masc:)

उत्तरदेशम् iii. 52 The new or other or next place or space.

उत्तरदेशे iii. 53 In the succeeding or other place.

उत्तरपरिणामोपजनः iv. 2 The birth, origin, germination, commencement, of the succeeding transformation, aspect, manifestation.

उत्तरभाविनः iii. 52 Of the next-occurring (moment).

tence.

उत्तरस्य iii. 53

उत्तरा i. 24 Subsequent (fem:)

उत्तरामलकसहक्षणदेशात् iii. 53 From the space marked by the moment, or from the space and the moment, associated with the other or next myrobalan. [A particular position or situation of such an undistinctive-looking fruit as a myrobalan—all myrobalans look alike—is associated with a particular spot of space and a particular moment of time—always. And these three, the time-moment, the space-point, and the substance-motion (or rest), help to fix and identify each other].

उत्तराः कुरवः iii. 26 'The northern Kurus'—a legendary happy people and blessed land.

उत्तरे ii. 30; iii. 55 Subsequent ones.

उत्तरेण iii. 17

उत्तरेषाम् ii. 4 Of the subsequent, the others.

—उत्तरेषु iv. 15 'उत्तरक्षणेषु' इति पाठान्तरः

उत्पतन्तम् ii. 54; iii. 38 Uprising, flying.

उत्पतन्ति ii. 54 (उत् up + पत् to fall) Leap up, fly.

—उत्पत्ति—i. 9

उत्पत्ति—i. 9

—उत्पत्तिः iii. 13

उत्पत्तिकारणम् ii. 28 The cause of birth.

उत्पत्तिधर्मस्य i. 9 Of the property of birth.

उत्पत्तिबीजम् ii. 23 The seed of birth, production.

उत्पत्तिस्थित्यभिव्यक्तिविकारप्रत्ययाप्तयः ii. 28 Birth, preservation, manifestation, transformation, belief, gain.

उत्पत्तौ iii. 33 (उत् + पद् to go, to happen) In the birth.

उत्पद्यते iii. 18, 21 (उत् + पद् to go) Arises; is produced.

उत्पद्यन्ते iv. 29

उत्पद्यमानस्य iv. 15 Of the arising.

उत्पद्यमानाः iii. 37 Arising, originating (plural:)

उत्पद्यमानेन iii. 18

उत्पद्येत iv. 16 May arise.

—उत्पन्नम् iii. 54

—उत्पन्नता iv. 11

उत्पन्ना i. 35 Born; produced; arisen.

उत्पन्ना i. 35, 36

उत्पन्नाः i. 35

—उत्पल—ii. 5; iii. 26

—उत्पादः ii. 23

उत्पादः ii. 27 Birth; production.

उत्पादयति i. 35; iv. 12 Produces.

उत्पादयिष्यामि ii. 24 I shall produce.

—उत्पादात् ii. 34

—उत्पादाय iv. 21

—उत्पादे ii. 27

उत्पित्सु iv. 12 'Wishing to,' ready to, arise (neu:).

उत्सर्गस्य ii. 13 Of the general rule, 'the (fiat) gone forth' or 'sent forth'.

उत्सहन्ते iv. 11, 32 (They) dare.

उत्सहेत iv. 10 May venture.

उत्साहः i. 13 Assurance; courage; eonfidence; enterprise; high spirit.

उत्सृज्य iv. 14 Having cast forth, abandoned.

—उदक—ii. 19; iii. 26

उदके iii. 45 In the water.

—उदधिना iii. 26

उदधीनाम् iv. 22 Of the oceans.

उद्पत्स्यत् iv. 12 Would arise or would have arisen.

—उदयः iv. 9

उदयः iii. 11 (उत् up + ई to go) Appearance; rise; uprising.

—उदयात् ii. 13

उदयात् iv. 32

उदये i. 16, 43; iii. 33

—उदयौ iii. 11

उदरम् iv. 16 Abdomen.

—उदाचरति ii. 4

—उदाचरन्ति ii. 4

उदानः iii. 39 The 'up-breathing' vital force, nerve-force, prāna-current.

उदानजयात् iii. 39 By conquest of the Udāna-force.

उदारः ii. 4 (उत् above + आर goad, 'above' the need for a 'goad') Noble; generous; grand.

—उदाराणाम् ii. 4

उदाहरणम् iii. 13 (उत् + आ + हर्) Citation; illustration.

उदाहार्याः iv. 3 To be cited, brought forward, as illustrations.

—उदित—iii. 14

—उदित—i. 44; ii. 27; iii. 49; iv. 33.

उदितः iii. 12 Uprisen, active.

उदितधर्मविशिष्टम् i. 44 Characterised or defined by the risen or active, developed,| manifest ḍharma i. e. function or attribute.

उदिताः iii. 14

—उदितौ iii. 12

उदियात् iv. 9 Would or may arise.

उदीचीनाः iii. 26 Northern.

उद्घाटयति ii. 24 Opens out; makes clear; discloses; leads off; exposes; ridicules.

उद्घाटितम् iv. 31 Awakened; uncovered; opened up.

उद्घाट्यते i. 12 Is opened up.

उद्घातः ii. 50 ('उत्+हन् to strike) 'Upstriking, upbreaking'; opening; stage or resting place (after an eruption, explosion, effort).

उद्दिश्य iv. 33 Having regard to; referring or with reference to.

उद्दिष्टः ii. 1 (उत्+दिश् to point, to show the direction) Declared, indicated, pointed out.

उद्धरिष्यामि i. 25 I shall lift out, liberate, save.

उद्भेदेन iv. 25 By the up-breaking, the shooting out.

उद्यानभूमिः iii. 26 'Going-up or going-out ground'; picnicing place; play-ground; pleasure-ground; garden-land.

उद्यानानि iii. 26 Resorts (of pleasure); gardens.

उद्वेजयति ii. 15 Agitates; perturbs; troubles; repels.

उन्नमयन्ति ii. 3 'Upraise'; arouse; stimulate; set going.

उन्नयनात् iii. 39 Because of upraising.

उन्मज्जति iii. 45 Emerges; floats.

उन्मार्गप्रवणवितर्कज्वरेण ii. 33 By the fever of excited thought leading on to the wrong path.

उपकरणम् ii. 34 Instrument; means; appliance.

—उपकरणे ii. 5

—उपकरणेषु ii. 5

—उपकार—ii. 30

—उपकारि i. 4; ii. 17

—उपकारिणः ii. 18

—उपक्रमः i. 43

उपक्रान्तम् iii, 55 Transcended; crossed; passed beyond; superseded; commenced; begun.

—उपक्षयम् i. 25

उपक्षिप्यते iii. 16, 53 Is 'dragged up'; is 'put down', put forward, stated.

—उपगम् i. 2

—उपगतः iii. 14

—उपगतानाम् ii. 11

—उपगतेषु ii. 12

—उपगमः ii. 4, 26; iv. 20

—उपगमात् iii. 13

—उपगम्यते iv. 23

—उपग्रह—ii. 20; iv. 22 (Holding; seizure: eclipse; shadow).

—उपघाताय i. 31; ii. 30

उपचरितभोगाभावः iii. 55 Absence of superimposed, imaginary, supposititious, artificial, unreal, spurious experiences.

—उपचर्यः iii. 51

—उपचितस्य i. 32

उपचिनोति ii. 15 Gathers, picks out and together: developes: strengthens accumulatively.

--उपजनः iv. 2, 11

—उपजननयोः iii. 11

—उपजनने iv. 12

उपजनापायधर्मकाः ii. 19 Having the properties of birth and 'passing away' or death.

—उपजात—i. 20

उपजातायाम् i. 35 In or on (a certain state) having been born or arisen.

उपजायते ii. 20, 33; iii. 15 Is born, generated; springs up; grows up.

उपजायन्ते ii. 19

उपतिष्ठते i. 20, 44, 50 Waits on, attends on, presents itself to, appears before.

उपतिष्ठन्ते ii. 37; iii. 49, 55

उपदर्शितः iii. 13 Shown.

उपदर्शितसन्निधानाः ii. 18 Displaying proximity or presence (prominently).

उपदिश्यते i. 7 Is taught, communicated.

—उपदिष्ट—i. 35

—उपदेश—i. 35

—उपदेशेन i. 25 By teaching.

—उपदेशैः i. 35

उपद्रष्टा ii. 20 Supervisor; spectator, witness.

उपध्मानम् iii. 40 Blowing up (as of fire); filling out; swelling.

—उपनिमन्त्रणे iii. 51

उपनिमन्त्रयन्ते iii. 51 Invite (pl).

उपनीयमानान् ii. 18 (All modes) being 'brought up', assigned, imputed, assimilated.

—उपपत्तिः i. 32; iii. 53

--उपपन्नाः iii. 26

उपपन्नान् ii. 18 Ready-provided; supplied.

उपपादयिष्यामः i. 7 We will expound or explain.

उपभोगः ii. 15 Sufferance, enjoyment, experience.

उपभोगेन ii. 16 By experiencing.

उपभोक्ता i. 32 Sufferer, enjoyer, 'taster, eater'.

—उपमम् iv. 14

—उपमः iii. 51

—उपमेभ्यः iii. 51

—उपयोगेन i. 19

—उपरक्त—ii. 18

—उपरक्तम् iv. 23

—उपरक्तम् i. 37, 41; iv. 23

उपरक्तम् iv. 17, 23 Coloured, tinged, stained; affected.

—उपरक्ता i. 43

उपरञ्जयति i. 44; Colours, tinges.

उपरञ्जयन्ति iv. 17

उपरतस्य ii. 31 Of the ceased, the become indifferent, the reposing, the withdrawn, the retired.

उपरताः iii. 14 Ceased; indifferent.

—उपरमः ii. 25

—उपरमात् ii. 47

—उपराग—iv. 17

—उपरागः iv. 15

—उपरागात् i. 7

उपरि iii. 26 Up; upper; above.

उपरिष्टात् i. 1, 7 Further up or on, later on, afterwards.

उपलक्षितप्रचाराः iii. 26 With observed or observable movements.

उपलब्धम् iii. 18 Found, gained, experienced, comprehended.

—उपलब्धि—ii. 17

—उपलब्धिः ii. 23 ; iii. 13

उपलब्धिः ii. 23 (उप + लभ् to gain) Apprehension, knowledge, cognition, experiencing.

उपलब्धिः ii. 23

उपलभ्यते i. 43 Is found, perceived, sensed, cognised.

उपलभ्यन्ते ii. 4

उपले ii. 50 In or on a stone.

उपशान्तिः ii. 15 Pacification; peace; stillness.

उपष्टम्भात् ii. 5 From the (need for) support; from (the quality of) the nourishment (needed).

उपसंहरन् i. 32 Summing up; concluding.

उपसंहारः i. 49 Conclusion ; summary; summation.

—उपसंहारे i. 25

उपसंहृतध्वनिक्रमाणाम् iii. 17 Of the summed or gathered up successions of sound.

उपसङ्ख्यातः i. 46 Enumerated; counted.

उपसम्पद्यमानम् iii. 13 Accumulating; developing.

उपसम्पद्यमानः iii. 13

उपसम्पद्येत iii. 52 May attain, come to, achieve.

उपसर्गाः iii. 37 (उप + सृज् to cast forth, to emanate) Epi-phenomena, bye-products, secondary results; additions; (prefixes); excrescences; hindrances.

उपसर्गाः iii. 37

—उपसर्जन—ii. 13

—उपसर्जनी—i. 1 Become secondary.

उपस्थस्य ii. 30 Of the genital organ.

—उपस्थानम् ii. 37

—उपस्थानि ii. 19

—उपस्थाप्य iii. 17

—उपस्थित—ii. 1

—उपस्थितम् iv. 14

उपस्थितम् iii. 22 (उप near + स्था to stand) Present; arrived; standing near; come up.

उपस्थितः i. 32

—उपस्थिताः iv. 16

—उपहत्य ii. 15

—उपहताः ii. 4

उपहन्ति ii. 15 ; iv. 11 Kills.

—उपहतम् ii. 15

—उपाख्यानेन ii. 24

उपागतः ii, 33 Come to; arrived; arrived at.

उपात्तम् ii. 15 (उप + आ + दा) Taken up; accepted; endured.

उपात्तभेदावयवानुगतः iii. 44 A collection or compound with parts or components whose separateness is indicated or admitted.

उपादत्ते iv. 10 Takes up; admits; waits on; depends on.

उपाददानम् ii. 15 Taking up.

—उपादानम् i. 41

उपादानम् ii. 1 (उप + आ + दा) Taking up.

—उपादानात् i. 24; iv. 7

उपादाने ii. 15 In (case of) taking up, accepting.

उपादाय iii. 54; iv. 4, 9, 14 Having taken up.

उपादीयन्ते ii. 30 Are taken up.

—उपादेय— i. 15

उपादेयम् ii. 15 To be taken up.

उपाध्यायः iii. 6 Sub-teacher; assistant teacher; guide; counsellor.

उपाय— i. 19, 20.

—उपायः ii. 26

—उपायः i. 18, 21; ii. 26, 27, 28

उपायः i. 12, 18, 23; ii. 26 (उप + इ to go) Way of approach; approach; means, method; device.

उपायद्वयेन i. 17 By a pair of means; by two methods; in two ways,

उपायप्रत्ययः i. 19, 20 Produced; caused by, (having reference to, connected with a belief in), means or methods.

उपायस्य i. 22

—उपायाः i. 21

उपायानाम् i. 21

उपायान्तरम् ii. 54, 55 Another means.

उपायेन ii. 11

—उपारूढम् iii. 49, 54

—उपारूढाः ii. 17; iii. 52 (उप + आ + रुह् to mount, to grow—upon the understanding).

—उपारोही i. 9

उपार्जितम् iii. 51 Earned.

उपार्जितमूर्त्तयः ii. 18 That have acquired forms or defining sheaths.

उपार्जितसुखदुःखमोहप्रत्ययाः ii. 15 Which have acquired the nature of (being causes of) pleasure, pain, and perplexity or infatuation.

उपावर्त्तते i. 20, 26, 42; ii. 39; iv. 10 (उप + आ + वृत् to be, to revolve) Comes round; returns, recoils.

उपावर्त्यते iii. 53 Is brought around; is placed.

—उपाश्रयम् ii. 46.

उपाश्रयभेदात् i. 41 From variety of the juxtaposed; because of variation of the setting, the supporting substance, the receptacle.

उपाश्रयरूपाकारेण i. 41 In, with, by, the form which is the form of the juxtaposed, i. e., the thing on which (the gem or crystal) rests.

—उपाश्रयेण ii. 18

उपासीत ii. 13 May stand (in abeyance); may keep waiting.

उपेक्षा iii. 23 (उप near, or on all sides + ईक्ष् to see; to see all sides equally; to stand by indifferently, Indifference; endurance; quiet sufferance; resignation.

—उपेक्षाणाम् i. 33

उपेक्षातः iii. 23 By or from resignation.

उपेक्षाम् i. 33

—उपोद्बलन—i. 35 (Strengthening, supporting, confirming, developing, expanding, evolving).

—उभय—i. 11; ii. 15

उभय—iv. 20

उभय—ii. 15

उभयकोटिस्पृक् i. 30 Touching both sides, points, ends, edges, extremes; swinging between opposite poles.

उभयतः i. 12 From or on both sides; in both or opposite ways.

उभयथा ii. 23, 51 In both ways.

उभयप्रत्याख्याने ii. 15 In or on the refutation or repudiation of both.

उभयस्य ii. 23 Of both.

उभयाक्षेपपूर्वकः ii. 51 Preceded by contraction, reduction, diminution, transcendence of both.

उभयाधीनः i. 12 Dependent on both.

उभयाभावः ii. 49, 50 Absence of both.

उभयीम् i. 40 To the two, the duad, the pair.

उभये iii. 44 Both; the two.

उभयोः i. 44; ii. 51; iii. 12 Of both.

उररीकृत्य ii. 18 Taking to heart; accepting.

उरसि iii, 31 In the chest.

उवाच iii. 18 Said; spoke.

उष्ट्रनिषदनम् ii. 46 The camel-seat, camel-posture.

—उष्ण—ii. 48

उष्णः iii. 45 Hot.

उष्णता iii. 44 Heat.

—उष्णे ii 32

ऊ

ऊनत्वम् i. 24 (Comparative) lack; deficiency; smallness.

ऊर्णनाभितन्तुमात्रे iii. 42 On the mere thread of the "wool-navelled" spider.

ऊर्णतन्तुः ii. 15 Spider-thread, cobweb; wool-thread.

ऊर्द्ध्वम् iii. 26 Upwards; above.

ऊर्द्ध्वरेतसः iii. 26 Those whose semen, seminal energy, is directed upwards; utterly abstinent and continent celibates. (The yoga-doctrine is that by practice, the seminal secretion, after forming in the testicular glands, is resolved back into the brain-substance and creates brain-and-mind-energy).

—ऊह—ii. 18 (ऊह् to suppose) "Detection of details, particulars, minutiae"; postulation;

conjecture; guess; supposition; arguing from a hypothesis.

ऋ

ऋच्छति iv. 13 (ऋच्छ to go, to reach) Attains; comes into.

ऋतम्भरप्रज्ञः iii. 51 He who has or is possessed of the truth-seeing, truth-bearing, truth-yielding consciousness, or the faculty of intuition or insight.

ऋतम्भरा i. 48 (ऋतम् right and भृ to bear, to hold, to nourish, to supporr, to maintain) Truth-apprehending; right-bearing.

ऋतम्भरा i. 48

ऋभवः iii. 26 A race of high devas.

—**ऋषयः** iii. 51

ऋषयः ii. 44 (ऋ गतौ अर्थात् ज्ञाने, गमने, प्राप्तौ to know, to go, to reach) They who have "arrived", "reached", gone to, known, attained (the Supreme); Seers.

—**ऋषि**—ii. 12

—**ऋषिः** i. 25

ऋषीन् iv. 33

ए

—**एक**—iii. 2

एकः i. 43; iii. 13, 15, 44, 51; iv. 14. One (mas:)

एकक्षणोपारूढम् iii. 54 'Mounted on', concentrated in, appearing, uprising, in one moment; all together at once.

एकचन्द्रदर्शनेन i. 8 By the beholding of one moon.

एकचित्ततन्त्रम् iv. 16 Dependent on one mind.

एकचित्तपरिकल्पितम् iv. 15 Formed, imagined, supposed, formulated, ideated, shaped, by one mind.

एकचित्ताभिप्रायपुरस्सरा iv. 5 "Having going in front", having as leader, following after, guided and governed by, the purpose or intention or will of one mind.

एकजातिसमन्वितानाम् iii. 44 Of the (bhūtas, elements) pervaded, strung together, threaded by, one genus or generic attribute.

एकतत्त्वाभ्यासः i. 32 The practice of one tattva, being, thing, object; practice with one object; persistent practice of the contemplation of some one thing (see तत्त्व)

एकतत्त्वावलम्बनम् i. 32 That which has for support some one thing; pending from, depending on, fixed on, hanging on to, some one thing.

एकतमस्य ii. 18 Of one of the lot; of one of the group; of one out of the number.

एकतानता iii. 2 "One-stretch-ed-ness"; stretching, streaming, extending unbrokenly as one; con-tinu-ity; incessant and rapid repetition.

एकत्र iii. 4 In one place; together; collectively; jointly.

एकत्र iii. 16

—एकत्वात् iv. 14

एकत्वेन iii. 15 By oneness.

एकदेशः i. 35 One place; one part.

एकदेशश्रुतित्वम् iii. 41 The quality or condition of hearing 'one-place-sound' or one and the same sound. (Some editions read **एकश्रुतित्वम्**, which seems better).

एकद्वित्रिचतुष्पञ्चलक्षणाः ii. 19 Having, respectively, one, two, three, four and five characteristics, attributes, qualities.

एकप्रघट्टकेन ii. 13 By one effort, by one 'knocking together'; at one blow; with one heave; at or by one operation; (by 'a pull all together').

एकप्रत्ययविषयः 1. 32 The object of one understanding, one cognition, apprehension, idea, perception, concept, faith. (See प्रत्यय)

एकप्रयत्नाक्षिप्तम् iii. 17 'Flung together', dragged in, brought up, by one effort (of the mind).

एकबुद्धिनिर्ग्राह्यम् i. 44 Comprehensible by or in one act of consciousness, cognition, intelligence; comprehensible as a unity, with the sense or consciousness of unity.

एकबुद्धिविषयम् iii. 17 Object of one awareness, one act or mood of consciousness, one intellection; object of the consciousness of unity; apprehended as a one.

एकबुद्ध्युपक्रमः i. 43 Arousing, commencing, giving rise to one cognition.

एकभविक: ii. 13 Single-birthed; resulting in, bringing about, only one birth.

एकम् iv. 5 One (Neu:)

एकम् i. 1; ii. 13, 22; iii. 13, 17; iv. 5, 14, 15.

एकमनस्काः iv. 4 "One-minded"; inspired, animated by, subordinate to, governed by, one mind, one chiṭṭa, one soul.

एकरूपत्वात् iv. 9 Because of "one-formed-ness", of having one form, the same form.

एकविपाकारम्भी ii. 13 Initiatory of one fruit, product, resultant, maturation or matured effect.

एकविषयाणि iii. 4 Having one object.

एकसमयासम्भवित्वात् iii. 17 Because of impossibility (i. e., being impossible to pronounce all) at one time, in simultaneity.

एकसमये iv. 20 In or at one time.

एकस्मिन् i. 24, 32; iv. 20 In one.

एकस्मृत्यनवधारणम् iv. 21 Non-ascertainment, absence of discriminate cognition, of each separate reminiscence, each act of memory.

एकस्य i. 24; ii. 13, 28; iii, 9, 14, 15, 17; Of one.

एकस्याम् ii. 4; iii. 13 In one (fem:)

एकस्वरूपापत्तिः ii. 6 "Attainment of one-form"; assumption; (of the appearance) of identity.

एकाकारः iii. 17 Of one form; of the form of a unity.

एकाग्रम् i. 1, 28, 32, 33 "One-fronted"; "one-pointed"; single-minded; pointed or directed towards, concentrated on, one object.

—एकाग्रतयाः iii. 11

एकाग्रता i. 32; iii. 11 One pointedness; single-mindedness.

एकाग्रतापरिणामः iii. 12 The consequence, development, resultant, product, of one-pointedness.

एकाग्रतायाः iii. 11 Of one-pointedness.

एकाग्रे i. 1 In the (state of being) one-pointed.

एकात्मता ii. 6 "One-souledness" "one-natured-ness"; identity.

एकात्मिका i. 17 "One-souled"; "one-ness-souled"; of the nature of oneness, unity, (separate) individuality.

एकादशम् ii. 19 Eleventh.

एकान्तानभ्युपगमात् iii. 13 Because of non-acceptance, non-supposition, non-postulation, of extreme or one-sided or utter (changelessness or eternity). (Some editions read एकान्ततानभ्युपगमात्)

एकाशीतिभेदा ii. 34 Of one-and-eighty divisions or kinds.

एके ii. 23 'Ones'; one set or class of thinkers; some.

एकेन i. 32; iii. 52 By one.

एकैकम् ii. 13 One by one; each; (neu:)

एकैकः iii. 17 One by one (mas:) each.

एकैका ii. 34 One by one (fem:); each.

एजयति i. 31 (एज् to agitate, shake) Shakes; makes restless; causes to vibrate, tremble, move.

एतत् i. 24, 32; ii. 1, 18, 25; iii. 4, 41; iv. 12, 15, 19, 23. This (neuter).

एतदर्थम् i. 35 For this sake or purpose.

एतया i. 44 By this (fem:)
एतया ii. 9; iv. 15
एतयोः i. 24; ii. 6 Of these two.
—एतऽयम् iv. 19
एतस्मात् i. 23. 24 From or because of this.
एतस्य i. 16 Of this.
एतस्याम् ii. 27; iii 55 In this (fem:)
एतान् iv. 21 These (mas:)
एतानि ii. 15; iii. 36 These (neu:)
एताम् ii. 27 To this (fem:)
एतावताम् iii. 17 Of so many or thus much.
एतावद्भिः ii. 50 By so many or thus much.
एताः i. 11, 35; ii. 13; iii. 48 These (fem:)
—एति iii. 13
एते i. 8; ii.4; iii. 13, 17; iv. 10 These (mas:)
एतेन iii. 13 By this (mas:)
एतेन i. 35; ii. 5; iii. 21 By this.
एतेषाम् i. 30; ii. 4; iii. 17 Of these.
एतेषु iii. 14 In these.
एतैः iv. 11 By these.
एतौ ii. 18 These two.
एनम् ii. 55 To this
एभिः ii. 31 By these.
एव i. 44, 46; ii. 15, 21; iii. 3; iv. 8 Even; only.
एव i. 2; ii. 4; iii. 6; iv. 3 etc,
एवम् i. 5; ii. 5; iii. 1; iv. 1 etc. Thus.
एवंजातीयक: iii. 17 Of such species or kind,
एवंभूतम् i. 5 "Thus-become"; Of this nature.
एवंस्वरूपम् i. 44 Of this form.
एषः i. 26 This (mas:). (Some editions make this word part of the immediately preceding *Bháshya*).
एषः i. 18; ii. 13; iii. 13; iv. 11
एषा i. 36; ii. 5; iii. 13 This (fem:)
एषाम् iv. 11, 28 Of these.
एषाम् ii. 4; iii. 17, 29

ऐ

ऐकभविकम् iii. 22 "One-birth-producing"; resulting in one birth.
—ऐकाग्र्य—ii. 41
ऐकाग्र्यम् ii. 41 One-pointed-ness.
—ऐकाऽग्यात् ii. 55
—ऐश्वर्य—iii. 26
ऐश्वर्य—i. 2
ऐश्वर्यम् i. 15, 24; ii. 35; iii. 55 Lordliness; sovereignty; sovereign might; superphysical or occult powers. (See ईश्वरः)
ऐश्वर्यविषयप्रियम् i. 2. That to which the ways, the objects, the domains, of power are dear.
ऐश्वर्यस्य i. 24
ऐश्वर्याणि iii. 45

ऐश्वर्यान्तरेण i. 24 By another sovereignty; by another's authority.

ओ

ॐ iv. 33 Yes. (Also the *Praṇava*; this sound, as *sound*, is supposed to be the primal sound in Nature and the very first *manifestation* of Universal Consciousness when it, so to say, begins to become particularised or individualised. As *word*, it is the most mystic of all in Samskṛt, being composed of अ + (इ) + उ + म्, each letter standing for one member of the countless triads and quartettes of which the world-process is made up).

—ओषधि—iv. 1 (ओषं दोषं दहन्ति, which burn up faults, diseases; ओषः प्लोषः दीप्तिः धीयते अत्र, that in which special energy resides) Medicine; chemico-physical substance having special properties.

—ओषधि—iv. 6

ओषधिभिः iv. 1 By medicinal substances.

औ

—औकार—iii. 17 The letter or sound 'au'.

औदकान् iv. 3 Aqueous; watery.

—औपदेशिकम् iii. 54

औपपादिकदेहाः iii. 26 With imagined, ideated, self-made, self-created bodies (not born of parents.)

—औष्ण्य—iv. 14 Warmth.

क

कः i. 12; ii. 4; iii. 13; iv. 10 etc. Who; what,

कक्षे iii. 22 In a straw-heap.

कणमृत् iii. 15 "Speck-earth"; the earth composing a small grain of dust.

—कण्टक—iii. 39

कण्टकस्य ii. 17 Of a thorn.

कण्ठः iii. 30 Throat.

कण्ठकूपे iii. 30 In the 'throat-well'; (a nerve-centre orgland in the throat, some part of the sympathetic system connected with the esophagus or the appetitive apparatus; the thymus gland?)

कति ii. 28 How many.

कथम् i. 4; ii. 1; iii. 6; iv. 3 etc. How.

कथंचित् i. 32; ii. 34; iii. 51 etc. Anyhow; somehow.

—कथंता—ii. 39 (How-ness; cause; manner.)

कथंस्वित् ii. 39 How indeed.

कन्या ii. 5; iii. 51 Girl; virgin.

कपालमृत् iii. 15 "Shell-earth"; "pot-sherd earth"; the earth composing a pot-sherd.

—कपाले iii. 32 (Shell; shard; concave fragment; skull).

कमनीयः iii. 51 Desirable (mas:)

कमनीया ii. 5; iii. 51 Desirable; lovable; lovely; (fem:)

—कम्पनीयाः iv. 23

कम्पयति i. 31 Shakes; makes restless; moves.

—करः iv. 21

—करण—ii. 2; iii. 48

—करण—i. 30; ii. 23, iii. 17.

—करणम् iii. 51

करणपञ्चकस्वरूपजयात् iii. 48 By conquest of the essential nature of the five indriyas, organs. (Some editions read करणपञ्चकरूपजयात्)

करणभावेन iv. 14 In the form of instrument.

— करणात् ii. 2, 23.

—करणानाम् iii. 17 (Some editions read करणकर्मणाम्)

—करणाय ii. 30

—करणीयः iv. 33

—करणे iv. 12

—करणेषु ii. 5

करिष्यति i. 50; ii. 2, 13, 24 Will make or do.

—करुणा—i. 33

करुणा iii. 23 Pity; compassion.

करुणाबलम् iii. 23 The power of compassion.

करुणाम् i. 33; iii. 23

—करोति ii, 2

करोति i. 1; ii. 13, 24, 30; iii. 13, 45; iv. 4 Makes; does.

—कर्णः iii. 22

—कर्त्तरि ii. 18

—कर्त्तव्यम् iii. 26 (Some editions read करणीयं)

—कर्त्तव्यतया ii. 18

कर्त्तव्यसाधनादिमान् iii. 51 Possessed of means of accomplishing what has to be done.

कर्त्तुम् ii. 13, 15; iv. 10 To do.

कर्त्तृकर्मकरणानाम् iii. 17 Of doer, deed, and means of doing; of subject, object, and instrument. (Some editions read कर्त्तृकरणकर्मणाम्)

कर्त्तृषु ii. 18 In the doers.

—कर्म—i. 24; iv. 30

—कर्म—ii. 1, 12, 15, 17, 32; iii. 17, 26, 43, 50; iv. 31

कर्म iii. 22; iv. 7 (कृ to do, to create) Act; action; deed; (good or evil deed regarded as the cause of joy or sorrow to the doer himself, later on, by reaction).

कर्म ii. 13, 52; iii. 22; iv. 9

कर्मक्लेशविपाकस्वरूपेण iii. 50 By the form of karma and (sin as the cause of) misery and fruits. (See i. 24).

कर्मगतिः ii. 13 The path, the way, of karma; the operation of karma.

कर्मजातिः iv. 7 Kind, species, of karma.

कर्मणः ii. 13; iii. 14, 38; iv. 8, 12 Of karma.

कर्मणा ii. 13; iv. 10.

कर्मणि ii. 17.

कर्मणी ii. 13 Two (kinds of) karmas.

कर्मबन्धक्षयात् iii. 38 By "consumption", abrasion, attenuation, decay, wearing away, exhaustion, of the bonds of karma.

कर्मबन्धनानि i. 1. The bonds of karma.

कर्मभ्यः ii. 15.

कर्मरूपताम् ii. 21 "To the formness of karma"; to the condition of being the "accusative", the acted on, the object of all action or activity (of the subject, the self).

कर्मवासनानुरूपाः iv. 9 Following imitating, the form of, being in accordance with, karma and vāsanā, deed and propensity; (or, conforming with tendency to action of a particular kind).

कर्मविपाकम् ii. 3; iv. 8 The maturation, ripening, fruiting, of karma

कर्मविपाकाभावः iii. 55 Absence of fruition of karma.

कर्मविषयताम् ii. 22 To the condition of being object of action.

कर्मसु ii. 13.

कर्मस्थत्वात् ii. 17 Because of being "seated", present, in an "accusative", an object (in the technical sense, in grammar, of karma, viz. 'the object of action').

कर्माणि i. 24; ii. 13.

कर्माभिनिर्वर्त्तितम् iv. 25 Matured, completed, created, fully developed, by (good) karma.

कर्माभिव्यञ्जकम् iv. 9 Indicator, manifestor, of karma.

कर्माशयः ii. 12 The "sleeping-place" of karma; the germ, seed, seed-pod, 'ganglion', 'gland', 'cell', reservoir, of karma.

कर्माशयः ii. 12, 13, 15; iv. 6 (See आशय). (The commentator explains that धर्माधर्मौ are, or constitute, the कर्माशयः; he seems to mean that the conglomerate of the tendencies to sin and sacrifice, vice and virtue, demerit and merit, is the karma-seed).

—कर्माशय: ii 12.

—कर्माशयप्रचयः ii. 13.

कर्माशयप्रचय: ii. 15; iv. 7 The growth of the seed-germ of karma, its formation, accumulation, shaping, development.

कर्माशयप्रचयक्षेत्रीभूताः i. 5 Those (moods of mind) which have become the field, the soil, wherein the seed-germ of karma grows, thrives, is nourished, or developed. (Some editions read कर्माशयप्रचये क्षेत्रीभूताः)

कर्माशयवशात् iii. 38 By force of the karma-germ, the karma-nucleus, the instinct or appetite for karma, the tendency to karma.

कर्माशयवृत्तिलाभवशात् iv. 9 By means, process, force, of gaining, securing, operation or functioning as karma-germ; or, by force of the karma-germ obtaining operance, becoming active or operant.

कर्माशयस्य i. 32; ii. 5.

कर्माशयाः iv. 30.

कर्मेन्द्रियाणि ii. 19 The organs of action; the motor-organs.

—कर्ष—i. 26.

—कर्षति iv. 3.

कलाम् ii. 42 (कल् to sound 'count', move, energise, throw about, go, act; whence also कालः, "Dark Time," which counts in succession, drives, and finally also swallows up all). Part; digit; piece; portion; aspect; facet; phase; (a portion of the infinite glories of the absolute, manifestable only by some activity; hence, also fine art).

—कल्पम् i. 4, 36; ii. 17; iv. 10, 23.

—कल्पः i. 9.

—कल्पानाम् ii. 4 (Some editions read कल्पितानाम्)

—कल्पः ii. 15.

कल्पते i. 18; ii. 6 (क्लृप् to be able, to be able to do, to design, devise, imagine, plan, ideate, fashion, 'clip' into shape). Suffices; prevails; becomes able; becomes fit or appropriate; commends itself as fit to the mind; becomes feasible.

—कल्पते i. 36.

कल्पद्रुमाः iii. 51 "Wishing-trees", "imagination"-trees, (which yield whatever is desired; the imaginative power of the mind, which devises, ideates, whatever is desired, is itself this "Wishing-tree" planted in the "Garden of Heaven", the higher mind).

—कल्पना iv. 14.

कल्पप्रलयमहाप्रलयेषु i. 25 (कल्पः, a great period, a vast eonian cycle, of time, demarcated, clipped-off, cut-off, by the Mind of Brahmā, the Ideator). In kalpa-pralayas and in mahā-pralayas, eonic dissolutions or obscurations of a part of a globe or of a whole globe of a world-system, and in great dissolutions of a whole world-system, (solar, sidereal, and so on, grade after grade).

कल्पयन्तः iv. 21 Imagining; supposing; originating; forming; postulating; positing.

कल्पशतेन iv. 9 By a hundred kalpas, eons, cycles.

कल्पसहस्रायुषः iii. 26 Living a thousand kalpas; having lifetimes extending over a thousand kalpas.

कल्पस्य Of a cycle, (a period of time marked out by Brahma's Consciousness, Will-and-Imagination, as appropriate for a manifestation).

—कल्पा iv. 17.

—कल्पाः ii. 10, 11, 18; iii. 26.

—कल्पान् ii. 2.

—कल्पानि iii. 50.

कल्पायुषः iii. 26 Living for the period of a kalpa, a Day of Brahmā.

—कल्पिकः iii. 51.

कल्पितम् iv. 14 Imagined; assumed.

—कल्पितम् iv. 15.

कल्पितः iv. 33.

कल्पितया iii. 43.

—कल्पिता iii. 43 (See also विकल्प)

कल्पिता iii. 43.

—कल्पिताम् iii. 43.

कल्पितेषु ii. 23.

कल्पिष्यते ii. 2 Will be ready, fit, able, competent.

—कल्प्य iv. 21.

कल्याणवहा i. 12 Bearing, carrying, flowing towards good fortune, happiness, blessings, blessedness, (here) Moksha, the final Blessedness.

कल्याणाय i. 12 For or towards well-being, good fortune, virtue, good, merit, auspiciousness, blessing, moksha.

कल्याणी i. 20 Beneficent; benignant; auspicious; blessed.

कवयः ii. 13; iv. 22 (कु, to sound, hum, sing). The poets; wise ones; seers; sages; knowers; all-knowers. (Brahmā, the Universal Mind, is the greatest and primal Poet, Dramatist, and Singer, who manifests in the 'sound-word' primarily).

कश्चित् i. 23; ii. 24; iv. 30 etc. Any one; some one.

कषिताः iv. 30 Uprooted.

कष्टम् iii. 26 (कष्, to rub, grind, scratch, pull out, kill). Pain; painful.

कष्टतमम् ii. 30 Greatest pain; most painful. (Some editions read कष्टं तमः).

कस्मात् i. 8; ii. 4; iii. 6; iv. 9, etc. Why; wherefore; whence; from whom.

कस्य ii. 5; iv. 15 etc. Whose.

कस्यचित् iv. 19 Of some one or other.

का ii. 4, 15 Who (feminine).

काञ्चनः iii, 26 Golden.

—कान्त—iv. 17.

कान्तिमान् iii. 46 (कम्, to desire), Radiant; bright; lovely.

—काम—iii. 45.

कामगः iv. 1 Able to go anywhere at will, as desired.

कामभोगिनः iii. 26 Enjoyers of (objects of) desire (sensuous and sexual, principally);

enjoyers at will; having at command whatever objects of enjoyment they desire.

कामरूपी iv. 1 Able to assume any form as desired, at will.

कामलोभमोहक्रोधप्रसवः ii. 12 Born of lust, greed, infatuation, and anger. (Some editions read लोभमोहक्रोधप्रभवः)

कामसुखम् ii. 42 The joy of love, of desire fulfilled, of sense-gratification.

कामिते i. 24 In the desired.

कामितार्थप्राप्तिः i 24 Attainment of the desired object.

कायः iii. 51 (कस्य ब्रह्मणः अयः, आयश्च, गतागतं जीवरूपेण, यस्मिन्, that into and out of which the Spirit comes and goes). The body; the tenement, vesture, garment, vehicle, of the jivātmā or purusha, the soul, the spirit, and also the Paramātmā or Brahman, the Supreme Spirit, the One Principle of all Life.

—**कायः** iii. 45.

काय—ii. 40.

कायम् ii. 5, 40.

कायरूपसंयमात् iii. 21 By meditation on the form, or the visibility, of the body.

कायरूपे iii. 21 In or on the form, or the visibility, of the body. (Some editions read कायस्य रूपे)

कायव्यूहम् iii. 29 The organization of the body.

कायव्यूहज्ञानम् iii. 29 Knowledge of the organisation of the body.

कायशुद्धिम् ii. 40 The purification of the body.

कायसम्पत् iii. 45, 46 The wealth, perfection, richness, fullness, of body, the physical vehicle of life.

कायसिद्धिः ii. 43 Perfection, accomplishment, super-power, of body.

कायस्य i. 30; iii. 48.

कायस्वभावावलोकी ii. 40 Examiner, inspector, beholder, discriminator, cogniser, of the 'own-form', the (impure) nature, of the body.

कायाकाशयोः iii. 42 Of the body and ākāsha, ether, space.

कायान् iv. 4.

कायानभिष्वङ्गी ii. 40 Unattached to the body. (स्वज् to embrace.

कायावद्यदर्शी ii. 40 Seeing, perceiving, conscious or cognisant of, the defects, impurities, of the body.

काये ii. 5.

कायेन ii. 15; iv. 11.

कायेन्द्रियप्रकृतयः iv. 2 The prakṛtis, 'material causes', substrata, of the body and the organs.

कायेन्द्रियसिद्धिः ii. 43 Accomplishment, perfection, of the body and the organs.

कायेन्द्रियाणाम् iv. 2 Of the body and the organs.
—कायैः ii. 40.
—कार—iv. 10, 23.
—कारम् iv. 22.
—कारक—iii. 17.
कारकम् iv. 20 Doer, actor; that which causes another to do or act; moving cause; (the object or person in which a prepositional relation resides).
कारकवाचकम् iii. 17 'Subject-expressing'; denoting the 'actor', the mover; meaning something or someone which or who is the locus of a prepositional relation (i. e. a noun).
—कारकाणाम् iii. 17.
कारकार्थः iii. 17 'Noun-signifying;' meaning an object or person (who or which is or can be related to another person in one of the active ways signified by the various prepositions).
कारके iii. 17.
—कारण—iii. 38.
—कारण—ii. 3, 24, 25; iv. 34.
—कारणम् ii. 13, 15, 23, 24, 25, 28; iii. 13, 44; iv. 4.
कारणम् i. 43; ii. 13, 17, 19, 23, 28; iv. 3, 30 (कृ to do; to create; that which causes to do or act). Cause; reason, motive.
कारणत्वम् ii. 28 Causeness; causality; motivity; causativeness.
—कारणस्य ii. 23; iii. 38.
कारणानि ii. 28.
कारणान्तरेषु ii. 23 Amongst other causes; on other causes (being supposed).
—कारणे ii. 27.
—कारि—iv. 24.
—कारि—iv. 22.
—कारित—ii. 34.
कारिता ii. 34 Caused (to be done by another: fem).
—कारित्वात् ii. 20
कारुण्यात् i. 25 By or from or because of compassion.
—कार्य—ii. 23.
कार्यकारणस्रोतः ii. 3 The stream of cause and effect.
कार्यकारणात्मनाम् iv. 34 Of the (guṇas, primal Nature-attributes, having the) nature of cause and effect. (Some edns. read कार्यकारणात्मकानाम्)
कार्यनिष्ठाम् ii. 24 To finality, cessation, coming to a stand-still, of all activity.
कार्यस्वभावानुपातिनः iii. 44 Following the nature of the effects, (कार्यस्य स्वभावं अनुपतन्ति); or permeating, pervading, all effects which are, and because they are, but modifications, transformations, transmutations, new shapes and forms, developments and evolutions, of their own-nature, (कार्यस्य स्वभावे अनुपतन्ति).

कार्या ii. 27 To be caused; achievable by effort; (fem:).

—कार्यात् i. 50.

—कार्ये ii. 52.

कार्ये ii. 5, 44.

कार्येण iv. 3.

—काल—i. 14; ii. 31, 50; iv. 9.

—काल—i. 44, 51; ii. 13, 51; iii. 14, 18, 48.

—कालम् iii. 14.

कालः i. 26; iii. 52 (See कलाम्; कल्, to move). Time; the ('dark', 'black', mysterious, unfathomable) "Mover", the driver, of all.

कालविदः iii. 52 Knowers of Time; knowers of the essential nature, and the measures and cycles of time.

—कालसूत्र—iii. 26.

कालाक्षी iii. 53 Black-eyed.

कालान्तरे ii. 45 In or at some other time.

कालावच्छिन्ना ii. 31 Conditioned, limited, marked or divided off, by time; having limits in time; temporary; not timeless, either as everlasting or as eternal; having a beginning and an end.

—कालीनाः ii. 13.

—काले ii. 4, 14; iii. 13, 39.

कालेन i. 26 By Time.

कालेन ii. 50; iii. 22.

काश्चित् iv. 10 Some (fem:)

—काषम् iv. 30

काष्ठमौनाकारमौने ii. 32 "Wood-like" silence (i. e. avoidance of all expression), and avoidance of only speech or oral expression (as distinguished from signs or gestures).

काष्ठा i. 16 Stage, grade, degree; final goal; quarter of the heavens; one of the (four or six or eight) directions (of space); (a measure of time equal to eighteen winks of the eye).

काष्ठाप्राप्तिः i. 24, 25 Attainment or finding of highest grade or degree, i. e. finality, culmination, climax, completeness.

—काष्ठाम् ii. 19.

किम् iv. 16 What.

किम् i. 9; ii. 13; iii. 18; iv. 3 What; does it ?; is it ?; is it that ?

किंच i. 25; ii. 40; iii. 13; iv. 12 etc. Moreover; and what is more;.

किंचित् i. 2 Anything.

किन्तु i. 45; ii. 4; iii. 13; iv. 8 etc. But rather; but; rather.

किंनिमित्तम् i. 24 Proved or produced by what reason or authority.

किंनु i. 45 Is it that ?

किमर्थम् ii. 24; iii. 14 What for; why; what is the meaning that; for the sake of what.

किमुपायः i. 18 'Of what means'; attainable by what means.

किम्पुरुषम् iii. 26 Name of a land 'of imperfect men.'

किंविषया i. 41 Having what object.

किंस्वभावः i. 3, 18 Of what nature.

किंस्वरूपा i. 41 Of what form

किंस्वित् ii. 39; iv. 25 Whether; how indeed; how verily.

कियन्तः i. 30; ii. 3 (Plural of कियत्) How many ?

कीदृशः iii. 9 "Looking like what," (दृश् to see); of what kind; like what.

कुक्षयः iv. 22 (Plural of कुक्षिः). Hollows; flanks; bowels; deeps.

कुतः ii. 4; iii. 6; iv. 9, 25 Whence; wherefore; wherefrom.

कुमारः ii. 12 Boy; child; unmarried youth.

कुमुदाः iii. 26 A race of devas of a high order.

कुरवः iii. 26 (See उत्तराः).

कुरण्टकाभः iii. 26 Coloured, tinted, like the yellow kurantaka flower. (Some editions read कुरुण्डक)

कुरुते iv. 12 Makes; does, (कृ).

कुर्यात् ii. 6; iii. 51 May do; should make; would do.

कुर्वन्ति i. 50; iii. 53 (कृ, to do). (They) make; cause; create.

—कुश—iii. 26.

कुशलम् ii. 13, 22.

कुशलः ii. 4, 27; iv. 33 The 'weeder'; (कुशान् लाति, he who pulls out, cuts away, kushas, grasses, tares, or weeds, from a corn-field); skilful and careful agriculturist; wise; good; skilful; happy; comfortable; he who is well.

कुशलस्य ii. 13; iv. 25, 33 Of the righteous and virtuous, the thoughtful, wise, foresighted person (who is careful to pull out and cast away the 'weeds' from his own nature and character).

कुशलाकुशलयोः ii. 9 Of the skilled and the unskilled.

कुशलाकुशलानि i. 24 Good and evil.

कुशलाकुशलाः iv. 30.

—कुशलान् ii. 22.

कुशलानुष्ठानम् iv. 12 The performance of, the engagement in, good and wise work.

—कुसीदस्य iv. 29 (सीदता दीयते, सीदतः आदीयते, तस्मात् कुत्सितः, 'interest' paid by one in misfortune, on loan taken by him because of his needs; blameworthy, because the interest is taken by a well-to-do person from an unfortunate one).

—कूट—ii. 27, iii. 26 (Some editions read—तट—in ii. 27).

कूटस्थनित्यता iv. 33 (कूट, mountain-peak, स्था, to stand, नित्य, permanent, eternal). Rock-seated rock-like permanance;

changeless eternity; immutability.

कूटस्थनित्येषु iv. 33 In the changelessly eternal, (i. e., purushas, jīvas, souls).

कूपः iii. 30 Well; hole; hollow.

कूपात् iii. 31.

—कूपे iii. 30.

कूर्मनाड्याम् iii. 31 On or in the nerve named kūrma.

कूर्माकारा iii. 31 Of the shape of a turtle.

—कूष्माण्ड—iii. 26.

कृच्छ्रचान्द्रायण—ii. 32 (A special, difficult, कृच्छ्र, painful, kind of 'penance' or austerity', involving certain vows, fasts, and vigils, and extending over two चन्द्र, 'lunar', fortnights; a 'fastcure' and 'nature-cure').

—कृत—i. 51.

—कृतम् i. 27; ii. 27, 55; iii. 20; iv. 21;

—कृतः i 50 ii. 15, 17.

कृतः ii. 12, 13 Done.

कृतकारितानुमोदिताः ii. 34 Done, caused to be done, and consented to, approved, acquiesced in.

कृतपरिचाराः iii. 26 Done service to; attended; served. (Some editions read कृतपरिवाराः Having retinue made up of; surrounded).

कृतभोगापवर्गाणाम् iv. 34 Of those who have done, experienced, achieved, both pursuit and renunciation; (भुज्, to eat; अप + वृज्, to cut away); those souls which have tasted the world and put it away; have known both bondage and salvation. (See भोगand अपवर्ग);

कृतभोगापवर्गाः iv. 32 Those (souls) which have achieved, experienced, the world-process as well as retirement therefrom.

कृतरक्षाबन्धः iii. 51 Having (or he who has) made protective 'bounds', 'boundaries', all round himself.

कृतसंकेतः i. 49 One who has made a sign, an agreement, a contract; (a word) connected by convention or usage (with a particular meaning)

कृतसंयमः iii. 31, 42 One who has made the threefold meditation.

कृतसंयमस्य iii. 41.

कृतस्य ii. 13; iii. 14.

—कृता ii. 19.

कृता ii. 34 Done.

—कृतान् ii. 2.

—कृतानाम् i. 51.

कृताग्राम् ii. 21.

कृतार्थम् ii. 22 To him who has done his work, whose work is done, whose business is finished, office ended, interest achieved, aim, object, or end secured, purpose fulfilled

कृतार्थानाम् iv. 32 Of those (guṇas) which have finished their work, served their purpose.

—**कृताः** i. 50, ii. 11.

—**कृतेभ्यः** ii. 30.

कृतोपक्षयम् i. 25 Come to a close; finished; completed.

—**कृत्य** iv. 33.

कृत्वा iii. 13, 14, 26, 27, 29, 40, 47 Having done.

कृत्स्नः iii. 52 All; the whole.

कृपणजनप्रार्थनीयेभ्यः iii. 51 To or for (things) desired by pitiable (pitiful, miser-able, miser-ly) people.

—**कृपणेषु** ii. 12.

कृमेः ii. 9 Of the worm; (Skt. vamrī, the white ant)

—**कृष्**—iii. 38 (To pull, drag, take out.)

—**कृष्णम्** iv. 10.

—**कृष्णम** iv. 7.

कृष्णस्य ii. 13 Of the dark or black.

कृष्णा iv. 7 (The kind or class of actions which is) dark; black; evil. (**कृष्** to draw, to attract; **कर्षति** 'that which attracts', drags down the soul into ever grosser 'matter', promotes passions, passionate attachments, whence 'blindness', darkness).

के i. 30; 39; ii. 3; iii. 74 Who; what; which. (Plural of **कः**)

केचित् ii. 23; iv. 21 etc. Some.

केतुमालाः iii. 26 Name of a land of 'flag-rows', 'comet-rows'. (Some editions read **केतुमाल**—).

केदारात् iv. 3 From a bed, plot, sunk and ridged-in piece of land.

केदारान्तरम् iv. 3 Another field or plot

केदारे iv. 3.

केन i. 9; ii. 5; iii. 14; iv. 10 By whom, by what.

केनचित् iv. 16 By some one.

केवलम् i 51; iii. 13 Only.

केवलः i. 29; 51 One; alone; sole; on (e) ly.

केवला iv. 34 (Fem:).

केवलिनः i. 24 (Plural of **केवली**) Possessors of Oneness; the Lonely Ones; Soli-taries; Those who have achieved Unity, (who see only the One Supreme Self al-one, everywhere, everywhen, everyway, in all, and also above, beyond, including, all).

केवली ii. 27; iii. 55.

केवले iv. 7.

केशेषु iii. 51 In the hairs; by the hairs.

कैवल्यम् i. 16; 24; ii. 6.

कैवल्यम् ii. 25; iii. 50; 55; iv. 34 ('Leave me alone'—the harrassed person's cry!). Soleness,

Solitude, Oneness, Aloneness, Loneliness, Onlyness, Solitariness, Uniqueness, All-One-ness.

कैवल्यकारणम् ii. 23 The cause of, or caused by, kaivalya.

कैवल्यपदम् i. 19 The 'foot-rest', 'standing-place', seat, conditions, state, status, of kaivalya.

कैवल्यप्राग्भारम् iv. 26.

कैवल्यप्राग्भारा i. 12 (Ending in) the mountain face of, heading towards, 'bulking forwards' to, kaivalya.

कैवल्यभागीयैः i. 51 By those (who or which are) partaking of the nature of Oneness.

कैवल्यापेक्षया iii. 18 By comparison with kaivalya; looking at kaivalya. (Some editions read कैवल्यसुखापेक्षया).

कैवल्ये i. 3.

कैश्चित् iii. 13 By some (plural).

—कोटि i. 30; iii. 26 (Point; tip; side; also crore or ten millions).

कोटिम् i. 40 To the tip, side, part, edge, end, aspect.

—कोटिः i. 24.

कोष्ठ्यम् (or कौष्ठ्यम्) i. 31 Thoracic; pertaining to the 'hollow', the 'box'.

कोष्ठ्यस्य i. 34; ii. 49.

कौटस्थ्यम् iii. 13 The state of कूटस्थ (see कूटस्थनित्यता).

कौटस्थ्यप्रसङ्गदोषः iii. 13 The fault of the 'association', 'attachment', supervention, of rock-seatedness or un-changeability.

कौटस्थ्येन iii. 13.

कौशलानि ii. 15 Skilfulness; skills; powers; capacities; abilities.

—क्रम iii. 52; iv. 22; 32.

—क्रम—i. 51; ii. 13, 19, 28; iii. 49; iv. 33, 34.

—क्रमम् iii. 54.

—क्रमम् ii. 29; iii. 17, 18.

—क्रमः iii. 15.

क्रमः iv. 33 Succession; 'step', 'step after step'.

क्रमः iii. 15.

क्रमशः iii. 22 Successively; one after another; gradually.

क्रमसमाप्तिः iv. 33 Cessation of succession.

—क्रमसमाप्तौ iv. 34.

—क्रमाणाम् iii. 17.

क्रमानतिवृत्तेः ii. 19 Because of not overpassing, not disregarding, ignoring, neglecting, transcending, violating, the order of succession.

क्रमाननुरोधी i. 47 Not following, not restricted by, succession or order; characterised by simultaneousness.

क्रमानुरोधिनः iii. 17 Observing, following, restricted by, confined to, an order or succession; appearing in succession or time-sequence.

क्रमान्यत्वम् iii. 15 Otherness of

order; difference, variation, of order or succession.

क्रमावलम्बी iii. 52 Pending, depending on, lengthening out on, supported by, hanging on, order or succession.

—क्रमाः iii. 32.

क्रमाः iii. 15.

क्रमेण ii. 13, 15, 51; iii. 13, 15 iv. 33.

—क्रान्त—i. 26.

—क्रान्तम् iii. 55.

—क्रान्तिः iii. 39.

—क्रियते i. 18.

क्रियते i. 27 Is done.

क्रियन्ते i. 5, 43 Are made, done, created.

क्रियमाणस्य iii. 13 Of the (thing) being made.

—क्रिया—ii. 18.

—क्रिया—ii. 18; iii. 44, 47; iv. 14.

—क्रिया ii. 17; iii. 13.

क्रिया iii. 17, 39; iv. 20 Act; action; doing; deed.

क्रियाकारकात्मा iii. 17 Of the nature of action and actor or mover.

—क्रियाणाम् ii. 1.

क्रियाधर्मकः i. 43 Having the property of activity.

क्रियाफलाश्रयत्वम् ii. 36 The state of being the receptacle of action (viz. dharma and adharma) and its fruit (viz. happiness and misery, or heaven and hell).

—क्रियाम् iv. 33.

—क्रियाम् iii. 45.

क्रियायाम् iii. 17.

—क्रियायाः ii. 17.

क्रियायोगः ii. 1 Actional, practical, active yoga; yoga of the nature of special practices or exercises; yoga-practices; yoga-exercises.

क्रियायोगः ii. 2.

क्रियायोगेन ii. 11.

क्रियार्थः iii. 17 Signifying action; verb; having action for object; for the sake of action.

क्रियावाचकम् iii. 17 Denoting, expressive of, naming, speaking of, action.

क्रियाशीलम् ii. 18 Of the nature of, having the characteristic of, tending to, activity.

क्रुद्धः iv. 19 (क्रुध्, to be angry), Angered; angry.

—क्रोध—ii. 34.

—क्रोध—ii. 12.

क्रोधः ii. 4, 8; iv. 19 Anger.

क्रोधकाले iii. 13 In, during, at the time of, anger.

क्रोधस्य ii. 4.

क्रोधेन ii. 34

—क्रौञ्च—iii. 26.

क्रौञ्चनिषदनम् ii. 46 The posture, 'seat', manner of standing or sitting, of the krauncha-bird, the flaming.

क्लान्तम् i. 10 (क्लम्, to become

tired; cf. 'clammy' with perspiration born of fatigue). Tired, fatigued.

क्लिश्नाति ii. 15 Torments; distresses; causes pain.

क्लिष्टच्छिद्रेषु i. 5 In the 'holes', interstices, intervals, between the painful (moods or functionings of the mind).

क्लिष्टप्रवाहपतिताः i. 5 'Fallen into', intermixed with, the stream or flow of the painful (moods of mind).

क्लिष्टाः i. 5 Painful; miserable (moods, functionings).

क्लिष्टाऽक्लिष्टाः i. 5 Painful and non-painful; miserable and non-miserable.

क्लेदयन्ति iii. 45 Moisten; wet.

—क्लेश—i. 1; ii. 1, 4, 13, 26; iii. 18, 49, 55; iv. 6.

—क्लेशः ii. 4, 13.

क्लेशः ii. 4, 6, 9 (क्लिश्, to torment). Pain; affliction; misery; cause of pain and misery. (Cf. 'original sin' of Christian theology with अविद्या, Avidyā, the first seed or root क्लेश, the Great Error, the Great Primal Original Sin, the cause of the 'fall' of Spirit into Matter. The mis-take, of taking the part for the whole, the perishing and impure body for the Eternal and Pure Self, is the prime cause, the root, the seed, of all the miseries, kleshas, of the world; therefore, it is, by a figure of speech, as it were, itself called the first and greatest 'misery', 'affliction', klesha. The uses of the English word 'miserable', —Latin, miserari, to have mercy, to pity,—which means "exceedingly unhappy, also worthless, despicable, wretched", and of the word 'wretched',—"Anglo-Saxon wrecca, an outcast, one driven away"—cf. Skt. vrātya—which also means "a most miserable person, one sunk in vice, distressingly bad, despicable";—these uses are similar to those of klesha. In Samskṛt, kṛpā means pity, kṛpaṇa is pitiable, 'pitiful', compassionate, feeling pity, also exciting pity, also despicable, miser-ly, avaricious).

क्लेशकर्मक्षये iii 50 On the wearing away, the destruction, of affliction and action.

क्लेशकर्मनिवृत्तिः iv. 30 'Retirement', 'turning back or away', cessation, of affliction and action.

क्लेशकर्मविपाकत्रयम् iii. 43 The triplet of affliction, action, and fruit.

क्लेशकर्मविपाकानुभवनिमित्ताभिः ii. 13 By (the instincts which are) the causes of (and are, again, in turn, caused by) the experience of 'sin', 'action', and 'fruition'. (Some editions read निर्वर्त्तिताभिःfor नमित्ताभिः,which would mean 'caused by').

क्लेशकर्मविपाकाशयैः i. 24 By the afflictions, (moral worth, e.g. Dharma and Adharma based on) activities, (virtuous and sinful deeds), their maturation or fruition (e.g. jāti, āyuh, and bhoga), and the corresponding seed-germs.

क्लेशकर्मावरणैः iv, 31 By the veils, envelopes, wrappings, screens, (made up of, consisting of, of the nature of) afflictions and actions.

क्लेशक्षयहेतुत्वात् i. 50 Because of being the cause of the decline, shrinkage, crumbling away, decay, destruction, consumption (i. e. becoming consumed), of the afflictions.

क्लेशतनूकरणार्थः ii. 2 Having for its object the attenuation of the afflictions.

क्लेशतिमिरविनाशी iii. 51 Destroyer of the darkness of the miseries or afflictions.

—**क्लेशबीजस्य** iii. 55.

क्लेशबीजानि iii. 50 The seeds of misery or affliction.

क्लेशमूलः ii. 12 Rooted in misery; or the root of misery.

क्लेशवत् iv. 28 Like the miseries, the calamities, the afflictions.

क्लेशविषयत्वम् ii. 4 The 'objectness' of, the state of being within the reach, ramification, domination, purview, province, range, domain, comprehension, application, of, (the word) 'misery', affliction.

क्लेशसन्तानस्य ii. 5 Of the continuity, continuous stream, progeny, of afflictions; (see क्लेशाः).

क्लेशहेतुकाः i. 5 Caused by the afflictions; (or causing and giving rise to the afflictions; or both).

क्लेशाः ii. 3 'Miseries'; afflictions; 'original sins'; sorrows; wretchednesses.

क्लेशाः i. 8, 16, 24; ii. 3, 4, 10; iv. 28.

क्लेशान् i. 1; ii. 2; iii. 51.

—**क्लेशानाम्** ii. 12; iv. 7, 11.

क्लेशानाम् ii. 4, 11.

क्लेशाभावात् iii. 55 By or because of absence of afflictions.

क्लेशावनद्धः ii. 13 Enwrapped in afflictions, bound with afflictions.

क्लेशावस्था ii. 4 The condition, state, or kind, of affliction.

—**क्लेशेन** ii. 12.

क्लेशेषु i. 11; ii. 13.

क्लेशैः ii. 2.

क्वचन iv. 21 Somewhere.

क्वचित् ii. 4; iii. 13; iv. 30 Somewhere; here and there; in a few places.

—क्षण— iii. 9.

—क्षण—iii. 54.

—क्षणम् ii. 34; iii. 9; iv. 11.

क्षणम् iii. 13; iv. 32 Moment.

—क्षणः iii. 53.

क्षणतत्क्रमयोः iii. 52 Of the moment and its order (in the succession or flow of moments); of the moment and the succession.

क्षणपरम्परानुपातिना iii. 15 By the (succession, the process,) following the 'one after anotherness' of moments.

क्षणप्रतियोगी iv. 33 Having 'moment' for its 'counterpart'.

क्षणानन्तर्यात्मा iii. 52; iv. 33 Of the nature of uninterrupted flow of moments; of the nature of an unbroken series of them; of the nature of immediacy of moment.

क्षणानाम् ii. 50.

क्षणान्तरे ii. 16 In another moment.

क्षणिकत्वात् i. 32 Because of momentariness.

क्षणिकम् i. 32 Momentary; lasting for only one moment.

क्षणिकवादिनः iv. 20 Of the theorist who says (or of him whose doctrine is) that existence is momentary, from moment to moment.

—क्षणे ii. 16.

—क्षणे iv. 20.

—क्षणेषु iii. 9, 13.

क्षणेषु iv. 15.

क्षत्रियाणाम् ii. 31 Of kshattriyas (men of the soldier-class, 'men of action'; क्षतात् त्रायते, he who protects the weak from hurt and harm).

—क्षय—i. 50; ii. 15, 30, 42.

—क्षयम् ii. 32.

—क्षयः iii. 43.

क्षयः ii. 28; iii. 11 (क्षि, to waste away, to decay; to kill). Becoming consumed; consumption; (the disease of phthisis, as well as any decay); wasting away.

क्षयक्रमानुरोधिनी ii. 28 Depending on, following, the succession, the successive or gradual progress, process, advance, of decay.

—क्षयात् ii. 43.

—क्षयात् iii. 38; iv. 29.

—क्षये ii. 28; iii. 50.

—क्षये ii. 23, 28.

क्षयोदयौ iii. 11 Decay and rise.

क्षिणोति i. 1 Attenuates; consumes; wears down; kills; destroys.

—क्षिपति iii. 38.

—क्षिप्तम् iii. 17, 38.

क्षिप्तम् i. 1 (क्षिप्, to throw, to fling). Flung about; fickle; "explosive", (as used by W. James, to describe the stage or state in which the mind jumps, is flung about, from one object to another).

—क्षिप्य iv. 21.

—क्षिप्यते iii. 16.

क्षिप्रपरिणामि ii. 15 Quick-changing.

—क्षीण—ii. 32.

—क्षीणक्लेशः ii. 4 He whose afflictions have decayed, been whittled away.

क्षीणक्लेशत्वात् iv. 6 Because of the decay of the afflictions.

क्षीणक्लेशानाम् ii. 12; iv. 7 Of those whose afflictions have thinned, have been consumed.

क्षीणक्लेशबन्धनः iii. 49 With bonds of affliction loosened, worn out; he whose bonds, of the nature of the afflictions, have become feeble.

क्षीणतृष्णः iv. 33 He whose desire has decayed.

क्षीणविपर्ययः iv. 30 He whose error has decayed.

क्षीणवीर्यम् ii. 34 Vigorless; depleted, devoid, of vital energy.

क्षीणवृत्तेः i, 41 Of him whose mental activities, psychic functionings, have thinned, weakened.

क्षीणाः i. 16; ii. 27 Decayed; attenuated; consumed.

क्षीयते ii. 52 Decays; perishes; dissolves; disappears; becomes absorbed. (see क्षयः).

क्षीयते ii. 28.

क्षीयन्ते ii. 4.

क्षीयमाणबीजेभ्यः iv. 27 From (purva-samskaras, old 'impressions', impressed habits) whose germs are decaying.

क्षीयमाणाम् ii. 4 Wearing away; being eroded.

—क्षीर—iii. 26.

क्षुत्पिपासानिवृत्तिः iii. 30 'Turning away', suspension, cessation, of hunger and thirst.

क्षुत्पिपासे iii. 20 Hunger and thirst.

क्षेतव्यम् ii. 27 The to-be-consumed; the consumable.

क्षेतव्याः i. 16.

क्षेत्रम् ii. 4 Field (which 'preserves the seed from decay'; क्षयात् त्रायते बीजं); the mind-body.

क्षेत्रज्ञम् iii. 49 To the knower of the field (of consciousness).

क्षेत्रज्ञे ii. 17 In the apperceptive Jiva, the knower of the field.

क्षेत्रिकः iv. 3 The field-owner; tiller; cultivator.

क्षेत्रिकवत् iv. 3 Like the 'field-man', the cultivator.

क्षेत्री—i. 5.

—क्षेपः iii. 17.

क्षेपीयसा iii. 22 By very quick.

क्षोभः i. 31 Excitement; agitation.

ख

खद्योतः iii. 26; iv. 31 'Sky-illuminator'; fire-fly; star.

खलु i. 10; ii. 15; iii. 12; iv. 15 etc. Verily; indeed.

खिलीक्रियते i. 12 Is attenuated, thinned, scattered, dispersed, weakened.

—ख्या— i. 2.

—ख्यातम् ii. 20; iii. 41.

—ख्याताः iii. 26.

—ख्याति— iii. 49.

—ख्याति—i. 2; ii. 27; iv. 27.

—ख्यातिः ii. 5, 26.

—ख्यातिः i. 16; ii. 2, 5, 28; iv. 33.

ख्यातिः i, 4 (ख्या, to tell, to make known). Knowledge, cognition, consciousness; general or public or common knowledge; proclamation; fame; (mental); 'clearing up'; declaration; publication.

ख्यातिक्रियास्थितिशीलाः iii. 44 Having the nature or characteristics, characters, properties, of knowability (self-declar-ation, publication), of mobility, motility, or activity, and of tenacity (steadiness, stability, clinging, persistence, 'sitting down', perseverence, holding on, inertia); having the properties of cognition, action, and ('steady') desire. (See i. 2; ii. 15, 18, 52; iii 43, 47; iv. 14; etc. and गुणाः).

ख्यातिपर्यवसानम् i. 50 Ending with discriminative knowledge.

—ख्यातिम् ii. 5, 24.

ख्यातिम् i. 2.

ख्यातिविषयाः i. 5 Moods of consciousness of the nature of (सत्त्वपुरुषविवेकः, सत्त्वपुरुषान्यताख्यातिः) discrimination (between the Purusha, the Spirit, the Self, and Saṭṭva (here used in the way of a part for the whole, i. e., standing for the whole of Prakṛṭi with all its three properties, Saṭṭva being the finest).

—ख्यातेः i. 16; ii. 28; iv. 29.

—ख्यातेः ii. 27.

—ख्यापन—ii. 23.

—ख्याप्यते i. 2; ii. 19, 20, 27; iv. 22.

—ख्यापयिष्यन्ते ii. 19.

ग

गकारौकारविसर्जनीयाः iii. 17 (The constituent sounds) ga, au, and aspirate.

गच्छति i. 5 Goes. (गम्, to go)

गच्छन्ति ii. 10, 27, 44; iii. 59 Go (plural).

—गच्छन्ते iv. 21.

गच्छेत् ii, 13 May go.

—गत—iv. 31.

—गतम् iv. 12.

—गतः i. 49; iii. 13, 14; iv. 23.

गतः ii. 13 Gone.

—गताः ii. 23; iv. 13.

—गति— iii. 28.

—गतिः ii. 13; iii. 39, 42, 44.

गतिः i. 49; ii. 13 'Going'; movement; way; path; mode of development; fate; ultimate destiny; finale; end.

गतिनिवृत्तौ i. 9 In or on the cessation of 'going', 'movement', 'procession'.

गतिमत् i. 7 Possessed of motion.

गतिलाभः iii. 48 Gain or attainment of motion.

गतिविच्छेदः ii. 49 Cessation or break of movement.

गतिसंस्काराभिव्यक्तिः ii. 23 Manifestation, development, of the tendency, faculty, habit, to 'move', 'go', 'operate', 'function.'

—गतौ iv. 12.

गत्यभावः ii. 50, 51 Absence of movement.

—गत्या i. 26.

गत्या ii. 23; iv. 33 By 'going'.

—गन्ध—i. 35; ii. 19; iii. 36 Smell; scent; fragrance.

—गन्धः i. 48; iv. 15.

गन्धतन्मात्रम् i. 45; ii. 19 The 'root-matter', or 'primal-matter' of smell; smell-in-itself; the 'that-alone' of smell; the sensation of smell alone, pure, mere, simple; smell-continuum; (गन्धसामान्यं, गन्धमात्रं).

गन्धमादनसीमानः iii. 26 Bounded by the Gandha-mādana mountain, 'the mountain of the maddening or intoxicating fragrances'. (मद्, to madden).

—गन्धर्व—iii. 26 A class of nature-spirits specially devoted to the æsthetic arts.

—गमः iv. 20.

—गमन—iv. 1.

—गमनम् iii. 42.

—गमनम् ii. 13.

—गम्यते iv. 23.

गम्यते i. 9; iii. 17 (गम्, गच्छ्, to go). Is approached; is gone to; is understood.

—गम्यन्ते iii. 48.

—गर्द्धः i. 30; ii. 7; 'Greed'. (गृध्, to covet, to be greedy of or for).

—गर्भ—iii. 18. (Womb. गृभ्, to grip, to hold).

—गर्भाभ्याम् ii. 5.

गवादिः i. 43; ii. 20; iv. 23 Cow etc.

गवाद्यर्थः i. 42 The signification, sense, meaning, connotation or denotation, (of the word) cow; the thing or object 'cow'.

गवाम् ii. 19 Of cows.

—गवेधुक—iv. 3 A kind of grass,

गाढम् i. 10 Deeply; densely; soundly; intensely; profoundly.

गात्राणि i. 10 Limbs.

गात्रावयवेषु ii. 15 In or on the

other parts of the body or the limbs.

गावः ii. 9; iii. 44 Cows.

गिरिशिखरकूटच्युताः ii. 27 Slipped from the pinnacle of a mountain-peak. (Some editions read तट, surface, for कूट).

गिरीणाम् iv. 22 Of mountains.

—गुण—ii. 18.

—गुणम् i. 2; ii. 15.

—गुणः iii. 18.

—गुणत्वात् ii. 20.

गुणत्वे ii. 18 In the state of being (inherently, indefeasibly, constituent) guṇas, 'strands', properties, attributes (of Praḍhāna or Prakṛṭi).

गुणधर्मेषु iii. 33 Amongst the properties, functions, of the guṇas, (the three main attributes of Prakṛti).

गुणपर्वाणि ii. 19 The 'joints', stages, of developement of the guṇas.

गुणपुरुषस्वरूपविज्ञानात् ii. 28 (Till the rise of) discriminative knowledge of the respective natures, the 'own-forms', of the guṇas and the Spirit.

गुणप्रधानभावकृतः ii. 15, (Their distinguishability is) made (possible) by their (different) states or conditions, (now) as (subdominant or ordinary) guṇas and (then) as predominant, (one over the other two).

गुणवियोगः iii. 50 Separation from guṇas.

गुणवृत्तम् ii. 15; iii. 9; iv. 15 The 'ways of existence', doings, of the gunas; their character, conduct, doing, being, circling, turning, rotating.

गुणवृत्तिविरोधात् ii. 15 Owing to the mutual contradictions, conflicts, (inherent) in the (various) aspects, forms, functionings, of the guṇas.

गुणवैतृष्ण्यम् i. 16 Absence of desire for the guṇas.

गुणसम्बन्धातीतः ii. 27 Transcending the bond, relation, connection of or with attributes.

गुणसंयोगे ii. 23 In the conjuction of or with the guṇas.

गुणस्वाभाव्यम् iii. 13 'Guṇa-natureness'; the totality of the nature of the guṇas; or that which is born of that nature.

—गुणा ii. 20.

—गुणाः ii. 15.

गुणाः ii. 15, 18, 19, 27; iii. 44, 47, 49, 55; iv. 14 Attributes; primal attributes; qualities; properties; 'strands'. (गुण्, to multiply; गुणः, a string, cord, rope, twisted of 'multiple' threads, strands. This is one of the most important words in the whole of Samskṛṭ Philosophy. The three guṇas, primal attributes, strands, of which Prakṛṭi, Nature, the Nature of the Supreme Principle of Consciousness, Purusha or Paramāṭmā or Brahma (n), is made up, viz., Saṭṭva, Rajas, Ṭamas, simply pervade the whole of Samskṛṭ thought and literature. A correct understanding of their significance is indispensable to see clearly what otherwise remains obscure and confused. A long Note at the end of ch. xi of Bhagavan Das' *The Science of Peace*, endeavours to ascertain that significance precisely, by comparing scores of passages, from different works, in which the three words occur. The conclusion arrived at is, briefly, that the three correspond to or signify, respectively, the principles of cognition (knowledge, en-'light'-enment), action (volition), and desire ('blindly' clinging tenacity), the three all-comprehensive functions of mind-body or life. The usual rendering, by the words luminosity, activity or passion, darkness or inertia, is unsatisfactory and catches only partial aspects.

गुणातीतत्वात् ii. 27 Because of transcendence of the guṇas; because of 'having gone beyond' the guṇas. (अति + इ, to go).

गुणात्मानः iv. 13 Of the nature of guṇas.

गुणाधिकारक्रमसमाप्तौ iv. 34 On the conclusion of the succession or process of the functionings of the guṇas.

गुणाधिकारम् ii. 3 The functioning of the guṇas; their 'office', 'right and authority,' momentum, term of being in force or in action, period of dynamicity.

गुणाधिकारविरोधिन्यः i. 5 Opposed or hostile to, or counteractive of, the functioning of the guṇas.

गुणान् ii. 38.

—गुणानाम् iv. 8.

गुणानाम् iv. 32, 34 Of the primal attributes.

गुणानाम् ii. 19, 20, 23; iii. 13, 50; iv. 13, 14, 33.

गुणान्वयिनीभिः ii. 19 By the (manifestations) following or accompanying the guṇas.

गुणिनित्यत्वे iii. 13 In the state of the permanence of the substratum of the guṇas; that, to which the guṇas belong, being Eternal.

गुणेभ्यः i. 16.

गुणेषु ii. 18; iii. 44; iv. 33.

—गुणैः iii. 51.

गुणैः ii. 25.

गुप्तेन्द्रियस्य ii. 30 Of the private organ; also, of him, or by him, all whose organs are well-controlled and guarded from straying.

गुरवः i. 26.

गुरुः i. 26 Teacher, master; 'weighty'; 'one of weight'; important.

गुरुत्वात् i. 30 Because of heaviness, dullness, denseness.

गुरूणि i. 10 (Plural). Heavy; weighty.

गुरोः iv. 21.

—गुरौ ii. 1, 32.

गुहा iv. 22 Cave.

गृहवत् iv. 24 Like a house.

—गृहीत—iv. 16.

गृहीतम् iii. 51 Held, caught; apprehended.

—गृहीतत्वात् iv. 11.

—गृह्णाति iv. 11.

गृह्णाति iii. 41, 54 (गृह्, to 'grip', 'grab', catch, take). Seizes, grasps; apprehends.

गृह्यते iv. 21, 33 Is apprehended.

गृह्येत iv. 16, 21 Would be apprehended.

गोधा iii. 31 Lizard.

गोमयपायसीयम् i. 32 The 'logic' which argues that milk and cowdung are the same, because both come from the cow.

—गोष्पदम् ii. 5.

गोष्पदमात्रम् ii. 5 Only a 'hoof-print'; a trifle; (of the size of) merely a 'cow-hoof'; (a small puddle or obstacle which can be easily stepped over).

गोष्पदाभावः ii. 5 Absence of a 'hoof-print'.

गौः i. 9, 42; iii. 17, 53; iv. 14 (That which 'goes'. Hence, a sun-beam; the earth; a star; an arrow; the voice; cattle; etc.) Cow. (गम्, to go).

ग्रन्थिभिः ii. 13 With or by knots.

—ग्रह–i. 35, 36; iii. 17; iv. 10,22.

—ग्रहण— i. 41.

—ग्रहण—i. 11; iii. 41; iv. 15, 23.

—ग्रहणम् i. 25; iv. 12 (another reading is—ग्रहम्, in iv. 12).

ग्रहणम् i. 42, 49 (ग्रह्, to 'grab'). Taking, grasping, seizing; apprehending; thinking; sensation; the fact or meaning sensed or apprehended.

ग्रहणधारणोहापोहतत्त्वज्ञानाभिनिवेशाः ii. 18 Apprehension or cognition, retention (in memory), acceptance by inference, rejection by refutation, exact knowledge, and insistent conviction.

ग्रहणसमर्थम् iv. 31 Able or competent to apprehend.

ग्रहणस्वरूपास्मितान्वयार्थवत्त्वसंयमात् iii. 47 By concentration on the (successive five stages, viz.,) apprehension, the '(own-form', here the) sensing organ, egoism, (the 'through-running') attributes, and subservience to the purposes, the interests, the aims (of the self, the jīva, the individualised spirit or soul or ego).

ग्रहणाकारपूर्वा i. 11 That wherein the form of apprehension is first, foremost, predominant.

ग्रहणात्मकम् i. 43 Of the nature of apprehension or comprehension.

ग्रहणात्मकानाम् iv. 14 Of (the guṇas of) the nature of apprehension or apprehendors.

ग्रहणालम्बनोपरक्तम् i. 41 'Tinged by the supporting apprehension'; having reference to, coloured by, an awareness of the fact of apprehension.

ग्रहणेषु i. 41 Amongst the apprehendors, 'receivers', sense-organs.

ग्रहनक्षत्रतारकाः iii. 26 Comets (?), planets, (or constellations), stars; or planets, asterisms, and stars.

—ग्रहीता ii. 20.

ग्रहीता ii. 20 Apprehendor; cogniser; subject.

ग्रहीतृग्रहणग्राह्यस्वरूपचित्तभेदात् iv. 23 Because of the difference of the forms, (the various moods, activities, functionings, of the mind (tinged by, or when it assumes, or is) in the forms of apprehendor, apprehension, and apprehended.

ग्रहीतृग्रहणग्राह्येषु i. 41 Amongst the apprehendor, the apprehension, and the apprehended; in the subject, (the) relation (between the two), and the object.

ग्रहीतृपुरुषालम्बनोपरक्तम् i. 41 Tinged by (awareness of) the apprehending subject as 'support'.

—ग्रामम् ii. 15.

ग्रावाणः ii. 27 Stones; boulders.

—ग्राह्य—iii. 21.

—ग्राह्य—iv. 23.

—ग्राह्यम् iv. 19.

—ग्राह्यः iv. 33.

ग्राह्यः iii. 47 Object of apprehension; apprehensible.

ग्राह्यग्रहणभेदभिन्नयोः iv. 15 Of the (two) distinguished by the distinction between the 'apprehensible' and the 'apprehension' (or the means, the organ, of apprehension).

ग्राह्यग्रहणोभयाकारनिर्भासः i. 11 Showing forth the form of both the object of apprehension and of the act of apprehension. (Like the English word 'sensation', the word ग्रहण covers the object which is sensed, the act or fact and also the organ of sensing, and the subjective feeling. That this is so, is due to the inseparability of all the three or four, though their natures are distinguishable.)

ग्राह्यग्रहणोभयात्मिकाम् i. 11 Of the nature of both apprehended and apprehendor.

ग्राह्यशक्तिस्तम्भे iii. 21 On suspension of 'the power of the apprehensible', i. e., the capacity of apprehensibility.

ग्राह्यसमापन्नम् i. 41 'Arrived at', 'gone to' (the state of), become, accomplished into, identified with, the object, the apprehensible.

ग्राह्यस्वरूपाकारेण i. 41 In or by the form which is the form of the apprehensible object.

ग्राह्यस्वरूपापन्ना i. 43 Attained to the form of the apprehensible.

ग्राह्यस्वरूपोपरक्ता i. 43 Tinged, affected, by the form of the apprehensible.

ग्राह्या iii. 21 Apprehensible. (Fem.)

ग्राह्याकारपूर्वा i. 11 'Preceded by', 'giving first place to', having for predominant factor, the form of the object apprehended.

ग्राह्यात्मकानाम् iv. 14 Of the (guṇas when) of the nature of, or when taking the form of, apprehensibles.

ग्राह्यालम्बनोपरक्तम् i. 41 Tinged, affected, by (awareness of) the apprehensible on which it depends, as (on a) support.

—ग्राह्येषु i. 41.

ग्राह्योपरक्तः i. 11 Coloured, tinged, affected, shaped, by the object to be grasped, apprehended.

—ग्रीवः iv 31.

— घ —

घटः iii. 13, 15 Jar; pot.

घटप्रासादप्रदीपकल्पम् iv. 10 Like the lamp (now placed) inside a pot and (again) in a palace.

घटमृत् iii. 15 Pot-earth; the earth composing a pot.

घटस्य iii. 15.

घटाकारः iii. 13 Pot-shaped; of the form of a jar.

घटादिः i 43; ii. 20, iv. 23 Jar etc; pot etc.

घनसलिलानलानिलाकाशतमःप्रतिष्ठाः iii. 26 Established in or on, or supporting, or connected and corresponding with, or composed of, ghana, the dense, gross, compact, (*solid*), i. e. earth; salila, (*liquid*), water; anala, (*fluid*), fire; anila, (*gaseous*), air; ākāsha, (*etheric*) radial substance (?); and ṭamas, 'darkness', (*black space*).

—घाटयति ii. 24 ('Opens out'; expresses; makes plain; illustrates; (causative of घट, to happen).

—घातम् iv. 30.

—घातः iii. 45 (From हन् to strike, to slay.)

—घातः ii. 50.

घातात्—iv. 33

घोरम् ii. 15 Active; dire; turbulent; furious; intense; raging.

घोरेषु ii. 33; iii. 51.

घोषम् iii. 22 Sound.

—घ्राण—ii. 19 (Nose; also smell. From घ्रा to smell).

— च —

च i. 29, 44, 45; ii. 2, 15, 41, 53; iii. 20, 22, 38, 39, 42, 45, 48, 49, 54; iv. 10, 11, 15, 16, 20, 21 And; also.

च i. 1; ii. 1; iii. 36; iv. 2, etc.

—चक्रम् i. 5; iv. 11 Wheel; disc; 'cycle'; 'circle'; (these last two words seem to be etymologically the same as the Skt. chakra, Gr. kuklos).

—चक्रे iii. 29.

—चक्रे iii. 1, 29.

—चक्षते iii. 52.

—चक्षुः—ii. 19.

चक्षुः—iii. 21.

चक्षुःप्रकाशासम्प्रयोगे iii. 21 On non-meeting of eye and light; on non-contact (of an object) with the light of or from the eye, the visual or optic light.

—चक्षुषी iii. 51.

चतस्रः i. 17, 46 Four (fem:).

—चतुः— ii. 19.

चतुर्थम् iii. 44, 47. Fourth (neu:).

चतुर्थः ii. 51 Fourth (masc:).

चतुर्थः i. 17; iii. 26, 51.

चतुर्थे ii. 18.

चतुर्दश्याम् ii. 31 On the fourteenth (day of the moon).

चतुर्धा i. 46 In four ways; quadruple; four-fold.

चतुर्विधः ii. 26 Of four kinds; four-fold.

चतुर्विधकल्पितानाम् ii. 4 Formed, fashioned, imagined, made up, classified, sub-divided, in four ways; grouped in four groups; occurring in four forms.

चतुर्व्यूहम् ii. 15, 16 Four-organed; organised with four component parts or organs.

चतुष्टयानुगतः i. 17 Accompanied by the quartette.

चतुष्टयी ii. 27 Quartette.

चतुष्पदा ii. 5 four-footed; four-fold.

चतुष्पात् iv. 7 Four-footed; four-fold.

चत्वारः iii. 26, 51 Four (pl., mas.).

—चन्द्र—ii. 5.

चन्द्रतारकम् i. 7 Moon and stars.

चन्द्रम् ii. 5 The moon.

चन्द्रमसम् iii. 45 To the moon.

चन्द्रादित्यग्रहमणिप्रदीपरत्नादिषु i. 35 In or on the moon, the sun, the planets, gems, lamps, precious things etc. (Some edns read प्रदीपरश्म्यादिषु, i. e., in or on lamps and rays, or rays of lamps etc., for प्रदीपरत्नादिषु, 'lamps, jewels, etc.'; cf. 'crystalgazing').

चन्द्रे iii. 27.

चन्द्रे iii. 27.

—चयः iv. 7.

—चरः iv. 14.

चरमदेहः ii. 4 One who is in his last body, has no more rebirths before him.

चरमदेहानाम् iv. 7 Of those who are in their last incarnation.

—चरित—iii. 55.

चरिताधिकारा ii. 24 (fem:).

चरिताधिकाराः ii. 27; iii. 55 Those who have done their duty, finished their business, completed their work, exhausted their force or momentum, run their course.

चरिताधिकारे ii. 10 In (the mind) whose actional or functional tendency or dynamicity has been exhausted, which has finished its 'office' work; whose office is over, whose term has expired.

चरितार्थानाम् iii. 50 Of those whose object is gained, purpose fulfilled, work over, business done.

चरिष्यामि iv. 21 I will move, wander, act, pursue, follow.

चर्चः ii. 23; iv. 8 Talk; consideration; argument; case; affair.

—चर्म—ii. 34 (skin).

चलम् ii. 15; iii. 9, 13; iv. 15 Moving, going; moveable; fickle, restless, unstable, unsteady.

चलितः iii. 52 Moved, disturbed, set going.

—चार—iv. 19.

— चारिणाम् iii, 32.

चिकित्साशास्त्रम् ii. 15 The science of medicine; (चिकित्सा, विचिकित्सा, is doubt, hesitation, conjecture; hence, the science wherein life and death are in doubt, and treatment proceeds by guesses).

– चित् i. 20; ii. 23, iv. 21, 23 See किंचित्, केनचित्, क्वचित्, केचित्, कश्चित् etc.

चितिः i. 9 Consciousness.

चितिमात्ररूपः iii. 35 Of the form of pure and mere consciousness.

चितिशक्तिः iv. 34. The power of (i. e. known as) Consciousness. (चित्, to be conscious, to perceive, to remember; चि, to gather, to col-lect; That which is aware of every thing and all things, that in which all the past, the present, the future, the there behind, the here, the there in front, is all gathered up and col-lect-ed, bound up, in the Eternal Now and Infinite Here, That is the Principle of Consciousness, God's Changless Memory, Chiti).

चितिशक्तिः i. 2, 3; iii. 50; iv 34.

चितेः iv. 22 Of Consciousness.

चित्त—i. 2, 30, 33; ii. 54; iv. 15, 18, 21.

—चित्त— iii. 9, 19; iv 4, 16.

—चित्त—i. 37, 51; iii. 6, 9; iv. 5, 15, 16, 23.

—चित्तम् i. 25; iii. 12; iv. 6.

चित्तम् i. 37; iv. 5, 23, 26 The mind; the individual mind; the psyche; individualised Chit or Chiti.

चित्तम् i. 2, 4, 5, 10, 11, 18, 19, 28, 32, 33, 35, 36, 37, 38, 40, 50, 51; ii. 13, 15, 47; iii. 9, 11, 13, 38; iv. 5, 6, 10, 17, 19, 21, 23, 24.

—चित्तः ii. 1.

चित्तकारणम् iv. 4 The cause of the mind; or caused by the mind, i. e. that of which the mind is the cause.

चित्तचेष्टितम् i. 50 The actings, movements, workings, of the mind; its gestures, expressions.

चित्तधर्मः iii. 11 A property, characteristic, function, attribute, of the mind.

चित्तधर्माः iii. 9, 18.

चित्तधर्मैः iv. 25.

चित्तनदी i. 12 The stream, the river, the flow, the current, of the mind, i. e., of the mind's workings, of consciousness.

चित्तनिरोधे ii. 54, 55 In or on the restraint or inhibition of the (functionings of the) mind; (when the mind is held poised, is held in hand).

चित्तनिवृत्तिम् ii. 24 To the reversion, returning, retiring, withdrawal, of the mind.

चित्तनिवृत्तिः ii. 24 The retirement of the mind.

चित्तपरिकर्म i. 35 The 'toilette', 'finish and polish', refinement, adornment, decoration, purification, of the mind.

चित्तपरिणामः iii, 9 The or a transformation, or the or a resultant of the transformation, of the mind; a sequential change, a development, of the mind.

चित्तपरिणामेन iii. 13.

चित्तप्रतिसर्गः iii. 51 Reabsorption, involution, in-turning, of the mind.

चित्तप्रसादनम् i. 33 The calming, stilling, tranquilising, composing, of the mind; making the mind peaceful, 'placid', restful, cheerful, pleasant.

चित्तप्रसादनम् ii. 1.

चित्तबलव्यतिरेकेण iv. 10 Apart from, in the absence of, without, the might, the force, the energy, of the mind.

चित्तभेदात् iv. 15 Because of the separateness of minds.

चित्तमलप्रसङ्गेन i. 8 In or by connection, association, contact, juxtaposition with, or influence of, the impurities, scum, dirt, 'excretions', grossness, (the obscuring and distracting factors, passions, likes and dislikes, prejudices,) of the mind.

चित्तमात्रम् iv. 23 Only the mind.

चित्तमात्राधीनम् iv. 10 Dependent on the mind only.

चित्तवत् ii. 54; iv. 18 Like the mind.

चित्तविक्षेपाः i. 30 'Flingings about', distractions, of the mind.

चित्तविमुक्तिः ii. 27 The vi-mukti, the special or complete liberation of, or from, the mind; the abolition of the mind.

चित्तवृत्तयः iv. 18 The functionings of the mind, the psyche; 'psychoses', i. e., psychic functionings generally, (not in the special technical sense, of psychic disease, in which the word 'psychosis' is now specially used by the psycho-analysts in contrast with 'neurosis' or nervous disease).

चित्तवृत्तयः i. 4, 30; iv. 18.

चित्तवृत्तिनिरोधः i. 2 Restraint, check, restriction, obstruction, prevention, barring, damming up, stopping, of the functionings, modifications, activities, of the mind; inhibition of mental moods, of psychic workings.

चित्तवृत्तिनिरोधः i. 2, 12.

चित्तवृत्तिबोधः i. 7 Awareness of psychic moods; apperception.

चित्तवृत्तिबोधे i. 4 In or on or for the awareness, cognisance, consciousness, of psychic activity; in or on or during apperception, or self-reference.

चित्तवृत्तिभिः i. 30 By psychic functionings.

—**चित्तवृत्तेः** i. 17.

चित्तवृत्त्या ii. 15.

चित्तसंवित् iii. 34 Consciousness, awareness (by the self), of the mind.

चित्तसत्त्वम् i. 2 The sattva or cognitional element, factor, aspect, of the mind.

चित्तसारूप्येण iv. 23 By similiformity with or of the mind.

—**चित्तस्य** i. 20, 48; ii. 1, 23; iii. 12, 20, 37.

चित्तस्य ii. 54; iii. 1, 11, 12, 38; iv. 17.

चित्तस्य i. 1, 5, 7, 13, 17, 18, 30, 32, 40, 51; ii. 27; iii. 1, 9, 10, 11, 12, 15; iv. 15, 25, 27.

चित्तस्वरूपानुकारः ii. 54 Imitation of the form of the mind.

चित्तात्मवादिनाम् iv. 19 Of those who hold that the mind itself is the Self, and that there is no Self other than or separate from the mind. (Some editions omit this word).

चित्ताधिकारसमाप्तिम् iv. 28 The exhaustion, completion, finishing, closing, of the office, officiousness, restlessness, functioning, activity, 'duty', force, energy, of the mind.

—**चित्तानि** iv. 4.

चित्तानि iv. 16.

चित्तान्तरदृश्ये iv. 21 In or on being, cognisable by another mind; or, in that which is apprehensible by another mind.

चित्तान्तरेण iv. 21 By another mind.

चित्ते iv. 16.

—चित्तेन ii. 23; iii. 20; iv. 15.

चित्तेन i. 19, 32; iv. 16, 24.

चित्तेषु i. 32.

चित्तैकाग्र्यात् ii. 55 From the one-pointedness of the mind.

चित्तैः iv. 15.

चित्तोपरागः iv. 15 Coloring, tinging, affection of the mind.

चित्रम् iv. 24 Variegated, (multicolored, like a 'picture', imagined by the mind. चित्तं त्रायते, that which protects, helps, pleases the mind).

—चित्रः iv. 13, 25.

चित्रा ii. 13.

—चित्रा ii. 1.

चित्रीकृतम् ii. 13; iv. 34. Variegated, multicolored.

चिन्त्यन्ते iv. 28 Are considered.

चिरम् ii. 13; iii. 6 Long.

चिरेण iii. 22. Slowly; in a long time

चूर्णमृत् iii. 15 Powdered or loose earth.

चेत् i. 42; iv. 16, 23 etc. If; may be; if it be.

—**चेतन**—i. 29 The conscious; the conscious Self.

or

—**चेतना**—i. 29 Consciousness.

—चेतनम् iv. 23.

चेतनम् iv. 23.

—चेतनस्य ii. 24.

—चेतना—ii. 32.

—चेतना ii. 20.

चेतनाचेतनम् ii. 34 Living and non-living; conscious and unconscious.

चेतनाचेतनसाधनाधीनः ii. 14, 15 Dependent on animate and inanimate instruments.

चेतनाचेतनस्वरूपापन्नम् iv. 23 Attained to, arrived at, evolved or developed or changed into, the form of animate and inanimate.

चेतनाचेतनेषु ii. 5 In the animate and inanimate.

चेतसः i. 20, 31, 41 Of the mind.

चेतसि i. 1, 3, 19; ii. 4, 10.

चेष्टा iii. 15, 18 Effort; volition; striving; movement.

—चेष्टितम् i. 50 Movement; gesture; expression.

—चैतन्य—iv. 22.

चैतन्यम् i. 9 Consciousness.

चैत्रः ii. 4 Chaiṭra (a proper name).

चैत्ररथम् iii. 26 The Garden of Kubera.

चैत्रवत् i. 7 Like Chaiṭra.

चैत्रस्य i. 9.

चैत्राग्नितण्डुलानाम् iii. 17 Of Chaiṭra, fire, and rice.

चोद्यते iii. 13 Is put forward; pressed; obtruded; urged; argued.

—च्युता ii. 27.

—छ—

छन्दः iii. 17 Metre; Scripture (because 'chant'-ed metrically).

छित्त्वा i. 24 Having severed.

—छिद्य ii. 4.

—छिद्रम् iii. 32.

छिद्रान्तरप्रेक्षी iii. 51 One who is on the look-out for, who is a seeker of, holes, loopholes, weak points.

—छिद्रेषु iv. 27 (छिद् to pierce, cut; छिद्रं, hole, interstice, crack, rent, tear.)

—छिद्रेषु i. 5; iv. 27.

छिन्नः i. 16; ii. 4 Severed, cut, broken.

—छिन्न—ii. 4, 13.

—छिन्नाः ii. 4, 31, 50; iii. 14, 17.

—छिन्नानाम् iii. 17.

—छेदः iii. 52.

—छेदात् iii. 53..

—छेदाद् i. 16; iv. 9.

—छेदेन iii. 14.

छेद्यस्य ii. 28 Of the divisible; of that which has or requires to be cut, to be severed.

—ज—

—जं iii. 52, 54.

—ज—iii. 52. 54; iv. 26.

जगतः i. 1 (गम् to go) Of 'that which goes ever, unceasingly'; of the world, the world-process.

जङ्गमानाम् iii. 14 Of the moving.

जङ्गमेषु iii. 14.

—जन—ii. 19; iii. 51.

—जनः iv. 2, 11.

जननमरणान्धकारे iii. 51 In the darkness of (the blind round of involuntary) births and deaths.

जननी i. 20 Progenitress; mother.

—जनने iv. 12.

जनयति i. 11 Produces, gives birth to, brings forth. (जन्, to be 'gen'-erated; to 'gen'-erate).

जनलोकः iii. 26 The superphysical plane or world named Jana.

जनलोके iii. 26.

जनान् i. 47 People; (Lat. 'gens').

—जनितम् ii. 32.

जनित्वा i. 16 Having come forth; having been born.

जनिष्यते iv. 33 Will be born.

जन्तोः iv. 10 Of 'the born,' the animal.

—जन्म—ii. 9, 12, 13.

—जन्म—ii. 12, 13.

जन्म ii. 13 Birth.

जन्मकथंतासम्बोधः ii. 39 Knowledge of 'the how' of birth.

जन्मनः ii. 13.

जन्मना iv. 1.

जन्मपरिणामक्रमम् iii. 18 The course or succession of the transformations of births.

जन्मप्रायणान्तरे ii. 13 Between birth and death.

जन्मसु ii. 13.

जन्मायुर्भोगहेतुत्वात् ii. 13 Because of being the source of birth, life-term, and experience.

जन्मायुर्भोगाः ii. 14 Birth, life-period, and experience.

जन्मौषधिमन्त्रतपःसमाधिजाः iv. 1 'Born of,' arising from, birth, herbs, appliances, (chemical processes etc.), mantra, magic chant, (the physics of sound), austerity, (developement of will-power by asceticism), and trance-meditation.

जन्मौषधिमन्त्रतपःसमाधिजाः iv. 6.

—जपः i. 28 Recitation; repetition; reiteration; repeated utterance (loud or silent).

—जपः ii. 32.

जपः i. 28; ii. 1.

जपतः i. 28 Of him who recites.

जम्बूः iii. 26 The blue-plum tree.

जम्बूद्वीपः iii. 26 The continent of the earth called Jambu (in the Purāṇas).

—जय—ii. 41.

जयम् iii, 47.

—जयः iii. 44, 47, 48.

—जयः i. 24; ii. 18, 41, 55; iii. 47, 48.

जयः i. 24, 44; ii, 18 Victory; conquest; mastery (जि, to conquer).

—जयवत् ii. 54, 55.

—जयात् iii. 5, 39, 40.

—जयात् ii. 48, 51; iii. 39, 44, 47, 48.

जयात् iii. 5.

—जयी iii. 44, 51.

—जये ii. 49.

—जरम् iii. 51.

जरामृत्युम् iii. 51 Age and death.

—जल—ii. 32.

जलम् ii. 50; iii. 44 Water, (whence living things are born, जायन्ते, and into which they dissolve, लीयन्ते).

जलधौ iii. 26 In the 'reservoir of waters', the ocean.

जलपङ्ककण्टकादिषु iii. 39 In water, mire, thorns, etc.

जलपङ्ककण्टकादिषु iii. 39.

जलभूम्योः iii. 14 Of water and earth.

जले iii. 42.

—**जवित्वम्** iii 48. (Speediness).

—जवित्वम् iii. 48.

जह्यात् iii. 25 May abandon, quit, give up. (हा, to give up).

जाग्रत्समये i. 11 In the time of waking; during the waking condition.

जातम् ii. 15 Born (neu:).

जातः iv. 30, 33 Born (masc:).

जातमात्रस्य ii. 9; iv. 10 Of the just-born.

—जाताग्राम् i. 35.

जाति—ii. 13.

—**जाति**—iii. 18.

—जाति iii. 18, 44, 53.

—जातिः iv. 7, 33.

जातिः ii. 13 (जन् to be born) Birth; birth-type; type; kind, species, genus; 'gens', clan, tribe.

जातितः iv. 23 By, or because of, or from, class, species, con 'geni'-tal nature.

जातिदेशकालव्यवहितानाम् iv. 9 Of (the vāsanā-s, instincts,) divided off, walled off, separated, intervened, veiled, hidden, by special type (form), space, and time.

जातिदेशकालसमयानवच्छिन्नाः ii.31 Unlimited, not 'cut-off', not-defined, unconditioned, by (reservations of) species or kinds, places, times, and other conditions; not restricted by conditions or circumstances of kind, time, place, or other cause or condition.

जातिदेशकालसमयैः ii. 31 By species, place, time, conditions.

जातिभेदः iii. 53 Difference of species.

जातिलक्षणदेशैः iii. 53 By species, characteristic marks, and place.

जातिलक्षणसारूप्यात् iii. 53 From similarity of species and marks.

जातिशतेन iv. 9 By hundred births (in other species).

—जातीय—ii. 18; iv. 2.

—जातीयकम् i. 11.

—जातीयकः iii 17 Of or belonging to (a particular) species.

—जातीयकाः i. 5.

—जातीयत्वे iii. 53.

—जातीयस्य iv. 8.

—जातीयानाम् iv. 14.

—जातीयेभ्यः i. 7.

—जातीये ii. 18.

—जातीयेषु i. 7.

जात्यनुच्छेदेन iii. 14 Without uprooting, abolition, destruction, of the (characteristic) type or species.

जात्यन्तरपरिणामः iv. 2 Transmigration, development, transformation, mutation, variation, into another species, genus, race, (natural) kingdom.

जात्यवच्छिन्ना ii. 31 Conditioned by species; limited to, marked off by, type.

जात्यायुर्भोगाः ii. 13 Species (into which birth takes place), life-period, and experience.

जानाति i. 20; ii. 45; iii. 20. 22, 33, 54 Knows. (ज्ञा, to know).

—**जानाति** ii. 45.

जानामि iv. 27 I know.

—**जानीयात्** iii. 27, 29, 35.

जायते i 16, 47, 48, 50; iii. 35 Is born; comes forth.

—**जायन्ते** ii. 19.

जायन्ते iii. 36 Are born; are produced. (जन्, to be born)

जायन्ते iii. 23, 26, 36.

जायेरन् i. 32; ii. 33 If (they) are born; if they occur or appear; (they) may be born.

—**जालम्** ii, 13. (Mesh; net-work).

—**जालः** ii. 32.

—**जाला** ii. 1.

जिघत्सापिपासे ii. 32 Wish to eat and wish to drink; hunger and thirst.

जिघांसा ii. 8 Wish to slay.

जिज्ञासमानाय i. 25 To or for him who 'wishes to know'; for the enquiring or inquisitive (person).

—**जिज्ञासा** ii. 39.

—**जित**—iii, 6.

जितभूमेः iii, 6 Of him who has conquered, mastered, won, (a) stage. (See जयः)

जितसमानः iii. 40 He who has conquered, mastered, subjugated the (nerve) force named Samāna.

जितसम्बन्धः iii 42 He who has mastered the relation (between the body and space).

जितोत्तरभूमिकस्य iii. 6 Of him who has won the next or higher stage.

जित्वा iii. 42, 44 Having conquered, subjugated.

जिहासुः ii. 40 Wishing to abandon, to throw off.

—**जिहः** iv. 31.

—**जिह्वा**—ii. 19.

जिह्वाग्रे i 35; iii. 1 In front of, on the tip of, the tongue.

जिह्वामध्ये i. 35 In or on the middle of the tongue.

जिह्वामूले i. 35 In, on, at, the root of the tongue.

जिह्वायाः iii 30 Of the tongue.

जीवति iii. 17 Lives.

जीवन् iv 30 Living.

—**जीवन**—iii. 18.

जीवनम् iii. 15, 39 Life.

जीवलोकम् ii. 5 The world of jīvas, the living; the living world; all living beings in their totality.

जीवितव्यपरोपणात् ii 34 By taking away, deprivation, of or from life.

जीवितात् ii. 34 From living; from life.

जीवितात्यये ii. 34 At the passing of life; in the throes of death.

—जुगुप्सा ii. 40 'Wish to hide'; shame at; contempt of; shrinking from; dislike; abhorrence.

जुगुप्सायाम् ii. 40.

जैगीषव्यः ii. 55; iii. 18 Name of a Ṛṣhi (mentioned in the Upanishaṭs and Purāṇas, as a great yogī; (Bṛhaḍ Āraṇyaka; Vishṇu Bhāgavaṭa; Maṭsya, etc.).

जैगीषव्यस्य iii. 18.

—ज्ञ—i. 25.

—ज्ञः iii. 17, 49, 51.

—ज्ञा i. 47, 48, 50; ii 27; iii. 5, 35, 51.

—ज्ञा—i. 25, 49, 50; iii. 26; iv. 23.

—ज्ञाम् ii. 27.

—ज्ञात—ii. 20.

ज्ञातत्वम् iv. 18.

—ज्ञातम् ii. 27; iii. 17.

—ज्ञातः i. 16; ii. 20; iv. 17.

ज्ञातः ii. 20; iv. 17 Known.

ज्ञातव्यः iii. 6. To be known; knowable; what ought to be known.

ज्ञाताः iv. 18 Known. (Pl:).

ज्ञाताज्ञातम् iv. 17 (Partly) known and (partly) unknown.

ज्ञाताज्ञातविषयत्वात् ii. 20 Because of its knowing some and not knowing other objects; because of its cognisance of objects being broken, not all-inclusive.

ज्ञाताज्ञातस्वरूपत्वात् iv. 17 Because of its 'own-form' its nature, its characteristic of being known (in part) and unknown (in other parts).

ज्ञाताज्ञाताः iv. 18 (Successively, interruptedly.) known and unknown.

—ज्ञातारम् iii. 35.

ज्ञातुः iii. 53 Of the knower.

—ज्ञातृत्वम् iii. 49.

—ज्ञातृत्वम् iii. 49.

—ज्ञान—i. 9, 38, 42.

—ज्ञान—i. 1, 2, 38, 42, 43; ii. 18, 24, 52; iii. 6, 55; iv. 14, 26.

—ज्ञानम् i. 8; iii. 16, 17, 18, 19, 22, 25, 26, 27, 28, 29, 35, 52.

—ज्ञानम् i. 43, 49; ii. 23, 26, 28, 55; iii. 17, 34, 36; iv. 15.

ज्ञानम् iii. 54. (ज्ञा, to 'know'; Lat. gnoscere; Gr. gnosis). Knowledge; (spiritual knowledge particularly).

ज्ञानम् i. 42, 43; ii 24, 38; iii. 17, 18, 22, 49; iv. 12, 14, 24, 55.

ज्ञानदीप्तिः ii. 28 The flaming up, blazing forth, illumination, luminosity, radiance, effulgennce, en-'light'-enment, shining out of knowledge.

—ज्ञानधर्माः i. 42

ज्ञानधर्मोपदेशेन i. 25 By teaching of (the truths of final spiritual) knowledge and duty.

ज्ञानपरिकल्पनामात्रम् iv. 14 Only a form, a construction, a projection, an imagination, supposition, ideation, assumption, of or by (the faculty or power of) knowledge

ज्ञानप्रसादमात्रम् i. 16 Only the placidity, lucidity, cheerfulness and vigor, e-lucid-ation, blossoming and efflorescence, of knowledge; the true or highest knowledge.

—ज्ञानयोः iv. 15.

ज्ञानवृत्तिः ii. 20; iv. 22 The mood of knowledge; cognitive functioning; cognitional activity awareness; self-consciousness.

ज्ञानवैराग्ये iv. 10 Knowledge and renunciation.

ज्ञानसंस्काराः iv. 28 Knowledge-producing impressions,'tendencies; the tendencies to, the instincts of, (spiritual) knowledge.

ज्ञानसत्त्वम् iv. 31 (The element or factor of) cognitional or cognitive saṭṭva.

ज्ञानसहभूः iv. 16 Born together with knowledge.

—ज्ञानस्य ii. 26, 28; iii. 55.

ज्ञानस्य iv. 31.

ज्ञानस्य i. 16, 25; ii. 28, 52; iii. 33; iv. 12, 31.

—ज्ञाना ii. 26.

—ज्ञानाः iii. 26.

ज्ञानाग्निना iv. 28 By the fire of knowledge.

—ज्ञानात् ii. 28; iii. 14, 53.

ज्ञानात् iii. 55.

ज्ञानान्तरम् ii. 5 Another knowledge.

ज्ञानार्थम् iv. 24 For the sake of knowledge.

—ज्ञानेन iii. 14, 53.

ज्ञाने iii. 55.

—ज्ञाभ्याम् i. 49.

ज्ञायते ii. 5 Is known; seems.

—ज्ञायाम् i. 42; ii. 26: iii. 49; iv. 23.

—ज्ञायाः ii. 27, iii. 5.

—ज्ञालोकः iii. 6.

—ज्ञेयम् ii. 5, 27.

ज्ञेयम् iv. 31. Knowable (neu:).

ज्ञेयम iv. 12, 31.

—ज्ञेयः iv. 23.

—ज्योतिः ii. 27; iii. 51.

ज्योतिः iii. 22, 32 Light.

—ज्योतिषि iii. 32.

ज्योतिषि iii. 1 In the light.

ज्योतिष्मती i 36 Luminous; (a technical name for an illuminated state of mind in yoga, in which there is a vision of colored light, within the head, as it were, amongst other experiences).

ज्योतिष्मती i. 36; iii. 25.

—ज्वरेण ii. 33.

ज्वलति iii. 40 Blazes; shines; glows.

ज्वलनम् iii. 40 Blazing, shining.

—त—

तच्छिद्रेषु iv. 27 In the holes, intervals, interstices, breaks of it.

तच्छुद्धिप्रविवेकाप्यायितबुद्धिः i. 16 (The world-surfeited practiser of yoga) whose intelligence has been nourished, filled, strengthened by and with clear and strong discrimination (between Purusha and Prakriti, Spirit and Matter, Subject and Object) born of true vision (of the Pure stainless Purusha or Self.)

तज्जः i. 50 Born of it.

तज्जपः i. 28 Repetition, 'telling', (as with beads) of It (i.e., the Praṇava, AUM).

तज्जयात् iii. 5 By subjugation of it.

—तण्डुलाः ii. 13 (Grains; paddy-grains.)

—तण्डुलानाम् iii. 17.

तत्—, —तत्—i. 8, 12, 28, 32, 41, 50; ii. 11, 13, 21, 25, 35; iii. 5, 17, 21, 22, 28, 45, 50, 52; iv. 8, 11, 16, 17, 18, 22, 27.

—तत्—ii. 20.

तत् i. 16; ii. 22, 25; iii. 3, 8, 20; iv. 19, 24 That.

तत् i. 2; ii. 1; iii. 8; iv. 6; etc. That; so then.

ततः i. 22, 29; ii. 48, 52, 55; iii. 12, 36, 43, 45, 48, 53; iv. 3, 8, 30, 32 Thence; therefore; from it.

ततः i. 22; ii. 15; iii. 26; iv. 3 etc.

तत्कृतम् ii. 34 Done by that.

तत्क्रियासाक्षिणि ii. 18 In the witness of their activity.

तत्क्षणोपारूढाः iii. 52 'Mounted on', occurring in, that moment.

तत्क्षये ii. 28 On the decay of that.

तत्तच्छास्त्रानुमानाचार्योपदेशैः i. 35 By the several sciences, by reasonings and inferences, and by the teachings of the experts, adepts, teachers.

—तत्त्व—i. 32.

—तत्त्व—ii. 18; iii. 13.

—तत्त्वम् iv. 14.

—तत्त्वम् i. 35; ii. 5, 19.

तत्त्वम् iv. 33 'That-ness'; thing-in-itself; the exact thing; the thing as it is; thing; fact; truth; reality; element; essence; substance; first principle; principle.

तत्त्वज्ञानम् ii. 28 True-knowledge; knowledge of the truth, the 'that-ness', of a thing as it really is.

तत्त्वज्ञानेन iii. 53.

तत्त्वानभिघातात् iv. 33 Because of non-destruction of the substratum, the substance, the essence.

तत्त्वान्तरम् ii. 19 Another ṭaṭṭva.

तत्त्वान्तरपरिणामः ii. 19 Transformation into another ṭaṭṭva.

तत्परः iii. 26 Next to that; beyond it. (Another reading is ततः परः, meaning the same).

तत्पूर्वकः ii. 51 Preceded by it.

तत्प्रतिपक्षान् ii. 33 Their enemies, antagonists, opponents, foes.

तत्प्रतिपादनार्थं ii. 30 For the propounding, expounding, exposition, of it.

तत्प्रतिषेधः ii. 30 Refutation, contradiction, prevention, prohibition, of it.

तत्प्रतिषेधार्थम् i. 32 For the prevention, the checking, the 'prohibiting' of (distractions).

तत्प्रभवाः i. 50 Born of it.

तत्प्रभोः iv. 18 Of their Lord, Master, Sovereign.

तत्प्रवाहाविच्छेदः iii. 52 The non-breach, unbrokenness, unceasingness, continuance, incessance, of its flow.

तत्प्रविभागसंयमात् iii. 17 By meditation on their separateness, their distinctness.

तत्प्रस्तारः iii. 26 (स्तॄ, to 'stretch'). Its extent.

तत्फलम् i. 24 The fruit thereof.

तत्फलसंन्यासः ii. 1 The renunciation of the fruit thereof.

तत्फलस्य i. 24; ii. 18.

तत्र i. 13, 25, 42, 48; iii. 2; iv. 6 There; in that place; in it.

तत्र i. 1; ii. 4; iv. 2; etc.

तत्संयमात् iii. 22 By meditation on it.

तत्संयोगहेतुविवर्जनात् ii. 17 By, from, through, because of, avoidance of the cause of the connection, 'conjunction', identification, of them.

तत्संश्रयाणाम् iv. 11. Of (the appetites, the instinctive desires) supported by, resting or depending on, them.

तत्संस्कारमान्द्ये iii. 10 On the dulling, slowing, weakening, of that tendency; when that impress, that cultivated habit, predilection, disposition, is weak.

तत्सङ्करात् iv. 21 By mixture, confusion, adulteration, of them.

तत्सदृशः iii. 12 Like that; similar to it.

तत्सन्निधौ ii. 35 In his vicinity.

तत्समानम् i. 24 Equal to its or his.

तत्समाहारः iii. 52 Gathering up, collection, aggregate, totality, of them.

तत्सम्पिपादयिषया i. 13 With or by the wish to bring about, achieve, accomplish, fulfil, collect or accumulate it.

तत्सम्बन्धः i. 24 Relation or connection with them.

तत्साधनानुष्ठानम् i. 13 The practice, the following out, of the means which will secure it.

तत्साधनाय i. 18 For its accomplishment..

तत्साधने ii. 7, 8.

तत्सिद्धिपरतया ii. 30 Because of, or as, leading to its success.

तत्स्थतदञ्जनता i. 41 The taking on of the form or color of that on which it rests.

तत्स्मृत्यभावः iii. 14 Absence of memory of that.

तत्स्वरूपम् ii. 21; iv. 34 That form, or its form. (Some editions read तत् as a separate word).

तत्स्वरूपाकारमात्रतया i. 42 Only in or by the form of that object.

तथा ii. 9 So; thus; similarly; in the same way.

तथा i. 3; ii. 4; iii. 5; iv. 3; etc.

तथाजातीयकम् i. 11, 19 Of that or corresponding or similar genus or species.

तथाजातीयकाः i. 5.

—तदञ्जनता i. 41.

तदनुगुणाः i. 24 Consequent on and reproducing or reflecting the properties or characteristics thereof; having qualities corresponding with it.

तदन्तरेषु iii. 26 In the interstices between them.

तदप्रमाणकम् iv. 16 Unwitnessed, unsupported, by it.

तदभावः iv. 11 Absence of that or those.

तदभावात् ii. 25 By or from absence, non-existence, abolition or elimination of it or that.

तदभावात् iii. 6.

तदभावे iii. 8.

तदभिध्यानात् i. 23 By that or his well-wishing.

तदभ्यासपूर्वम् i. 18 Preceded by practice thereof.

तदभ्यासात् i. 20 By practice thereof.

तदर्थः ii. 21 For its sake.

तदर्थः i. 13; iii. 17.

तदर्थभावनम् i. 28 Dwelling on, reflection on, realisation of, its meaning.

तदर्थविषया i. 7 Having for object the meaning thereof.

तदर्थस्य iii. 6 Of the meaning, purport, purpose, thereof.

तदर्थावसायः ii. 18 The finishing, completing, of that purpose.

तदर्द्धेन iii. 26 By half of it.

तद्वदातकरणाय ii. 30 In order to make it of perfect form, to refine it.

तदवस्थम् i. 2 In that state.

तदवस्थे i. 2.

तदविशिष्टवृत्तिः i. 4 Having a 'mode of existence', not-different, not-distinguishable, from that of those (moods, functionings, workings, states, of the mind, chitta).

तदा i. 3; iv, 16, 26, 31 Then.

तदा i. 32; ii. 4; iii. 3; iv. 3; etc.

तदाकारम् i. 37 Of that same form.

तदाकारानुरोधी ii. 17 'Imitator of its form'.

तदाकारापत्तिः i, 41 Attainment to the form thereof.

तदाकारापत्तौ iv. 22 On the attainment of that form.

तदाकाराम् i. 11 Of that same form (fem.).

तदात्मकः ii. 20 Of its nature; having the same nature as that.

तदानीम् i. 3; iii 13; iv. 16, 26 At that time; during that time.

तदाश्रिताः i. 10 Dependent thereon.

तदुद्देशेन iv. 12 By or with reference to it; with it as object, end, aim.

तदुपघाताय i. 31 For the destruction of which or it.

तदुपदिष्टार्थैकदेशप्रत्यक्षत्वे i. 35 On some one part or portion of the matters taught by them being brought within direct sensuous cognition, within immediate personal experience.

तदुपरागापेक्षित्वात् iv. 17 Because of dependence on coloring, tinging, by it.

तद्गतिज्ञानम् iii. 28 Knowledge of its motion.

तद्ग्राह्यशक्तिस्तम्भे iii. 21 On suspension of its power or capacity of being apprehended; in case of suspension of its apprehensibility.

तद्दर्शनम् i. 42 Seeing of that; the vision of it.

तद्दर्शनप्रत्यनीकत्वात् iii. 37 Because of being hostile to the vision of that.

तद्देशानुपपत्तौ iii. 53 On the non-propriety or non-perceiving of (that atom being in) that position or place.

तद्देशानुभवः iii. 53 Experience of that position or place.

तद्द्वारेण iii. 15 By that 'door', that means.

तद्धर्मानभिघातः iii. 45 (See अभिघातः) The non-overcoming (of the yogi's body) by the powers, attributes, functions, of them (i. e. of the five bhūṭas).

तद्बीजसत्ता iv. 25 The existence of the germ thereof.

तद्वत् ii. 50 Like that.

तद्वशीकारात् i. 40 By that control; or, by control of that.

तद्विकलः i. 17 Deprived, devoid, of that part.

तद्विपाकः ii. 13 Its maturation, fruition.

तद्विपाकस्य ii. 13.

तद्विपाकानुगुणानाम् iv. 8 Of (desires) con-natural, con-sonant, con-forming, cor-respondent, with its (karma's) maturation, its fruitage.

तद्विरुद्धः ii. 5 The opposite or contradictory of it; hostile to it.

तद्विषया i. 7 Pertaining to it; having it for object.

तद्विषयात् i. 20.

तद्विषयायाम् i. 35.

तद्विषयाः i. 10; iv. 18.

तद्वृत्तयः ii. 11 Their formulations, existences, manifestations, functionings, (i.e. workings of the psyche).

तद्वृत्तिम् ii. 20; iv. 22.

तद्वैराग्यात् iii. 50 By revulsion, 'dis-affection', therefrom.

तनवः ii. 4 (Plural of तनुः).

—तनु—ii. 4.

—तनु—ii. 4.

—तनुः i. 1.

तनुः ii. 4 'Thin'; at-'tenu'-ated; 'tiny'; fine-drawn; (तन् to stretch); also (the living) body.

तनुत्वम् ii. 4 'Thin'-ness.

तनुधरः iii. 18 Wearing a body.

—तनू—ii. 2.

तनूकृताः ii. 11 Made 'thin'; at-'tenu'-ated.

—तन्तु—iii. 42.

—तन्तुः iii. 18.

तन्तुः ii. 15; iii. 30 Strand; thread; (तन् to stretch); warp and woof; string; cord; catgut.

—तन्त्रम् iv. 16.

—तन्त्रम् ii. 17 (Dependent on, interwoven with).

तन्त्रम् i. 25 (तन् to stretch, spread, as warp and woof). Science; web or network of knowledge; systematised, organised, knowledge.

—तन्त्री—ii. 3, 15.

तन्निरोधः i. 12 The inhibition or control of it.

—तन्मात्रम् i. 45; ii. 19.

तन्मात्रम् iii. 44 (मा, to measure; माता, the 'mother', who sets the measure of the progeny; मात्रा, 'matter', that which 'measures', defines, delimits, the immeasurable, indefinable, limitless Spirit). 'That-measure';

'that only'; that-in-itself; 'that-matrix'; 'that-measurer'; 'measurer-of-that'; the sensations of sound, tact, sight, taste, smell, in-themselves; the sensations as such, pure and simple; (शब्दमात्रम्, स्पर्शमात्रम्, etc., see Bhāgavaṭa, iii. xxvi); sense-continua or, rather, sensation-continua, sound-continuum, tact-continuum, light-continuum, taste-continuum, smell-continuum.

तन्मात्रभूतभौतिकेषु iii. 44 Through or in the ṭan-māṭras, and the bhūṭas (the five elements), and the bhūṭa-products or compounds.

—तन्मात्राणाम् ii. 19.

तन्मात्रावयवः iv. 14 Having (five) ṭan-māṭras as component parts.

तन्मूलाः ii. 30 Rooted in that.

—तपः—ii. 32; iv. 1.

—तपः—ii. 12; iv. 6.

तपः ii. 1, 32, 43, 52 (तप् to burn; to be hot; to glow; to suffer). Self-denial; suffering; abnegation; asceticism; austerity; penance; burning (of the lower or selfish heart, with the fire of renunciation, resignation, unselfishness); repression of the lower self; 'burning' up of selfishness; 'glowing' with noble motive and aspiration; will-force developed by austerity; ('credit-account' accumulated with the 'Lord of Karma' by austerities).

तपःस्वाध्यायध्यानवताम् iv. 7 Of those who are practising, or have practised, austerity, study, and contemplation.

तपःस्वाध्यायेश्वरप्रणिधानानि ii. 1 Asceticism, and study, and resignation or surrender of the will to God.

तपसः ii. 43 Of or from or because of ṭapas.

तपसः ii. 1.

तपसा i. 14.

तपसि iii. 26 In the loka or world or plane called Ṭapas, Tapo-loka.

—तपस्विनः ii. 1.

तपस्विषु ii. 12 In or towards the ascetics.

तपिक्रिया ii. 17 The act of austerity, self-denial, penance.

तपिक्रियायाः ii. 17.

तपोलोकः iii. 26 The superphysical world or plane called Ṭapas or Ṭapo-loka,

तप्ते ii. 50 In the heated; on being heated.

—तप्यते ii. 17.

तप्यम् ii. 17 The (thing) capable of, or to be, or being heated, energised; the to-be-stimulated.

तप्यमाने ii. 17 In the (thing) being heated.

तम् i. 23; iv. 31 Him.

—तमः—iii. 43, 49, 55.

तमः i, 8; ii. 18 Darkness; inertia; heaviness; density; substantiality; dense dark blind desire.

तमःप्रतिष्ठाः iii. 26 Based in, seated or founded on, ṭamas.

तमसा i. 2; iv. 31.

—तमसो iii. 35.

—तमोभ्याम् i. 2, 47.

तयोः iv. 15 Of those two or in those two.

तयोः ii. 6; iii. 9; iv. 10; etc.

तर्हि i. 4; ii. 4; iv. 3 etc. Then; if so.

—तल—iii. 39.

—तलस्य ii. 17.

—तलातल—iii. 26.

तल्लाभात् iv. 30 By the gain of that.

तस्मात् i, 4; ii. 13; iii. 13; iv. 10; etc. From him or it; therefore; thence.

तस्मिन् ii. 49 In him or it.

तस्मिन् i. 48; ii. 13; iii. 2; iv. 3; etc.

तस्य i. 27, 51; ii. 24, 27; iii. 6, 10, 20 Of him; his; its.

तस्य i. 2; ii. 4; iii. 5; iv. 6; etc.

तस्याम् i. 2; iii. 23.

तस्याः i. 43; ii. 5; iii. 25; iv. 11; etc.

ताः i. 46 Those (fem.).

ताः i. 5; ii. 11; etc.

तान् ii. 33.

तानि ii. 28; iii. 50.

तान्त्रिकी iii. 4 Technical; special to one science; scientific; belonging to a Ṭantra. (See तन्त्रम्).

—ताप—ii. 15.

—ताप—ii. 5; iii. 18.

तापकस्य ii. 17 Of the cause of suffering; of the heater, energiser, stimulator, oppressor disturber.

तापत्रयम् iii. 50 Three-fold suffering; the three kinds of suffering (mental, physical, and mixed or 'superphysical').

तापदुःखता ii. 15 The state of pain of sorrow and suffering, (with an implication of remorse, पश्चात्-तापः, 'after-suffering', 'subsequent-grief').

तापानुभवः ii. 15 Experience of suffering.

तापाः ii. 15 Pains; sufferings.

ताभ्याम् i. 32; ii. 5; iii. 44.

ताम् i. 2; ii. 24; iii. 13.

तामिस्रः i. 8 Composed of 'deep darkness.' grosser ṭamas.

—तारकम् i. 7.

तारकम् iii. 54 That which helps to 'cross over', to win across.

तारकम् iii. 53, 34.

—तारका ii. 5.

—तारकाः iii. 26.

—तारा—iii. 26.

ताराः iii. 26 'Stars'.

ताराव्यूहम् iii. 27 The co-ordination', 'inter-linking', organisation, system, of stars.

ताराव्यूहज्ञानम् iii. 27 Knowledge of the sidereal system, of the organisation of stars.

तालुनि i. 35 In the palate; in a brain-centre placed near or above the palate.

तावत् i. 24, 29, 35; ii. 13, 34; iii. 26 So long as; till then; indeed; so much that.

तावन्त्यः iv. 21.

तासाम् iv. 10 Of them (fem:).

तासाम् iv. 8.

—तिमिर—iii. 51.

तिरोभवति i. 43 'Goes below'; goes under the surface; disappears.

तिरोभावः iii. 11 Disappearance.

तिरोभूताः iii. 17 Hidden; disappeared.

—तिर्यक्—iii. 18; iv. 8

—तिर्यक् ii. 34.

तिर्यक्त्वेन ii. 12 By animal-ness; as a lower animal. (तिर्यक् means sidewise, horizontal; thus, the reptiles and quadrupeds etc., are तिर्यक्स्रोतस्, i. e., their alimentary camals are horizontal).

—तिष्ठ—iv. 19.

तिष्ठति i. 9, 10 (स्था, to stand). Stands.

—तिष्ठन्ति iii. 26. (Some editions read प्र-तिष्ठन्ते instead of प्रतितिष्ठन्ति).

—तिष्ठन्ते ii. 37; iii. 26, 49, 55.

तिस्रः iii. 23, 48 Three.

तीर्थे ii. 31 In a holy place, (where the jīva can 'cross over' from this to another world, or from sin to virtue).

—तीव्र—i. 21.

तीव्रक्लेशेन ii. 12 By intense suffering or misery

तीव्रमध्यः ii 34 Of the middle type in intense degree.

तीव्रमृदुः ii. 34 Of the mild type, kind, of an intense degree.

—तीव्र; i. 22.

तीव्रः ii. 50 Sharp; intense.

तीव्रसंवेगः i. 21 Of sharp or intense speed, energy, force, impulse, passion, earnestness.

तीव्रसंवेगानाम् i. 21 Of those whose wish (for samadhi) is intensely strong, passionate, earnest.

तीव्रसंवेगेन ii. 12 By intense force.

तु i. 14; iv 3 Verily; indeed; on the other hand

तु i. 1; ii. 4; iii 6; iv. 4; etc.

—तुच्छकम् iv. 13.

तुल्यः ii. 33 Equal. (तुल्, to weigh to measure; तुला, a weighing balance; तुल्यः, that which is 'weighable' equally against or with an other, hence is 'equal' to another.)

तुल्यजातिलक्षणदेशस्य iii. 53 Of the (atom) with equal or similar genus, mark or characteristic, and position or place or location.

तुल्यजातीयातुल्यजातीयशक्तिभेदानुपातिनः ii 18 Following the distinction of the functions, forces, or powers, (as in the case) of things of one and the same kind, and things of different kinds. (each producing its own effect, exercising its own function, so that the total result includes the consequences of the operations of all three guṇa-s).

तुल्यजातीयेषु i. 7 'Among the equal-genus-ed', i. e , in objects belonging to the same genus.

तुल्यदेशजातीयत्वे iii. 53 On place or position or location and genus or species or kind being equal or same; when these are the same or similar; in the case of these being alike.

तुल्यदेशत्वे iii. 53 Place, space, position, location being the same.

तुल्यदेशश्रवणानाम् iii. 41 Of (persons) with equal or similar position and audition.

तुल्यप्रत्ययौ iii. 12 Two equal concepts; similar or coincident or equivalent ideas, cognitions, perceptions.

तुल्ययोः iii. 53 Of the two equals.

तुल्ययोः i 24 iii. 53 Of the two equals.

तुल्यातुल्यजातीये ii 18 In (the purusha who is) the same as well as different in kind or species.

—तुषाः ii. 13.

तुषावनद्धाः ii. 13 'Bound with', enclosed in, husk; unhusked.

तुषिताः iii. 26 A race of ḍevas called Ṭushiṭa.

—तूल— iii. 42.

तूलादिषु iii. 42 Amongst or in cotton, etc.

तृणराशौ iii. 22 In a heap of grass.

तृणाङ्कुरस्य iv. 25 Of the grass-sprout.

तृतीयम् iii. 44, 47 Third.

तृतीयः i. 17; ii. 50, 51; iii. 13, 26, 51.

तृतीये iii. 26.

तृप्तेः ii. 5 From appeasement, satiation, satisfaction.

—तृष्णः iv. 33.

तृष्णा ii. 7 'Thirst'; craving; desire (for bodily enjoyments, for the experiences of the separate individuality).

तृष्णाक्षयसुखस्य ii. 42 Of the happiness of, i. e., arising from, the wearing away, perishing, disappearance, annihilation, of desire.

तृष्णातन्तुः iii. 18 The thread, strand, cord, of desire.

तृष्णादुःखसन्तापापगमात् iii. 18 By the departure, the passing away, of the burning heat of the pain of desire; from the disappearance of the hot pains, the sorrows and sufferings, caused by desire.

तृष्णायोनयः iii. 51 The 'wombs' i. e. producers, and also the products, of 'thirst', desire.

ते i. 30; ii. 10, 14; iii. 37; iv. 13 They.

ते i. 19; ii. 3; iii. 9; iv. 9; etc.

तेजसः iii. 40 Of tejas, 'fire', light, heat, radiance.

तेन i. 9; ii. 4; iii. 16; iv. 11; etc. By it or him.

तेन तेन iv. 15 By 'that and that'; by the appropriate.

तेषाम् i. 45; ii. 2; iii. 18; iv. 2; etc.

तेषु ii. 19; iii. 16; iv. 3; etc.

तैः iv. 23.

तैजसस्य i. 45 Of the 'luminous'; of that which consists of, or is born of, tejas, light and heat, fire.

तैर्यग्यौन— ii. 28 (Belonging to the animal kingdom).

त्यक्तम् ii. 15 Given up; abandoned.

त्यक्तस्य ii. 33.

त्यक्त्वा i. 1, 43; ii. 33 Having abandoned.

त्यजन्तम् ii. 15 Giving up.

—त्यागः ii. 35.

—त्रय— iii. 16.

—त्रयम् iii. 4, 7, 8, 16, 43, 50.

त्रयम् iii. 4, 7 Three; triplet, triad, trinity.

त्रयम् ii. 17; iv. 12, 23.

त्रयः ii. 50; iii. 14, 26, 29 (In iii. 14 some editions read ये in place of त्रयः).

त्रयस्य iii. 4.

त्रयाणाम् ii. 19; iii. 13; iv. 12.

त्रयी ii. 13, 27 Triplet (fem:).

त्रस्यति iv. 21 Fears.

—त्राण— ii. 17.

—त्रासः ii. 9.

—त्रि—ii. 19.

त्रिगुणम् i. 2; ii. 15; iv. 15 Having three 'strands', attributes; (neu:).

त्रिगुणः iii. 18 Having (the) three properties, attributes, qualities (masc:).

त्रिगुणत्वात् ii. 20 Because of possessing (the) three attributes.

त्रिगुणा ii. 20 Having (the) three properties, attributes (fem:).

त्रित्वोपलब्धिसामर्थ्यात् ii. 17 By the power of knowledge of the triplicity.

त्रिदशाः iii. 26 The 'three-tens'; (the word is explained in other ways also); the devas.

त्रिदशानाम् iii. 26.

त्रिधा i. 48; ii. 34 In three ways; three-wise; trebly.

त्रिपर्वाणः ii 15 Three-jointed.

त्रिभिः ii. 31; iii. 13 By three.

त्रिभूमिकः iii. 26 Three storeyed, three-layered, three-planed.

त्रिलक्षणम् iii. 13 Having three marks.

त्रिलक्षणः iii. 13.

त्रिविधम् iv. 7 Threefold (neu:).

त्रिविधम् iii. 22.

त्रिविधः i. 21; ii. 13; iii. 13, 26.

त्रिविधाः ii. 34.

त्रिविधात् iv. 8.

त्रिविपाकः ii 13 Having three maturations, fruits, consequences, results.

त्रिषु ii 18.

त्रीणि i. 24; iii. 4, 26 Three.

त्रेधा ii. 34 Three-wise; in three ways.

त्रैलोक्यम् iii. 13 The triple world; the triad of worlds; the three worlds together.

त्रैलोक्यमध्ये iii. 26 Within the triple world.

त्र्यध्वा iii. 13 Having three paths.

त्र्यध्वानः iii. 13; iv. 13 (Plural of above).

—त्वक् ii. 19.

त्वग्लोहितमांसस्नाय्वस्थिमज्जाशुक्राणि iii. 29 Cutaneous (dermal) tissue, blood (liquid tissue), flesh (fibrous tissue), cartilege (cartilaginous tissue), bone (osseous tissue), marrow (oleaginous or fatty tissue), semen-ovum (reproductive tissue). (This septenary is a little different from that mentioned in the Āyurvedic medical works, viz., rasa (chyme-chyle), rakṭa (blood), māṁsa (flesh), méḍas (fat), asṭhi (bone), majjā (marrow), shukra (semenovum).

त्वया iii. 18 By thee.

—द्—

दक्षिणः ii. 26. South; southern.

दक्षिणतः iii. 26. To the south.

दक्षिणपार्श्वे iii. 26. On the right or the southern side.

दक्षिणभागः iii. 26. Southern part. (Most editions read दक्षिणः भागः).

दग्धक्लेशबीजम् iii. 55. With seed of misery burnt, consumed.

दग्धक्लेशबीजस्य ii. 4; iii. 55. Of (the wise person) whose seed of misery has been burnt, i. e. sterilised (by true knowledge).

दग्धबीजकल्पान् ii. 2.

दग्धबीजकल्पाः ii. 10, 11. Like, having the form of, similar to, resembling, burnt i. e. sterilised seeds.

दग्धबीजभावम् ii. 26. To the being, the state, of burnt seeds.

दग्धबीजभावः iv. 28. Reduced to the state of a burnt seed.

दग्धबीजभावा ii. 4. Being in the state of a burnt seed; (fem:).

दग्धबीजभावाः ii. 13; iv. 28.

दग्धबीजभावोपगमः ii. 26. The coming on, supervention, assumption, attainment, of the condition of burnt seeds.

दग्धबीजस्य ii. 4. Of the burnt seed.

दग्धबीजानाम् ii. 4. Of burnt seeds.

दग्धम् ii. 4. Burnt.

दग्धशालिबीजकल्पानि iii. 50. Like burnt paddy-seeds.

दण्डकारण्यम् iv. 10. The forest named Ḍandaka.

दण्डासनम् ii. 46. 'Rod-posture'; (a particular yogic posture in which the practiser is 'stretched out like a rod').

—दत्ते iv. 10. (दा, to give).

—ददानः ii. 33.

—दधाति ii. 23. (धा, to 'do', to place, to put).

—दधाति iv. 21.

—दधि—iii. 26. (Curd).

दरिद्राणम् ii. 19. Impoverishment. (Some editions read दरिद्रता, poverty).

दरिद्राति ii. 19. Becomes poor.

—दर्श— iii. 36.

—दर्शन—i. 30; ii. 6, 41.

—दर्शन— i. 12, 16; ii. 17, 23, 24, 43; iii. 37; iv. 15, 25.

दर्शनकार्यावसानः ii. 23. Ending with the act of vision.

दर्शनज्ञानम् ii. 23. Vision-knowledge; illumination; the knowledge that is identical with, is of the nature of, or arises from, direct vision.

—दर्शनम् iii. 32.

—दर्शनम् i. 29; ii. 15, 23, 24.

दर्शनम् i. 4, 43; ii. 18, 23, 44; iii. 32. (दृश्, पश्य, to see). Seeing; view; vision, recognition, of the Self; vision; doctrine; system of philosophy.

दर्शनवर्जिताः iii. 15. Deprived of, beyond, vision.

दर्शनशक्तिः ii. 6, 23. The power of seeing, knowledge, cognition, awareness.

—दर्शनस्य ii. 23, 25.

दर्शनस्य ii. 23.

—दर्शना ii. 24.

—दर्शनात् ii. 4, 17, 30; iii. 41.

दर्शनात् ii. 24.

—दर्शनाद्या ii. 43.

—दर्शनानाम् iii. 52.

दर्शनाभावः ii. 23. Absence or lack of vision.

दर्शनार्थम् ii. 23. For the sake of vision.

दर्शनीयः iii. 46. Worthy to see.

दर्शयति ii. 20 Shows.

दर्शितविषयत्वात् i. 4; ii. 17; iii. 35 Because of having objects shown to it.

दर्शितविषयस्य ii. 23 Of (the Self,

the soul, the purusha) to which objects have been exhibited.

दर्शितविषया i. 2 That (Chiṭi-Shakṭi, Principle or Power of Consciousness, the Self, Purusha) to which objects, sensuous things, have been or are exhibited; spectatress.

—दर्शितः iii. 13.

—दर्शिनः iv. 25.

—दर्शिनः iv. 23, 25.

दश iii. 13 Ten.

दशसु iii. 18.

दशस्थाने iii. 13. In the place of tens.

दष्टः ii. 15. Bitten, stung.

दहति iii. 45. Burns.

दहरम् iii. 34. Hollow; empty space; subtle, small, infinitesimal; the cairty of the heart; the heart.

दहेत् iii. 22. may burn up.

—दा—iv. 4.

—दात—ii. 30.

—दान—iv. 10.

—दानात् iii. 42; iv. 7.

—दानानि iv. 14.

—दानेन ii. 33.

—दाय iii. 54; iv. 4, 9, 14, 33.

दारेषु ii. 33. In, among, the wives.

—दिक्—ii. 37.

—दित्सते ii. 30.

—दित्सा—ii. 32.

—दिवम् iii. 26.

दिवि iii. 26. In heaven.

दिवौकसः ii. 5. Dwellers of heaven; gods. (Gr. *theos*, god, *oikos*, house).

दिव्यगन्धविज्ञानम् iii. 36. Knowledge, experience, of 'divine', superphysical, subtle, fragrances.

दिव्यगन्धसंवित् i. 35. Consciousness, awareness, 'sensing' of 'divine', subtle, superphysical scents; 'clair-olfaction'.

दिव्यम् iii. 4. 'Divine', heavenly, superphysical.

दिव्यम् ii. 42; iii. 41.

दिव्यरससंवित् iii. 36; i. 35. Consciousness, awareness, 'sensing' of 'divine', subtle, superphysical taste; 'clair-guestation'.

दिव्यरूपसंवित् iii. 36. Do. of forms, sights, shapes; clair-voyance.

दिव्यशब्दश्रवणम् iii. 36. Do. of sounds; clair-audience.

दिव्यस्पर्शाधिगमः iii. 36. Do. of tacts, touches; 'clair-palpation'.

दिव्यादिव्यविषयसम्प्रयोगे i. 15. In or for the contact, engagement, experience, proximity, enjoyment, or employment, of 'divine' or superphysical and non-divine or physical objects.

दिव्ये iii. 51. In the 'shining', the 'divine'.

—दिश्य—iv. 33. (Here some editions reed अधिकृत्य in place of उद्दिश्य).

दिशा iv. 14. By this direction; in this way, this manner.

दिशिदिशि iii. 26. In direction upon direction; in every direction; in quarter after quarter.

—दिश्यते i. 33, 35.

—दीप—i. 35; iv. 10.

—दीपयति ii. 20.

—दीपः iii. 51, 54.

—दीप्तस्य iii. 51.

—दीप्तिः ii. 28.

दीप्तिः ii. 28, 52 Shining; radiance; shining forth; luminosity; effulgence.

—दीप्तेन ii. 33.

—दीयन्ते ii. 30.

दीर्घकालनैरन्तर्यसत्कारासेवितः i. 14. 'Served', followed, tended, observed, propitiated, practised, for a long time, and unremittingly, unintermittently, (without break, interruption), and with 'reverent trust', 'loving faith', fervour, ardour, (not doubtfully, or in the spirit of levity or play).

दीर्घकालासेवितः i. 14 Practised, 'served' for, a long time.

दीर्घम् iii. 26 Long.

दीर्घसूक्ष्मः ii. 50 Long and subtle or fine; prolonged and attenuated.

दीर्घसूक्ष्मः ii. 50, 51.

—दुःख— i. 33; ii. 5.

—दुःख—i. 11, ii. 9, 15, 55; iii. 18, 26.

दुःख—i. 11; ii. 8, 14, 15, 17, 25 34; iii. 18; iv. 10, 15.

दुःख—i. 31, ii. 8.

—दुःखम् ii. 9.

दुःखम् ii. 15, 16. Pain; painful.

दुःखम् i. 10, 31; ii. 5, 14, 15, 16, 17, 25, 34; iii. 18; iv. 11.

दुःखकारणनिवृत्तौ ii. 25 On the 'retirement', cessation, removal, abolition, of the cause of pain.

दुःखज्ञानम् iv. 15 Knowledge, experience, feeling, of pain.

—दुःखता ii. 15.

दुःखत्वे ii. 28. In painfulness.

दुःखपक्षे iii. 18 On the side of pain; in the category of pain.

दुःखपङ्के ii. 15 In the mire, quagmire, of pains and sorrows. (Cf. 'slough of despond').

दुःखप्रतीकारः ii. 17 Remedy, 'counter-action', of pain.

दुःखफलाः ii. 14 Having pain for fruit; painful in the result, in effect.

दुःखबहुलः ii. 15 Painful; full of pains; with pain preponderant.

दुःखयति ii. 15, 34 Pains; distresses; causes pain.

—दुःखयोः iii. 18.

दुःखविपाकस्य ii. 34 Of the maturation or fruit of pain; or, of that of which pain is the fruit.

दुःखसंस्काराशयः ii. 15 Germ of

the tendency or disposition to or of pain.

दुःखसमुदायस्य ii. 15 Of the 'coming together', 'gathering', crowding, accumulation, of pains. (सम् + उत् + आ + ई, to go; going or coming together).

दुःखसाधनानि ii. 15 The 'accomplishers', makers, means, of pain.

दुःखस्य ii. 17.

दुःखस्रोतः ii. 15. Stream of sorrow.

दुःखस्वरूपः iii. 18 Of the 'own-fom', the nature, of pain.

दुःखहेतोः ii. 17 Because of pain; from the cause of pain.

दुःखाज्ञानानन्तफलाः ii. 34 With endless fruit of pain and ignorance; fruiting, fructifying, resulting, in endless pains and errors.

दुःखाज्ञानानन्तफलाः ii. 34.

दुःखात् iv. 11.

दुःखानि ii. 15.

दुःखानुभवात् ii. 15 Because of, from, experience of pain.

दुःखानुशयी ii. 8 'Sleeping with', accompanying, pain; going with, following upon, pain.

दुःखानुशयी i. 11.

दुःखानुस्मृतिपूर्वः ii. 8 Preceded by remembrance of pain.

दुःखाभिज्ञस्य ii. 8 Of him who knows pain, who has experienced pain.

दुःखितेषु i. 33; iii. 23 Amongst the miserable; amongst those who are in pain.

दुःखे ii. 5, 8, 15.

—दुःखे iv. 11.

—दुःखैः ii. 15.

—दुःखैः ii. 5.

दुःखोत्पादात् ii. 34 From the creation, production, or causing to others, of pain,

दुःखोपरमः ii. 25 Cessation of pain.

दुरात्मनाम् iv. 7 Of the evil-souled.

दुर्बलम् ii 52 Of 'poor strength'; weak.

दुर्बलाः iii. 13.

दुर्विज्ञाना ii. 13 Difficult to know.

दुहिता iii. 13 Daughter.

दूरदेशतया iv. 9 By distance of place; because of distance; in consequence of being far off.

दूरात् ii. 43 From a distance.

दृक्शक्तिः ii. 6, 20 The power of, i. e., known as, 'seeingness', 'seer-ness', Consciousness, Awareness (mere, pure).

दृग्दर्शनशक्त्योः ii. 6 Of the (two) powers (of) Consciousness (pure and simple, mere Awareness) and cognitive intelligence.

दृग्दर्शनशक्त्योः ii. 17, 22.

दृढभूमिः i. 14 Firm-grounded.

दृढभूमिः i. 14.

दृढाम् i. 35 To the strong, firm, dense, hard (fem:)

दृढीभविष्यति iii. 51 Will become firm, strong, hard.

दृशिमात्रः ii. 20 Pure consciousness; simple awareness.

दृशिमात्रः ii. 20.

दृशिरूपस्य ii. 17, 21, 23 Of that which has the form of Awareness.

दृशेः ii. 25 Of the Principle of Consciousness.

दृशेः ii. 22, 25.

—दृश्य— iv. 23.

—दृश्य—iii. 49.

—दृश्यः iii 45.

दृश्यः iii. 35 'Visible'; the 'seen'; the object-world; object (as contrasted with the Subject, the knower, the Self).

दृश्यते i. 9; ii. 5, 9, 17, 21, 23; iii 15, 35; iv. 10, 19, 30 Is seen.

दृश्यत्वात् iv. 19 Because of 'seeability', 'visibility', objectivity.

दृश्यत्वात् iv. 19.

दृश्यत्वेन i. 4; ii. 17; iii. 55 By seeableness, visibleness; by reason of being 'object', being the seen, the known.

दृश्यधर्मत्वेन ii. 23 By the quality of possessing, or being of, the nature of object; because of having objectivity; by reason of having the property of 'object-ness'.

दृश्यप्रत्ययापेक्षम् ii. 23 Depending on, relative to the idea, notion, belief, hypothesis, assumption, of object'; dependent on the idea that there is an object (contraposed before the subject).

दृश्यम् ii. 18 The to-be-seen, seeable, visible; the object-world (neu:).

दृश्यम् ii. 17, 18, 20, 21, 22, 23.

दृश्यमानः ii. 4 Being seen; visible; appearing.

—दृश्ययोः ii. 17.

दृश्यस्य ii. 21 Of the seen; the visible, the to-be-seen or seeable.

दृश्यस्य ii. 21, 23.

दृश्यस्वरूपम् ii. 18 Of the own-form' or nature of object.

दृश्याः ii. 17.

दृश्यानाम् ii. 19.

—दृश्ये iv. 21.

दृश्ये ii. 23.

दृश्येते iv. 25 (Two) are seen.

दृश्येन ii. 23.

—दृष्ट—ii. 12, 13.

—दृष्टः ii. 50.

—दृष्टः ii. 50, 51; iii. 14.

दृष्टः i. 7; iv. 19, 33 Seen (masc.) (दृश्, पश्य, to see).

दृष्ट—i. 7, 15, 41; ii. 12, 13.

दृष्टजन्मवेदनीयः ii. 12, 13 To be experienced, realised, in the 'seen' or immediate present birth.

दृष्टजन्मवेदनीयस्य ii. 13.

दृष्टम् i. 8, 42; ii. 30; iii. 14, 17, 26.

दृष्टविषयवितृष्णस्य i. 15 Of him who has ceased to 'thirst' for things seen, i. e., the things of sense, the things of this world.

—दृष्टस्य i, 32.

—दृष्टाः ii. 50; iii. 15.

दृष्टादृष्टजन्मवेदनीयः ii. 12 To be 'felt', 'experienced', realised in or as belonging to seen and unseen (present and future) births.

दृष्टानुमितार्थः i. 7 He by whom a 'meaning', 'a thing intended', a fact, has been seen or inferred.

दृष्टानुमितार्थे i. 7.

दृष्टानुश्रविकविषयदोषदर्शी i. 16 One who sees the evil inherent in all objects of enjoyment, 'seen', or 'heard', sensuous as well as supersensuous, mundane and celestial.

दृष्टानुश्रविकविषयवितृष्णस्य i. 15 Of him who has ceased to crave for objects 'seen' or 'heard' (physical or super-physical, 'visible' or 'revealed')

दृष्टान्तः iv. 19 Illustration; example; instance; 'that of which the end, the finality has been seen'.

दृष्टान्तेन iii. 53.

दृष्टान्तोपादानम् i. 41 The taking of an example, an instance, an illustration; 'to take an example'.

दृष्टिपथम् iv. 13. The path of vision.

दृष्ट्वा ii. 15 Having seen.

देवः i. 1 A god, a superhuman being, 'who shines'. (दिव् , to shine, to play, to be glad).

—देवता— ii. 44.

—देवता—ii. 12.

देवत्वेन ii. 12 By 'god-hood', 'god-ness', 'godship', divinity.

देवदत्तः ii. 19 (A proper name, 'God-given', 'Theoatus').

देवनिकायः iii. 26 A race, group, class, of minor ḍevas; spirits; sub-gods; demi-gods.

देवनिकायाः iii. 26.

देवब्राह्मणार्थे ii. 31 For the sake of the gods and the brāhmaṇaṣ' i. e., 'the men of Brahma, spiritual knowledge'.

देवमनुष्याः iii. 26, 44 Gods and men.

देवमनुष्येषु iii. 18.

देवसभा iii. 26 The hall of the gods.

देवाः ii. 44; iii. 51.

देवान् iv. 33.

देवानाम् i. 19; ii. 12; iii. 51.

—देश— ii. 31; iv. 9.

—देश—iii 41, 48, 53.

देशः ii. 5, 50 Country; place;

direction; space (दिश्, to direct to point out).

देशकालनिमित्तानवधारणात् ii. 13 Because of the indefinability, unascertainability, of (its) space, time, and causality.

देशकालनिमित्तानुभवावच्छिन्नेषु i. 44 Defined, delimited, characterised, by experience, awareness, cognisance, of space, time and causality.

देशकालनिमित्तानुभवैः iii. 18 By experience of space, time, and causation.

देशकालाकारनिमित्तापबन्धात् iii. 14 By the 'un-tying', the absence, keeping away removal of (the proper) place, time, form, and cause.

देशकालसङ्ख्याभिः ii. 50 By (extent or reach or length in) place, by duration, and by number.

देशकालसङ्ख्याभिः ii. 51.

—देशतया iv. 9.

देशबन्धः iii. 1 'Place-binding'; 'tying down to one place'; confinement to one definite spot; limitation of or to a place; definition of centre, sphere, spot or place; circumscription.

देशभेदः iii. 53 Difference of place or space.

—देशम् iii. 52.

देशलक्षणभेदः iii. 53 Difference of position and charactering works.

देशलक्षणसारूप्ये iii. 53 On similarity of place and mark.

—देशस्य iii. 53.

देशान्तरप्राप्तेः i. 7 Because of 'reaching' another place.

देशान्तरे ii. 45 In another place.

देशावच्छिन्ना ii. 31 Conditioned, defined, marked off, divided off, by place or space.

देशे iii. 2.

देशेन ii. 50.

—देशेभ्यः iii. 14.

देशेषु iii. 1.

—देशैः iii. 53.

—देश्याः iii. 14.

—देहा iii. 43.

—देहाः iii. 26.

—देहानाम् i. 19; iii. 48; iv. 7.

देहान्तरिता iv. 1 Belonging to, screened off by, 'intervened' by, another body or birth.

देहान्तरे ii. 45 In another body.

—देहे iii. 22.

—दैवतानि ii. 28.

दैवम् iv. 8 Divine; heavenly.

दैवानुगुणाः iv. 8 'Following', in keeping with, in accord with, consonant with, divinity; having the qualities that resemble divine qualities.

—दैविकम् iii. 22.

—दोष—i. 15; ii. 13, 30.

—दोषः iii. 13.

दोषः iii. 13 Fault, defect, vice.

दोषबीजक्षये iii. 50 On the 'consumption', destruction, of the seeds of sin.

दोषाः iii. 29 Faults; (the principal materials or constituents which make up the body-called faults because of the reasons given in ii. 3, 15).

दोषात् iv. 25.

—दोषान् iii. 51.

—दौर्मनस्य—i. 31 ('Ill-minded'-ness; restlessness; deperession of mind).

द्यावापृथिव्योः iii. 32 Of sky and earth.

—द्योतयति i. 1.

द्योतयन्ति iii. 17 (They) light up, illumine.

द्योत्यते i. 43 (दिव्, द्यु, to shine) is illuminated, is shown forth, indicated, lighted up.

द्यौः ii. 5 Heaven, sky.

द्रढयन्ति ii. 3 Make hard, firm; strengthen; confirm.

द्रव्यम् ii. 33; iii. 44, 47, 52 Substance; 'that which can melt, run'; thing.

द्रव्यतः iv. 12 From substance

द्रव्यत्वेन iv. 12 By substantiality; in the shape of, or as, substance.

द्रव्यपरिणामः iii. 13 Modification, change, of or into or as substance.

द्रव्यस्य iii. 13.

द्रव्याणाम् ii. 30,

द्रव्यान्तरतः iii. 13 Because of, from, another, substance; because of being another substance, something else (than before).

द्रव्यान्यथात्वम् iii. 13 Otherwiseness of substance; change of an object into another object, another substance, something else.

द्रष्टव्यम् i. 41 Should be seen, noted; is observable.

—द्रष्टा ii. 20.

द्रष्टा ii. 20 Seer; knower.

द्रष्टा ii. 17.

द्रष्टुः i. 3. (दृश्, पश्य, to see) Of the seer, spectator, (silent and inactive) watcher, (mere) witness.

द्रष्टुः ii. 20, 23.

द्रष्टृदृश्ययोः ii. 17 Of seer and seen.

द्रष्टृदृश्योपरक्तम् iv. 23 Colored with, tinged with, seer and seen.

द्रष्टृदृश्योपरक्तम् iv. 23.

द्राक् i. 14 Rapidly; quickly; readily; at once.

—द्रुमाः iii. 51.

—द्रोहः ii. 30.

द्वन्द्वः ii. 32 Two-and-two; pairs of opposites.

द्वन्द्वसहनम् ii. 32 Endurance of pairs of opposites.

द्वन्द्वानभिघातः ii. 48 Not being 'stricken' by, non-oppression by, the opposites; not-feeling of, not being affected by, the pairs of opposites.

—**द्वन्द्वौ** ii. 23.

द्वन्द्वैः ii. 48.

द्वयम् i. 16 Duad; two; pair; (neu).

द्वयी i. 11, 36; iv. 33 Do: (fem:)

द्वये iii. 15, 18 Two pairs.

द्वयोः i. 24; ii. 18, 50; iii, 15, 52, 53 Of two.

—**द्वारा** iii. 13.

द्वारा iv. 16 By (this) 'door', way, path.

द्वारीभवन्ति i. 35 Become or act as 'doors', gate-ways, paths, passages, means, helps.

—**द्वारे** iii. 26.

—**द्वारेण** iii. 15, 55; iv. 7.

—**द्वि**—ii. 19.

द्विगुणद्विगुणोत्तरायुषः iii. 26 With successively 'double and double' life-periods; each succeeding class having a life-time twice as long as that of the preceding.

द्विगुणाः iii. 26 Twofold; double, (plu:).

द्विगुणेन iii. 26 By double as much.

द्विचन्द्रदर्शनम् i. 8 (The optical hallucination of) seeing two moons.

द्वितीयम् iii. 44 Second; (neu:).

द्वितीयः i. 17; ii. 50, 55; iii. 13, 44, 51 Do: (masc.).

द्वितीया ii. 13 Do: (fem:).

द्वितीये iii. 26.

द्विधा ii. 28 In two ways.

द्विविधम् iii. 22; iv. 10 Of two kinds; (neu:).

द्विविधः i. 2, 19; iii. 44 Do: (masc:)

द्विविपाकारम्भो ii. 13 Beginner, initiator, cause 'maturatious', fruitious, of two results.

द्विष्ठः iii 44 Seated in, dependent on, two; established in two ways.

द्विसहस्रायामाः iii 26 Two thousand (yojanas) high or long.

—**द्वीपः** iii. 26.

द्वीपेषु iii. 26 In islands, continents.

द्वे ii. 13 Two; (fem: and neu:).

—**द्वेष**— ii. 3.

—**द्वेष**—i. 8; ii. 55.

—**द्वेषः** ii. 8.

द्वेषः i. 11; ii. 8, 28; iv. 11 ('Two'-ness; feeling of 'two'-ness, separateness; separativeness; desire to put another away, to 'divide' off; dislike; disaffection; repulsion; hate.

—**द्वेषौ** iv. 11.

द्वेषजः ii 15 Hate-born.

द्वेषदुःखानुस्मृतिनिमित्तः iv. 10 Caused, occasioned, generated, by the recollection of hate and pain, or of pain accompanied with hate or dislike

द्वेषमोहकृतः ii. 15 Produced by hate and perplexity, error (or confusion, fear).

द्वेषानुविद्धः ii. 15 Pervaded, permeated, threaded and pierced, by hate.

द्वेष्टि ii. 15 Hates.

द्वौ iii. 52. Two; (masc.)

—ध—

—धर्म—iii. 14, 45.

—धर्म—i. 2, 25, 44; ii. 19; iii. 10, 15, 45; iv. 10, 12.

—धर्मः i. 9; ii. 33; iii. 11; iv. 3.

धर्मः i. 1, 9, 32, 33, 43; ii. 23, 28, 34; iii. 13, 14. 15, 18, 50; iv. 3 (From धृ, धर्, to hold, support, bind together). 1. That which holds together; supports, preserves, makes a thing what it is; constituent principle; function; property, characteristic; the attribute which is the essence of a thing, its substratum, as it were; the law of the nature of a thing; nature. 2. Law, (*legere*, to bind), which binds human beings together in the bonds of rights and duties; binding, governing, guiding force, internal and external; moral law, imposed by conscience, or ordained and imposed by the compelling power of human authority, legal or other. 3. Religion, (*re*, back, *legere* to bind), which binds souls together and to God in the bonds of love and devotion. 4. Merit acquired by obeying such legal, moral, religious guidance and authority; the helpful power and property of good deeds, helpful to doer as well as object and recipient; virtue.

—धर्मकम् iii. 13.

—धर्मकः i. 43.

—धर्मकस्य ii. 9; iv. 10.

—धर्मकाः ii. 19.

—धर्मकेभ्यः i. 16.

—धर्मकेषु i. 44.

धर्मज्ञानवैराग्यैश्वर्योपगम् i. 2 Going, approaching, tending, towards virtue and wisdom and detachment and sovereignty.

धर्मतः iii. 13 From ḍharma.

धर्मत्वम् iii. 13 Attributeness; the condition of (being a) quality.

धर्मत्वे iii. 13 In the state of (being a) ḍharma.

—धर्मत्वेन ii. 23; iii. 49.

धर्मद्वारा iii. 13 By the 'door' of attributes; through the ḍharma.

धर्मधर्मिणोः iii. 13. Of property and thing; of attribute and substance (possessing the attribute).

धर्मधर्मिभेदात् iii. 13 By the difference of or between attribute and substratum.

धर्मधर्मिभेदे iii. 15 In the difference of 'phenomenon and noumenon', property and thing, attribute and substance.

धर्मपरिणामः iii. 13 Succession of the attributes (of exhibition and inhibition).

धर्मपरिणामक्रमः iii. 15 Order of change of property.

—धर्मम् iv. 3.

धर्मम् iv. 3, 10.

धर्ममात्रम् iii. 13, 14 Only or the whole of the attribute; the exact measure of the total property; neither more nor less than the property.

धर्ममात्रव्यावृत्तिः iii. 44 Change, alteration, of function or property only.

धर्ममात्राणाम् ii. 22 Of all attributes only.

धर्ममेघः iv. 29 'The cloud which showers virtues'; 'the cloud of holiness'. The kind or stage of samāḍhi, or trance, named Ḍharma-megha, in which the ḍharmas, laws of nature, laws of the world-order, the secrets of God's Nature and Nature's God, rain upon, become clear to, the mind of the en-tranced yogi.

धर्ममेघः iv. 29.

धर्ममेघध्यानोपगम् i. 2 Inclining, approximating, to the state of trance-meditation called ḍharma-megha.

धर्ममेघस्य iv. 32.

धर्मयोः iii. 11, 13 Of two ḍharmas.

धर्मलक्षणाभ्याम् iii. 15 From property and mark.

धर्मलक्षणावस्थापरिणामाः iii. 13 Transformation of ḍharmas (i. e., the 'form'-attribute, the attribute of form, as e. g. of 'clay-ness' into 'jar-ness', i. e. of a lump of clay into a jar), and sequential changes of lakshaṇas (i. e.) the three stages, special characteristics, viz., past 'unbornness', present 'createdness', future 'destroyedness'), and developements of the successive avasṭhās, states or conditions, (as e.g., at first newness, then oldness; first freshness, then worn-out decay). (This looks very obscure jargon and 'logomachy' as translated, more or less literally. The significance is seen in the process of evolution and involution. Modern science with or despite its ever-changing and conflicting theories and speculations, has approached the fact that *all* potentialities are present in every atom, at least in every 'living atom' or biophore or zygote; these potencies have been named 'ids' or 'genes'. Ancient science only adds what modern science is also beginning to think to be very likely, that all atoms, super-atoms etc., are *living*. And it says that evolution consists in the gradual unfoldment of these potentialities. The technical expressions used by the *Yoga-Bhāshya* seem intended only to indicate the three implications of this faith; viz. (i) that the unfoldment of any one potentiality implies the becoming latent of another that was before patent; (2) that this means that what was formerly hidden in the 'future' has now become the 'present', and the 'present' become the 'past'; (3) that this again means that what was manifesting dynamically is weakening into staticity, while what was static is strengthening into dynamicity. This is suggested as a possible way of interpreting intelligibly, in modern terms, the language of the old passage, which is undoubtedly very technical and obscure).

धर्मलक्षणावस्थापरिणामाः ii. 19; iii. 13.

धर्मलक्षणावस्थापरिणामेषु iii. 16.

धर्मलक्षणावस्थापरिणामैः iii. 13.

धर्मलक्षणावस्थारूपेण iii. 13 By or in the shape or form of attributes, stages and conditions.

—धर्मवत् iii. 18.

—धर्मस्य i. 9; iv. 3.

धर्मस्य iii. 13, 15.

—धर्मा i. 9; iii. 35.

—धर्मा: i. 42; iii. 9, 18.

धर्माः ii. 17; iii. 13, 14, 15, 52; iv. 12.

—धर्माणः ii. 18.

धर्माणाम् iv. 12 Of ḍharmas.

धर्माणाम् iii. 13.

धर्मात् iii. 13; iv. 11.

—धर्मात् iii. 13; iv. 17.

धर्मादि iv. 2 Merit etc.

धर्मादिनिमित्तापेक्षम् iv. 10, 15 Dependent on merit etc. as its cause, condition, occasion.

धर्मादेः iv. 11 Of ḍharma etc.

धर्माधर्मरूपाः iii. 18 Of the form or nature of merit and demerit

धर्माधर्मौ ii. 15; iv. 11 Merit and demerit; virtue and vice; piety and sin.

धर्मानभ्यधिकः iii. 13 Not more than, not other than, the attribute.

धर्मान्तरम् iii 13 Another property.

धर्मान्तरेभ्यः iii. 14 From other properties.

धर्मान्तरोत्पत्तिः iii. 13 The birth of another property.

धर्मान्तरोदये i. 43 On the arising of another Dharma. (Some editions read धर्मान्तरोदयः, and others, धर्मान्तरस्य कपालादेरुदये).

धर्मान्यथात्वम् iii. 14 'Otherwiseness', change of property.

धर्मापेक्षम् iv. 15. With reference to, because of, depending on, merit.

—धर्मापेक्षम् iv 15.

—धर्मिणः ii. 2.

धर्मिणः iii. 12, 13, 14, 15 Of the possessor of the ḍharma or ḍharmas.

—धर्मिणा iii. 10.

धर्मिणाम् ii. 22 Of substrata, functionaries; (sometimes the primal three guṇas, attributes, which serve as the unmanifest substrata of all manifest attributes).

धर्मिणि iii. 13, 15.

धर्मित्वेन iii. 11 By the condition of (being) the substratum.

धर्मिविक्रिया iii. 13 The transformation, change, 'curdling,' of the substratum.

धर्मिसमन्वागतौ iv. 12 (The two) accompanying, latent, co-existent, in the substratum.

धर्मिस्वरूपम् iii. 13 (To) the 'own-form,' nature, character, of the substratum.

धर्मिस्वरूपमात्रः iii. 13 Of only the own-form, the essence, the very nature or substance, of the substratum.

धर्मिस्वरूपमात्रत्वात् iii. 14 Because of being of only the own-form of the substratum.

धर्मिषु iv. 33.

धर्मी iii. 14 The possessor of ḍharma or property; substrate; functionary.

धर्मी iii. 13, 14, 15; iv. 12.

—धर्मेषु iv. 33.

धर्मेषु iii. 14.

—धर्मैः iv. 25.

धर्मैः iii. 13, 44.

धातवः iii. 29 (धा to 'do', to put, place, keep in place, 'do up', make up, con-sti-tute, compose, keep up, hold up, maintain. The seven ḍhāṭus, 'tissues', of the body, 'chyle, blood, flesh, fat, bone, marrow, semen-ovum', are so called because they constitute and maintain the body: एते सप्त स्वयं स्थित्वा देहं दधति यन्नृणाम्। रसासृङ्मांसमेदोऽस्थिमज्जाशुक्राणि धातवः ॥ Bhāva-prakāsha I. i. 131). Tissues; constituent substances. (The word ḍhāṭu, in grammar, means the verb).

धातुरसकरणवैषम्यम् i. 30 Dis-ease, ill-health, disturbance of proportion and equilibrium, of tissues, liquids, and organs or 'instruments.'

धात्वर्थमात्रम् i. 9 Only the sense

or meaning of the root or verb.

—धान—iii. 17.

धान्यमूलानि iv. 3 The roots of grain-plants.

—धारण—i. 7; ii. 18, 19, 20.

—धारणम् iv. 20.

—धारणम् i. 34; ii. 18; iv. 21.

—धारणा— ii. 29.

धारणा iii. 1. (धृ, धर्, to hold; causative धारय्, to cause to hold; to hold firm, steady, still). Causing (the mind) to hold firm, steady, still, fixed to one spot; concentration; fixed ideation; retention; retentiveness; holding on to one object, one idea, in the mind or by the mind.

धारणा iii. 1, 43.

—धारणात् ii. 13, 51.

धारणातः iii. 43 From, by means or because of, concentration.

धारणाध्यानसमाधित्रयम् iii. 4, 7,16. The triplet of concentration, contemplation and rapport.

—धारणाभ्याम् i. 34.

—धारणाभ्याम् ii. 53.

धारणासु ii. 53.

धारयतः i. 35, 36 Of (the person) concentrating, 'holding'.

धारयति iii. 17 Supports, holds, maintains, keeps on or up.

धार्मिकः ii. 36 Virtuous; meritorious.

—धार्यते iv. 23, 24.

—धार्यन्ते ii. 29.

—धार्येत iv. 23.

—धीयमानैः iii. 17.

धूमज्ञानम् ii. 28 The knowledge, the perception, of smoke.

—धूयते ii. 11.

—धृतयः ii. 28.

धृतिकारणम् ii. 28 The supporting or maintaining cause; the cause of fortitude, of holding on.

—ध्यान—ii 29.

—ध्यान—i. 2; iii. 4, 7, 16, 26.

ध्यान—i. 48.

ध्यानजम् iv. 6 Born of contemplation.

ध्यानजम् iv. 6.

ध्यानम् iii. 2 (ध्यै, ध्याय्, to dwell upon, to 'think' of, a thing). Intent observation; continuous attention; contemplation. (By the dictionary and etymology, 'con-templa-tion' is marking out an area, a templum, for observation; and this fits in exactly with the technical definition of धारणा in the text. And, on the other hand, 'con-centra-tion,' 'confining to a centre, may be said similarly to fit in with the technical defiinition of ध्यानम् as continuous, unbroken, 'one-pointed' or single-minded 'stretching' of an idea, a belief, a thought or conception or cognition. Yet, on the whole, considering all the associations and conventional uses of the two words, it seems best to render धारणा by concentration, and ध्यान by contemplation. Martial phraseology is analogous. Forces are 'concentrated' at a particular spot or point, as the chiṭṭa-mind is concentrated at some spot or point in the body or outside; and as a military operation, a march, an attack, is 'contemplated,' against, or on, a fort or other distant object, so the mind 'contemplates' one object with the intention, as it were, of throwing itself on or into it, to grasp and conquer the whole of it, to discover all its ins and outs, to seize hold of and identify itself with it, to make it not only 'mine', but that final degree of 'mine', viz, 'me', which constitutes समाधि, occupation or 'possession' of, rapport or identification with, the object, 'collected absorption' or 'absorbed collectedness' of the mind, rapture, raptness.

ध्यानम् iii. 2, 3.

—ध्यानवताम् iv. 7.

—ध्यानहेयाः ii. 11 Avoidable, destructible, by contemplation.

ध्यानात् i. 39.

ध्यानाभ्यासरसेन i. 48 By the growing 'taste' for, joy in, the practice of contemplation.

ध्यानाहाराः iii. 26 Feeding on, nourished by, contemplation; having contemplation for food. (The old live in memory; the young in action).

ध्यानेन ii. 11.

ध्यायिनः i. 2 The contemplators; yogis.

ध्यायिनाम् iv. 10.

ध्यायेत् i. 39 May contemplate.

ध्येयस्वभावावेशात् iii 3 By the incoming, entrance, influx, inspiration, 'obsession', 'possession', of or by the nature of the object contemplated.

ध्येयाकारनिर्भासम् iii. 3 Showing forth the form of the object contemplated.

ध्येयालम्बनस्य iii. 2 Of the (idea) which 'supports' the contemplated object, or is supported by and hangs on it.

ध्रुवा ii. 5 Fixed; steady; certain; permanent.

—ध्रुवात् iii. 26.

ध्रुवे iii. 28 In or on the pole star.

ध्रुवे iii. 28.

—ध्वनि—iii. 17.

ध्वनिपरिणाममात्रविषयम् iii. 17 Having for object, cognising, only the transformations, changes, developements, results, of inarticulate sound.

—न—

न iii. 20; iv. 16, 19 No; not.

न i. 1; ii. 1; iii. 6; iv. 3; etc.

—नक्षत्र—iii. 26.

—नदी i. 12.

ननु i. 45 Surely; but surely.

नन्दति ii. 3 Rejoices.

नन्दनम् iii. 26 'The place which gives joy'; the heavenly garden of Indra the king of the gods; elysium.

नन्दीश्वरः ii. 12 Nand-īshvara, the name of one of the chief officers of the staff of Shiva-Rudra. (By very great tapas, he was suddenly transformed from a very low birth to the chief servant of Shiva).

नन्दीश्वरवत् ii. 13 Like Nandīshvara.

नन्दीश्वरादयः iv. 3 Nandīshvara etc.

नभसः iii. 26 Of the sky.

—नमयन्ति ii. 3.

नयनात् iii. 39 Because of leading.

—नरक—iii. 26.

नरकतिर्यक्प्रेतादिषु ii. 34 In purgatory, in the animal kingdom, and in (earthbound) ghosts. (नरकः, the 'small man', the 'evil man'; इ, to go, प्र-इतः, the 'departed', the 'gone on'; तिर्यक्, slanting, horizontal, the animals whose alimentary canals run slantwise or horizontally).

नरकतिर्यग्गर्भसम्भवम् iii. 18 Born of purgatories and of animal wombs.

नरकतिर्यग्भवम् iii. 18 Arising from, born of, purgatory and the animal kingdom.

नव i. 21, 30; ii 28; iii.26 Nine.

नवः i 50 New; (masc:).

नवम् i, 24 Do: (neu:).

नवधा ii 28 Nine-fold; in nine ways.

नवपुराणताम् iii. 13 Newness and oldness.

नवस्य iv. 33 (Some editions omit this word).

नवा ii. 5 New; (fem:).

—नश्यति ii. 21.

नश्येत् ii. 13 May perish; may be destroyed.

—नष्टम् ii. 22.

नष्टम् ii. 22 Destroyed; perished. (नश्, to perish, to disappear).

नहुषः ii. 12 Nahusha; (the name of one of the famous kings, in the Puranas. He officiated as king of the gods for a period, when Indra was in hiding, after having been defeated by the titun-king Bali. But he grew proud and grossly insulted the ṛshis. They cursed him, and he was suddenly transformed into a great serpent).

नहुषवत् ii. 13 Like Nahusha.

नहुषाजगरादयः iv. 3 The Nahusha-serpent etc.

नाडी iii. 31 Nerve; nerve-centre; ganglion.

—नाड्याम् iii. 31.

नादानुसंहारबुद्धिनिर्ग्राह्यम् iii. 17 Graspable, comprehensible, cognisable, by the intelligence which follows sounds, spoken syllables, and gathers them up and retains (memory of) them (running) through their (successive) appearance and disappearance.

—नाभि—iii. 39.

नाभिचक्रे iii. 29 In or on the 'navel-disc', the solar plexus; (some say, the epigastric plexus).

नाभिचक्रे iii. 1.

नाम i. 12, 24; ii. 15, 20, 23; iii. 33, 43, 49; iv. 29, 33 Name; by name.

नामाख्यातसारूप्यात् iii. 17 By similarity of nouns and verbs, (name or form and action or function).

नारकतिर्यङ्मनुष्यवासनाभिव्यक्तिनिमित्तम् iv. 8 The cause, condition, occasion, of the manifestation, exfoliation, unfolding, of purgatorial or animal or human tendency.

नारकाणाम् ii. 12 Of the purgatorial (jīvas).

—नाशः iv. 12.

नाशः ii. 13, 21, 23. 28 Destruction.

नाशम् ii. 22.

—नाशिकः iv, 24.

—नाशिकैः iv. 21.

—नाशी iii. 51.

—नासिका—iii. 39.

नासिकाग्रे i. 35; iii. 1 In or on the 'front' of the nose; at the root of the nose (between the eyebrows, where the ājñāchakra is placed; some interpret the word as 'on the tip of the nose', or looking towards the heart).

नासिकापुटाभ्याम् i. 34 By or from the nostrils, the 'pots', the 'utensils' of the nose.

—निकायः iii. 26.

—निकायाः iii. 26.

निक्षिपति iii. 38 Deposits, places; transfers. (नि + क्षिप्, to fling).

निक्षिप्तम् iii. 18, 38 Flung, cast down, deposited, transferred.

निक्षिप्य iv. 21 Casting down; having thrown aside.

निगृहीतस्य ii. 50 Of the (breath) restrained, controlled.

नित्यः i. 27 Continuous; permanent.

नित्यख्यातिः ii. 5 'Permanence-belief'; (the mistaken) awareness, belief, notion, consciousness, that (that which is not permanent) is permanent.

—नित्यतया i. 27.

नित्यता iv. 33 Permanence; eternity.

नित्यत्वम् iv. 33 Eternity; permanence.

नित्यत्वप्रतिषेधात् iii. 13 By or because of the negation or denial of eternity or permanence.

नित्यत्वात् iv. 10 Because of permanence, constancy, everlastingness.

नित्यत्वात् ii. 22.

—नित्यत्वात् ii. 23.

—नित्यत्वे iii. 13.

नित्यम् i. 1; iii. 36, 51; iv. 33 Ever; always; eternally.

नित्यमुक्तः ii. 32 Ever-free.

नित्यशुचिसुखात्मख्यातिः ii. 5 'Awareness of the permanent, the pure, the pleasurable and the self'; (the erroneous belief that that which is the very opposite of these, is eternal, is pure, is happy, and is the Self).

—नित्या ii. 19.

नित्या ii. 9, 19 Constant.

नित्येषु iv. 33 In or amongst the permanents, the eternals, the infinites.

—निदानेभ्यः ii. 30.

—निद्रा—i. 6, 38.

—निद्रा—i. 11.

निद्रा i. 10 Slumber; dreamless sleep; sleep.

निद्राज्ञानालम्बनम् i. 38 'Pending' on, 'supported' by, connected with, relating to, having for object, the knowledge of slumber, or the knowledge gained in slumber.

निधनात् ii. 5 Because of, from (the fact of), death.

—निपातेन ii. 34.

निबद्धाः iii. 26 Bound; tied.

निबध्नन्ति i. 35 Tie, bind, fix. (बध, बन्ध्, to 'bind').

—निबन्धनः i. 9.

—निबन्धनम् ii. 52.

—निबन्धनी i. 35 (Some editions read निबन्धिनी)

—निबन्धनी i. 36 (Do:).

निमग्नः ii. 15 Sunk; immersed.

निमज्जति iii. 54 Sinks; merges. (मस्ज, to 'merge', to sink).

—निमन्त्रयन्ते iii. 51.

—निमित्त—i. 44; iii. 18; iv. 10.

निमित्त—iv. 15.

—निमित्तः i. 24; iv. 10.

—निमित्तम् i. 24; ii. 23, 25; iv. 2, 8 (Some editions read iv. 2 as a separate word and not part of a compound).

निमित्तम् iv. 3 Cause; condition; occasion; reason; motive;

efficient cause; sake; final cause; object; proof; authority.

निमित्तम् i 24; ii. 13, 19; iv. 2, 3, 12.

निमित्तनैमित्तिकभावानुच्छेदात् iv. 9 By non-breaking, non-disruption, i. e., by continuity, of the condition or relation of cause and effect, condition and conditioned, occasion nnd occasioned.

निमित्तवशात् iv. 10 By power of the cause; 'by force of circumstances'.

—निमित्ताः ii. 15.

—निमित्तानाम् iii. 14.

निमित्तानुरूपस्य iv. 15 Of (the notion) appropriate to the cause or (the idea) of condition; accordant with, assonant with, congenial to, the cause, the occasion.

—निमित्ताभिः ii. 13 (Some editions read—निर्वर्त्तिताभिः).

निमित्तीभूतम् iv. 9 (That which has) become the cause, condition, occasion.

निमित्तेन iv. 12 By cause.

निम्नतरस्य iv. 3 of the lower, the hollower.

—निम्नम् iv. 26.

निम्नम् iv. 3 Low; hollow; downwards.

—निम्नस्य iv. 27.

—निम्ना i. 12.

—नियतत्वात् i. 32.

—नियतम् i. 32.

नियतविपाकः ii. 13 Having a definite, fixed, pre-ordained, certain, assured 'ripening', 'maturation', fruit, result, effect, consequence, product.

नियतविपाकप्रधानकर्मणा ii. 13 By a principal karma, a principal act or deed, of unfailing operation and effectiveness and assured fruit.

नियतविपाकवेदनीयत्वात् ii. 34 Because of being experienced through or by an assured consequence.

नियतविपाकस्य ii. 13 Of (karma-germ) having a definite, fixed, pre-ordained, certain, assured fruit, result, effect, consequence, product.

नियम—ii. 29.

नियमः ii. 13 Rule; law; vow; ordainment; fixed habit; fixed observance; (technical name for a special set of vowd observances) (नि+यम्, यच्छ, to check, to restrain; to fix, to tie down; to lay down as a fixed rule, a binding law, which must be observed; to control, to subdue).

नियमविकल्पसमुच्चयभेदात् ii. 34 Because of difference of options and combinations of vows.

—नियमाः ii. 30, 46.

नियमाः ii. 32.

—नियमात् ii. 13, 19.
—नियमानाम् ii. 33.
नियमार्थः iii. 17 For the sake of, having the purpose of, 'specification, 'tying down', limitation.
—नियमेन iii. 26.
नियमेषु ii. 40.
नियुक्तम् ii. 52.
नियुङ्क्ते ii. 52 (Some editions read नियुक्तम्). 'Enjoins; 'en-gages'; appoints.
निरतिशयम् i. 25 Unexcelled; unsurpassed.
निरतिशयम् i. 45.
—निरनुग्रह—iii. 17; iv. 10.
निरन्तरासेवितः i. 14 Served, observed, practised, unremittingly, uninterruptedly, without 'intervals' or breaks.
निरन्वयम् iii. 14 Without a 'through-going', persisting (residuum, thread).
—निरपेक्षा iii. 43.
निरवस्थानाः ii. 27 Without a stop or resting-place.
निरसत् ii. 19 Not-unreal; not-non-existent.
निरालम्बनम् i. 18 Supportless; not having anything to depend on.
निराश्रया iv. 11 Support-less; without anything to rest on.
निरुणद्धि i. 2; iii. 45 Obstructs, hinders, prohibits, inhibits, restricts, restrains. (नि+रुध्, to oppose, to besiege).
निरुद्धचित्तवृत्तेः i. 17 Of him whose mind-functions are restrained, controlled, inhibited, shut off.
—निरुद्धम् iv. 21.
निरुद्धम् i. 1 Restrained; controlled; shut off; focussed; inhibited from all other directions and concentrated on one object; collected; poised; held in. (From क्षिप्त to निरुद्ध is one continuous unbroken process. The last is the highest degree of attention, when it has become effortless, as it were, natural).
निरुद्धा ii. 23.
निरुद्धाः iii. 9.
निरुद्धानि ii. 54.
निरुद्धे iv. 16.
निरुपक्रमम् iii. 22 'Without intensive activity'; without quickening and stimulating accessories; slow-working.
निरुपाख्यम् iv. 12 Unspeakable; indescribable; unknowable; incognisable; ineffable.
निरोद्धव्या i. 10 To be restrained; fit to be inhibited; inhibitable.
निरोद्धव्याः i. 5, 11, 32 Do: (pl:).
—निरोध—i. 51; 18.
निरोध—iii. 9
—निरोधः i. 2, 12.
—निरोधः i 12.

निरोधः i. 18; iii. 13 (नि + रुध्, to oppose, besiege, obstruct, hedge round, enclose). Restraint; control; inhibition; stoppage.

निरोधक्षणचित्तान्वयः iii. 9 The following, by the mind, of the inhibitional or inhibitive moment, mood, tendency; or the coming into the mind of, the permeation of the mind by, the inhibitive, cessational, or restward mood

निरोधक्षणम् iii. 9 The inhibitional moment or mood.

निरोधक्षणेषु iii. 13.

निरोधचित्तकृतसंस्कारास्तित्वम् i. 51 The existence of (inhibitive) tendencies set up by the 'inhibition-mind'. (Cf. such modern expressions as war-mindedness, air-mindedness, peace-mentality, slave-mentality).

निरोधचित्तक्षणेषु iii. 9 In the moments of the inhibitional mind, i. e. when the mind is inclined towards inhibition of functions, towards restfulness; or in the inhibitional or inhibitive moments of the mind, i. e of the mind's existence; or in the moment when the mind is completely inhibited, restrained, paralysed.

निरोधजः i. 51 Born of restraint

निरोधधर्मसंस्कारः iii. 10 The impression, stamp, tendency, faculty of the inhibition-property, quality or function.

निरोधधर्मसंस्काराः iii. 15 (The three, viz.) inhibition, and sin-and-merit or karma, (ethical property), and impressed or implanted tendency.

निरोधपरिणामः iii. 9 Consequence or result of, or of the nature of, inhibition.

निरोधपरिणामः iii. 9.

निरोधम् i. 1.

—निरोधयोः iii. 13.

निरोधसंस्कारपाटवापेक्षा iii. 10 Looking to, dependent on, proportionate to, the skill in, or the perfection of, the practice of inhibition.

निरोधसंस्काराः iii. 9, 13 The inhibitive tendencies or potencies.

निरोधसंस्कारात् iii. 10 (Some editions omit this).

निरोधसमाधिना ii. 27 By inhibitive trance.

निरोधसमाधौ iii. 9 In the inhibitional trance.

निरोधस्थितिकालक्रमानुभवेन i. 51 By experience of succession of time during fixity or steadiness of inhibition.

—निरोधात् i. 51.

—निरोधे i. 1, 11, 50; ii. 54, 55; iii. 9.

निरोधे i. 51 On, or in the state of, inhibition (thereof).

निरोधे i. 12.

—**निर्ग्राह्यः** iv. 33 (Perceptible; apprehensible).

—**निर्ग्राह्यः** i. 49; iv. 33.

—**निर्ग्राह्यम्** i. 44; iii. 17.

निर्णये iv. 25 In or for decision, established conclusion.

निर्दिश्यते i. 33, 35; ii. 17 Is pointed out. (निर् + दिश् to direct).

—**निर्दिश्यन्ते** iii. 13.

—**निर्देशः** ii. 55.

निर्धूतरजस्तमोमलम् iii. 55 That (intelligence) which has shaken off the 'dust and dirt' of rajas and ṭamas, restlessness and infatuated clinging

निर्धूतरजस्तमोमलस्य iii. 49.

निर्धूयते ii. 11 Is washed off, shaken off. (धु, to shake).

निर्निमित्तः i. 24 Without reason; without cause or occasion

निर्बीजः i. 51 Seedless. (This word requires some consideration. Etymologically and by definition it means that final trance-extasis in which there is no seed, no germ, left of a world-process, no appetite for externalisation, or for anything other than Self-Puruṣha, no ālambana for the chiṭṭa. It is equivalent to Kaivalyam, al-one-ness, soleness. On the other hand, when we ask, does this condition belong to the chiṭṭa, or is the chiṭṭa completely annihilated before or at the time this final extasis is achieved ?—then the Yoga system indicates that there is no final annihilation of anything; that this condition of quiescence is a condition of the chiṭṭa and the corresponding condition of Purusha is that of 'Sol-itude', eternal and changeless; that 'seedless' here implies only that the three guṇas have, by praṭi-pra-sava, 'in-volu-tion', 'reversal of out-going-ness', been reduced to, have 'gone back to', the seed-condition, but the burnt-seed-condition, the samskāra or condition of sāmya, equilibrium, wherein there is no movement. Now, if this be so, the word nir-bīja 'seedless', is a misnomer. What is perhaps meant is that there is no bīja, seed, *outside* the individual subject, no leaning-crutch, ālambana, no peg to hang on, no leg to rest on, as *object* to it. This latter is the case in the other kind of samāḍhi, sa-bīja or samprajñāṭa, in which, in its perfection, the jīva-chiṭṭa is, as it were, *identified* with some one *object*, instead of all objects disappearing altogether and leaving the individual jīva-chiṭṭa or purusha (?) केवल, 'al-one'. But this explanation does not clear up the inconsistencies and self-contradictions involved at the bottom. Those ultimate cruxes can be satisfactorily explained and solved only with the help of the Veḍānṭa).

निर्बीजः i. 2, 18.

निर्बीजस्य iii. 8.

—निर्भासः i. 11.

निर्भासते i. 41 Shines out ; shows forth ; appears. (भास्, to shine, to appear, to become clear).

—निर्भासम् iii. 3.

—निर्भासम् iii. 3; iv. 33.

—निर्भासा i. 43,

निर्मलः ii. 26 Taintless; stainless; pure.

निर्माणचित्तम् i. 25; iv-6 (4) 'Construction-mind'; a mind full of the wish to construct, a constructive or constructing mind; or, a 'mind' constructed, artificially created, by yoga-power, (to serve as an instrument, a 'receiver'); a manufactured mind. (निर् + मा, to measure, to 'map' out).

निर्माणचित्तानि iv. 4.

—निर्मिता ii. 5.

निर्मिमीते iv. 4, 5 Constructs, creates, frames, forms, fashions.

निर्वर्त्तयति ii. 13, 47 Brings about.

—निर्वर्त्तयन्ति iv-10.

—निर्वर्त्तितम् iv. 25

निर्वर्त्तितः ii. 12 Made to exist; realised, perfected, completed, matured. (निर् fully, वृत्, to exist, to act, to revolve, Lat. *vertere*).

—निर्वर्त्तितानि ii. 13.

निर्वर्त्यमानम् ii. 43 Being achieved; fulfilled, realised, secured.

निर्वस्तुकः i. 18 Substanceless.

निर्विचारवैशारद्ये i. 47 On the perfect lucidity, purity, refinement, of the non-reflectional (meditation, raptness).

निर्विचारस्य i. 47 Of the non-reflectional.

निर्विचारा i. 44 Non-reflectional; (fem:).

निर्विचारा i. 44.

निर्वितर्कः i. 46 Not tinged with vi-ṭarkas, passions, or attachments to gross objects. (See निर्वितर्का).

निर्वितर्कया i. 44.

निर्वितर्कसमाधिजम् i. 43 Born of non-emotional or non-perceptional meditation or absorption.

निर्वितर्का i. 43 (The attainment, samāpaṭṭi, of that stage in or) that kind of meditation, in which there is no confusion of word and meaning with the apprehension of that word and that meaning. (This is the interpretation in the Bhāshya; sa-viṭarkā having been previously explained as that kind in which there is confusion of and non-discrimination between the three. But in ii, 33. the word viṭarka is used in the sense of emotional, passionate, affective, bias or mood of mind. Thus nir-viṭarkā may also be interpreted as 'free from all affective or emotional bias').

निर्वितर्का i. 44.

निर्वितर्कायाः i. 43.

निर्विप्लवः i. 7 'Unfloating'; not bobbing up and down; steady, stable, unshaking. (प्लु, to 'float').

निर्विषयम् iv. 12 Without object. (निर् + वि + सि, to bind; विषयाः, objects which bind or attract the senses to themselves)

—निर्भेदाय iv. 21.

—निर्हरन्ति ii. 4.

—निवर्त्तते i. 51; iv. 25

निवर्त्तते ii. 24; iii. 55; iv. 25 Returns; retires; ceases from pursuit; turns back; turns away; withdraws; draws back. (नि, back, वृत्, to वृत् turn).

निवर्त्तमानः ii. 30 Returning, retiring, retreating.

निवर्त्तिष्यन्ते iv. 12 Will retire.

—निवासाः iii. 26.

—निवासिनः iii. 26.

—निविशन्ते ii. 54; iii. 38

निविशमानम् ii. 54; iii. 38 'Sitting down', resting, coming to rest. (विश्, to enter).

निविशमानस्य i. 40 (The mind) of the (yogi) who is 'entering into', concentrating upon, contemplating.

निविष्टाः iii. 26 'Firm-seated'; placed, situated.

—निवृत्त ii. 26.

निवृत्तः ii. 4; iii. 13 Retired.

निवृत्तादर्शना ii. 24 With its non-vision (of the truth) removed.

—निवृत्तिः iii, 30; iv 25, 30.

—निवृत्तिः ii. 24.

निवृत्तिः ii. 13, 15 Retirement; withdrawal. (See निवर्त्तते).

निवृत्तिमात्रे iv. 3 In or of only the turning away, the retreat, the cessation or remission.

निवृत्ते i. 51; iii. 55.

—निवृत्तौ i. 9; ii. 25; iii. 13.

निवेदयिष्यामः i. 1 We will state, explain, declare, expound.

—निवेश— iv. 13.

निश्चितमतिः iii. 51 One whose

opinion is fixed, whose mind is made up, who has a decided view.

—निषदनम् ii. 46.

निषधहेमकूटहिमशैलाः iii. 26 (Names of three mountains) Nishadha, Hèma-kūta, and Himālaya.

निष्कृष्य iii 38 Having taken out, pulled out. (कृष्, to drag, pull, draw).

निष्क्रियः i. 9 Action-less.

निष्क्रिये ii. 17.

—निष्ठाम् ii. 24.

—निष्पन्नः ii. 12

निस्तरङ्गमहोदधिकल्पम् i 36 Like the waveless ocean.

निस्सत्तासत्तम् ii. 19 Devoid of both being and non-being.

निस्सदसत् ii. 19 Neither existent nor non-exist nt.

निस्सारणम् ii. 49 Expulsion.

निस्सारयति i. 31 Expels, drives out. (Causative of सृ, to go, to move, to 'slide').

निस्सृता ii. 5 Come forth; issued.

निस्स्यन्दात् ii. 5 Because of excretion, perspiration, exudation.

निहितम् iv. 22 Deposited. (धा).

—नीत— ii. 18.

नीलश्वेतशृङ्गवन्तः iii. 26 Possessed of blue and white peaks (or, perhaps, three proper names of three mountains, Nīla, Shvēta and Shṛṇgavān).

नीलोत्पलपत्रश्यामः iii. 26 Dark like the petal of the blue-lotus.

नीलोत्पलपत्रायताक्षी ii. 5 Having large eyes like the blue-lotus-petal

नेत्री iv. 11 (Fem:). Leader; turner; turning or churning string.

नेत्रे iii. 22 In or on the eye (being closed); when the eye (is closed tightly, or closed and pressed slightly).

—नैमित्तिक— iv. 9.

नैमित्तिकस्य iv. 12 Of the occasional; of that which is due to special occasion, cause, condition, motive, aim.

—नैरन्तर्य— i. 14.

न्यस्तम् ii. 50; iii. 50 (नि + अस् to fling), 'Flung'; dropped; cast.

न्यस्तः ii. 15; iii 18, 22.

न्यस्ताः iii. 26.

—न्यस्य iii. 25.

न्यायम् i. 32 (नि + इ, to go; according to which, by the rule or light or guidance of which, people go). Law; rule; rule of thought; logic; proverbial law; proverb; common saying; the logic of common sense; maxim.

न्यायेन iv. 2.

न्याय्या ii. 55 Logical; reasonable; rational; proper; just.

—न्यासः iii. 29.

—न्यासाः iii. 26.

—न्यासात् iii. 25.

—न्यासात् iv. 7.

—न्यासिनाम् iv. 7.

—प—

—पक्षे ii. 16; iv. 15, 25.

—पङ्क— iii. 39.

—पङ्क— iii. 39.

—पङ्के ii. 15.

पचति iii. 17 Cooks.

—पच्यमानम् iv. 8.

पच्यमानेन ii. 33; iii. 51 By (me) who was being 'cooked', 'roasted', burnt alive.

—पञ्च—ii. 19.

पञ्च ii. 3 Five.

पञ्च ii. 3, 10, 19; iii. 1, 44; iv. 21.

—पञ्चक— iii. 48.

पञ्चतयी iii. 39 Group of five.

पञ्चतय्यः i. 5 Pentads; quintettes; groups of five; five-fold.

पञ्चधा i. 5 In five ways; five-fold.

पञ्चपर्व्वणः ii. 28 Of the five-jointed, five-branched.

पञ्चपर्व्वा i. 8 Five-jointed.

पञ्चमम् iii. 44, 47 Fifth; (neu:).

पञ्चमी ii. 4 Do: (fem:).

पञ्चरूपजयात् iii 47 By conquest or subjugation of the five forms.

पञ्चरूपेषु iii. 44 In the five forms.

पञ्चविधम् iv. 6 Of five kinds; five-fold; (neu:).

पञ्चविधः iii. 26 Do: (masc:).

पञ्चसु iii. 44.

पञ्चाशद्योजनकोटिसङ्ख्याताः iii. 26 Measured by, amounting to, fifty crore (=five hundred million) yojanas; (one yojana = four kroshas = eight miles).

पण्डिताः ii. 5 The possessors of pandā, i.e., discernment between good and evil; the wise.

पतञ्जलिः iii. 44 Pataňjali, the author of the *Yoga-Sutras*.

—पतन्तम् iii. 38.

—पतति ii 20; iv. 22 (Falls).

—पतन्ति iii. 38.

—पतितः iii. 52.

—पतिताः i. 5.

—पत्र— ii. 5; iii. 26 (Leaf, petal; wing).

—पथम् iv. 13.

पथि ii. 32 In the 'path', the way.

—पद— iii. 17.

पदपदार्थयोः iii. 17 Of word and its meaning, i.e. the object meant.

—पदम् i. 33; iii. 31.

पदम् iii. 17 A full and complete word.

पदरचनम् iii. 17 Arrangement of complete words.

पदात्मा iii. 17 Of the nature of a or the word; ensouling a word; constituent of the word.

पदार्थः iii. 17 The meaning of a word; an object.

पदार्थमात्रस्वरूपा i. 43 (The intelligence, which has taken on, is) of the form of the object only; when it has identified itself with the object pure and simple; is shaped like the object; has no other form than the 'object'.

—**पदार्थयोः** iii. 17.

पदार्थविपर्यासम् iii. 45 Derangement, perversion, reversal, inversion, upsettal, of objects.

पदार्थान्तरेषु ii. 28; iii. 13 Amongst other objects, things.

पदार्थाभिव्यक्तिः iii. 17 The showing forth of an object meant, a thing named (Some editions read. पदपदार्थाभिव्यक्तिः).

—**पदेषु** iii. 17.

पद्मासनम् ii. 46 The 'lotus-seat,' (a special yoga-meditation-posture).

—**पद्यताम्** iii. 51.

—**पद्यते** ii. 15, 26, 28; iii. 13; 14. 31.

—**पद्यमानस्य** iv. 15.

पन्थाः iv. 15 'Path'.

पन्थाः i. 42.

—**पन्न—** iv. 11.

—**पन्नम्** iii. 13; iv. 23.

—**पन्नः** i. 43.

—**पर—** iii. 22; iv. 20.

परः i. 40; iv. 24 Highest; 'farthest; utmost; beyond; onwards; afterwards; other; another (person).

परकायैः ii. 40 With other bodies, or, with others' bodies.

परचित्तज्ञानम् iii. 19 Knowledge of another mind, or, of another's mind.

परचित्तज्ञानादिषु iii. 6 In knowledge of another or another's mind, etc.

परजातिसंवेदनम् iii. 18 Knowing, bringing into consciousness, remembering, of other births.

परतः ii. 30 From another.

परतन्त्रम् ii. 17 Dependent on, 'woven' up with, others.

—**परतया** ii. 30.

परत्र i. 7; ii. 30; iii. 17, 18 Elsewhere; to another.

परपीडानुग्रहद्वारेण iv. 7 By the way of, by means of, through, (giving of) pain or (of) help, kindness, i. e., pleasure, to another.

परप्रतिष्ठम् iv. 19 Supported by, established in, founded on, resting on, another.

परप्रत्ययमात्रम् iii. 23 Only another's thought, idea, belief.

परप्रत्ययस्य iii. 20 Of another's thought.

परम् i. 16 Final, ultimate; extreme.

परम् i. 2, 18, 43, 45; ii. 6, 15, 19, 25, 52; iv. 11. (see परः)

—परम— i. 40.

परमगुरौ ii. 1, 32 In or to the Supreme Teacher.

परमबीभत्से ii. 5 In the supremely, extremely, disgusting.

परमम् iv. 13 Supreme.

परममहत्त्वान्तम् i. 40 Ending with the vastest, the greatest, the infinite.

परमर्षिः i. 25 The highest or very high Ṛshi.

परमा ii. 55 Supreme; superlative.

परमा ii. 55.

—परमाणुः iv. 14.

परमाणुः iii. 44, 52 Atom, ultra-atom, super-atom, 'extreme' atom.

परमाणुपरममहत्त्वान्तः i. 40 Ending with, extending to, extreme smallness (on the one side) and extreme largeness (on the other).

परमाणुभ्यः iii. 42.

परमाणोः iii. 53.

परमाण्वन्तम् i. 40 Ending with the atom, the infinitesimal.

परमात्मा i. 28 The Supreme Self.

परमापकर्षपर्यन्तः iii. 52 Down to, ending with, extreme division, differentiation, separation, involution, descent, downward regress (अपकर्ष, 'down-drag', as the opposite of उत्कर्ष, 'uplift', progress).

परमार्थतः iii. 13, 15, 55; iv. 13, 14 From the supreme 'meaning', 'intention'; in the supreme aspect; from the transcendental standpoint; really, verily, truly, in reality.

—परम्परा— iii. 15 (One after another; unbroken succession; continued tradition).

पररूपेण ii. 21, 22 By means of another's form or being.

परशरीराणि iii. 43 Other bodies.

परशरीरावेशः iii. 38 Entrance into another or another's body.

परशुः ii. 28 Axe.

परस्परम् ii. 28 'Other with other'; in respect of one another or each other; mutually; reciprocally.

परस्परनिरनुग्रहात्मानः iii. 17 Of non-interdependent nature; of natures not mutually helpful.

परस्पराङ्गाङ्गित्वे ii. 18 In (the condition of) being mutually (related as) organ and organism; while (connected as) part and whole.

परस्परानुग्रहतन्त्रीभूत्वा ii. 3, 15 Becoming bound to the (work of) favouring or helping each other; by mutual help or support.

परस्परार्थत्वात् ii. 28 Because of being for the sake of each other; from mutual subservience; by reason of mutual helpfulness.

परस्परेण ii. 15; iii. 13.

परस्परोपरतप्रविभागाः ii. 18 With parts colored by each other.

परस्य iv. 24.

परस्याम् ii. 26; iii. 49 In the final, or extreme, or supreme; (fem:).

—परा ii. 30.

परा i. 16 Final, ultimate, extreme; (fem :).

पराजयः i. 24; ii. 18 Defeat.

परान् iv. 7 To others.

परानुग्रहपीडाभ्याम् ii. 15 By the favoring or oppressing of others.

—परान्त—ii. 39.

पराम् iii. 15 Extreme.

—परामृष्टम् iv. 16.

—परामृष्टः iii. 2; iv. 25.

—परामृष्टा ii 20.

—परामृष्टा ii 2.

परार्थत्वात् iii. 35 Because of subservience to another's interest; because of being a means.

परार्थत्वात् ii. 17.

परार्थम् iv. 24 For the sake of another; (neu:).

परार्थम् iv. 24.

परार्था ii. 20 Do/: (fem).

—परिकरः i. 1.

—परिकर्म i. 35.

परिकर्म i. 33, 40 Refining, improving, beautifying 'action on all sides'; toilette, purification, ornamentation.

—परिकल्पना—iv. 14.

—परिकल्पितम् iv. 15.

परिकल्प्य iv. 21 Having formulated, imagined. (क्लृप्, क्ऌप्, कल्प्, to 'clip', shape, form, imagine).

परिक्षीणवितर्कजालः ii. 32 With the network, tangle, of doubts and fancies and evil thinkings perished and fallen away; freed from all evil thoughts and feelings.

—परिग्रहः ii. 30.

—परिग्रहाः ii. 30.

परिग्रहेषु ii. 33 In 'holdings', possessions, interests, properties.

परिज्ञातम् ii. 27 Learnt, found out, recognised.

परिज्ञेयम् ii. 27 (That which is) to be understood, recognised.

परिणतम् iii. 35 Transformed; resulted in; (neu.).

परिणतः ii 12 Do: (masc:).

—परिणतानाम् iv. 2.

परिणमते ii. 18; iii. 13 Is transformed.

परिणमेत iv. 18 Would be transformed; if (it) be transformed.

परिणम्यमाने iv. 33 (Which) undergoing change, being changed.

—परिणाम—iii. 15,17; iv. 2.

—परिणामः iii. 9, 11, 12; iv. 2.

—परिणामः ii. 19; iii. 9, 11, 12, 13; iv. 3.

परिणामः ii. 19; iii, 13, 15, 47;

iv. 14, 25 'Bending on all sides'; change; transformation; evolution; development; unfolding; consequence; sequential condition; result. (परि on all sides, all round, नम्, to bend).

परिणामक्रमः iv. 32 Order of the successive changes.

परिणामक्रमनियमात् ii. 19 Because of (fixed) law of succession of transformations; definite law of serial evolution, law of evolutionary series.

परिणामक्रमसमाप्तिः iv. 32 Conclusion, closing, cessation of the succession of changes.

परिणामचेष्टानिरोधशक्तिजीवनधर्मवत् iii. 18 Like the properties of change, volition or effort, inhibition or inhibitedness or latency, power, or energy, and vitality. See iii 15).

परिणामतापसंस्कारदुःखैः ii. 15 By means of, because of, the pains of change, of suffering, and of tendencies; (i. e. (1) the immediate consequence of satisfying one's own desire for sense-pleasures, viz., hurt to others, and increase of one's own greed for such pleasures; (2) the farther result in sin and merit, with their further consequences; (3) the still more distant result in the formation and confirmation of long-lasting 'tendencies', 'instincts', which cause further rebirths, etc.).

परिणामतापसंस्कारदुःखैः ii. 5.

परिणामत्रयम् iii. 16 The triplet of transformations or consequences.

परिणामत्रयसंयमात् iii. 16 By or from meditation on the three transformations or consequences.

परिणामदुःखता ii. 15 The painfulness of the consequences.

—परिणामम् ii. 12.

परिणामम् ii. 3, 12; iii. 52.

परिणामस्य iv. 33.

परिणामाः iii. 13.

—परिणामाः ii. 19.

परिणामान्यत्वे iii. 15 In otherness of transformation; with another transformation; if or when there is another change or consequence.

परिणामान्यत्वे iii. 15.

परिणामान्विताः iii. 52 Accompanied, threaded, pervaded, by transformation.

परिणामापरान्तनिर्ग्राह्यः iv. 33 Apprehensible as and at the later end of a change, of an event.

परिणामापरान्तनिर्ग्राह्यः iv. 33.

—परिणामि ii. 15.

परिणामि iv. 17 Changeful.

—परिणामित्वम् ii. 20.

परिणामित्वम् ii. 20 Changefulness.

परिणामित्वात् iv. 18 Because of do:.

परिणामिनः iii. 35.

—परिणामिनि ii. 17.

परिणामिनि ii. 20; iv. 22.

परिणामिनित्यता iv. 33 Ever-changing permanence; the permanence of the changeful (like that of a river); ever-lastingness.

—परिणामिनी ii. 20; iv. 22.

परिणामिनी ii. 20 Changing; changeful; (fem.).

—परिणामी iii. 50.

—परिणामे iii. 13.

—परिणामेन iii. 13.

—परिणामेषु iii. 16.

—परिणामैः iii. 13.

परिणामैकत्वात् iv. 14 Because of oneness, unity, singularity, of resultant transformation.

—परिताप— ii. 14.

परिदीपयति ii. 20 Illuminates.

परिदृष्टः ii. 50 'Seen all round'; seen thoroughly; examined; measured precisely; scrutinised.

—परिदृष्टः ii. 50.

परिदृष्टः ii. 51; iii. 14.

परिदृष्टाः ii. 50; iii. 15.

—परिदृष्टाः iii. 15.

परिनिर्मितवशवर्त्तिनः iii. 26 (The designation, probably descriptive, of a race of dévas).

—परिनिर्मितवशवर्त्तिनः iii. 26.

परिनिष्पन्नः ii. 12 Completed, matured, accomplished. (परि + निः + पद्, to go, to fall, to attain, to happen).

परिपच्यते ii. 12 Is ripened, cooked; ripens, bears fruit.

परिपालनीयाः ii. 31 To be protected, cherished, observed, carried out.

परिपूर्णम् i. 40; iii. 54 Filled up, full, complete, perfect.

परिपृष्टे iv. 33 On being questioned.

परिभाषा iii. 4 Definition; designation; technical name; conventional name; 'common speech', 'speech all around', (i. e., as men all round, all over, usually, call a thing).

परिभाषिताः iii. 44 (Technically and commonly) designated.

—परिमाण— iv. 10.

परिमाणवत् i. 25 'Like size'; 'as of measure'; as of a thing possessed of a definite size; as of a measurable thing.

—परिवर्त्तेत iii. 13.

—परिवाराः iii. 26.

—परिशुद्धौ i. 43.

परिसमाप्तक्रमाः iv. 32 With succession finished; having finished their successive changes.

—परिसमाप्तिः ii. 18.

परिसमाप्तिः iii. 54 Completion; finishing.

परिसमाप्यते iv. 32 Is closed, finished, wound up.

परिस्पन्दते ii. 14 Vibrates, acts, behaves, struggles. (स्पन्द्, to throb, shake, vibrate).

परिस्पन्दमानः iv. 11 Vibrating; moving; operating; acting; striving.

परिहारः ii. 17; iii. 13 Removal; avoidance. (हृ, to take away).

परिहार्यस्य ii. 17 Of the evitable, avoidable, remediable, removable.

परीक्ष्य ii. 30 Having looked at, inspected, examined. (ईक्ष्, to see).

परे ii. 26; iii. 49 In the final, extreme, supreme.

परैः ii. 40 With or by others.

परैः iii. 13.

परोक्षम् i. 35 Out of sight; vicarious; indirect; unrealised. (अक्ष्णोः परम्, 'away from the eye's).

पर्यङ्कम् ii. 46 Bed; (a meditation posture).

—पर्यन्तम् iii. 52.

—पर्यन्तः iii. 52.

पर्यन्वेष्या i. 25 To be sought or looked for. (परि + अनु + इष्, to wish, to seek).

—पर्यवसानम् i. 45.

—पर्यवसानम् i. 50.

—पर्यवसानः iv. 33.

पर्यायैः iii. 54 By equivalents, synonymns; or sub-divisions, subordinate forms. (परि, round, इ, ई, to go; 'things which go round and round', words which can be used, by turns, in place of each other).

—पर्यासम् iii. 45.

—पर्वणः ii. 28.

पर्वतः iv. 14 Mountain.

—पर्वत— iii. 26.

पर्वतराजः iii. 26 The king of mountains.

पर्वताः iii. 26.

पर्वतेषु iii. 26.

—पर्वा i. 8.

—पर्वाणः ii. 15.

—पर्वाणि ii. 19.

—पवित्राणाम् ii. 1 (Of the pure, the purifying).

पशून् iv. 33. Animals.

पश्चात् ii. 11 Afterwards.

पश्चिमः iii. 26 Western; later.

—पश्चिमता iii. 14.

—पश्चिमतायाः iii. 14.

—पश्यः ii. 20.

—पश्यः ii. 20.

—पश्यतः iii. 18.

—पश्यता iii. 18.

—पश्यति ii. 20.

पश्यति ii 23; iii. 22, 35 Sees; beholds. (दृश्, पश्य, to see).

—पश्यन् ii. 6. 20, 40.

—पश्यन्तः iii. 51.

पश्यामि i. 32 I see.

—पाक— iv. 8 (पच्, to cook, to ripen).

पाक्यस्य ii. 28 Of the cookable, the to-be-cooked or ripened.

—पाटव— iii. 10.

—पाणि— ii. 19.

पाणिना iv. 3 By the hand.

—पात् iv. 7.

—पाताल— iii. 26.

पातालम् iv. 22 The under-world; the name of one of the seven worlds or planes, 'below' the (surface of the) earth.

पातालानि iii. 26.

पाताले iii. 26.

पाति i. 20. Protects; fosters; cherishes; nourishes; preserves; maintains. (पा, to protect).

—पातिना iii. 15.

पाती— i. 9; iii. 14.

—पाती iii. 14.

—पातौ iv. 25.

—पात्र— ii. 15.

—पाद्— ii. 19; iii. 39.

—पादः ii. 1.

पादतलस्य ii. 17 Of the surface, the bottom, the sole of the foot.

पादत्राणव्यवहितेन ii. 17 By or with an interposing 'foot-protector', or shoe; (a thorn) screened off, walled off, kept out, by a shoe.

पादानधिष्ठानम् ii. 17 Non-retention in the foot; non-penetration into the foot.

पादाभ्याम् iii. 42 By, with, the two feet.

—पादाय (iv. 21).

—पाप— iv. 6.

पापकर्माशयः ii. 12 The germ, the seed-pod, cyst, capsule, of evil deeds.

पापकस्य ii. 13 Of miserable, petty, mean, contemptible sin.

पापम् ii. 30 Sin; evil; crime; de-merit; liability to future punishment, to painful experience, stored up, seed-like, superphysically as sub-conscious 'prick of conscience,' in the depths of the soul, the ego. (Cf: "Thy sin will find thee out", "Murder will out").

पापवहा i. 12 'Sin-bearing'; 'flowing with sin': sinful.

पापशीलेषु iii. 23 On, in, among the (men of) sinful character.

पापाय i. 12 For or towards evil, sin.

—पायसीयम् i. 32.

—पायु—ii. 19.

पारिणामिकम् iii. 14 Transformational.

पार्थिवस्य i. 45 Of the earthy or earthly.

पार्थिवाद्याः iii. 44 Earthly etc.

—पार्श्वे iii. 26.

—पालनीयाः ii, 31.

पिण्डः iii. Lump; clod.

पिण्डमृत् iii. 15 Lump-clay; clay in a lump; lumped up clay.

पिण्डस्य iii. 15.

पिण्डाकारात् iii. 13 From the 'lump-formed;' from the 'property', 'attribute', of being in the form of a lump, a clod.

—पिण्डितम् iii. 22.

पिता i. 27 Father.

पितापुत्रयोः i. 27 Of father and son.

पितॄन् iii. 22 The forefathers; the lares and penates.

—पित्त—iii. 29 ('Bile': 'yellow'; digestive and assimilative juices (? salivary, gastric, hepatic, pancreatic, and intestinal, corresponding to the five पित्त's: पाचकं रंजकं चापि, साधकाऽलोचके तथा। भ्राजकं, चेति पित्तस्य नामानि स्थानभेदतः॥ "The digestion of food; pigmentation; stimulation of the intelligence and general vitalisation; strengthening of the eyesight; increase of the general warmth of the body; these are the five functions, respectively, of the five kinds of piṭṭa; *Sushruta*).

—**पिपासा**—iii. 30 (Thirst).

—पिपासे iii. 30.

पिप्लावयिषुः iv. 3 Wishing to 'flood', to irrigate. (प्लु, to 'flow', to 'flood'; to swim, to 'float').

पिबेत् iv. 10 May drink up. (पा, to drink).

पिहितकर्णः iii. 22 With ears closed.

पीडयित्वा iv. 7 Having caused pain.

—पीडा—iv. 7.

—पीडाभ्याम् ii. 15.

पुण्डरीकम् iii. 34 Lotus.

—पुण्डरीके i.36; iii. 1.

—**पुण्य**—i. 33 (**पू**, to purify, to cleanse. पुण्यम्, virtuous deed; act of merit; merit as opposed to sin or demerit; superphysical right to future reward or pleasurable experience); an asset superphysically registered in the soul, as contrasted with a similar debit. See पापम्).

—पुण्य—i. 33.

पुण्यकर्माशयः ii. 12 The 'seed-pod', the germ, of merit.

पुण्यकृतः ii. 13 Made, created, brought about, by merit.

पुण्यपापाभिसम्बन्धः iv. 6 The connection with, the binding or connecting up with, the relating on to, merit and sin.

पुण्यप्रतिरूपकेण ii. 30 The inverted 'copy', the opposite reflection, of merit; false or hypocritical 'appearance' of virtue

पुण्यप्रत्ययः ii. 5 The notion of merit.

पुण्यशीलेषु iii. 23 Amongst the virtuous-charactered.

पुण्यहेतुकाः ii. 14 Caused by, or causes of, merit.

पुण्या iii. 51 Holy, sacred, blessed; (fem:).

पुण्यात् ii. 34 From merit.

पुण्यात्मकेषु i. 33 Amongst the,

towards the, virtuous-souled ones.

पुण्यात्मानः iii. 26 Virtuous souls; holy-souled persons.

पुण्यापुण्यकर्माशयः ii 12 The 'seed pod', the germ, of merit and de-merit.

पुण्यापुण्यकर्माशयप्रचयः ii. 13 The gradual growth or formation of the 'seed-pod' of merit and sin.

पुण्यापुण्यहेतुत्वात् ii. 14 Because of being caused by merit and sin, or, being causes of virtuous and vicious deeds.

पुण्याभासेन ii. 30 By the merit-simulating, the merit-seeming, (not being real merit).

—पुण्ये ii. 5.

पुण्ये ii. 31 In, on, a holy, meritorious, sacred (day).

पुत्रः i. 27 Son.

—पुत्र ii. 24.

—पुत्रयोः i. 27.

पुनः iii 12, 51 Again.

पुनः i. 5, 11, 19, 30, 43; ii. 2, 4, 15, 24, 25, 27, 33, 34; iii. 12, 17, 18, 47, 51, 55; iv. 9, 11, 15, 16, 21, 34.

पुरम् iii. 26 Town.

पुरस्तात् ii. 19 Before; before hand; in front.

—पुरस्सरा iv. 5.

पुराणम् i 24 Ancient; old; as before.

पुराणता iii. 15; iv. 33 Oldness.

—पुराणताम् iii. 13.

—पुरुष—iii 49.

—पुरुष—i. 2, 24, 41; ii. 2, 22, 25, 26, 28; iii. 35, 49; iv. 16, 27.

पुरुषः i. 3, 4, 7, 9, 29, 45, 51; ii. 6, 17, 20, 23, 25, 27; iii. 13, 35, 50, 55; iv. 18, 23, 24, 25. (पुरि शेते, he who 'sleeps' in the 'town', i. e. the body; पुरति, goes before all; पूरयति, fills everything; the Spirit, soul, self, ego, 'person', in-divid-ual).

पुरुषख्यातिपर्यवसानां ii. 24 To (practice) ending in, finishing with, self-consciousness; ending with awareness of the (true nature of the) Self.

पुरुषख्यातिम् ii 24 To the knowledge, awareness, consciousness, of the Ego.

पुरुषख्यातेः i. 16 By or from awareness or consciousness of Self.

पुरुषगतः i 49 'Gone into', included in, inherent in, the Ego.

पुरुषज्ञानम् iii. 35 Knowledge of the Self.

पुरुषदर्शनाभ्यासात् i. 16 By perseverent practice of Self-vision.

पुरुषधर्मत्वेन ii. 23 By the state of being the property of, or being of the nature of, the Self.

पुरुषप्रत्ययापेक्षम् ii. 23 Looking to, dependent on, the consciousness, cognition, idea, ideation, notion, concept, awareness, of the Self, the Ego.

पुरुषप्रत्ययेन iii. 35 By the idea, notion, belief of the Ego.

पुरुषम् ii. 6, 22; iv. 21 To the Ego.

—पुरुषयोः iii. 35, 55.

—पुरुषयोः ii. 15.

पुरुषविशेषः i. 24 Special or peculiar Purușha.

पुरुषविशेषः I. 24, 25.

पुरुषविषया iii. 35 Relating to Spirit, Ego.

पुरुषस्य iv. 18.

पुरुषस्य i. 4, 9, 45; ii. 17, 18, 20, 21, 23, 25; iii. 35 50, 55; iv. 10, 16, 18, 33, 34.

पुरुषाणाम् ii. 23.

पुरुषान् i. 25; ii. 22.

—पुरुषान् iii. 22.

पुरुषान्वयी i. 9 'Accompanying', 'following', residing in, the Purușha.

पुरुषार्थः ii. 19 The meaning, intention, purpose, interest, wealth, object, end, aim, of the Ego; or, (that which is) for the sake of the Ego.

पुरुषार्थकर्त्तव्यतया ii. 18 Because of the discharge or fulfilment (by the guṇas) of the need or purpose of the Self.

पुरुषार्थकृता ii. 19 'Made' by the purpose, end, or aim of the Ego.

पुरुषार्थता ii. 19, 28 The state of being the aim etc. of the Ego; subservience to the Ego.

पुरुषार्थवत्त्वम् iii. 47 The state of being possessed of subservience to the Ego; having the quality or property of subservience to the Ego.

पुरुषार्थशून्यानाम् iv. 34 Of the (guṇas) devoid of (subservience to the) Self's purpose.

पुरुषार्थशून्यानाम् iv. 34.

पुरुषार्थापरिसमाप्तिः ii. 18 Non-completion of the goal, the purpose, of the Ego.

पुरुषे i. 24; ii. 18.

पुरुषेण ii. 21; iv. 23.

पुरुषेन्द्रियभूतेषु i. 41 In the Self, the sense-organs, and the sense-objects.

—पुरुषेषु iv. 33.

पुरुषोपकरणे ii. 5 In the (mind which is the) instrument of the Self.

—पुरे iii. 34.

—पुष्कर— iii. 26 (Name of a continent).

पूरणात् iv. 3 From the 'filler', the reservoir. (Some editions read पूर्णात्, the 'filled up'; this seems the better reading in view of the context).

—पूरेण iv. 2.

—पूर्णम् iii. 54.

पूर्णात् iv. 3 (See पूरणात्).

—पूर्व— ii. 9; iv. 2, 11, 12.

—पूर्वः—i. 18.

—पूर्वः ii. 7, 8.

पूर्वः iii. 17, 26 Eastern; that which is in front, is 'before' one; that which has gone or occurred 'before'; the earlier; the first; the past. (When a person 'faces', stands 'before', the rising sun, he is looking 'east', where the sun rises 'first').

—पूर्वकः i. 20.

—पूर्वकः i. 20; ii. 50, 51.

—पूर्वकम् ii. 30.

पूर्वजन्मानुभवः ii. 9 Experience of a previous birth.

पूर्वजन्मानुभूतम् ii. 9 Experienced in a previous birth.

पूर्वजातिज्ञानम् iii. 18 Knowledge of previous birth.

पूर्वजातिज्ञानम् iii. 18.

पूर्वतत्त्वानतिक्रमात् iii. 13 By non-transcendence of the preceding tattva; because it does not give up its former reality, its 'thatness', its peculiar character.

पूर्वदेशम् iii. 52 The former space, place, position, situation.

पूर्वदोषानुषङ्गः ii. 13 'Addiction to, attachment of or to, pursuit by, the previous fault'; the same fault, flaw in the argument, difficulty, persists; the same objection applies.

पूर्वधर्मनिवृत्तौ iii. 13 On the disappearance or removal of the former quality or property.

पूर्वपक्षे iv. 25 In or towards the first side (of the two-sided question); in the former view or alternative.

पूर्वपरतायाम् iii. 15 In (the consideration of) the condition of before and after; 'in beforeness and afterness, earlierness and laterness, precedingness and succeedingness'.

पूर्वपरमाणुदेशसहक्षणसाक्षात्करणात् iii. 53 By or from observation, visualisation, envisaging, of the moment associated with the (former) position in space of the former atom.

पूर्वपरिणामापाये iv. 2 On the passing away of the former transformation, mode, manifestation, unfoldment.

पूर्वपश्चिमता iii. 14 'Before-and-afterness'; 'eastness and westness.'

पूर्वपश्चिमतायाः iii. 14.

पूर्वप्रत्ययः iii. 12 The preceding perception, notion, concept, belief; the previous 'way of approach.' (प्रति, towards, इ, to go; 'approach towards.')

पूर्वभवाभिसंस्कृताः iii. 18 Formed, shaped, impressed, moulded, stamped, in previous existences or births.

—पूर्वम् i. 18 iv. 12.

पूर्वम् ii. 11; iii. 29, 53; iv. 7 (See पूर्वः).

पूर्वरूपम् iii. 33 Previous or preliminary form.

पूर्वसंस्कारः iv. 28 Former impressed tendency, pro-disposition, acquired character.

पूर्वसंस्कारेभ्यः iv. 27.

पूर्वसिद्धस्य iii. 45 Of the (yogi who has become) 'perfected earlier'.

पूर्वस्मात् iii. 52.

—पूर्वा i. 11.

पूर्वा i. 24 Preceding, antecedent; (fem:).

पूर्वानुभूतवृषदंशविपाकाभिसंस्कृता iv. 9 'Impressed,' pre-disposed, with the formerly-experienced cat-manifestation; with tendencies or predispositions formed during birth, 'fruition', 'maturation,' as a cat.

पूर्वान्तपरान्तमध्येषु ii. 39 In or at the 'preceding end,' the 'succeeding end,' and the middle; concerning the earlier, former, past limit, the future, and final limit, the middle or present (stage of births).

पूर्वापरावस्थाभेदम् iii. 13 The difference of preceding and succeeding conditions.

पूर्वामलकसहक्षणः iii. 53 The moment associated with the first or former myrobalan.

—पूर्विकाः ii. 13.

पूर्वे i. 26 The Elders.

पूर्वेण iii. 17.

पूर्वेभ्यः iii. 7 Than, as compared with, the preceding ones.

पूर्वेभ्यः iii. 7.

पूर्वेषाम् i. 26 Of the Elders, Formers, Ancients.

पूर्वेषाम् i. 26.

पूर्वोक्ताः i. 30 Afore-mentioned; (plu:).

पूर्वोक्तेन iii. 13 By the afore-said.

पूर्वोत्तरक्षणाः iii. 52 Earlier and later moments; preceding and succeeding points of time.

पूर्वोत्तरेषु iv. 16 Amongst the earlier and later.

—पृथक्त्वम् iii. 53.

पृथिवी ii. 5; iv. 14 The earth (-globe)

पृथिवीपरमाणुः iv. 14 'Earth-atom'; an atom of the earth-element.

पृथिव्यादिना ii. 18 By (way of, in the form of) the earth-element, etc.

—पृथिव्योः iii. 32.

पृथ्वी iii. 45 (See पृथिवी).

—पृष्ठे iv. 33.

—पृष्ठम् iii. 26.

पृष्ठम् iv. 16 Back.

—पृष्ठात् iii. 26.

—पृष्ठेन iv. 33.

पौरुषेयः i. 7; iii. 35 Belonging to the Ego.

प्रकर्षगत्या i. 26 By 'upward progress'; in the way of greatness; by possession of or in respect of, grandeur, glory, splendour; with regard to progressive gradation of advance (i. e., very, or, indeed, incomparably, high stage of spiritual perfection).

प्रकर्षम् ii. 28 To growth, progress, elevation, uplifting. (प्र, much, कृष् , to draw, drag, lift, attract, plough, cultivate).

प्रकल्पयन् i. 48 Forming, improving, refining, cultivating, polishing. (कृप् , क्लृप् ; see कल्पते).

—प्रकारः ii. 27.

—प्रकाश— iii. 21.

—प्रकाश— iii. 21.

—प्रकाशवत् i. 27.

प्रकाशः iv. 19 Light; luminous; obvious; visible; seen; cognised. (प्र, much, काश् , to shine).

—प्रकाशक iv. 19.

प्रकाशक्रियास्थितिशीलम् ii. 18 Having the characters, characteristics, properties, functions, of 'luminosity', 'activity' and 'steadiness', (i. e., cognition, action and desire). (See प्रख्या-क्रिया-स्थिति—, प्रख्या-प्रवृत्ति-स्थिति—, and गुणाः; also प्रकाशः, and क्रिया; कृ, to make, do, act, 'create'; स्था, to 'stand', sit, be 'steady').

प्रकाशक्रियास्थितिशीलाः iii. 47.

प्रकाशते i. 28 Shines forth.

—प्रकाशम् iv. 19.

प्रकाशयति iv. 19 Discloses, discovers, enlightens, illuminates, makes visible, shows forth, makes cognisable; (causative of प्र-काश्).

प्रकाशशीलम् ii. 18, 52 Having the characteristic, the nature, the property or quality of light, en-lighten-ment, illumination, i. e., intelligence.

प्रकाशात्मनः i. 47; iii. 43, 47 Of (the buddhi-sattva or intelligence which is) of the nature of luminosity.

प्रकाशावरणक्षयः iii. 43 Decay, destruction, erosion, 'consumption', wearing thin, wearing away, removal, of the veil of or on the 'light'.

प्रकाशावरणम् ii. 52 The 'screen' or veil of or on the 'light'.

प्रकाशावरणम् ii. 52.

प्रकाश्यप्रकाशकसंयोगे iv. 19 In or on the conjunction of the illuminated and the illuminator.

—प्रकृतयः iii. 44.

प्रकृतयः iv. 3 Natures; substrates;

primaries. (प्र, much, कृ, to 'create', do, act, maker; प्रकृतिः is that Nature which does, makes, acts, gives birth to, creates; cf. Lat., *natura naturans*).

—प्रकृति— i. 19.

—प्रकृति—iii. 48.

प्रकृतिप्रवृत्तौ iv. 3 In or on the setting in motion, the beginning to function, of Prakṛṭi.

—प्रकृतिलयाः iii. 26

प्रकृतिलयाः i. 19 'Lying in', dissolved, absorbed, merged in, Prakṛṭi, Matter, Nature. (Three kinds of Moksha are mentioned in the *Yoga-sūṭra* and *Bhāshya*:—Viḍéha, Prakṛṭi-laya and Kaivalya. The commentary of Vāchaspati, quoting from the Purāṇas, shows that the viḍéhas are a class of *ḍévas*. One current notion of Moksha is that all distinctions of 'individuality' cease in that condition. Another is that they do not disappear altogether, but are more and more lost, in increasing degrees, in the feel of 'universality'; whence grades of Moksha. The three grades of Kaivalya, viveka-khyāṭi, ḍharma-megha, and kaivalya, with their summation in Svarūpa-praṭishṭhā Chiṭiḥ; the three kinds of Moksha, Sālokya, Sārūpya, Sāyujya, to which some add a fourth, Sāmīpya, after Sālokya, and also a fifth, Sārshti, before Sāyujya; the three kinds of Mukṭi, mukṭi, vi-mukṭi, a-vi-mukṭi, and their summation -vide *Praṇava-Vāḍa* ; and various 'triplets' under each; also, sa-viṭarka, nir-viṭarka, sa-vichāra, nir-vichāra, asmitā-nugaṭā, ānanḍā-nugaṭā, ṛṭambharā, maḍhu-bhūmikā, etc., of the Yoga; and sa-vikalpa, nir-vikalpa, etc. of the Véḍanṭa; various forms of ḍhyāna mentioned by Yogī Yājñavalkya, etc; all such require to be synthesised).

प्रकृतिलीनस्य i. 24 Of (the soul) 'merged in Prakṛṭi', the soul which has become a Prakṛṭi-laya.

प्रकृतिलीने i. 19.

—प्रकृतीनाम् iii. 45.

प्रकृतीनाम् iv. 3 Of 'natures', natural tendencies, powers, faculties, potentialities. (See प्रकृतयः).

प्रकृतीनाम् iv. 3.

प्रकृतौ i. 51 In (its own) nature.

प्रकृत्यापूरात् iv. 2 From the 'flooding up', 'up-welling', 'over-flow', of nature, or natural tendency or potentiality; from the uprush, the surging up into patency and manifestation, of natural potentialities lying dormant or latent, static, seed-like, overlaid and overpowered by other tendencies and potencies which were in manifestation, operant, dynamic.

प्रकृष्टम् iv. 10 Very high; elevated; up-drawn; fine-drawn; progressed; attracted upwards. (See प्रकर्षम्).

प्रकृष्टसत्त्वनिमित्तम् i. 24 Having the finest (degree, grade, quality of) sattva for cause.

प्रकृष्टसत्त्वोपादानात् i. 24 By the donning of (a veil of) the most refined and 'progressed' sattva.

—प्रकृष्टस्य i. 49.

—प्रकृष्टे iii. 25.

प्रक्षीणक्लेशराशिः i. 1 He who destroys the hosts of miseries, sins, afflictions, of others; or he whose own 'sins', faults (of a-vidyā) have all been washed away (and who is now full of vidyā).

प्रक्षीणमोहावरणम् i. 2 With the veil of 'confusion' (i. e., conflictful desire which causes 'perplexities') worn away.

प्रख्याक्रियास्थितिशीलानाम् iv. 14 Of the (guṇas) characterised by knowledge, activity, and 'steadiness' (or tenacity of *desire*). (See प्रकाशक्रियास्थिति-शीलं; प्र + ख्या, to tell, inform, make clear).

प्रख्यातम् iii. 41 Well-known.

प्रख्याप्रवृत्तिस्थितिरूपाः ii. 15 Of the 'form' or character or nature of (the three i. e.) cognition, 'going forward' or action, and 'sitting' down (clinging 'steady' *desire*). (प्र + वृत्, Lat. *vertere*, to 'turn', 'roll', 'revolve'; प्रवृत्तिः, turning out, rolling out, revolving and evolving forth).

प्रख्याप्रवृत्तिस्थितिशीलत्वात् i. 2 Because of possessing the characteristics of cognition, action, and desire.

प्रख्यारूपम् i. 2 Of the form, nature, or aspect of knowledge.

प्रख्याशीलम् iii 35 Having the characteristic of cognition.

—प्रघट्टकेन ii. 13 (Violent combination; collision; spasm; sudden effort).

—प्रचय—i. 5, 43.

—प्रचयः ii. 13, 15; iv. 7.

प्रचयविशेषः i. 43 Special or peculiar collection, accumulation, grouping, combination. (प्र + चि, to 'choose', select, gather).

—प्रचार—iv. 19.

प्रचारसंवेदनम् iii. 38 Knowledge of (lines, tracts, channels, ways of) movement, passage, wandering. (प्र+चर्, to move about).

प्रचारसंवेदनात् iii. 38 From do:.

प्रचारसंवेदनात् iii. 38.

—प्रचारात् iii. 26.

—प्रचाराः iii. 26.

—प्रचितः iii. 17.

—प्रचितस्य ii. 13.

प्रचिताभाः iii. 26 'Of accumulated glory', luminosity, brilliance, resplendence, effulgence; (a race or class of gods).

प्रच्छर्दनम् i. 34 'Vomiting', throwing out.

प्रच्छर्दनविधारणाभ्याम् i. 34 By expiration and retention (of the breath).

प्रच्छर्दनविधारणाभ्याम् ii. 53.

प्रच्यवते iii. 15 Drops off; falls; slips away. (च्यु, to go, to drop, to fail).

प्रजाः iii. 26 Progenies; creatures. (प्र+जन्, to be born).

प्रजानाति ii. 45 Knows lucidly, clearly. (प्र+ज्ञा, to 'know').

—प्रज्ञः iii 51.

प्रज्ञया iv. 23 (See प्रज्ञा).

—प्रज्ञा— i. 20.

—प्रज्ञा—i. 47, 49, 50, 51.

—प्रज्ञा iii. 5.

—प्रज्ञाः iii. 51.

प्रज्ञा i. 48; ii. 27 'High knowledge'; the highest *cognitive* consciousness; the 'pure reason'; the higher mind or intelligence. (प्र, high, much, great+ज्ञा, to 'know').

प्रज्ञा i. 20, 43, 44, 48, 49, 50; ii. 2, 27, 45; iii. 35.

प्रज्ञाम् i. 10, 48.

—प्रज्ञाम् ii. 27.

प्रज्ञाकृतः i. 50 Made, created, produced, caused, by intelligence.

प्रज्ञाकृताः i. 50

प्रज्ञाकृतानाम् i. 51.

प्रज्ञाज्योतिः iii. 51 (The technical name of the Yogī in the third progressive stage of Yoga); 'the (yogi) lighted by his own lucid mind'.

—प्रज्ञात—i. 1, 17.

—प्रज्ञातः i. 2, 11, 18, 20.

—प्रज्ञातस्य iii. 7.

प्रज्ञाप्रसादम् i. 47 To the lucidity or placidity of intelligence.

—प्रज्ञाभ्याम् i. 49.

प्रज्ञाभ्याम् i. 49.

प्रज्ञायते i. 24 Is known, cognised.

—प्रज्ञायते i. 2.

—प्रज्ञायाः iii 5.

प्रज्ञायाः iii. 27.

—प्रज्ञायाम् i. 35, 42, 43, 44; iv. 23.

प्रज्ञायाम् iv. 23.

प्रज्ञारूपम् i. 43; iv. 23 The form, the function, of cognisance; intellection.

प्रज्ञाऽऽलोकः iii. 5 The light, or the

enlightenment, of the higher intelligence, the lucid mind. (आ, all round, लोक्, to see, to shine)

प्रज्ञालोकः iii. 6.

प्रज्ञाविवेकः i. 20 Discrimination, discernment, by or of the intelligence.

प्रज्ञेयः iv. 23 Cognisable; to be cognised.

प्रणवः i. 27 The Praṇava; "A-U-M", (pronounced Om, as a humming sound). (प्र + नु, नू; प्रणौति, प्रणुवति, praises, sings, hymns, the Supreme Self; प्रणूयते, is lauded, eulogised, by all; प्राणान् अवति, protects the vital forces; प्रकर्षेण नवीकरोति, re-'nov'-ates, re-juven-ates, every thing; makes everything new, renews the soul, as it were; makes the world process appear in a new light, when its meaning is duly understood; see *The Science of Peace*, and *Praṇava-Vāda or The Science of the Sacred Word*)

प्रणवम् i. 28.

प्रणवजपः ii. 32 The recitation, repetition, of the Praṇava.

प्रणवस्य i 27, 28.

प्रणवादिपवित्राणाम् ii. 1 Of the pure and purifying Praṇava etc.

प्रणवाभिधेयस्य i 28 Of that which is named by the Praṇava.

प्रणवार्थम् i. 28 To the meaning of the Praṇava.

—प्रणामित्व—iv 14.

प्रणामी iii. 44, 45 The bender.

—प्रणालिकया i. 7.

प्रणिदधीत ii. 34 Let him put, place, deposit, surrender, submit, yield (the mind to thoughts).

—प्रणिधानम् ii. 1, 32.

—प्रणिधानात् i. 23; ii. 45.

प्रणिधानात् i. 23 From 'attaching the mind to', 'laying down the mind in'; from submission, resignation, surrender; (a special kind of devotion, where-in God is regarded as the 'repository', 'source and fount' of all one's own life and actions and of all others, in a constant remembrance).

—प्रणिधानानि ii. 1, 32.

प्रतनूकरोति ii. 2 Attenuates, wears away. (See तनुः).

प्रतनूकृतान् ii. 2 To the attenuated.

प्रतर्दनाः iii. 26 (A race of gods).

प्रति ii. 22 To; for; in the presence of; in front of; confronting.

प्रति ii. 22, iii. 49.

प्रतिकूला ii. 15 Antipathetic; hostile; confronting inimically.

प्रतिकूलात्मकम् ii. 14 Of an opposite 'self' or nature; antipathetic.

प्रतिकूलात्मकत्वात् ii. 15 Because of antipathy.

प्रतिक्षणम् ii. 34, 52; iii. 9, 13; iv. 11 Every moment.

प्रतिघः ii. 8 'Back-striking'; hostility; hate. (प्रति, back, against, हन् to strike, to kill).

—प्रतिघात् ii. 38.

प्रतिजानते i. 27 (They) 'know in face of another'; they promise, declare as true.

प्रतितिष्ठन्ति iii. 26 Reside; stay; become fixed, established.

प्रतिद्वन्द्वी ii. 23 Opponent; rival; match; foe; 'the other of the two and two'.

प्रतिनिर्दिश्यते ii. 16 Is pointed out. (प्रति + निर् + दिश्, to point out, to direct).

प्रतिनिर्दिश्यन्ते iii. 13 Do: (plural). Are specified, distinguished.

प्रतिपक्षभावनम् ii. 33, 34 Realisation of, imagination of, dwelling in mind on, the opposites

प्रतिपक्षभावनम् ii. 34.

प्रतिपक्षभावनात् ii. 34 From do:

प्रतिपक्षभावनातः ii. 4 From do:

प्रतिपक्षभावनोपहताः ii. 4 Beaten down, defeated, destroyed, by vivid thought of the opposites.

—प्रतिपक्षाः i. 30; 32; ii. 11.

प्रतिपक्षाः iii. 51 Adversaries. (प्रति, opposite, पक्ष, side, wing).

—प्रतिपक्षान् ii. 33.

—प्रतिपयेत्त iii. 16.

प्रतिपत्तारम् ii. 15, 16 To the cogniser, the experiencer.

—प्रतिपत्तिः i. 25; ii. 55.

प्रतिपत्तिः iii. 53 'Fitting' (in to the mind); understanding (प्रति + पद्, to go, to approach).

प्रतिपत्तिः ii. 55; iii. 53.

—प्रतिपत्ति—i. 27.

प्रतिपत्तिवन्ध्या ii. 30 Barren of sense; devoid of apprehension.

—प्रतिपत्तौ i. 25.

—प्रतिपत्त्या iii. 17.

प्रतिपद्यताम् iii. 51 Let (it) be approached; or let (him) find.

प्रतिपद्यते iii. 13, 39 Arrives at; attains to; obtains.

प्रतिपन्नः iii. 13 Arrived at; come to; understood.

प्रतिपन्नम् iii. 13.

प्रतिपन्नाः iv. 10.

—प्रतिपादन— i. 35.

—प्रतिपादनाय ii. 30.

प्रतिपाद्यन्ते ii. 30 Are expounded.

प्रतिपिपादयिषया iii. 17 By the wish to expound, to make others understand.

प्रतिपुरुषम् iv. 16 To, with, or in, each Ego, soul, individual person.

प्रतिप्रसवः iv. 34 Re-tire-ment; in-volu-tion; retreat; re-duction; re-absorp-tion; re-mergence; im-mer-gence. (प्रति,

back, सू, to bring forth, to impel, to drive).

प्रतिप्रसवः iv. 34.

प्रतिप्रसवहेयाः ii. 10 Capable of being cast off, reduced, abolished, by a counter-process of involution, absorption, re-emergence.

प्रतिप्रसवाय ii. 2.

प्रतिप्रसवे ii. 27; iii. 50.

प्रतिबध्नाति iii. 21 'Binds over against'; ties up; inhibits; suspends; bars; prevents. (प्रति + बंध्, to 'bind').

—**प्रतिबन्धी** i. 50 (Pre-vent-er).

—प्रतिबन्धी i. 51.

—प्रतिबन्धेन i. 35.

प्रतिबिम्बीभूतः iv. 23 (That which has) 'become a reflection', an image, a 'counter-disc'.

—प्रतिबुद्धः ii. 5.

—प्रतिभा—iii. 54.

प्रतियन्ति ii. 19 (प्रति + इ, to go). (They) go back.

—प्रतियोगित्वात् iii. 17.

—**प्रतियोगी** iv. 33 (Cor-respondent; relative or related, because of or by means of contrast and opposition, as white and black, heat and cold, pleasure and pain, sin and merit).

प्रतिलब्धस्वरूपाः iii. 15 Those (successions, orders) that have gained their 'own-forms', found their realisation, have become realised.

प्रतिलब्धात्मकम् ii. 17, 21 That which has found, gained, realised itself.

प्रतिलभ्य iv. 10 Having regained, recovered. (प्रति + लभ्, to gain).

—प्रतिलम्भे i. 30, 50; ii. 6.

प्रतिवसन्ति iii. 26 Dwell. (वस्, to dwell).

प्रतिषिद्धवस्तुधर्मः i. 9 That which has repudiated, refuted, rejected, forbidden and denied, all properties, functions of things, substances, particular realities.

—**प्रतिषेध—** i. 32 ('Counter-proof', countermanding, rejection, denial, inhibition, prohibition, stopping, checking; (प्रति to, against, in the face of, सिध् to be proved, accomplished).

—प्रतिषेध—i. 32.

—प्रतिषेधः ii. 30.

—प्रतिषेधात् iii. 13.

—प्रतिष्ठः i. 51; ii. 25.

—**प्रतिष्ठम्** i. 8.

—प्रतिष्ठम् i. 2, 43; iv. 12, 19.

—प्रतिष्ठस्य iii. 43, 49.

—**प्रतिष्ठा** iv. 34.

—प्रतिष्ठा i. 3, 30; iii. 50; iv. 34.

प्रतिष्ठा iii. 38, 41 Fixing; steadying; establishment; dwelling-place; support; seat. (प्रति + स्था, to 'stand').

—प्रतिष्ठाः iii. 26.
—प्रतिष्ठानाम् ii. 4.
—प्रतिष्ठायाम् ii. 35, 36, 37, 38.
—प्रतिष्ठित—iii. 26.
—प्रतिष्ठेषु iv. 33.
—प्रतिसंक्रमायाः iv. 22.
—प्रतिसंक्रमा i. 2; ii. 20; iv. 22.

प्रतिसंक्रान्ता ii. 20; iv. 22 Moved, transferred, passed, from one to another; reflected; transformed. (क्रम्, to step).

प्रतिसंद्धाति iv. 21 Re-forms, re-shapes, counter-ranges, re-arrays, re-arranges. (प्रति + सं + धा).

—प्रतिसंवेदनात् iv. 19.
—प्रतिसंवेदिनम् iv. 21.

प्रतिसंवेदी i. 7, 29; ii. 17, 20 The ap-perceiver; the self-conscious; the (Self) possessed of reacting or reflecting consciousness; apperceptive; co-efficiently aware; reflective; mirroring; 'back-well-knowing'. (This word seems to mean the same thing as प्रत्ययानुपश्यः, which also occurs in the Yoga system, and as अनुव्यवसायी of the Nyāya, and साक्षी and उपद्रष्टा of the Vedānta; जानाति च, अहं जानामीत्यपि च जानाति; विज्ञातं विजानाति, इच्छति, वदति, करोति).

प्रतिसंसृज्यमानाः ii. 19 Being 'counter-led', led backwards, involuted, de-manifested, re-absorbed, de-manated (the opposite of e-manated).

—प्रतिसर्गः iii. 51.
—प्रतिहत— iii. 26.
—प्रतीकाः iii. 48.
—प्रतीकारः ii. 17.

प्रतीकारदर्शनात् ii. 17 From seeing, learning, of the way of counter-action; by knowledge of the remedy.

प्रतीकारम् ii. 17 To the counter-action, the remedy.

प्रतीचीनाः iii. 26 Western.

—प्रतीत्य ii. 5.

प्रतीयते ii. 9; iii. 17 Is approached, understood, believed. (Passive of प्रति + इ; see प्रत्ययः).

प्रत्यक्चेतनस्य ii. 24 Of the 'in-turned', 'in-drawn', introspective, Self-conscious Ego.

प्रत्यक्चेतनाधिगमः i. 29 (प्रति, against, in the opposite direction, अञ्च्, अञ्चति, goes, draws). Attainment of the inturned or introspective consciousness; or of the abstract conciousness; or consciousness of the abstract Self. (Vāchaspaṭi's explanation is very labored, and can be reconciled with the Bhāṣhya only by much hair-splitting; he makes the word mean 'the knowledge of the fact that the soul has been pulled away in the wrong direction, is suffering from a-vidyā).

प्रत्यक्चेतनाधिगमः ii. 32.

—प्रत्यक्षत्वे i. 35.

प्रत्यक्षबलेन i. 32 By the power of sense-perception.

प्रत्यक्षम् i. 7, 43 (प्रति, to, towards, fronting, अक्षम्, sense-organ). 'To each sense'; direct, immediate, sense-cognition; sensation; sense-evidence.

प्रत्यक्षस्य i. 32 Of sensation; of the direct evidence of the senses.

प्रत्यक्षानुमानागमाः i. 7 Sensation or direct perception or observation, and inference, and testimony or 'tradition', 'that which has come'.

प्रत्यक्षानुमानागमैः ii. 9.

प्रत्यक्षीकरणाय i. 35 For realisation; in order to secure direct sense-perception.

प्रत्यक्षीकर्त्तव्यः i. 35 Should be realised, brought into direct knowledge.

—प्रत्यक्षेण i. 49.

—प्रत्यनीकत्वात्—iii. 37.

—प्रत्यभिज्ञानात् iii. 14.

प्रत्यभिज्ञायते iii. 14 Is recognised.

प्रत्यमुञ्चत् iv. 31 (He did) put on; 'let go (on the body)'.

—प्रत्यय—i. 10, 18.

—प्रत्यय—i. 10, 32; ii. 4, 23, 26, 28; iii. 17, 20, 55.

—प्रत्ययः i. 19.

—प्रत्ययः i. 18, 19, 20; ii. 5, 26; iii. 12, 35, 50, 53.

प्रत्ययः i. 11, 32; iii. 17, 18, 35 (प्रति, to, इ, to go). An 'approach', a going to (an object)'; understanding; notion; concept; idea; opinion; belief; conviction; confidence; faith; trust; an inducing or motivating idea; (cf: 'ideas move the world)'; a cause (since the primal cause is Imaginative-Will or Volitional Imagination, 'the faith which moves mountains'); also an affix or suffix in grammar, because it is that which 'fixes', is the cause of the definition of the indefinite root-verb).

प्रत्ययकारणम् ii. 28 The cause of the idea, belief, conviction.

प्रत्ययनिरोधे i. 50; iii. 9 On the restraint of ideas, inhibition of concepts.

प्रत्ययप्रसूः iv. 28 Idea-generating; ideation-causing; productive of new causes (of em-bodiment of the soul).

प्रत्ययम् ii. 15, 18, 20; iii. 20, 35.

—प्रत्ययम् iii. 53.

प्रत्ययमात्रम् i. 32 Only and all or mere idea.

प्रत्यययोः iii. 17.

प्रत्ययविवेकनिम्नस्य iv. 27 Of (the

'mind' which is) 'low', 'hollow', 'empty', weak, in (respect of), the discrimination of ideas; which is no longer interested in and is turning away from dealing with, or discriminating between (worldly) ideas.

प्रत्ययविशेषः i. 10 A special, peculiar, particular notion.

—प्रत्ययस्य i. 41; ii. 28; iii. 20.

प्रत्ययस्य iii. 19.

प्रत्ययस्य i. 11, 32; iii. 2, 19; iv. 15.

—प्रत्ययाः ii. 15; iii. 17.

प्रत्ययाः i. 32, 50.

प्रत्ययात्मकाः iii. 9, 15 Of the nature of ideas

प्रत्ययात्मकेन iii. 3.

—प्रत्ययानाम् iii. 17.

—प्रत्ययानाम् iii. 17.

प्रत्ययानुपश्यः ii. 20 Co-perceiver, ap-perceiver, of ideas, thoughts; he who sees, is aware or conscious, of the mind's moods, functionings, ideations, ideas. (See प्रतिसंवेदी).

प्रत्ययानुपश्यः ii. 20.

प्रत्ययानुभवे i. 10 In or on experience, feeling, of a notion or idea.

प्रत्ययान्तराणि iv. 27 Other notions or ideas.

प्रत्ययान्तराणि iv. 27, 29.

प्रत्ययान्तरानुत्पादे ii. 27 On the non-birth of another idea.

प्रत्ययान्तरेण iii. 2.

प्रत्ययाविशेषः iii. 35 Non-distinction between the ideas or awarenesses.

प्रत्ययाविशेषः iii. 35.

प्रत्ययिनम् i. 32 To the ideator or subject.

प्रत्ययिनि i. 32.

प्रत्यये iii. 19.

—प्रत्ययेन iii. 35.

प्रत्ययैकतानता iii. 2 Unbroken continuity, 'single-stretchedness' of idea, cognition, thought.

—प्रत्ययौ iii. 12.

प्रत्यर्थनियतत्वात् i. 32 (See the next word). Because of being confined to only one thing, being limited to each percept.

प्रत्यर्थनियतम् i. 32 Confined to, limited by, beginning and ending with, each 'object', each 'presentation'; unique.

प्रत्यवभासते ii. 20; iii. 15 Appears, shines out.

प्रत्यवभासन्ते ii. 19.

—प्रत्यवमर्शः ii. 13.

प्रत्यवमर्शः i. 10. Inferential, reasoned, reflective recollection. (प्रति + अव + मृश्, to touch; 'to touch again all round'; to recognise, recollect, clearly).

प्रत्यवमर्शात् i. 10.

प्रत्यवस्थिताः iv. 12 Contra-posed; placed face to face. (प्रति + अव + स्था).

प्रत्यवैमि iii. 18 I believe, understand, feel, think. (प्रति + अव + ई, to go).

प्रत्यस्तभेदावयवानुगतः iii. 44 Accompanied by, consisting of, parts, the differentiation of which has disappeared; showing no indication of separate parts.

प्रत्यस्तम् ii. 19; iii. 50 To remergence, setting, abolition, disappearance.

—प्रत्यस्तमये i. 18.

प्रत्यस्तमितप्रत्ययस्य i. 41 With belief or ideation sunk, set, disappeared; devoid of ideas.

—प्रत्याख्याने ii. 15 (In refutation, re-joinder, counter-manding).

प्रत्याम्नायः ii. 27 'Re-thinking-back'; mental envelopement, involution, 'in-drawal in thought'.

प्रत्याशा ii. 24 Hope.

प्रत्यासन्नम् ii. 19 (प्रति, to, towards, आ, near, up to, सद् to sit). Near; close; proximate.

—प्रत्याहार—ii. 29.

प्रत्याहारः ii. 54 (प्रति + आ + हृ, to take away), Abs-trac-tion.

प्रत्याहारः ii. 54.

प्रत्याहृत्य i. 32 Having abstracted, drawn away.

—प्रत्युत्पन्न—i. 25 (Ready-born, ready-formed).

प्रत्युत्पन्नता iv. 11 'Ready-born-ness'; appearance; existence; operativeness; manifestness.

—प्रत्युपपन्नम् iii. 54.

प्रत्युदितख्यातिः i. 16; iv. 33 He in whom the cognisance has arisen.

प्रत्युदितख्यातेः ii 27.

प्रत्युपस्थितम् iv. 14 Present; standing in front.

प्रत्युपस्थितविषयजाला ii. 1 With 'ever standing' network of sense-objects; matted with the tangle of sense-objects; (i. e. full of cravings for sensuous experiences).

—प्रत्येक—i. 25.

प्रत्येकम् iii. 17 Each one; singly; one by one.

प्रत्येतव्यः i. 26 To be believed. (masc:).

प्रत्येतव्यम् iv. 19.

प्रथमः i. 17; ii. 50; iii. 51 The first.

प्रथमकल्पिकः iii. 51 (Name of a Yoga-stage, the first).

प्रथमम् ii. 34; iii. 13, 44 Firstly; at first.

प्रथमे iii. 26.

—प्रदानेन ii. 33.

—प्रदीप—i. 35; iv. 10.

—प्रदीपः iii. 51, 54.

प्रदीपप्रकाशवत् i. 27 Like lamp and light.

प्रदीप्तस्य iii 51 Of the lighted, flaming, blazing. (दीप्, to shine).

प्रद्योतमानम् i. 2 Shining, luminous, radiant. (द्युत्, to shine).

प्रद्योतयति i. 1 Lights up; casts light on; brings to light; illuminates.

—प्रधान—ii. 13, 15.

प्रधानः iii. 39 Chief. (प्र + धा).

प्रधानकर्मणि ii. 13 In the principal 'karma'.

प्रधानचित्तस्य ii. 23 Of the pradhāna-ward mind; or of the mind which is of the nature of Pradhāna i. e., Prakṛti.

प्रधानजयः iii. 48 Conquest of Pradhāna.

प्रधानजयः iii. 48.

प्रधानपुरुषयोः ii. 15 Of Matter and Spirit.

प्रधानपुरुषव्यतिरिक्तः i. 24 Apart from, other than, Matter and Spirit.

—प्रधानम् ii. 23.

प्रधानम् ii. 19, 23 Prakṛti; Matter; Nature. (प्र + धा, to do, to place, to deposit; 'that which does or makes all sorts of transformations, things, objects of the senses', or 'that in which all things are deposited ultimately').

प्रधानवशित्वम् iii. 18 Control, mastery, of Primal Matter.

प्रधानवशिनः iii. 26 Lords, masters, controllers of Pradhāna.

प्रधानवेलायाम् ii. 18 At the time, during the period, of predominance.

प्रधानव्यवहारम् ii. 23 Behaviour, functioning, as principium-pradhāna.

प्रधानशब्दवाच्याः ii. 18 Designated, denoted, by the word pradhāna.

प्रधानस्य ii. 23; iii. 26.

—प्रधाना i. 7.

प्रधानान्तर्णीतानुमितास्तिताः ii. 18 (They) whose existence, merged in the principal (one), is only inferred.

प्रधाने i. 45.

प्रधानोपसर्जनभावेन ii. 13 In the form, 'being', state, of principal and bye-product.

प्रपञ्च्यते iii. 13 Is 'quintuplicated', spread out, detailed, made complex, complicated, heterogenised; multiplied. (पञ्च, five).

प्रपद्यते ii. 15 Approaches; arrives at; finds. (प्र + पद्, to go).

प्रबुद्धस्य i. 10 Of the awakened. (प्र + बुध्, to know, to awake).

प्रबोधः ii. 4 Awakening.

—प्रभवः i. 50.

प्रभवतः i. 43 (The two) come forth, are born.

प्रभवति i. 1; iv. 3 Prevails; manifests; comes forth; has power.

प्रभवबीजम् ii. 15 The production-seed; the source of birth.

—प्रभवाः i. 50.

प्रभवाऽप्ययव्यूहानाम् iii. 45 Of or over production or integration, and absorption or dissolution or disintegration, and organisation.

—प्रभवैः i. 51.

—प्रभा—i. 36; iii. 26.

प्रभा iii. 33 The dawn-glow.

प्रभास्वरम् iii. 32 Shining; brilliant; radiant.

प्रभुः iv. 18 (प्र+भू, to be). Master; lord; 'who is, predominantly'.

—प्रभृतयः i. 29.

प्रभृति iii. 26 'Beginning with'; 'et cetera'; 'and others'.

—प्रभोः iv. 18.

—प्रभोः iv. 18.

प्रमत्तः iii. 6.

—प्रमाण—iv. 14.

प्रमाणम् i. 7, 8; ii 5 Proof; 'that which measures' and so determines, makes sure (प्र+मा, to measure).

—प्रमाणकम् iv. 16.

—प्रमाणकम् iv. 16.

प्रमाणविपर्ययविकल्पनिद्रास्मृतयः i 6 Truth, error, (doubt or) fancy (or imagination), sleep, and recollection.

प्रमाणविपर्ययविकल्पनिद्रास्मृतीनाम् i. 11.

—प्रमाणस्य i. 8.

प्रमाणस्य i. 8.

प्रमाणानि i. 7 (प्र+मा to measure) The 'measurers'; proofs; evidence; facts; standards; tests; measures; authorities; truths; verities; realities; tested and attested facts; 'measured' truths.

प्रमाणान्तरम् i. 32 Another proof.

प्रमाणान्तरेण i. 32, 43.

प्रमाणाभावः ii. 5 Absence of proof, of proven verity, of verification.

प्रमाणेन i. 8.

प्रमाणोपारोही i. 9. Amounting to proof, truth, verity, reality.

—प्रमाद— i. 30.

प्रमादः i. 30. iii. 51 Carelessness. (प्र+मद्, to madden).

प्रमादकृतेभ्यः ii. 30 From (acts giving pain to others) caused by carelessness.

प्रमोषः—i. 11.

प्रयतन्ते i. 31 (They) endeavor. (यत्, to try).

—प्रयत्नैः ii. 40.

—प्रयत्न—iii. 17.

प्रयत्नः i. 13; iv. 11 Endeavor, effort, exertion.

प्रयत्नकृतम् ii. 55 Done with effort.

प्रयत्नविशेषात् i. 33 Because of a special, peculiar, effort.

प्रयत्नशैथिल्यानन्तसमापत्तिभ्याम् ii. 47 From relaxation of effort and attainment of the "Endless".

—प्रयत्नात् ii. 50.

प्रयत्नोपरमात् ii. 47 From cessation of effort.

प्रयुक्तसामर्थ्याः ii. 18 Projecting, exercising, their powers.

प्रयोग—i. 30; ii. 54.

—प्रयोगः ii. 44.

—प्रयोग ii. 55.

—प्रयोगे i. 15.

—प्रयोजकम् iv. 3.

प्रयोजकम् iv. 5 Inspiring, engaging, employing, moving.

प्रयोजकम् iv. 3, 5.

—प्रयोजनम् ii. 18.

प्रयोजनम् i. 25; ii. 18 (प्र+युज् to join). That which en-gage-s (a person in an action, 'joins' him to an endeavour); motive; incentive.

प्रयोजनाभावात् ii. 27 For lack of motive.

—प्ररोहः ii. 4.

प्ररोहः ii 4 Mounting, ascending; growing, sprouting. (प्र+रुह्, to grow).

प्ररोहसमर्थाः ii. 13; iv. 28 Capable of sprouting.

—प्ररोही ii. 13.

—प्रलय—i. 25.

प्रलयम् i. 5 To dissolution, reabsorption, (प्र+ली, to melt, to become absorbed, to 'lie' hidden).

प्रलयाभिमुखाः ii. 27 'Facing', tending towards, dissolution.

—प्रलयेषु i. 25.

—प्रलीनानाम् ii. 27.

प्रलीने ii. 10 On or in the (Yogi's mind when it has) become, 'absorbed', dissolved.

प्रलीनेषु iii. 50.

—प्रवण—ii. 33.

प्रवर्त्तते ii. 18; iii. 6, 41; iv. 25 Engages; becomes employed. (प्र+वृत्).

प्रवर्त्तन्ते ii. 18; iii. 13; iv. 16 Do: (plural).

प्रवर्त्तितम् iv. 31 Set going; started.

प्रवर्त्यते iv. 3 Is set in motion, set going, is made operative.

प्रवृत्ते i. 2; ii. 23 Came forth; went forth; issued into activity; became active.

प्रवादाः iv. 21 Declarations; doctrines; sayings; teachings. (प्र+वद्, to say, declare, affirm).

—प्रवाह—i. 5; iii. 52.

—प्रवाहः i. 47; ii. 26.

प्रवाहः iii. 2 Flow (प्र+वह्, to flow).

प्रवाहचित्तम् i. 32 The 'flow-mind'; the mind 'streaming' (with moods, tenses, functionings);

mind regarded as a stream of experiences.

प्रवाहचित्तस्य i. 32.

प्रवाहांशस्य i. 32 Of a part of the flow.

—प्रवाहिणः iv. 27.

—प्रवाही i. 32.

—प्रवाहेण i. 32.

प्रविभजन्ते iv. 23 (They) distinguish. (प्र + वि + भज्, भञ्ज, to divide, to break).

प्रविभज्य iii. 17 Having distinguished, separated.

प्रविभागः iii. 17 Separation; distinction; differentiation; difference; classification; division; sub-division.

प्रविभागज्ञः iii. 17 Knower of do:

—प्रविभाग— iii. 17.

—प्रविभागाः ii. 18.

प्रविभागानुपपत्तिः iii. 53 Inability, impossibility, non-feasibility of distinction.

प्रविलीयते i. 51 Dissolves; is dissolved.

—प्रविवेक—i 16 (Strong discernment).

—प्रविशन्ति iv. 3.

प्रवृत्तम् iv. 11 Ever-active, engaged, diligent.

प्रवृत्तमात्रज्योतिः iii. 51 With light just issuing, just arising, just beginning to be seen.

प्रवृत्तयः i. 35 (See प्रवृत्तिः)

प्रवृत्ता ii 30 Become operative.

—प्रवृत्ति—i. 2; ii. 15.

प्रवृत्तिः i. 35 Pursuit; functioning; occupation; activity; going forth into manifest existence; 'pro-version' (opposite of निवृत्तिः, 're-version'). (प्र + वृत्, to be, to exist, to revolve; Lat. *vertere*, to turn).

—प्रवृत्तिः i. 30, 35.

प्रवृत्तिः i. 35, 36; ii. 23; iii. 25; iv. 5, 19.

प्रवृत्तिकारणम् iii. 13 Cause of employment, engagement, activity.

प्रवृत्तिभेदः iv. 5.

प्रवृत्तिभेदे iv. 5 In (the state or fact of) diversity of pursuit, occupation, engagement.

प्रवृत्तेः ii. 23.

—प्रवृत्तौ iv. 3.

प्रवृत्त्यालोकन्यासात् iii. 25 'By directing the light of the super-physical activity'; by projection of the super-physical light (experienced within the head; see i. 36).

प्रवेदयिष्यामः i. 1 We shall 'cause to be known', i. e. explain.

—प्रवेशयितुम् iv. 3.

—प्रवेशात् iv. 2 (विश्, to enter).

प्रशान्तये iv. 21 For the great peace. (शम्, to be 'calm').

प्रशान्तवाहिता iii. 10 Peaceful flowingness; peaceful flow.

प्रशान्तवाहिता i. 13.

प्रश्नः iv. 33 Question; query.

प्रश्वासः i. 31; ii. 49 (श्वस्, to breathe).

प्रश्वासपूर्वकः ii. 50 Preceded by out-breathing.

—प्रश्वासयोः ii. 49.

—प्रश्वासयोः ii. 51.

—प्रश्वासाः i. 31.

—प्रश्वासैः ii. 50.

प्रसक्तः ii. 13 Attached; entailed; relevant; appurtenant; ensuant. (प्र+सञ्ज्, to cling, adhere, be addicted).

प्रसक्तम् i. 24 Supervenient.

प्रसक्ते iii. 15.

प्रसङ्ख्यानदग्धक्लेशबीजभावः ii. 13 (Tendency to or germ of action) whose quality of being the seed of misery has been burnt out by (truth-seeing) thought.

प्रसङ्ख्यानबलात् i. 15 From or by power of thought, meditation, 'calculation', 'counting up', 'accounting', considering.

प्रसङ्ख्यानम् i. 2 (प्र+सं+ख्या to declare, to make known, to 'count'). Highest knowledge; 'enumeration' (of ultimate causes and effects); meditation.

प्रसङ्ख्यानवतः ii. 4 Of the thoughtful (yogi).

प्रसङ्ख्यानाग्निना ii. 2 By the fire of cogitation, thought, meditation, true knowledge.

प्रसङ्ख्याने iv. 29.

प्रसङ्ख्याने iv. 29.

प्रसङ्ख्यानेन ii. 11.

—प्रसङ्ग—iii. 13.

—प्रसङ्गः iv. 21.

—प्रसङ्गः ii. 15; iii. 51; iv. 21.

—प्रसङ्गात् iii. 51 (See प्रसक्तः).

—प्रसङ्गेन i. 8.

प्रसन्नः i. 29 Placid; cheerful; pleasant; (masc:). (प्र, high, +सद्, to 'sit' down, to be weary, to approach; प्रसीदति 'sits' or rests in peace; 'sits on high'; is placid).

प्रसन्नम् i, 10, 33; iii. 18 Do: (neu:).

—प्रसव— ii. 10 (प्र+सू; see प्रतिप्रसवः).

—प्रसव—ii. 2, 10; 34 iii. 14, 50.

—प्रसवः ii. 12, 26; iv. 34.

—प्रसवः iv. 34.

प्रसवभूमिः ii. 4 Birth-place.

—प्रसवम् ii. 26.

—प्रसवाय ii. 2.

—प्रसवे ii. 27.

—प्रसाद—i. 16.

—प्रसादः i. 47 (See प्रसन्नः; cheerfulness; placidity; serenity; tranquillity; lucidity; purity; settling down, as of dust and mud; grace; favor).

—प्रसादः i. 20, 47.

—प्रसादनम् i. 33.

—प्रसादनम् ii. 1.

—प्रसादम् i. 47.

—प्रसादात् iii. 6.

प्रसाध्य ii. 13 Having accomplished. (प्र+साध्, to accomplish).

—प्रसाध्यम् iii. 13.

प्रसीदति i. 33 Is pleased; becomes cheerful, placid, serene.

प्रसुप्तः ii. 4 Asleep (प्र+स्वप्, to sleep; Gr. hypnos).

प्रसुप्ततनुविच्छिन्नोदाराणाम् ii. 4 Of the sleeping (dormant, quiescent, abeyant, static, latent, potential, germinal), and the 'thin', (slight, 'tenuous', attenuated, incipient, germinating), and the broken (sporadic, cut up, interrupted, intermittent); and the operant ('grand', 'generous', active, in full flush, dynamic, vigorous, splendid). (Cf: the terms of psycho-analysis, unconscious or sub-conscious or supra-conscious, and fore-conscious or pre-conscious, and conscious).

प्रसुप्ततनुविच्छिन्नोदाराणाम् ii. 4.

प्रसुप्ततनुविच्छिन्नः ii. 4.

प्रसुप्तिः ii. 4 Deep sleep.

—प्रसूः iv. 28.

—प्रसूतिः i 1.

—प्रसूतम् ii. 15.

—प्रस्तारः iii. 26.

प्राक् ii. 23 Before.

प्राकाम्यम् iii. 45 (Name of a super-physical power); 'will-success'; 'ability to do what one wishes'; 'irre-sistible will-power'. (प्र+कम्, to desire).

प्राकाम्यविघातात् i. 24 From defeat of will.

—प्राग्भारम् iv. 26 ('Front-heavy'; 'heavy forward'; heading towards).

—प्राग्भारम् iv. 26.

—प्राग्भारा i. 12.

प्राचीनाः iii. 26 Eastern; ancient; former. (प्राक्, before, former).

प्राजापत्यः iii. 26 Belonging to Prajāpaṭi.

प्राजापत्ये iii. 26.

प्राज्ञः i. 47 The wise one. (See प्रज्ञा).

प्राणः i. 31; iii. 39 Breath; vitality; vital force; life-breath. (प्र+अन्, to breathe; Lat. anima).

प्राणभृद्भेदस्य ii 34 Of the variety or multiplicity of living beings.

प्राणस्य i. 34 Of the life-breath.

प्राणस्य iii. 53.

प्राणादिलक्षणा iii. 39 Of the nature or character of Prāṇa etc.

प्राणान् iii. 17.

—प्राणायाम— ii. 29.

प्राणयामः iii 49 (प्राण + आयाम; यम्, to check; also to stretch.) Regulation of the life-breath; lengthening of the breath; making it regular, slow, deep, long, or stopping it wholly for a time.

प्राणायामः i. 34; iii. 49, 51.

प्राणायामात् iii. 52.

प्राणायामान् iii. 52.

प्राणायामाभ्यासात् iii. 52, 53 From or by practice of breath-regulation.

प्राणिनः i. 31 Living or breathing creatures.

—प्राणिनः ii. 9; iii. 26.

—प्राणिनाम् ii. 35.

—प्राणिषु i. 33.

प्रातिभम् iii. 33 Intuitional.

प्रातिभश्रावणवेदनादर्शास्वादवार्त्ताः iii. 36 Intuition, clair-audience, clair-tact, clair-voyance, clair-gustation and clair-olfaction. (वार्त्ता here is explained by the Bhāshya as meaning experience of super-physical scents. But this is not at all the ordinary meaning of the word, which is 'means of existence living, livelihood, trade'; hence also, 'news'. The aphorism probably means 'news i. e., experiences, of intuition etc'; but the Bhāshya-kāra puts in 'olfaction' apparently for the sake of symmetrical completion of the 'five' sense-experiences).

प्रातिभस्य ii. 33.

प्रातिभात् iii. 33.

प्रातिभात् iii. 36.

प्रातिभाद्यः iii 37 The intuitional etc.

प्रादुरभवत् iii. 18 Came forth; issued forth; appeared; came into manifestation. (प्रादुः, 'forth', outwardly, visibly, भू, to be).

प्रादुर्भवति i. 43; iii. 44, 47, 52 Comes forth, etc.

—प्रादुर्भावः iii 45.

—प्रादुर्भावौ iii. 9.

—प्रादुर्भावौ iii. 9, 13.

प्रान्तभूमिः ii. 27 'End-ground'; 'bordering' province; tract of country; a definite stage; step; grade; plane; level; layer.

प्रान्तभूमिप्रज्ञा iii. 51 The consciousness of the stage or plane.

प्रान्तभूमिप्रज्ञाम् ii. 27.

प्रान्तभूमिषु iii 6.

प्रान्ते iii. 15 At one end.

प्रापणीयम् i. 16 To be attained.

प्रापितवस्तुमात्रसद्भावाः iii. 15 Given or proved to have existence as real entities.

प्राप्तः ii. 21 Arrived; attained to; (masc:). (प्र + आप्, to obtain).

प्राप्तचैतन्योपग्रहरूपायाः ii. 20 'Of (the mental mood) which has found the form of the support, handclasp, grasp, reflection, shadow, of the conscious'; of the intelligence on which the reflection of consciousness has fallen and which therefore appears now as if it were itself conscious (like a mirror imaging the sun).

प्राप्तचैतन्योपग्रहस्वरूपायाः iv. 22 (See ii. 20).

—प्राप्तम् i. 18.

प्राप्तम् i. 16, 43; ii. 22; iv. 13 Found; arrived; (neu:).

प्राप्तविवेकजज्ञानस्य iii 55 Of him who has found the knowledge born of discrimination.

—प्राप्त—iii. 55.

प्राप्ताः i. 24.

प्राप्तिः i. 24, 49; iii. 42, 45 'Finding'; (name of a superphysical power); 'the power to reach anywhere one likes'.

—प्राप्तिः i. 7, 25, 49.

प्राप्तिकारणम् ii. 28 Cause of attainment.

—प्राप्तेः i. 7.

—प्राप्तौ i. 15; ii. 6, 34.

प्राप्त्युपायः ii 26 Means, way of, going, finding, attainment. (उप near, इ, to go).

प्राप्नुयात् ii. 30 May find.

प्राप्नुवन्तः iii. 13 Arriving, attaining.

प्राप्नुवन्ति iv. 21 (They) arrive; find; come up; present themselves.

प्राप्नुहि ii. 36 Do thou gain; (imperative mood).

प्राप्नोति i. 32; ii. 24, 36; iii. 13 Finds; gains; attains; arrives at; results.

प्राप्य iii. 49 Having found.

—प्रामाणिकस्य i. 49.

—प्रायण— ii. 13 (इ, to depart).

प्रायणकाले iii. 39 At the time of 'passing away', death.

प्रायणस्य iii. 22 Of death, 'the great departure'.

प्रायणाभिव्यक्तः ii. 13 Manifested, shown, indicated clearly, in, at, or by, 'departure', death.

प्रायेण i. 43 Generally; nearly; almost; frequently.

प्रार्थनीयः iii. 51 Worthy to be requested, solicited, entreated, begged.

—प्रार्थनीयेभ्यः iii. 51.

प्रार्थयते iv. 29 Desires; prays.

प्रार्थयमानः ii. 11, 15 (One who is) craving, requesting, entreating, soliciting.

प्रावृषि iv. 25 In the rain-season.

—प्रासाद— iv. 10.

प्रासादः iii. 17, 26 Mansion. (प्र + आ + सद्; 'high-seated'; 'of high approach').

प्रियम् iii. 51 Dear; pleasing; desired.

—प्रियम् i. 2.

प्रीतये i. 1 For gratification, pleasure, affection.

—प्रेक्षी iii. 51.

—प्रेत— ii. 34; iii. 26.

प्रोवाच i. 25 Spoke, uttered.

—प्लवः i. 7.

—प्लवते ii. 4; iii. 13.

प्लवते i. 7; ii. 26 Floats; fluctuates; shakes; is shaky, unsteady; bobs up and down. (प्लु, to 'flow', 'float').

—प्लवन्ते ii. 15.

प्लवा ii. 26.

—प्लवा ii. 26.

—प्लावयन्ति iv. 3.

—फ—

—फल— iv. 11.

—फल— ii. 1; iv. 11.

फलक्रमानियमात् ii. 13 Because of the uncertainty, the unregulatedness, of the order or succession of fruits or results.

फलप्रसवभेदानुमितसद्भावः iii. 14 That of which real existence or reality of existence is inferred from the difference of fruit-production, or of the fruits produced; (a cause or property) inferred as something distinctive from the distinctive character of the effects produced by it.

—फलम् i. 21, 22, 24; ii. 34.

फलम् i. 23; iv. 11, 12 Fruit; result.

फलसन्यासात् iv. 7 From renunciation of fruit.

—फलस्य i. 24; ii. 18.

फलस्य iv. 12, 18.

—फलाः ii. 14, 34.

—फलाः ii. 14, 34,

फलेन i. 43.

—ब—

—बद्धम् iv. 23.

बधिराबधिरयोः iii. 41 Of the deaf and the not-deaf.

—बध्नाति iii. 21.

—बध्य iv. 17 (Some editions read—बन्ध्य).

—बध्यते iv. 15.

—बध्यमानम् iv. 16.

—बन्ध—iii. 38.

—बन्धः iii. 1.

—बन्धः i. 24: iii. 51; iv, 6.

बन्धः ii. 18; iii. 1, 38 'Bondage'; tie; attachment. (बन्ध्, to 'bind').

—बन्धकस्य ii, 3.

बन्धकारणम् ii. 24 Cause of bondage,

बन्धकारणशैथिल्यात् iii. 38 From looseness of the cause of bondage; by relaxation of the cause of the attachment, the tie, viz. by weakening of desire.

बन्धकारणस्य ii. 23; iii. 38.

बन्धकारणाभावात् ii. 24 From absence of the cause of bondage.

बन्धकोटिः i. 24 State, stage, side, of bondage.

—बन्धनः iii, 49.

बन्धनानि i. 24 Bonds.

—बन्धने iii. 35

बन्धनोपरमः ii 24 Cessation of bondage; revulsion or satiation from the condition of being bound.

बन्धमोक्षौ ii. 18 Bondage and liberation.

—बन्धात् iv. 16.

बन्धाभावः ii. 23 Absence of bondage.

—बन्ध्य—iii. 23.

बन्ध्यप्रसवम् ii. 26 With progenition, issue, prevented, barred; sterile.

—बन्ध्या ii. 30.

—बल—iii. 24, 46.

—बल— iv. 10.

—बलः iii. 24, 46.

—बलम् iii. 23.

बलम् iii. 23 Force; strength; power.

बलवन्तः iii. 13 Powerful, strong.

—बलाः iii. 13.

—बलात् i. 15; iii. 38.

बलानि iii. 23 Forces; abilities; powers; (pl:).

बलानि iii. 23.

बलीयः iv. 10 The stronger.

—बले iii. 24.

—बलेन iv. 14.

बलेषु iii. 24 In or among forces, abilities, strengths, powers; (pl:).

बहवः i. 24 Many; (pl:; masc:).

बहिः iii. 43 Outside.

बहिः iii. 43.

बहिरंगम् iii. 8 External or outer limb or part.

बहिरंगम् iii. 8.

बहिरंगाणि iii. 1.

बहिर्भूतस्य iii. 43 Of the (mind i. e., soul which has) gone outside (the body).

बहिर्वस्तुबीजाः i. 46 'Seeded' with external objects; based on, springing from, dependent on, external objects.

बहिःसाधनसाध्या iv. 7 Achievable by external means.

बहु i. 25; ii. 13 Much; many.

बहुचित्तावलम्बनीभूतम् iv. 15 The (external thing) which is the 'support', the object, of many minds. (Some editions read बहुचित्तालम्बनीभूतम्).

—बहुत्वम् ii. 23.

बहुत्वे i. 5 In (the state of) manyness.

—बहुलः ii. 15.

बहून् iv. 4.

बहूनाम् iv. 5.

बहूनि ii. 30 Many; (plural).

बाधते i. 50; iii. 51; iv. 3 Oppresses; hinders, hampers, restrains, keeps off, opposes, restricts, gives trouble; traverses, contradicts. (बाध, to oppress, torment).

बाधनम् i. 8 Refutation.

—बाधने ii. 33.

—बाधमानम् ii. 1.

बाधमानाः iv. 16 Traversing, contradicting; (pl:; masc:). (Some editions include the sentence in which this word occurs, in the Bhāshya on iv. 15).

बाधेते iii. 30.

बाध्यते i. 8 Is refuted, destroyed; (passive of बाध्).

बाध्यमानः ii. 33 Being oppressed, disturbed, bothered.

बाह्यः ii 50 Outer.

बाह्यम् i. 31; ii. 32; iii. 29; iv. 10 External, outer.

बाह्यवस्तूपरागात् i. 7 Because of being tinged or affected by an external object.

बाह्यविषयः ii. 51 Having an external object; having the external for object; pertaining to the external.

बाह्यसाधननिरनुग्रहात्मानः iv. 10 Of a nature not dependent on the 'favors' of external means.

बाह्यस्य ii. 49.

बाह्याध्यात्मिकोभयनिमित्ताः ii. 15 Caused by external, or subjective, or both sorts of causes.

बाह्याभ्यन्तरस्तम्भवृत्तिः ii. 50 'Of the external, the internal, and the paralysed or suppressed or rigidified mode'; i. e, stopping of the breath (for a while) after expiration, after inspiration, and by sudden effort.

बाह्याभ्यन्तरविषयाक्षेपी ii. 51 (The word आक्षेपी is used here in some unusual and obscure sense, which makes the aphorism very difficult to understand. The most relevant interpretation of **आक्षेपी**, here, seems to be "that wich 'attacks', 'besieges', i. e, draws in, contracts, reduces, causes to shrink"). (The fourth kind of breath-regulation is the gradual) reducing of the external as well as the internal stretch or length of the breath, (making the expiration and the inspiration, both, less and less strong and long, till both disappear).

बाह्ये iii. 1.

बाह्योपकरणेषु ii. 5 In external instruments.

बिभर्त्ति i. 48 Bears, holds, carries; nourishes, cherishes. (भृ, to support).

—**बिम्बीभूतः** iv. 23.

—**बीज**—ii. 2, 10, 11, 13, 26, 32; iii. 50; iv. 25, 28, 29,

—**बीजः** i. 46.

—**बीजः** i. 2, 18.

बीजभावोपगतानाम् ii. 11 Of the Kléshas, afflictions, which have arrived at, gone back into, reverted into, the condition, state, nature, of seed or germ; i. e. when the primal instincts which lead to births and rebirths, have been deprived of their momentum or dynamicity, and been reduced back to their original seed-condition of staticity, i. e. have been reverted from patency to latency.

बीजभावोपगमः ii 4 Approach or approximation to, assumption of, the state or nature of seed or germ.

—बीजम् i. 25.

—बीजम् ii. 23; iii. 55; iv. 23.

बीजम् i. 43 Seed; germ; cause; root; source; secret essence; principle.

बीजसामर्थ्यम् ii. 4 The power of the seed; germinating power.

—बीजस्य ii. 4.

—बीजाः i. 46.

बीजात् ii. 5.

—बीजेभ्यः iv. 27.

—बीभत्से ii. 5 (Disgusting).

—बुद्धः ii. 5.

—बुद्धि— iv. 22.

—बुद्धि—i. 43, 44; iii. 17, 18, iv. 19.

—बुद्धिः i. 16.

बुद्धिः i. 11; ii. 6, 24, 27 The cognitive aspect, part, faculty, functioning, of the mind; the intellect; intelligence; also, the mind generally. (बुध्, to know, to understand, to think; to awake).

बुद्धिकृतौ ii. 18 (The two) made, caused, given rise to, 'created', by the mind.

बुद्धिगुणाः ii. 15 The attributes of the mind.

—बुद्धितः iii. 17.

बुद्धितः ii. 6 From intellect.

बुद्धिनिर्भासः iii. 17 Appearance in or to or before the intelligence; mental presentation.

बुद्धिनिर्माणः iii. 52 Created by the intellect.

बुद्धिनिवृत्तिः ii. 24 The retirement of the intellect; the cessation from functioning, the quiescence, of the mind.

बुद्धिपुरुषसंयोगाभावः ii. 25 Absence of conjunction of Ego or Spirit and mind.

बुद्धिप्रतिसंवेदिनम् iv. 21 The (Self, Ego, Spirit, which is the) apperceiver of the mind. (प्रतिसंवेदी, प्रत्ययानुपश्यः, see *supra*, अनुव्यवसायी of the Nyāya, साक्षी and उपद्रष्टा of the Vedānta, all signify the same fact, viz. that the soul, at the human stage, 'knows, desires, acts, and at the same time knows that it knows, desires, acts', i. e., it is aware of its own mental functionings'. 'Ap-perception' has been used in this sense by some western writers; and there seems no other better word available).

बुद्धिबुद्धीनाम् iv. 21 Of the awarenesses of the intellections; of the cognitions of the cognitions (pl:).

बुद्धिबुद्धेः iv. 21 Do: (Singular).

बुद्धिबोधात्मा 1. 3 Of the nature of simple witness, silent watcher or spectator, of the functionings of the mind.

—बुद्धिम् ii. 6.

बुद्धिम् i. 35.

बुद्धिवृत्तेः ii. 20; iv. 22 Of the mood or functioning of the intellect or mind.

बुद्धिवृत्त्यविशिष्टा ii. 20; iv. 22 Undifferentiated, undistinguished, indistinguishable, from the mood of the mind.

बुद्धिसंवित् i. 36 Awareness, consciousness, of the intellect or mind,

बुद्धिसत्त्वम् i. 36; iii. 35, 55 The saṭṭva-constituent, the saṭṭva-material, of the intellect or mind.

बुद्धिसत्त्वस्य i. 47; ii 41; iii. 18, 43, 47, 49.

बुद्धिसत्त्वात्मना iii. 35 By (an, or the, idea) of the nature of the saṭṭva-constituent of the buḍḍhi-mind.

बुद्धिसत्त्वानभिसम्बन्धात् iv. 34 Because of non-connection with the cognitional saṭṭva.

बुद्धिसत्त्वोपारूढाः ii. 17 'Mounted' to, understood by, reflected in, the saṭṭva component of buḍḍhi.

बुद्धिसमाहारः iii. 52 Mental summation, gathering up, synthesis.

बुद्धिसहगतः iii. 17 Inherently or inseparably connected with the intellect.

बुद्धीन्द्रियाणि ii. 19 Sense-organs.

बुद्धेः iv. 21.

—बुद्धेः iv. 19.

बुद्धेः i. 7, 29; ii. 17, 18, 20.

बुद्धौ ii. 18.

—बुध्द्या iii. 17.

बुध्द्यादिषु iv. 33 In intelligence etc.

बुभुत्सितार्थप्रतिपत्तये iii. 16 For the attainment of the object wished to be realised.

—बोध— i 3, 7; ii. 23.

—बोधः ii. 4.

—बोध्य— ii. 23.

बौद्धम् ii, 20; iii. 17 Mental, intellectual, ideal.

ब्रह्म iv. 22 Brahman; the Supreme, Eternal, and Infinite Spirit; the Universal Self; the Absolute.

ब्रह्मकायिकाः iii. 26 (A race of very high gods).

—ब्रह्मचर्य— ii. 30.

ब्रह्मचर्यप्रतिष्ठायाम् ii. 38 On fixity, permanence, stability, immutability, unshakeability, of Brahmacharya, sex-continence.

ब्रह्मचर्यम् ii. 30; iv. 21 Sexual continence (which is regarded as indispensable for successful 'pursuit and finding of Brahma', for 'living the godly Brahmic life').

ब्रह्मचर्येण i. 14.

ब्रह्मणः iii. 26 Of Brahmā.

ब्रह्मपुरे iii. 34 In the 'town' or 'house' of Brahman, i. e. the body' 'the temple of the Spirit, of the living God'.

ब्रह्मपुरोहिताः iii. 26 (A race of very high gods).

ब्रह्ममहाकायिकाः iii. 26 Do:

—ब्रह्मराक्षस— iii. 26 (A race of evil Spirits, generally the disembodied souls of black magicians).

ब्रह्मलोकाः iii. 26 The lokas, worlds, planes of Brahmā.

ब्राह्मः iii. 26 Belonging to Brahmā.

—ब्राह्मण— ii. 31.

ब्राह्मणः ii. 30; iv. 29 'Devotee of Brahma'; Yoga—aspirant seeking mergence in the Universal Supreme Spirit, the Absolute Self.

ब्राह्मणसङ्गः iii. 44 An assemblage or company of Brāhmaṇas.

ब्राह्मणस्य ii. 33; iii. 51.

ब्राह्मणानाम् iii. 44.

—भ—

—भक्तः iv. 15.

—भक्तिविशेषात् i 23 By a special form, kind or degree, of devotion.

भगवतः iii, 18 Of the Lord.

भगवान् i. 15; iii. 18 The Lord. (The possessor of भगः। ऐश्वर्यस्य समग्रस्य वीर्यस्य यशसः श्रियः। ज्ञानवैराग्ययोश्चैव षण्णां भग इतीङ्गना ॥ Vishṇu Purāṇa).

भगिनी ii. 24 Sister; 'born from the same womb'.

—भजन्ते iv. 23.

भद्राश्वाः or (भद्राश्व—) iii 26 (Name of a land, 'of good horses').

भद्रासनम् ii. 46 (Name of a yoga-meditation-posture).

—भय— ii. 33.

—भव— ii. 13; iii. 18.

—भवः iv. 12.

भवतः iii. 52; iv. 12 (Two) become. (भू, to be).

भवति i. 2, 4; iii. 3, 17; iv. 2; etc. Becomes; (also locative of भवान् and vocative of भवती).

—भवन— iii. 26.

भवनम् iv. 20 Becoming.

—भवनेषु iv. 1.

भवन्ति i. 5, 11; ii. 4, 34; iii. 13; iv. 4 etc. (They) become.

भवन्ती i. 3 Becoming.

—भवन्त्यः iv. 12.

भवप्रत्ययः i. 19 Caused by the 'fixed notion' of 'Becoming'; (a kind of असंप्रज्ञात समाधि, near to मोक्ष or कैवल्य, which is achieved by those yogis who meditate on and merge into an element, भूत, ākāsha, or vāyu, etc. or into an इंद्रिय, the universal principle corresponding to a sense-organ, ear, eye, etc).

—भवम् iii. 18.

भवसङ्क्रमः i. 16 The rotation of (the process of) Becoming; the succession or round of births and deaths.

भवस्य iv. 13 Of birth; of the world.

भवितव्यम् iii. 53; iv. 24 Ought to be.

भवितुम् ii. 15 To be.

—भविष्यति iii. 51.

भविष्यति ii. 34; iv. 19 Will be; will accrue; will happen; (sing:). (भू, to be).

भविष्यद्वृत्तिः ii. 4 Having existence or manifestation in future; (that which is) to manifest or come into operation in the future.

भविष्यद्व्यक्तिकम् iv. 12 That which will be manifested in the future.

भविष्यन्ति i. 35.

भविष्यामः ii. 39; iv. 25.

भविष्यामि ii. 33.

भवेत् i. 32; ii. 30; iii. 13; iv. 10 May be; if it be.

भव्यत्वात् iii. 18 Because of excellence, grandness, gloriousness.

—भाग— iii. 17.

—भाग— ii. 18.

—भागः iii. 17.

भागः iii. 26, 44 Share; part; portion; quarter. (भज्, to divide).

—भागम् iii 17.

भागाः iv. 16.

—भागिनः iii. 55.

—भागी ii. 32.

—भागीयम् iv. 25.

—भागीयस्य iv. 12.

—भागीयैः i. 51.

—भाजनस्य iii. 13.

भारतम् iii. 26 India.

—भारम् iv. 26.

भार्यया ii. 24 By the wife, the 'to-be-supported'. (भृ, to support, nourish, cherish, bear the burden of).

—भाव— iii. 49; iv. 25.

—भाव— i. 9; ii. 4, 11, 15, 39; iii. 15.

—भावः iii. 45, 48.

—भावः ii. 4, 25; iii. 11, 15, 55; iv. 10, 12, 28.

भावः iii. 13; iv. 12 Being; condition; also emotion and intention.

—भावनम् i. 28; ii. 33; 34.

भावनम् i. 28 'Making to be'; causing to exist; realising; dwelling upon in mind; cogitating; picturing; imagining.

—भावना— ii. 2; iv. 25.

—भावना— ii. 4.

भावनाः iii. 23 Ideations.

—भावनात् ii. 34 (Some editions read — भावनाहेतोः, and include the sentence in the commentary on ii. 35).

—भावनातः ii. 4.

भावनातः i. 33 By dwelling in mind upon; by realising; by evoking in one-self.

भावनातः iii. 23.

—भावनीयः iii. 51.

भावनीयः iii. 51 The (object or aim which is) to be 'realised', achieved, attained, 'brought into existence'.

भावनीयेषु iii. 51.

—भावम् ii. 26.

भावयतः i. 28, 33 Of (one who is) dwelling (in mind) upon

भावयति ii. 2 'Causes'; brings [about.

भावयन् ii 34 Picturing.

भावयित्वा iii. 23 Having imaged.

भावयिष्यति iii. 51.

भावयेत् i. 33; ii. 33; iii. 51.

—भावस्य ii. 45.

—भावा ii. 4.

—भावाः ii. 13, 18.

—भावात् iii. 15.

भावात् iii. 8.

भावान्यथात्वम् iii. 13 Otherwiseness, change, transmutation, mutation, of being, state, condition, mode, mood, manner.

भावितः ii. 27; iii. 51 Realised.

भावितस्मर्त्तव्या i. 11 That (memory) wherein the object called up by memory is 'realised', is invested with reality, is regarded as real.

भावितेषु iii. 51.

—भाविनः iii. 52.

भावी i. 24 (That which is) to become, to happen, in the future.

भावे ii. 23.

—भावेन ii. 13, 18; iv. 14.

—भावौ iii. 13.

—भासम् iii. 3; iv. 19 (Appearing; भास्, to shine, to appear).

—भासम् iv. 23.

—भासते ii. 20, 23; iii. 15, 52.

—भासन्ते ii 19.

भास्करस्य iii. 33 Of the 'lightmaker', the Sun.

भास्वरम् i. 36 Radiant; luminous.

भित्वा ii. 5; iii. 13 Having broken.

भिद्यते iii. 14 Is differentiated, distinguished, separated, 'cut off', 'broken up or away'; (passive of भिद्, to separate, break down, di-'vide'; Lat, *vid*, to separate).

भिद्येत iii. 14 Would be differentiated, separated, distinguished.

भिनत्ति iv. 3 Breaks through or away; removes. (भिद्).

—भिन्न— ii. 18.

भिन्नः iii. 53 Separate; different.

भिन्नजातीयेभ्यः i. 7 From (things or objects) of different genera or species.

—भिन्नयोः iv. 15.

—भिन्नाः i. 32.

भिन्ने iv.3 When (the obstructing dam has been) broken.

—भिन्ने iii. 53.

—भिन्नेषु i. 32.

—भीतः ii. 15.

भीतः iv. 19 Afraid; fear-stricken (भी, to fear).

भीतव्याधितकृपणेषु ii. 12 Towards the frightened, the sick, and the pitiable.

भुङ्क्ते iii. 50 Eats; tastes; experiences. (भुज्).

भुजगपरिकरः i. 1 With retinue of snakes 'which go by or on their arms'; having serpents for retinue.

भुवनज्ञानम् iii. 26 Knowledge of the cosmos.

भुवि iii. 26 On or in the Earth.

—भूः iv. 16 (Some editions include the sentence in which this occurs in the commentary on iv. 15).

—भूत— iii. 17.

—भूत— ii. 30, 33; iii, 18, 44; iv. 9. (भूतं, living beings, elements).

—भूतः i. 1; iv. 23.

भूतः i. 24 That which has become; the occurred; the past.

भूतकारणम् iii. 44 Cause of the elements.

भूतग्रामम् ii. 15 The host of living beings.

भूतजयः iii. 44 Conquest of the elements.

—भूतत्वात् iii. 20.

—भूतत्वात् iv. 23.

भूतप्रकृतयः iii. 44 The 'natures', 'origins', or 'substrata' of the elements.

भूतप्रकृतीनाम् iii 45 Of the 'origins', 'natures', or 'substances' of elements.

भूतभाविनः iii. 52 Past and future; (pl:).

भूतभावेन ii. 18 In the form or state of the elements.

भूतभौतिकेषु iii. 45 In, among, over, elements and compounds.

—भूतम् i. 1, 5, 35; ii. 23; iii 20; iv. 11, 15, 16, 31.

—भूतयोः iii. 11.

भूतसूक्ष्मगतः i. 49 Gone to, existing in, subtile elements.

भूतसूक्ष्मम् i. 44 Subtile elements; subtle forms of the elements.

भूतसूक्ष्मसमापन्नम् i. 41 Arrived at, resolved or accomplished into, a subtile element.

भुतसूक्ष्मस्वरूपाभासम् i. 41 Appearing in or with the form of a subtile element.

भूतसूक्ष्माणाम् i. 43.

भूतसूक्ष्मेषु i. 44

भूतसूक्ष्मोपरक्तम् i. 41 'Tinged' by a subtile element.

—भूतस्य iii. 38.

—भूताः i. 5; iii. 17.

—भूतानाम् ii. 30.

भूतानाम् iii. 44; iv. 7 Of living beings or elements.

भूतानि ii. 15, 19 Beings, creatures.

—भूतानि ii. 28.

भूतानुग्रहः i. 25 Compassion for all beings.

भूतान्तरेषु iv. 14 Among other elements.

भूतार्थविषयः i. 47 With a real existent object.

भूतार्थविषयत्वात् i. 8 Because of the object (of pramāṇa) being something which 'has come into existence', i. e., is real.

—भूते ii. 4.

भूतेन्द्रियजयी iii. 51 Conqueror of elements and of the sensor and motor organs.

भूतेन्द्रियप्रकृतिवशिनः iii. 26 Lords or masters of the elements, of the sensori-motor organs, and of the 'substrates' (ṭanmāṭras)

भूतेन्द्रियवशिनः iii. 26 Controllers, masters, of the elements and the sensori-motor organs.

भूतेन्द्रियाणि ii. 19 Elements and sensori-motor organs.

भूतेन्द्रियात्मकम् ii. 18 Of the nature or form of the elements and sensori-motor organs.

भूतेन्द्रियेषु iii. 13 Amongst the elements and the sensori-motor organs.

—भूतेषु i. 41.

भूतेषु iii. 23 Amongst or towards beings.

भूतोपघातपरा ii. 30 Bent on, tending towards, leading to, the slaughter of creatures.

भूतोपघाताय ii. 30 For the destruction of creatures.

—भूत्वा ii. 3, 15; iv. 12.

—भूमयः i. 1; ii. 19; iii 26.

—भूमि—iii. 51.

—भूमिः ii. 27 (Condition, state; stage; level).

—भूमिः i. 14; ii. 4; iii. 6, 26.

भूमिः iii. 6, 26, 44 The earth; ground, foundation, stage, resting-place, halting place, standing ground; layer, level, plane; condition or mood, (of mind).

—भूमिकः iii. 26, 51.

—भूमिकस्य iii. 6.

भूमिजयात् ii. 51 From or by conquest of stage (after stage, in succession).

—भूमिम् iii. 6.

भूमिम् iii. 51, 54.

—भूमिषु ii. 31; iii. 6, 26.

भूमिषु iii. 6 In or on the stages (one after another).

भूमिष्ठान् i. 47 Standing on the (low) 'ground', in the valley, the plain.

—भूमेः i. 30; iii. 6.

भूमेः iii. 6.

भूमौ i. 30; iii. 45.

—भूम्योः iii 14.

—भूयते iv. 33.

भूयाः ii. 36 Be thou; (benedictive mood of भू, to be).

भूयासम् ii. 9; iv. 10 May I be; (do:).

भूर्लोक: iii. 26 The physical world or plane; the Earth.

भूवम् ii. 9, iv. 10 (अभूवम् with मा drops the अ). May I be.

भेत्तृत्वम् ii. 17 Penetrativeness.

—भेद— ii. 18, 19; iii. 14, 44, 47.

—भेदः iv. 3.

भेदजम् ii. 17 'Born of breaking' (of the skin); caused by penetration (of the foot by a thorn).

—भेदम् ii. 1; iii. 13.

—भेदाः ii. 4.

भेदाः ii. 34 Sub-divisons; kinds.

—भेदात् iv. 12, 15.

—भेदात् i. 41; ii. 34; iii. 13; iv. 23.

भेदाभेदविवक्षितः iii. 44 'Wished to be described', or describable, as 'with and also without difference', as 'separate and again as non-separate'.

भेदे i. 32 In separateness, difference. (भिद्, to divide).

—भेदेन iv. 25.

भेदेन iii. 13 By separation.

भेद्यता ii. 17 'Divisibility'; piercability, penetrability.

भैषज्यम् ii. 15 Medication; medical treatment; medicine.

भोः iii. 51: iv. 33 (A vocative exclamation); 'Sir'.

भोक्ता i. 24; ii. 18 Experiencer. (भुज्, to eat, taste).

भोक्तारम् iv. 21.

भोक्तुः ii. 18.

भोक्तृत्वेन iii. 14 By experiencership.

भोक्तृभोग्यशक्त्योः ii. 6 Of the (two) powers, potencies, of experiencer and experienced.

भोक्तृशक्तिः ii. 20; iv. 22 Experiencing power; the potency of the experiencer.

भोक्तृस्वरूपम् iv. 21 The own form or nature of the subject, the experiencer.

—भोग— ii. 32; iii. 55; iv 34.

भोगः iii. 35 Experience; 'eating'; 'tasting'; suffering-and-enjoyment; undergoing the ups and downs of life. (भुज्, to eat, taste).

भोगः ii. 6, 13, 18, 23; iii. 51; iv. 16.

भोगप्रत्ययः iii. 35 Feel, belief, awareness of experience.

भोगभागीयस्य iv. 12 Of (the karma, action); leading to experience, suffering-and-enjoyment.

भोगहेतुत्वात् ii. 13 Because of being the cause, or, being caused by, experience.

—भोगाः ii. 13.

—भोगाः ii. 14.

भोगाधिष्ठाने ii. 5 In the 'forum' or 'locus' of experience.

भोगापवर्गार्थता iii. 44 Subservience to 'experience' (of the world) and 'retirement' (therefrom) or 'abolition' thereof, i. e. moksha.

भोगापवर्गार्थतायाम् ii. 21.

भोगापवर्गार्थम् ii. 18 For the sake of 'experience' and 'retirement', pursuit of worldly experience and renunciation thereof.

भोगापवर्गार्थम् ii. 18; iv. 24.

भोगापवर्गौ ii. 18 'Experience', 'tasting', and 'retirement', 'renunciation'. (See **भोगः** and **अपवर्गः**).

भोगाभावः iii. 14 Absence of experience of enjoyment-and-suffering.

भोगाभ्यासः ii. 15 Practice, repetition, continuity, of experience.

भोगाभ्यासम् ii. 15.

भोगाभ्यासेन ii. 15.

भोगाय iv. 10.

भोगारूढम् ii. 16 Rising, 'mount'-ing, to experience; being experienced.

—**भोगिनः** iii. 26,

—**भोगी** i. 1.

भोगेन i. 24; iv. 24.

भोगेषु ii. 15.

—**भोग्य**—ii. 6.

भोग्यत्वात् iv. 15. Because of experiencability.

—**भौमः** i. 1.

भौमान् iv. 3 The earthly, the earthy; (chemical substances, particles, juices) belonging to the earth, or of the earth

—**भ्रमः** ii. 24.

भ्रमति i. 10 Wanders. (**भ्रम्**, to-wander, to err, to move about erratically, mistakenly).

भ्रान्ता ii. 30 Strayed; erred; erroneous; misled; mistaken; (fem:).

भ्रान्ताः iv. 23 Deceived; deluded; (pl:).

—**भ्रान्तिदर्शन**—i. 30 (Erroneous view).

भ्रान्तिबीजम् iv. 23 The seed of error, delusion.

—**भ्रेषात्** iii. 12.

म

मक्षिकाः ii. 54; iii. 38 Flies; bees.

—**मगध**— iii. 26 (Some editions read **गोमेध** or **प्लक्ष** in place of **मगध**; name of a continent).

—**मज्जति** iii. 45.

—**मज्जा**— iii. 29.

—**मणि**— i. 4. 35, 36; ii. 17, 18; iv. 17, 23.

मणिम् iv. 31 To the precious stone, crystal, gem.

—**मणिमयानि** iii. 26.

मणेः i. 41 Of the precious stone, crystal, gem.

—**मण्ड**— iii. 26.

मतिः iv. 21 Opinion; view; result of mentation; (**मन्**, to know, think, suppose).

मतिविभ्रमः ii. 24 Mind-wandering; error of opinion.

मत्स्यजालम् ii. 31 'Fish-net'; fishing-net.

मत्स्यबन्धकस्य ii. 31 Of the 'fish-catcher', the fisherman.

मत्स्येषु ii. 31 Amongst, in, towards, fishes.

मधुकरराजम् ii. 54 (To) the king of the 'honey-makers', i.e., bees (Modern western biologists and nature-students and observers have ascertained that the chief and leader of a hive of bees is a queen, and not a king. The word occurs in one of the admittedly oldest Upanishats, the *Prashna*; and subsequent writers, Shankara etc., faithfully, with shut eyes, copy and repeat. Are the Upanishaḍ-Ṛshis and Yogis in भ्रान्ति, 'error,' here, inadvertently ?).

मधुकरराजानम् iii. 38.

मधुप्रतीकाः iii. 48 (Name of certain 'superphysical', occult, Yogic powers).

मधुभूमिकः iii. 51 One belonging to a stage of yoga called Maḍhu-bhūmi.

मधुमतीम् iii. 51, 54 (To) The Maḍhumaṭi-stage.

—मध्य—i. 22; ii. 34.

—मध्य—i. 21.

मध्यः ii. 50 'Middle'.

मध्यतीव्रः i. 22; ii. 34 Middling intense.

मध्यतीव्रसंवेगस्य i. 22 Of one possessing energy or aspiration of middling intensity. (सं+ विज्, to fear, to tremble, to be agitated; वेगः, urge, velocity)

मध्यमध्यः ii. 34 Middling middle.

मध्यमृदुः ii. 34 Middling mild.

मध्यसंवेगः i. 21 (One) possessing medium energy, speed, aspiration.

—मध्ये i. 35.

मध्ये iii. 26 In the middle.

—मध्येषु ii. 39.

मध्योपायः i. 21 With, of, possessing 'middling means', i. e., means of middling efficiency.

मध्वमृतावयवनिर्मिता ii. 5 (A girl) composed of members, limbs, parts of the body, made all of honey and nectar.

—मनस्काः iv. 4.

मनः i. 10; ii. 19, 28, 30, 34; iv. 11, 19, 23 (मन्, to think, believe, imagine, intend, agree; to think highly of another, to honor; to think highly of oneself, to be proud; to think of or on some object persistently, insistently, to set the mind on, to crave; etc). Mind. (The word seems to be used in this aphorism as the equivalent of chiṭṭa. The distinction between the two, if any, is not pointed out in the Yoga-sūṭras or the Bhāshya. In the Sānkhya system, which is the 'theory', as Yoga is the 'practice', the anṭah-karaṇa, 'inner organ', is said to be three-fold, buḍḍhi-ahankāra-manas; chiṭṭa is not mentioned; in the Yoga-system, chiṭṭa is used, and is said to perform the three functions of the 'triple inner organ'. In Veḍānṭa, chiṭṭa seems to be the faculty of memory in particular, which 'stores up', चि, and, with the three others, makes the 'four-fold inner organ').

मनसः i. 35; ii. 53. Of the mind.

मनसः i. 34, 36; ii. 28; iii 25, 38, 43; iv. 18.

मनसा ii. 15; iii. 47, 50; iv. 11.

मनसि i. 24; ii. 5; iii. 50; iv. 7.

—मनसि ii. 30.

—मनुष्य— iv. 8.

मनुष्यजातिः iv. 33 The human race.

मनुष्यपरिणामम् ii. 12 (To) the human development, the human form, condition, transformation; evolution into the human condition.

—मनुष्याः iii. 26, 44.

—मनुष्येषु iii. 18.

मनो-जवित्वम् iii, 48 'Mind-speededness'; being possessed of the speed of the mind.

मन्तव्येन iv. 23 By the 'cogitable', the 'thinkable (object); by that which has to be thought about

—मन्त्र— iv. 1 (मननात् त्रायते, that which, being kept or revolved in mind, protects).

—मन्त्र— iv. 6.

—मन्त्रणे iii. 51.

मन्त्रतपःसमाधिभिः ii. 12 By manṭra-chants, by asceticism, and by meditation or rapt concentrated contemplation.

—मन्त्रयन्ते iii. 51.

मन्त्रैः iv. 1 By incantations, magic-words, or chants.

मन्दाकिनी iii. 51 (Name of a river in heaven).

—मन्यतया iii. 51.

मन्यते i. 16, 32; ii. 1 Thinks, believes; (pass:) is thought, supposed. (See मनः).

मन्यमानः ii. 5 Believing. (Some editions read मन्वानः).

मन्युः ii. 8 Anger, wrath; rage; grief.

मन्वानः ii. 5 Believing.

मम iv. 27 My; mine.

—ममकार— ii. 15.

मया ii. 33; iii. 18, 51 By me.

—मरण— ii. 9; iii. 51; iv. 10.

मरणत्रासः ii. 9; iv. 10 The dread of death.

मरणदुःखम् ii. 9 The pain of death.

मरणदुःखानुभवात् ii. 9 From experience of the pain of death.

मरणम् ii. 13, 34 Dying; death. (मृ, to die).

मरणात् ii. 19.

मरिष्यति iv. 33 Will die.

—मल— i. 2, 8, 47; ii. 27, 43.

—मलः ii. 27.

मलः ii. 11 Stain; grossness; refuse; dirt; excretion; excrement; scum; filth; taint.

—मलम् ii. 43; iii. 55.

—मलस्य iii. 49.

—मलाः i. 30.

मलानाम् ii. 52.

मलैः iv. 31.

महत् ii. 42 Great; (neu:).

महति ii. 15, 19; iii. 26 In the great or large; in the Mahaṭ-ṭaṭṭva or Buddhi-ṭaṭṭva, Universal Mind, Principle of Intelligence, Collective Intelligence.

महतः ii. 15, 19 (महतः आत्मनः, महति आत्मनि). Of the 'Great-Āṭmā', the Mahaṭ-ṭaṭṭva or Buḍḍhi-ṭaṭṭva.

महत्तत्त्वम् ii. 19 The Mahaṭ-ṭaṭṭva, the Great Principle of Conciousness manifesting in primal Universal Omniscient 'Immense' Mind.

—महत्व— i. 40.

महत्वादिव्यवहारापन्नः i. 43 Become the subject of usage as 'largeness' etc.; conventionally treated as possessed of largeness etc. (Some editions read महत्तत्वादि—).

महद्वस्तुविषया i. 44 Having large, gross, dense substance for object.

महर्लोकः iii. 26 The world or plane called Mahah.

महर्षयः iii. 51 Great Ṛṣhis. (See ऋषयः).

—महर्षि— ii. 12.

—महा— ii. 12.

महाकाल— iii. 26 (Name of a hell or rather purgatory).

महातल— iii 26 Name of an underworld.

महान् i. 43; iii. 26, 45 Great; large; the Great, i. e. Mahaṭ-ṭaṭṭva; the Mahar-plane or world.

महानरकभूमयः iii. 26 Layers, grounds, tracts, of great hells.

महानिर्वेदाय iv. 21 For the great Surfeit, the great Detachment or Renunciation.

महानुभावेषु ii. 12 Towards the Great, (those possessed) of great influence or power, the high, the mighty, the holy.

महाप्रतिपक्षाः ii. 11 Having great or powerful enemies (who require much exertion to defeat).

महाप्रलयेषु i. 25 In the Great Dissolutions (when Cosmos dissolves into Chaos).

महाभास्वराः iii. 26 (Name of a race of very high gods).

महाभूतवशिनः iii. 26 Those who have control over the great Elements.

महाभूतानाम् ii. 28 Of the great Elements.

महामोहः i. 8 Great Confusion, Error, perplexity, inertness, delusion.

महामोहमयेन ii. 52 By (this phantasmagoria) composed of utter delusion.

—महारौरव— iii, 26 (Name of a hell).

महाविदेहा iii. 43 The 'Great Incorporeal'; (name of a yoga-siḍḍhi, occult superphysical power, the power of going out of the gross physical body, in the form of a subtile body).

महाव्रतम् ii. 31 The great vow,

महासर्गेषु iii. 18 In great creations.

महिमा iii. 45 Greatness.

—महोदधि— i. 36.

मा ii. 9; iv, 10 No; not.

—मांस— iii. 29

मांसचर्मार्थेन ii. 34 For the sake of the flesh and the skin.

—माण— iv. 4.

माता iii. 13 'Mother', (the 'measurer' of the quality, capacity, 'field of consciousness', of the progeny; **मा,** to measure).

—मात्र— i. 43; ii. 19; iii. 3.

—मात्र— i. 4, 19, 28; ii. 4, 17, 18, 27; iii. 15, 17, 35, 44, 47, 51, 55; iv. 14, 22, 33.

—मात्रः ii. 20.

—मात्रः i. 17; ii. 19, 20; iii. 13.

—मात्रतया ii. 20.

—मात्रम् i. 2, 9, 16, 45; ii. 5, 19; iii. 20, 44; iv. 10, 13, 23, 24.

—मात्रया i. 2.

—मात्रस्य iii. 49.

—मात्रस्य i. 45; ii. 9, 19; iv. 10.

—मात्रा i, 44.

—मात्राणाम् ii. 22.

—मात्रात् iv. 4.

—मात्रे ii. 19; iii. 42; iv. 3, 19:

—मात्रेण i. 23, 43; ii. 18; iii. 43.

माध्यस्थ्यज्ञानम् iv. 15 Knowledge, awareness, consciousness, experience, of 'middle-seatedness', (i. e. of the condition which is above or midway between pain and pleasure, i. e. peace).

माध्यस्थ्ये ii. 28 In 'middle-seatedness', impartiality, the middle path or course.

मानसम् iv. 10 Mental.

—मानुष—ii. 28.

—मान्द्ये iii. 10.

—मापयति iv. 18.

माया iv. 13 (**या मा**, 'That which is not'). Illusion.

—मार्ग—ii. 33; iv. 25.

मार्गः ii. 26 Way; path of 'seeking.' (मृग्, to seek, hunt).

माल्यवत्सीमानः iii. 26 Bounded by the Mālyavān mountain.

—माहात्म्य—i. 9.

माहात्म्यम् i. 32 Great-souledness; large-heartedness.

—माहात्म्येन iv. 14.

माहेन्द्रः iii. 26 'Belonging to the Great Indra'; (name of a superphysical world or heaven).

माहेन्द्रनिवासिनः iii. 26 Dwellers of the Māhendra-world.

मित्रमात्रम् ii. 5 Only ' friend'.

मित्राभावः ii. 5 Absence of 'friend'.

—मिथ्या—ii. 26.

मिथ्याज्ञानम् i. 8 'Mythical', false, illusory knowledge.

मिथ्याज्ञानम् i. 43; ii. 26.

मिथ्याज्ञानस्य ii. 26.

—मिमीते iv. 4, 5.

मिलित्वा ii. 13 Having mixed, joined, or combined together. (Some editions omit this word).

मिश्रवनम् iii. 26 (Name of an Elysian garden).

—मिश्री—ii 25.

—मुक्तः ii. 32; iv. 30 (Some editions read युक्तः in ii. 32).

मुक्तः i. 24; ii. 27; iii. 22 (मुच् to release, loosen, liberate, set free; gladden, rejoice). Freed; free; let loose; emancipated; liberated; delivered; a person, soul, ego, who or which has achieved 'freedom'.

मुक्तपुरुषालम्बनोपरक्तम् i. 41 (The mind) 'colored' with the idea or image of a 'liberated' ego, soul, person, on which it may be resting, which it may be contemplating

मुक्तपुरुषेषु iv. 33 Amongst, towards, freed egos.

—मुक्तस्य iv. 31.

मुक्तस्य i. 24.

—मुक्तिः ii. 27.

मुक्त्वा ii. 25 Having let go, abandoned.

—मुख— iv. 11.

मुखनासिकागतिः iii. 39 Moving in the nostrils and the mouth

मुग्धया ii. 24 By the simple, the artless, the foolish, the ingenuous; (fem:).

—मुदिता— i. 33 (See Bhāgavata, iv. viii. 34).

मुदिता iii. 23 Gladness; respectful satisfaction; gratification; grateful satisfaction.

मुदिताबलम् iii 23 The power, the force, of reverence, reverent gladness.

मुदिताम् i. 33; iii 23.

मुद्गगवेधुकश्यामाकादीन् iv. 3 (Various cereals, pulses, etc.).

मुषितम् i. 10 Robbed; plundered; deprived of vitality. (मुस्, मुष्, to steal, despoil, spoil, break, destroy; whence मूषकः, 'mouse').

मुहूर्त्ताहोरात्रादयः iii. 52 Muhūrṭa (= 48 minutes), day, night, etc.

मुह्यति ii. 15 Fails, faints, errs, becomes perplexed. (See मोहः)

मूढः i. 10 Unconscious; fainted; swooned; confused; perplexed; erroneous. (मुह्).

मूढज्ञानम् iv. 15 Experience of confusion; confused knowledge; knowledge of confusedness, i. e. consciousness of being confused, perplexity.

मूढत्वे ii. 28 In confusedness.

मूढम् i. 1; ii. 15.

—मूढेषु ii. 9.

—मूर्त्तयः ii. 18.

—मूर्त्तस्य iii. 41.

मूर्त्तिः iii. 44 Form, shape, image.

मूर्त्तिव्यवधिजातिभेदः iii. 53 Distinction of shape or form, of intervening space or separating distance, and of genus or species or character.

मूर्त्तिसमानजातीयानाम् iv. 14 Of the same genus or species in respect of shape or form.

मूर्त्या iii. 45.

मूर्धज्योतिषि iii. 32 In the 'head-light', the light within, at, under the crown of the head or skull.

मूर्ध्नि iii. 1 In the head, the crown.

—मूलः ii. 12.

—मूलः ii. 13.

मूलपृथक्त्वम् iii. 53 Separateness of or in the root.

—मूलम् iii. 43.

मूलम् ii. 5; iv. 11 Root.

मूलवक्तरि i. 7 (In case of) the root-speaker, the original declarer being (trustworthy).

—मूलाः ii 30.

—मूलानि iv. 3.

—मूले i. 35.

मूले iii. 13 In (case of) the root-cause, the source (being present); when the root-cause (is present).

—मृग— iii. 51.

मृज्जलादिजनितम् ii. 32 Produced by earth, water, etc.

मृज्जलादिभिः ii. 40 By earth, water etc.

—मृत् iii 15.

मृत् iii. 13 Earth; 'mud'; ('mire').

मृतः ii. 24 Dead.

मृत्युना iii. 51 By death.

—मृत्युम् iii. 51 (Some editions read—मृत्यू).

मृत्वा i. 16; iv. 33 Having died.

मृदुः ii. 50 Mild

मृदुतीव्रः i. 22; ii. 34 Mildly intense; of small or low intensity.

मृदुतीव्रसंवेगस्य i. 22 Of one of middling intensity (of aspiration). (Some editions omit this word together with about half the sentence in which it occurs).

मृदुमध्यः ii. 34 'Mild-middling'; of average mildness; of lower middle (intensity of aspiration).

मृदुमध्याधिमात्रत्वात् i. 22 Because of, by reason of, softness or weakness, of moderateness or mildness or mediumness, and of excessiveness or intenseness.

मृदुमध्याधिमात्राः ii. 34 Mild or gentle, and medium or moderate, and excessive or powerful or intense.

मृदुमध्याधिमात्रोपायाः i. 21 ((Possessed of mild, medium, and powerful means.

मृदुमृदुः ii. 34 'Mild-mild'; very mild.

मृदुसंवेगः i. 21 Of mild or low speed, eagerness, aspiration.

मृदूपायः i. 21 Of mild or small or poor means.

—मृष्टः iii. 2; iv. 25.

—मृष्टम् iv. 16.

—मृष्टा ii. 20.

मे i. 10; ii. 13, 24, 34 My; mine; (possessive or genitive of अहम्).

—मेघः iv. 29 (See धर्ममेघः; धर्मान् मेहति; मिह, to rain, to sprinkle).

—मेघस्य iv. 32.

मेध्याभ्यवहरणादि ii. 32 Pure feeding etc.; eating of pure food etc.

मेरुपृष्ठम् iii. 26 The back or top of the Meru mountain.

मेरुपृष्ठात् iii. 26.

मैत्री iii. 23 Friendliness.

मैत्रीकरुणामुदितोपेक्षाणाम् i. 33 Of friendliness, of compassion, of reverent gladness, and of indifference (or ignoring or turning away or 'silent witnessing').

मैत्रीबलम् iii. 23 The (inspiring, influencing, compelling, infecting) force of affection.

मैत्रीम् i. 33; iii. 23.

मैत्र्यादयः iv. 10 Affection etc.

मैत्र्यादिषु iii. 23 On or in affection etc

मोक्षः ii. 15, 18, 23, 24 Deliverance; freedom. (See मुच्यते).

मोक्षकारणम् ii. 23 Cause of moksha.

मोक्षपदे iii. 26 In the locus, plane, 'foot', 'standing-place', precincts, or on the threshold, of Liberation; in a condition nearly the same as Liberation.

मोक्षमार्गश्रवणेन iv. 25 By or on hearing of the Path of Emancipation.

मोक्षशास्त्राणाम् ii. 32 Of the Sciences of Salvation.

मोक्षशास्त्राध्ययनम् ii. 1 Study of the Science of Deliverance.

मोक्षस्य ii. 26 Of deliverance, freedom.

मोक्षोपायः ii. 15 Means or method of moksha.

—मोक्षौ ii. 18.

मोचयति ii. 34 Frees; liberates; emancipates; releases. (**मुच्**).

—मोह— ii. 34.

—मोह— i. 2, 11; ii. 12, 15, 52.

—मोहः i. 8.

मोहः i. 8, 11 (**मुह्** to faint, swoon, fail, err, become confused, perplexed, stupefied). Confusion; perplexity; error; doubt; distraction; delusion; foolishness; vacillation (to and fro; swinging between extremes—the characteristic of Prakṛti); not knowing what to do; blind clinging.

—मोहाः i. 11; ii. 34.

मोहात् ii. 15.

मोहेन ii. 6, 34.

—मौन— ii. 32.

म्रियते i. 16 Dies; (sing: **मृ**, to die).

म्रियन्ते ii. 19 Do: (pl:).

—य—

यः i. 1; ii. 7; iii. 6; iv. 8; etc. He who; whoever, (masc:).

यज्जातीयस्य iv. 8 Of that genus, species, kind, of which.

यत् i. 16; ii. 4; iv. 6, 11 etc. That which; (neu:).

यतः i. 8; ii. 15; iv. 9, etc. The place whence; because; in as much as; for the reason that.

यतिः ii. 40 The man who refrains (from worldly enjoyment), and restrains himself in various ways; the man of vows; the ascetic. (**यम्**, to refrain; to restrain, to check).

यत्किंचित् iii. 18 Whatsoever.

—यत्न— iii. 17.

—यत्नः iv. 11.

यत्नः i. 13 Effort; endeavour. (**यत्**, to strive, to endeavour).

यत्नेन ii. 11 With or by effort, care, endeavour, or striving; strenuously, assiduously, carefully.

यत्नोपचर्यः iii. 51 To be watched with great care; to be attended to, guarded against, watchfully. (**उप** near + **चर्**, to move).

यत्र i. 24; ii. 13; iii. 13; iv. 21 etc. There where; at the place where.

यत्रकामावसायित्वम् iii. 45 'Determination where desire'; the power of enforcing, of realising, one's will and imagination, of shaping things at pleasure, at will, anywhere.

यत्रकामावसायिनः iii. 45 Of (another person) who has the power etc., (as above).

यथा— i. 39.

यथा i. 3; ii. 4; iii. 5; iv. 3 etc. As; so as.

यथाक्रमम् ii. 29; iii. 47 'As the order is'; in the order; according to the succession; in successive order.

यथाभिमतध्यानात् i. 39 By contemplation as desired, i. e., of or on whatever is agreeable

यथाभूतम् ii. 45 'As happened'; 'as has occurred actually'; according to actual fact.

यथाभूतार्थप्रतिपादनसामर्थ्यात् i. 35 From ability to expound or convey knowledge of facts as they actually are, as they have really taken place or occurred, as they verily are.

यथायोगम् ii. 32 As possible; as may be fitting; 'as may join in', fit in, well or appropriately with the surroundings; according to occasion, or opportunity.

यथार्थम् i. 20 'As the fact is'; according to fact.

यथार्थे ii. 30.

यथावत् i. 20 'As it is'. (Some editions read **यथार्थम्**).

यथासम्भवम् ii. 28, 34 As possible. (**भू**, to be).

यथासुखम् ii. 46 'As pleasure'; as may be pleasing; at pleasure; according to one's own pleasure; as convenient.

यथेष्टम् iii. 42 As desired or desirable. (**इष्**, to 'wish').

यदभिमुखीभूतम् iv. 11 (At first sight, this whole seems to be one compound word; but as such it is difficult to fit in with the rest of the sentence. It is best to read it as two words, **यत्** and **अभिमुखीभूतम्**, i. e., the thing which 'coming in front', being met with, presenting itself, arouses a desire, etc.).

यदा ii. 26; iii. 3; iv. 4; etc. At the time when; when.

यदि ii. 30; iii, 13; iv. 9 etc. If.

यद्यपि i. 35 (**यदि + अपि**; usually treated as one word). Al though.

—**यन्ति** ii. 19; iv. 21.

यम् iv. 11 etc. Him whom; (acc: of **यः**).

यम—ii. 29 (See **यमाः**).

यम—ii. 30, 33, 46.

यमपुरुषान् iii. 22 The 'men', the servants, of Yama, the Great Checker, Restrainer, Adjuster, Ruler, Giver of rewards and punishments, the God of Death and the Underworlds, (the astral plane).

यमस्थैर्ये ii. 39 'In or on stability of vows'; when the practice or observance of the vows, the self-restraint, has become confirmed, established firmly, habitual, natural.

यमादिसाधनेभ्यः iii. 7 (From or) than the ways or means of vows etc. (Some editions read यमादिभ्यः पञ्चभ्यः साधनेभ्यः).

यमाः ii. 30 Rules; restraints; regulations; vows. (See यतिः).

यया i. 36; ii. 45; iii 43; etc.

यस्मात् i. 51; iv. 30; etc.

यस्मिन् iv. 33; etc.

यस्य i. 1; ii. 38; iii. 14 iv. 11; etc.

यस्याम् iv. 22; etc.

यस्याः iii. 26; etc.

या i. 12; ii. 15; iii. 6; iv. 10; etc. She who; (fem: of यत्).

याः i. 4; ii. 11; etc.

यानम् iii. 51 'Means of going'; (the act of) going; vehicle; conveyance; car; (या, to go).

यानि iii. 50.

याम् iii. 49; iv. 11; etc.

यावत् i. 19; ii. 11; iii. 26 While; up to; as long as.

यावता iii. 52 By so much as.

यावत्सर्गायुषः iii. 26 With life-time as long as (a cosmic) creation; living as long as creation or manifestation lasts

यावन्तः iv. 21 (Pl: of यावत्).

—युक्तः i. 1; ii. 1, 23, 32; iii. 13.

युक्तः iii. 6, 13, 22; iv. 10, 15 'Joining in' (with the surroundings); fitted to the occasion; fitting, fit, appropriate; possessed of: filled or supplied and provided with; (see योगः).

युक्तम् iii. 13; iv. 19, 20.

युगपत् i. 24; ii. 13; iii. 13 'Two together'; simultaneously.

युज्येत iv. 12 Would be proper, feasible, fitting, possible; (युज्).

युतसिद्धावयवः iii. 44 With its parts or components in juxtaposition, but capable of independent and separate existence, each complete in itself (like a forest with trees); a mere collection.

युद्धे ii. 31 In battle.

यूथम् iii. 44 A crowd; a herd.

ये i. 29; ii. 13; iii. 52; iv. 10; etc. (Pl: of यः).

येन i. 20; ii. 47; iv. 17; etc.

येषाम् ii. 34; iii. 46; iv. 25; etc.

—योग—i. 28; ii. 23; iv. 21.

योग— i. 1.

योग—i. 1.

—योगः ii. 1, 44; iii. 6.

—योगः ii. 23.

योगः i. 2 The 'joining' of the mind to an object; the union of the individual soul with the Universal Soul; communion; junction, conjunction; con-ju-ga-tion; en-gage-ment; attune-ment, harmonisation, rapport; trance, ex-tasy (ecstasy);

fitness; regulation; attention; coming together; balancing; equilibrium. (युज्, Lat. *jugare*, to join, to yoke; *jugum*, युगं, a yoke. The *Amara-kosha* gives five meanings; the *Médinī-kosha*, eleven; Apte, in his Samskṛt-English Dictionary, gives thirty-eight. The root-idea of 'joining', runs through all the rest, which have grown up gradually).

योगः i. 1, 2; ii. 1; iii. 6.

योगदः i. 1. Bestower of yoga; giver of the bliss of union.

योगधर्मः ii. 33 The ḍharma, the way, the path of yoga.

योगपक्षे i. 1 'On the side of', help-ful to, yoga.

योगप्रतिपक्षाः i. 30 The 'other-side', 'opposite side', enemies, of yoga.

योगप्रदीपः iii. 51, 54 The light, the lamp, of yoga.

योगम् i. 28, 48.

योगमलाः i. 30 The 'stains, refuse, excretions, rubbish, dust 'and dirt', of yoga; that is, the obstacles which stand in the way of the successful achievement of yoga.

योगयुक्तः i. 1 Possessed of, full of, yoga.

—**योगस्य** ii. 23.

योगस्य iii. 8.

योगाङ्गानि ii. 28, 29 The 'limbs, members, parts', steps, of yoga. (See अङ्गानि).

योगाङ्गानुष्ठानम् ii. 28 Practice of the yoga-steps; 'following' of the yoga-disciplines, the yoga-exercises. (अनु, behind, स्था, to stand; to follow).

योगाङ्गानुष्ठानात् ii. 28 From or by following or practice of the successive steps of yoga.

—**योगात्** ii. 23.

योगात् i. 28; iii. 6.

योगान्तरायाः i. 30 The 'inter-rupters' or hinderers of yoga; the obstacles to yoga; the hindrances of, the difficulties in the way of, yoga.

योगिचित्तस्य iii. 20 Of the mind of the yogī.

योगिचित्तेन iii. 20.

—**योगित्वात्** iii. 17.

योगिनम् ii. 15, 16.

योगिनः iv. 7 Of the yogī.

योगिनः i. 21, 23, 28, 36, 37, 38, 40, 42, 43, 47, 50; ii. 10, 14, 35, 52, 55; iii. 16, 17, 18, 21, 41, 43, 45, 47, 51, 52, 53; iv. 6, 7.

योगिना iii. 26.

योगिनाम् i. 19; iii. 16.

योगिबुद्धिगम्यः iii. 53 Reachable, cognisable, by the intelligence of the yogi.

—**योगी** iv. 33.

योगी ii. 15; iii. 25, 33, 38, 49;

iv. 4 One who is practising yoga, or has achieved it,

—योगे iii. 21.

—योगे iv. 19.

योगे iii. 6.

योगेन iii. 6.

योग्यता ii. 53 'Yokability'; 'fitness to be employed or engaged'; fitness; ability; capacity; potency.

योग्यताऽवच्छिन्ना or **योग्यताऽवच्छिन्नाः** iii. 14 (Vāchaspaṭi explains this in two ways; as an adjective to शक्तिः, when it is to be read without the aspirate, as singular and feminine; or as an adjective to धर्मिणः, when it is plural and masculine and has the aspirate; the significance of the phrase itself remains the same either way). 'Cut off', 'marked off', delimited, characterised, defined, by capacity, ability, power, fitness, 'joinability'.

—योग्यत्वम् ii. 41.

—योग्यत्वानि ii. 41 (Fitness).

योजनशतसहस्रम् iii. 26 Hundred thousand yojanas; or extent of a hundred thousand yojanas. (A yojana is four krosha-s, roughly eight miles. Some editions read—साहस्रम्).

योजनसहस्राणि iii. 26 'Yojana-thousands'; thousands of yojanas.

योज्यम् ii. 33, 34; iii. 13 'To be applied'; 'applicable'; to be understood.

योज्यानि ii. 28.

योद्धृषु i. 24; ii. 18 'In, amongst', on, or to, the combatants, the soldiers, warriors, the actual fighters.

—योनयः iii. 51.

—र—

—रक्तम् iv. 23.

—रक्तम् iv. 17.

रक्तम् iii. 20.

रक्तः ii. 4; iii. 13 (रञ्ज् to color, tinge, affect, please). Affectionate; attached; enamoured.

—रक्तस्य iv. 29.

—रक्षण— ii. 30.

—रक्षा iii. 51.

—रचनम् iii. 17.

रजः ii. 18 The attribute of Rajas, restlessness, motility, mobility; the primal principle of all activity, motion, action, movement anywhere and everywhere in the world-process. (See गुणाः).

—रजस् iii. 49, 55.

—रजसः ii. 26.

रजसः ii. 17.

रजसा iv. 31.

रजस्तमसी iii. 35 Rajas and ṭamas.

रजस्तमोभ्याम् i. 2, 47.

रजस्तमोमूलम् iii. 43 Rooted in, having its root in, arising from, rajas and ṭamas.

रजोमात्रया i. 2 By or with a small measure or quantity of rajas.

रजोलेशमलापेतम् i. 2 'Moved away from', free of, the stain of the remnants of rajas (to the utmost extent possible, for entire abolition of any guṇa is impossible).

—रञ्जयति iv. 17 (See रक्तः).

—रत्न— ii. 37.

—रत्न— i. 35.

रत्नानि ii. 37 Gems; jewels; things valuable, unique, rare.

रमणकम् iii. 26 (Name of a country), 'the happy' or 'the enjoyable'.

रमते iii. 6 Rejoices; takes pleasure; revels. (रम्, to play, to rejoice, to amuse oneself).

रम्यताम् iii. 51 (You may) enjoy (yourself here).

रश्मिषु iii. 42 Among or in the rays (of the sun, moon, etc).

—रस— ii. 9 Sap, juice; hormone; humour (medical); taste; relish.

—रस— i. 30; ii. 9, 19; iii. 26, 36; iv. 21.

रसतन्मात्रम् i. 45; ii. 19 The 'root-matter' of taste; taste-in-itself. (See तन्मात्रम्).

रससंवित् i. 35 Consciousness of taste.

रसाः iv. 3 Juices; liquids.

—रसातल— iii. 26 Name of one of the seven underworlds.

रसादिवैश्वरूप्यम् iii. 14 'The all-formness of sap, etc'.; the property of being the universal, pervasive, continuous, generic substrata of all sorts of particular forms; the 'universality', continuity, continuum-ness, of the sensations of taste, etc.

रसान् iv. 3.

रसायनम् iii. 51 'The goal, home, locus, dwelling-place, of taste'; 'vital-fluid'; 'juice'; elixir; tonic medicine. (अय्, to go, to rotate).

रसायनेन iv. 1.

—राक्षस— iii. 26.

—राग— i. 37; ii. 3; iv. 17.

—राग— i. 8.

—रागः iv. 15.

रागः ii. 7 (रञ्ज्; see रक्तः). That which colors; or pleases, tinges, the mind with pleasantness; affection; love; liking.

रागः i. 11; ii. 4, 28; iv. 11.

रागकाले ii. 4 In, at, during, the moment, time, period, of affection, attachment, attraction, love.

रागजः ii. 15 Born of love.

रागद्वेषाभावे ii. 55 In the absence of both attraction and repulsion, attachment and repugnance, inclination and aversion.

रागद्वेषौ iv. 11 Love and hate; like and dislike; sympathy and antipathy.

रागधर्मकम् iii. 13 Having the property of affection.

रागस्य iii. 13.

—रागात् iii 26.

रागादिप्रवृत्तिः iv. 6 That from which love, etc., issue forth; or, by which love, etc., are set in motion; or, which 'pursues', goes forwards, operates, functions, in the way of love, etc.

रागानुविद्धः ii. 15 'Love-pierced'; threaded, shot through, penetrated, pervaded, permeated, with or by love.

रागाः ii. 15.

राजतवैदूर्यस्फटिकहेममणिमयानि iii 26 Made of silver, emerald, crystal, gold and precious stone.

—राजानम् iii. 38.

—रात्र—iii. 52.

रात्रिंदिवम् iii. 26 Night and day.

—राशि—iii. 26.

राशिः ii. 13 Heap, horde, crowd, host; class; group.

—राशिः i. 1.

रुचिः iv. 25 Predilection, inclination, disposition, pleasure, taste, agreeability, congeniality.

—रुणद्धि iii. 45.

—रुत—iii. 17 (रु, to sound, to make a sound, a noise; cf: to make a 'row'; animals' cries or voices.)

—रुद्धम् i. 1; iv. 21.

—रुन्द्धे iv. 16.

—रूढम् iii. 49, 54.

रूढः ii. 9 'Root'-ed; grown up, developed, matured; established; mounted up. (From रुह् to grow).

—रूढाः ii. 17; iii. 52.

—रूप— i. 17; ii. 23; iii. 21, 44, iv. 9

—रूप—i. 36; ii. 18, 19, 20, 27, 30; iii. 36, 48, 49, 50; iv. 20, 23, 33.

—रूपम् i. 2; ii. 22, 30; iii. 13, iv. 14. 16, 19.

रूपम् i. 1; iii. 44, 47; iv. 13 Form, figure, aspect; appearance; nature, state, characteristic; mode, manner; essence.

—रूपः ii. 20, 27; iii. 17, 18, 35, 52.

रूपज्ञानम् ii 28 Knowledge, sensing, apprehension, cognition, of form.

—रूपतः iv. 12.

रूपतन्मात्रम् i. 45, ii. 19 The 'that-only', the root-matter, of the sense-quality of visibility; 'color-form or vision-in-itself, sight-continuum'. (See तन्मात्रम्).

—रूपताम् ii. 21.

—रूपत्वात् iv. 9, 17.

रूपलावण्यवज्रसंहननत्वानि iii. 46 Beautiful form, fine complexion, and adamantine 'knit', 'binding together', articulation, (of the parts) of the bodily frame.

रूपसंवित् i. 35 'Consciousness of form'; optical sensation, sight, vision.

—रूपस्य ii. 21, 23, 28.

रूपस्य ii. 28; iii. 21.

—रूपाः i i. 15; iv. 9, 13.

—रूपा iii. 18.

रूपातिशयाः ii. 15; iii. 13 'Aspect-excesses'; manifestations, predominances, prevalences of 'forms'. (This and the word following it in the text, viz., वृत्त्यतिशयाः, are explained by Vāchaspaṭi in a special manner. He says, the rūpas are eight: ḍharma, jṇāna, vairāgya, aishvarya, and their opposites,—see i. 2; and that the vṛṭṭis are 'pleasure, etc.' i. e., pleasure, pain, perplexity, as the context shows. This is not very clear. Vāchaspaṭi's own comment on *Sānkhya-kārikā*, 12, helps us to a simpler explanation; the rūpas, forms, or natures, and the vṛṭṭis, activities, or functionings, of the three guṇas, when in excess, conflict with one another or each other; when not abnormally strong, but fairly balanced, (not exactly equilibrated either, for that means pralaya), they manage, each to have its proper turn. This explanation fits in better, it seems, with the context in ii. 15, and also in iii. 13; which Vāchaspaṭi's rather far-fetched explanation of rūpas, and cursory one of vṛtṭis, does not seem to do so well and easily).

—रूपायाः ii. 20.

—रूपी iv. 1.

रूपे iii. 21.

—रूपेण ii. 21, 22; iii. 13; iv. 24.

रेखा iii. 13 Line; stroke (of pen).

रोगः ii. 15 Disease. (रुज्, to break, destroy, kill).

रोगहेतुः ii. 15 The cause of disease.

रोमहर्षाश्रुपातौ iv. 25 'Horripilation', i. e., excitement, standing on end, of the down on the skin and the hair, and the falling of tears.

—रोह— iv. 28.

—रोहः ii. 4.

—रौरव— iii. 26 (A purgatory).

—ल—

—लक्षण— iii. 13, 53.

—लक्षण— ii. 19; iii. 13

लक्षणम् i. 43; iii. 13 That by means of, or because of, which, a thing is seen, recognised, distinguished; distinctive feature or mark; characteristic; differentia. (लक्ष्, to see, to aim at).

—लक्षणम् iii. 13.

—लक्षणः iii. 47.

लक्षणतः iii. 13 From, because of, by means of, the mark.

लक्षणपरिणामक्रमः iii. 15 Order, succession, sequence, march, of the changes, transformations, gradual unfolding, developement, evolution, of the characteristics or marks. (See धर्मलक्षणावस्थापरिणामाः).

लक्षणपरिणामः iii. 13 The transformation of the characteristics.

लक्षणपरिणामे iii. 13

लक्षणभेदः iii 13 Difference of characteristics.

—लक्षणयोः iii. 15.

—लक्षणस्य ii. 19.

लक्षणस्य iii. 13, 14.

—लक्षणाः ii. 19.

लक्षणानाम् iii. 13.

लक्षणान्तरम् iii 13 Another characteristic.

लक्षणाभिधित्सया i. 2 By, because of, wish to declare the distinctive marks; in order to define, to characterise.

लक्षणाभ्याम् iii. 13.

लक्षणैः iii. 13.

—लक्षिताः iii. 13.

लक्षिताः iii. 13 Distinguished; particularised; characterised; specified; marked; observed.

लग्नम् iii. 26 Attached, clasped, clinging, in contact.

लघिमा iii. 45 Lightness; the yogic power of becoming light at will.

लघीयसा iii. 22 By very light.

लघुः iii. 42, 45 Light (the opposite of heavy).

लघुतूलसमापत्तेः iii. 42 From, by, because of, rapport with, (concentration on and attainment of the lightness of) light cotton-down.

लघुत्वात् iii. 42 Because of lightness.

लघुषु iii. 42,

—लपद्भिः iv. 21.

—लपन्तः iv. 14.

—लब्ध— ii. 17, 21.

लब्धपर्यवसानः iv. 33 That which has found a conclusion, an ending. लभ्, परि + अव+सो, to end).

लब्धविवरः iii. 51 That which has found a hole, crack, breach, loophole, opportunity (for entrance).

लब्धवृत्तिः ii. 4 That which has

found existence, way of existence, livelihood, pa'ency, activity, functioning, manifestation, expression.

लब्धस्थितिकम् i. 39 That which has attained fixity, stability.

लब्धस्थितिकस्य i. 41,

लब्धायाम् i. 30 On or in (the stage or state) which has been gained, achieved.

लब्धायुष्कम् ii. 13 That (birth) which has secured (or got determined) a life-period, or long life. (The new incarnation has its span of life determined by Karma).

लब्धालोकः iii. 51 One who has found light.

—लब्धिः iv. 16.

लब्ध्वा iii. 42 Having found or gained.

लभते i. 32, 33, 36, 37, 38, 39, 40, 48; ii. 22, 23, 28; iii. 6 Finds, gains, obtains, attains. (लभ्, to gain, to find).

—लभ्य— iv. 10.

—लभ्यन्ते ii. 4.

—लम्बनैः iv. 11.

—लम्ब— iv. 23.

—लम्बन— iii. 2, 17, 20.

—लम्बनम् i. 32; iii. 35.

लवणोदधिना iii. 26 By the 'salt-sea'.

—लाभ— iv. 9.

—लाभः ii. 42 (लभ्, to gain. Gain; achievement).

—लाभः i. 21, 22, 23; iii. 43, 48; iv. 1.

लाभात् ii. 38.

लाभे i. 23.

—लावण्य— iii. 46 ('Saltiness'; crystal-like gleam of complexion).

—लिङ्ग— i. 45.

लिङ्गम् iii. 13, 41 Mark; characteristic quality; a manifestation. (From लयं गच्छति, that which goes into laya, absorption, dissolution, and therefore has come out of latency previously, by inference; or लीयते च गच्छति च, that which 'lies' hid, and also goes forth; i. e. all marks, qualities, which unfold and fold back, appear and disappear, emerge and immerge; see प्रलयम्). (Another and more common meaning of the word is 'the mark of sex', the reproductive male organ. The etymology indicates why this conventional meaning has arisen).

—लिङ्गमात्र— ii. 19,

—लिङ्गमात्रम् i. 45.

लिङ्गमात्रम् ii. 19 Only (a, or the, or as a) mark; a mere principle; a mere germ of productivity; a seed of manifesting power. (Dr. Ganganath

Jha translates it as 'solely mergent').
लिङ्गमात्रः ii. 19.
लिङ्गमात्रस्य i. 45.
लिङ्गमात्रे ii 19.
—लिङ्गस्य ii. 19.
लिङ्गस्य i. 45
लिङ्गात् i. 45.
—लीने ii. 10.
—लेखा ii. 5.
—लेश— i. 2.
लोकः i. 43; iii. 25; iv. 23 That which shines, is seen, is visible, is lighted up; the world. (लोक्, लोच्, to see, perceive; to shine).
लोकप्रत्यक्षेण i. 49 By the 'worldly', physical, familiar, sense-cognition or perception; by means of the ordinary physical senses.
लोकबुद्ध्या iii. 17 By the 'world-mind'; by public opinion; by 'common sense', common convention.
—लोकम् ii. 5.
लोकमध्ये iii. 26 In the 'middle' or 'midst' of, within or amongst, the lokas, worlds.
लोकस्य ii. 13.
लोकालोकपर्वतपरिवाराः iii. 26 'Having the Lokā-loka mountains for family'; surrounded by those mountains.
लोकाः iii. 26.
लोके ii. 17, 42; iii. 26.
लोचनाभ्याम् ii. 5 With the two eyes.
लोभमोहक्रोधप्रभवः ii. 12 Born of greed, perplexity (silliness and terror), anger.
लोभक्रोधमोहपूर्वकाः ii. 34 'Preceded by', due to, caused by greed, anger, or confusion (stupidity, and fear).
लोभः ii. 7 (लुभ्, to covet, to 'love'). Avarice; greed; craving.
लोभात् ii. 14.
लोभेन ii. 34
लोलीभूतस्य iii. 38 Of the restless, the ever-moving, the disturbed.
—लोहित— iii. 29.
लौल्यात् ii. 15 From, because of, restlessness, cupidity.

—व—

वः i. 1; iii. 51 You; (=युष्मान्; acc: pl:).
—वक्तरि i. 7.
वक्तव्यम् ii. 25 'Declarable'; to be declared.
वक्तव्या iii. 1 Do: (fem:).
वक्ता i. 7 Speaker.
वक्ति ii. 24 Says. (वच्, to speak, to 'voice').
—वक्त्रः i. 1.
वक्ष्यति ii. 5 Will say; will declare. (वच्).
वक्ष्यमाणा iii. 45 The 'being-declared'; to be declared in

a moment; (that which) is going to be said.

वक्ष्यामः ii. 29, 40, 46 We will say.

वक्ष्यामि ii. 33 I will say.

—वचनाः iv. 14.

वचनात् ii. 53 From the speech, the word.

वचनीयम् iv. 33 To be said; to be answered.

—वचनीयम् iv. 33.

वचनीयः iv. 33.

—वचनीयः iv. 33.

—वज्रसंहननत्वानि iii. 46 (Adamantine knitting together of the parts of the body).

वज्रोपमः iii. 51 'Diamond-like'; adamantine.

वञ्चितः iii. 51 Deceived; (masc:). (वञ्च्, to deceive; also, to go).

वञ्चिता ii. 30 Deceived; deceptive; (fem:).

वडवा iii. 53 Mare.

वत्सानुसारिण्यः iii. 44 'Calf-following'; (like cows) running after their calves.

वध्यस्य ii 34 Of the (animal or person) to-be-slain.

वनम् iii. 44 Forest.

वमनम् i. 34 Vomiting; throwing out; (वम्, to 'vomit').

—वरण— iv. 31.

—वरण— iv. 31.

वरणभेदः iv. 3 Breaking of the ridge (of the field); making a hole or passage through the ridge; breaking up, removal, of the hindering envelope, veil, screen, shell, obstacle, wall, bar; clearing the way; breaking through the obstruction; (वृ, to cover, surround, c nceal; also, to choose).

वरणभेदः iv. 3.

—वर्ग— iv. 24.

—वर्जिताः iii. 15.

—वर्ण— iii. 17.

वर्णः iii. 17 Letter; articulate letter-sound; (also color, and 'caste' or 'vocational class').

—वर्णम् iii. 17.

वर्णयन्ति iii. 53 (They) describe; say; (pl: ; वर्ण्, to paint, to describe).

वर्णाः iii. 17.

वर्णेषु iii. 17.

वर्णैः iii. 17.

—वर्त्तते ii. 18; iii. 6, 26, 41; iv. 3, 25.

वर्त्तते i. 1; ii. 16 Exists; (वृत्, to be, happen, act, turn round).

—वर्त्तन्ते ii. 15; iii. 26; iv. 16.

वर्त्तन्ते ii. 44; iii. 26. (pl:).

वर्त्तमानः i. 24, 32; ii. 18, 34; iii. 13, 14, 52 Existent; (masc:).

वर्त्तमानभावक्रमः iii. 15 'Succession into', 'striding into', passing into the condition of being the present.

वर्त्तमानभावात् iii. 15 Because of the condition of 'the present'; because of being present.

वर्त्तमानम् ii. 16, 23; iii. 13; iv. 12.

—वर्त्तमानयोः iii. 14.

वर्त्तमानयोः i. 24.

वर्त्तमानलक्षणम् iii. 13 The characteristic of being 'present'.

वर्त्तमानलक्षणयुक्तः iii 13 Possessed of do:.

वर्त्तमानसमये iii. 13 In the present time.

—वर्त्तमानस्य iv. 11.

वर्त्तमानस्य ii 26; iii. 13, 14, 49; iv. 12, 33.

वर्त्तमानाः i 24; ii. 18; iii. 14; iv. 13.

वर्त्तमानातीताभ्याम् iii. 13 From the present and the past.

—वर्त्तमानाभ्याम् iii. 13.

वर्त्तमानीकरणे iv. 12 In or for the 'making present', the manifesting (of something pre-existent but not manifest at present).

—वर्त्तमानेन iii. 51.

—वर्त्तमानेषु iii. 13.

वर्त्तमानौ ii. 18.

—वर्त्तयन्ति iv. 10.

—वर्त्तितम् iv. 25, 31.

—वर्त्तिष्यन्ते iv. 12.

—वर्त्तेत iii. 13.

—वर्त्त्यते iv. 3.

वर्धमानम् i. 25 Increasing; (वृध्, to increase).

वर्षम् iii. 26 A continent or large country (of the earth).

—वर्षम् iii. 26.

वर्षाणि iii. 26

वलयाकृतयः iii. 26 Ring-shaped, 'bangle'-shaped; (pl:).

वलयाकृतिना iii. 26.

—वव्रूते ii 23.

—वशावर्तिनः iii. 26.

—वशात् i. 19; iii. 38; iv. 9.

—वशित्वम् iii. 18, 48.

वशित्वम् iii. 45 Having control, command, mastery, (over the elements and their products; a mystic yogic power).

वशित्वेन iii. 39.

—वशिनः iii. 26.

वशी iii. 45, 49 Conqueror; controller; sub-jugator (of the elements).

वशीकारः i. 40 Control, command, mastery.

वशीकारः i. 40.

वशीकारसंज्ञा i. 15 (A stage of yoga, of utter desirelessness; the characteristic or quality or consciousness of perfect 'self-control, command, mastery'.

वशीकारसंज्ञा i. 15.

वशीकारसंज्ञायाम् i. 35; ii. 26; iii. 49.

—वशीकारात् i. 40.

वशीकृत्य iii 35 Having subjugated, brought under control.

वश्यता ii. 55 Controllability.

—वसन्ति iii. 26.

वसुमती iii. 26 'Wealth-possessing'; (a name of) the Earth.

—वस्तु— i. 9, 44, 46.

वस्तु iv. 16, 17 Thing; substance; reality; entity; fact; real object; a thing objectively and independently real; (वस् to abide, reside).

वस्तु i. 20; ii. 4; iv. 10, 11, 12, 14, 15.

वस्तुज्ञानयोः iv. 15 Of thing and thought, substance and knowledge, object and apprehension thereof.

वस्तुतत्त्वम् iv. 14 The 'thatness', essence, of a thing or substance; (its peculiarity, individuality, that which makes it a separate, distinctive thing).

वस्तुनः i. 49.

वस्तुपतितः iii. 52 Fallen within (the category of) substance.

वस्तुप्रत्यभिज्ञानात् iii. 14 Because of re-cognition of things.

वस्तुमात्रात्मकाः iii. 15 Of the nature of all, or only and mere, entity.

वस्तुरूपम् iv. 16 The form, or of the form of, substance.

वस्तुशून्यः i. 9 Empty of substance or reality.

वस्तुशून्यः iii. 52.

वस्तुशून्यत्वे i. 9 In the state of being do:.

वस्तुसतत्त्वम् ii. 5 (Having a 'thatness', a reality, an essentiality, 'like' that of, or in 'common' with, true and real substance); positivity (not mere negativity); substantiality.

वस्तुसमाहारः iii 52 Actual, real, substantial summation, gathering up, accumulation; (सम्, from all sides, + आ, together, up to, + हृ, to take, to carry).

वस्तुसाम्ये iv. 15 'In sameness, similarity, equality of things'; objects being or remaining the same; when the object is the same.

वस्तुसाम्ये iv. 15.

वस्तुस्वरूपः iii. 52 Of the form of substance, reality, objectivity; as if real, substantial.

वस्तुस्वरूपम् iv. 14 The 'own-form', characteristic essential nature of (a) substance; the reality of (an) object.

—वस्त्रम् iii. 22

वस्त्रस्य iv. 33 Of wearing cloth, garment, raiment; (वस, to wear).

वस्त्राणाम् ii. 11 Do:; (pl:).

वस्त्वन्तरम् ii. 5 Another thing.

वहति i. 12; iii. 45 Carries; flows; blows; blows away; (वह्, to flow, to carry).

वह्निः iii. 44 Fire.

वा i. 23, 34, 35, 36, 37, 38, 39; iii. 22, 33; iv. 34 Or.

वा i. 5; ii. 1; iii. 1; iv. 3; etc.

वाक्, वाग्, वाङ् ii. 30, 36; iii. 17 Speech; voice.

वाक्पाणिपादपायूपस्थानि ii. 19 Voice, hand, foot, excretory, and reproductive organs.

वाक्यशक्तिः iii. 17 The power, force, significance, effect, of the sentence, 'the to-be-spoken', the 'speakable'.

वाक्यशेषः ii. 41, 47 The rest of the sentence.

वाक्यार्थे iii. 17 In the meaning of the spoken sentence.

वाक्ये iii. 17 In the sentence.

वाङ्मनसे ii. 30 Speech and mind

—वाचक— i. 27, 28

वाचकः i. 27 Designator, declarer, speaker, signifier, indicator, denoter. (See वक्ति).

वाचकः iii. 17.

—वाचकत्वम् i. 27.

—वाचकत्वस्य i. 28

—वाचकम् iii. 17.

वाचकम् iii. 17.

वाचकेन i. 27.

वाचा ii. 15; iv. 11 By speech.

—वाच्य— i. 28.

वाच्यः i. 27; iii. 13 The designated, indicated, denoted; the to-be-declared.

वाच्यम् ii. 13.

वाच्यवाचकत्वम् i. 27 Relation, condition, of denoter and denoted, name and thing.

वाच्यवाचकशक्त्यपेक्षः i. 27 Looking to dependent on, the 'power' of the relation do:.

वाच्यस्य i. 27; iii. 17.

—वाच्याः ii. 18.

वातपित्तश्लेष्माणः iii. 29 'Wind, bile, and phlegm'; the vital currents of nerve-forces and gases, and of the digestive and assimilative juices, and of the mucous, albuminous, and other semi-solid and solid tissues. (See –पित्त–; the works on Āyurveda describe five kinds of vāta and five of shléshmá, also).

वातेन iii, 22 By the wind.

—वादन— iv. 10.

—वादाः iv. 21 (Doctrines; views; opinions; theories).

—वादिनः iv. 20.

वान्तावलेही ii. 33 'Vomit-licker'; (cf: "The dog returning to its vomit"; लिह् , to lick).

—वायवः iii. 51.

वायवीयस्य i. 45 Of the aerial or airy.

—वायु— ii. 19.

वायुः iii. 44, 45 Air, wind. (वा, to blow).

वायुबलः iii. 24 Possessed of the might of the wind.

वायुबले iii. 24 In or on the might of the wind.

वायुम् i. 31.

वायुविक्षेपनियमेन iii 26 By the law of the flow of the wind; by the laws of air-currents.

वायोः i. 34; ii. 49.

—वार्त्ताः iii. 36 (See प्रातिभ—).

वार्त्ततः iii. 36 From subtile, super, or clair-olfaction.

वार्षगण्यः iii. 53 (Name of a Ṛṣhi).

—वासना— ii 1, 15, 24; iii. 17; iv. 8, 9, 10.

—वासना ii. 24.

वासना ii. 9 'In-dwelling', 'deep-seated', desire; inherent propensity, tendency, proclivity, inclination, ' primal appetite, impulse, urge, yearning, craving, instinct, innate disposition, hormé, élan. (वस्, to dwell, occupy, abide, reside; वास्, to perfume, incense, spice, flavour; see आशयाः and संस्काराः .

वासनाः i. 24; ii 13; iv. 8, 9, 10, 11, 12 Do: (pl:).

वासनानाम् iv. 8 Of do:.

वासनानाम् iv. 10, 11.

—वासनाभिः iv. 24.

वासनाभिः ii. 13.

वासनाम् iv. 11

वासनारूपाः iii. 18 Of the nature of deep-seated desires, instincts, innate dispositions, inherent appetites.

—वासिता ii. 24.

—वाहयन्ति iv. 19.

—वाहिणः (नः) ii. 27.

—वाहिता iii 10.

वाहिनी i. 12 Flowing; carrying.

—वाही ii 9 (See वहति).

—वाही ii. 9.

विकरणभावः iii. 48 'Organ-lessness'; condition of being devoid of instruments or organs.

विकरणभावः iii. 48.

—विकलः i. 17.

—विकल्प— i. 6.

— विकल्प— i. 11, 42, 43; ii. 34.

विकल्पः i. 9 Doubt, (as opposite of संकल्प, resolve); alternative; hypothesis; imagination, fancy; illusion; supposition; theory; postulate.

विकल्पज्ञानबलेन iv. 14 'By or on the strength of imaginative or imaginary knowledge'; or knowledge of imagined, imaginary, fancied, fanciful, illusive, objects.

विकल्पते i. 36 Alternates; occurs as one or other (of such and such objects).

विकल्पबहुत्वम् ii. 23 Plurality, multitude, of alternative (theories).

—विकल्पस्य i. 43.

विकल्पहानिः i. 44 Abolition of all doubt and element of unreality.

विकल्पाः ii 23 Alternatives; possible views, ways of thinking; (pl:).

विकल्पितः i. 9 Imagined; postulated.

—विकल्पैः i. 42

—विकार— ii. 28; iii. 48.

विकारकारणम् ii. 28 Cause of transformation.

विकारम् iv. 2, 3 Product; transformation (with an implication of badness); ('specially created', 'artificial', as contrasted with प्रकृति, Nature, and the non-artificial, uncompelled, 'natural' state, and प्रकार, good form or manner; वि, prefix expressive of separation, division, particularisation, privation, opposition, + कृ, to 'cre-ate', to do).

विकारसंज्ञा iii. 13 The designation of 'product', effect, 'curdlement', 'precipitate'; or, the consciousness that (it) is a (specifiable) 'product', a 'transformation', (not the homogeneous, unspecifiable, indistinguishable original 'plasm', root, source. (संज्ञा means both 'consciousness', and 'name' by which we become 'conscious' of or recognise a thing).

विकाराकरणात् ii. 23 From the non-making of 'transformations', 'products', 'changes': because of not producing any transformations.

विकारनित्यत्वात् ii. 23 Because of 'permanent' or continuous, unremitting, incessant transformation.

—विकाशि (or सि) iv. 10.

—विकाशि (or सि) नी iv. 10.

विक्रियमाणः iii. 17 Being transformed, corrupted, changed, artificialised.

—विक्रिया iii. 13.

विक्षिप्तचित्तस्य i. 31 Of the distraught mind; of him whose mind is distracted, maddened; of one obsessed demented.

विक्षिप्तचित्तानुपपत्तिः i. 32 Impossibility of the distracted mind; (i. e , there could be no such thing as 'distraction' at all).

विक्षिप्तम् i. 1, 32 'Flung away'; carried away; possessed, obsessed, maddened (by some one fixed idea); monomaniacal; lunatic; mad. (वि + क्षिप्, to throw, fling).

विक्षिप्ते i. 1.

—विक्षेप— iii. 26.

विक्षेपप्रतिषेधार्थम् i. 32 For the sake of prohibiting, preventing, precluding distraction.

विक्षेपसहभुवः i. 31 Connate or

congenital with, or companions of, distraction.

—विक्षेपाः i. 30 (Distractions, diversions. 'flingings', away).

—विक्षेपा: i. 30

विक्षेपाः i. 30, 32 Obsessions.

विक्षेपोपसर्जनीभूतः i. 1 Become subsidiary or subservient to distraction; bye-product of obsession.

—विघातात् i. 24 (By defeat or destruction).

—विचार— iii. 26

—विचार— i. 17

—विचारः i. 17.

विचारः i. 17 Thought, reflection, cogitation, consideration, pondering; opinion, view; (वि + चर् to move about).

विचारणा ii. 13 'Revolving, moving about, (in mind)'; 'taking (the mind) about or around'; circumspection; consideration; question, problem, subject or matter for thought and reflection.

विचारविकलः i. 17 Devoid of thinking, cogitating, reasoning, argument.

—विचारा i. 44 (See निर्विचारा).

—विचारा i. 44.

विचारानुगतः i. 1 Accompanied with reflective thought, (especially regarding subtile objects).

—विचार्यते ii. 13 'Is taken round', revolved, considered.

—विचित्र— iii. 26.

—विचित्रः iii. 26.

विचित्रः ii 13; iv. 25 Variegated; 'much-imagined-in-special-ways'; marvellous; wonderful; (masc:).

—विचित्रया ii. 15.

विचित्रा ii. 13 (Fem: some editions read चित्रा).

विचित्रीकृतम् ii. 13 'Made multiform, multi-colored'; variegated.

विच्छिद्य ii. 4 Having broken; with breaks; (वि + छिद्, to cut, sever, divide).

—विच्छिन्न— ii. 4.

—विच्छिन्नः ii. 4.

विच्छिन्नः ii. 4 Severed; cut up; broken; scattered; dispersed; sporadic.

विच्छिन्नाः ii. 4.

विच्छिन्नादित्वम् ii. 4 The state of being broken etc.

—विच्छेदः ii. 49. (Break; stoppage; cessation).

विजयः ii. 18 Conquest; victory. (Some editions read जयः).

विजानीयात् iii. 27, 28, 29, 35 Let him know; (ज्ञा, to know).

विज्ञातपूर्वापरान्तस्य ii. 9 'Of him to whom are known the before and the after ends'; of one who knows the beginning and the end.

विज्ञातारम् iii. 35 (To; the knower, perceiver

विज्ञानधर्माः i. 42 The properties of perception. (Some editions read ज्ञानधर्माः).

—विज्ञानम् i. 49; iii. 36.

विज्ञानम् i. 30; iii. 34 'Special know'edge'; perception; concrete 'science'; concrete thought.

विज्ञानविसहचरः iv. 14 Apart from, 'not going with', unaccompanied by, perception or knowledge.

विज्ञानस्य ii. 28 Of concrete knowledge. (Some editions read ज्ञानस्य).

—विज्ञानात् ii. 28.

विज्ञानेन iii, 14.

विज्ञेयम् ii. 5 To be known; knowable.

—वितथम् ii. 45.

—वितर्क— i. 43; ii. 32, 33; iii. 26.

वितर्कः i. 17 (The Bhāshya explains this as) 'the gross, coarse, unrefined, occupation of the mind with a concrete, gross, non-subtile object'. But aphorism ii. 34 explains the plural form of the word as meaning 'impulse to kill, etc'. See वितर्काः).

वितर्कबाधने ii. 33 'On oppression by evil thoughts'; when evil passions disturb (the mind).

—वितर्कया i. 44.

वितर्कविकलः i. 17 Devoid of, free from, 'gross functioning'.

वितर्कविचारानन्दास्मितारूपानुगमात् i. 17 Because of association with, or accompaniment by, (a) 'gross activity', i. e., (doubt-tinged, emotion-biassed) perception, or thought, of some physical object; (b) more subtile (bias-free, purely rational) thought; (c) mere feeling of joy; (d) mere feeling of self. (These four progressively successive states and stages of samprajñāṭa or 'conscious' meditation or 'absorption' may be illustrated by an extract from a recent book, which happens to be at hand at the time of writing, on what has come to be known as 'psycho-analysis', also 'the *new* psychology'. The extract is in exact accord with the undisputed Sānkhya and Yoga doctrine, that saṭṭva-rajas-ṭamas, or jñāna-icchhhā-kriyā, are inseparable, though one prevails at a time; and some western exponents of the '*old* psychology' also have noted the fact. "The working of each instinct involves three mental processes, the cognitive, the affective or emotional, and the conative......A very large part of our actions and opinions are entirely determined by our complexes, and by far the largest parts are more or less colored by them, even when we are able to emancipate our judgments so far as to be able to act or judge to some extent independently of the bonds of our complexes. In *purely* rational thinking, which is a great deal rarer than most people imagine, the *affective* bond is of a different nature. The love of objective truth is here at least a part of the *affect* involved" : Tansley, *The New Psychology*, p. 68. 'Complex' is a newly technicalised word, with a special significance, which includes what is clearly indicated by the words 'emotional bias', 'passionate prejudice', 'interested thought', etc. One of the main objects of yoga-discipline is to loosen and dissolve these 'complexes', kāma-jatāh, 'matted roots of desire', hṛḍaya-granṭhayah', 'heart-knots'; and thereby to purify and maximise saṭṭva to the utmost, and free it from and minimise, first the lower and then also the finer, rajas and ṭamas, as much as possible, complete abolition being impossible. The first important exercise for this purpose is to learn to discriminate between a word, its meaning, i. e., the object meant, and the knowledge or consciousness of the word, on the one hand, and the object, on the other. By persistent practice of such discrimination, there arises the ability to discriminate, in the total mental mood or 'complex', what and how much is the element of the 'affective', 'emotional', 'passionate' bias or prejudice, and what and how much that of 'pure reason', i. e. 'cognitional', 'intellectual', judgment. (a) Sa-viṭarkā seems to be the meditation wherein this freedom from all such bias and passion, due to the coarser rajas and ṭamas, of hostility to any one and wish to hurt him, etc., has not been secured; e.g., the *odium theologicum*, and almost all political or commercial thinking i. e., 'meditation'. When such freedom is secured, the meditation becomes viṭarka-vikala or nir-viṭarkā, (i. 17, 43).

Apparently this nir-viṭarkā is the same as (b) sa-vichārā (i. 17 and 44), purely rational deep thinking, absorbed reflection, especially with reference to 'subtile' objects, ideas, opinions, or superphysical things. When even that disappears, we have vichāra-vikala (i. 17) or nir-vichārā; and this seems to be the meditative mood or state of mind in which there is no thinking, (i. 17) but only a voluminous feel of pleasant ease, positive joy, bliss, (c) ānanḍ-ānugaṭā, is left; as in the proximity of a loved person, or when resting in a comfortable bed after a hard day's work, to take a more common if less idealised experience (d) Asmiṭā-nugaṭā is the rapt, absorbed, mood in which even that feel of joy has disappeared, ānanḍa-vikala (i. 17), and only the feel of self-existence, 'I-am-ness', remains, something like the consciousness just before falling asleep, but, in this case, alert and wakeful consciousness, without any sleepiness).

—वितर्का i. 42, 43.

—वितर्का i. 42, 43, 44.

वितर्काः ii. 34. Evil thoughts and emotions; also, doubts; fancies; suppositions; arguings.

वितर्काः ii. 33, 34.

वितर्काणाम् ii. 34.

वितर्कान् ii. 33.

वितर्कानुगतः i. 1 Accompanied by viṭarka; (see वितर्का···नुगमात्, *supra*).

—वितर्कायाः i. 43.

वितर्केषु ii. 34.

—वितल—iii. 26.

वितानितम् iii. 22 Spread out; stretched out, (तन्, to stretch).

—वितृष्णस्य i. 15.

—वितृष्णस्य i. 15.

वितृष्णस्य i. 15 Of the 'thirst-less', the desireless.

—विदित— ii. 31.

विदुः ii. 5 They know; (विद्, to know).

विदुषः ii. 9 Of the wise man; the knower.

विदुषः ii. 9.

विदेहप्रकृतिलयाः iii. 26 The bodiless' and the 'merged-in-Prakṛṭi'; (see प्रकृतिलयाः).

विदेहप्रकृतिलयानाम् i. 19 Of the do:.

—विदेहा iii. 43.

विदेहानाम् i. 19; iii. 48 Of the Viḍéha-beings, the 'bodiless' ones; (a class of very highly advanced jivas, souls, gods, just short of, or on the threshold of kaivalya, moksha).

—विद्रुम् iv. 10.

—विद्वया— iii 17.

विद्यते iv, 6 Exists; is known.(विद्, to know; also to exist; cf: *esse ist percipii).*

विद्यमानम् ii. 24 Existent; being cognised.

विद्यमाने ii. 23.

विद्यया i. 14 By learning, knowledge.

—विद्या i. 4, 5.

—विद्या— ii. 46.

—विद्या i. 11; ii. 4, 5, 23; iv. 4. 11.

—विद्याम् ii. 4.

—विद्यायाम् iv. 25.

विद्याविपरीतम् ii. 5 Opposed to, reverse of, true knowledge.

—विद्वान् i. 25.

विद्वान् ii. 15; iv. 30 The knower; the wise man.

—विधम् iv. 6, 10.

विधमन्ति i. 35 (They) break, beat, tear, batter down; blow away. (ध्मा, to blow; to cast away).

—विधर्मा iii. 35 (Different-natured).

—विधारणाभ्याम् i. 34 (Holding of breath).

—विधारणाभ्याम् ii. 53.

—विधीयन्ते iii. 38.

विधूतक्लेशरजसः ii. 26 Of (the saṭṭva) which has shaken off the (taint of the) rajas-restlessness of the 'afflictions', 'sins', 'miseries'.

विना iii. 18 Without.

—विनायकाः iii. 26 (A race of ḍevas).

—विनाशः iii. 51 (Some editions read —विनाशी).

विनाशः iv. 12 Destruction; annihilation; loss. (नश्, to perish).

विनाशप्रतिषेधात् iii. 13 'Prohibition', denial, of annihilation.

—विनाशि iii. 13 (Transient; destructible'; 'perishable').

—विनाशी iii. 51.

विनाशिनाम् iii 13.

विनियोगः iii. 6 Application, employment, direction; appointment; (वि + नि + युज्).

विनिर्मुक्तम् i. 24 Freed; gone beyond; emancipated.

विनिवर्त्तते i. 51; iv. 25 Reverts, returns, retires, goes back, ceases, turns away. (Some editions read निवर्त्तते).

—विनिवृत्तिः iv. 25 (Cessation, because of satisfaction. Some editions read निवृत्तिः).

विनेयेषु ii. 38 In the 'teachable', 'guidable', 'leadable', the to-be-led or instructed; (pl:; वि + नी, to lead, guide).

विन्ध्यः i. 7 The Vinḍhya mountain.

विन्यस्य iii. 25 Having 'put down', laid down, thrown down; arranged in order. (वि + नि + अस्, to throw).

विन्यासः iii. 29 Placing; arrangement; laying out.

विपच्यमानम् iv. 8 Fruiting; being matured; (पच्, to cook).

विपरिवर्त्तन्ते iii. 26 (They) revolve; (pl:; वि+परि+वृत्).

विपरिवर्त्तमानेन iii. 51 By (me,) revolving.

विपरिवर्त्तेत iii. 13 May, or would, exist transformed (? into the unchanging from the changeful); or (interpreting the word in a sense which is the reverse of the usual sense) may 'specially' (वि), and 'all round' (परि), exist (वर्त्तेत) unchanged; or, would change while being unchanged (a self-contradiction); (the context requires some such peculiar interpretation). (Some editions read परिवर्त्तेत).

—विपरीतम् ii. 5.

विपरीतम् iii. 22 'Gone to the other, the opposite, way'; opposed, reversed, turned round; (वि+परि+ई, to go).

विपरीता i. 2.

—विपर्य्यय i. 11.

—विपर्यय— i 6.

विपर्ययः 8 'Turning the other way round'; inversion; perversion; distortion; error; 'erring'; 'straying'; mistake; delusion; 'turning the truth upside down'; topsy-turvy; (cf. 'demon est deus inversus', i. e. 'Satan is God inverted'. वि+परि+ई).

विपर्ययः iv. 30.

विपर्ययज्ञानम् i. 30 'Falsehood-knowledge'; false or erroneous knowledge.

विपर्ययज्ञानवासना ii. 24 The innate, ingrained, inherent, indwelling, 'infiltrated' 'infused', 'insteeped', 'in-soaked', 'permeating', 'pervading', tendency to erroneous knowledge. (See वासना).

विपर्ययज्ञानवासनावासितः ii. 24 Permeated with the propensity to erroneous apprehension.

विपर्ययस्य ii. 28.

विपर्ययाः ii. 3.

विपर्ययेण iv. 3.

विपर्य्ययोपारोही i. 9 'A-mount-ing' to error.

—विपर्यास— ii. 5.

विपर्यासगन्धः i. 48 A faint 'smell', flavor, savor, trace, distant touch, of error, perversion, reversal, 'throwing upside down', 'topsy-turvy-dom', thrusting away from the right course. (Some editions read विपर्यासज्ञानगन्धः; वि+परि+अस् to throw).

विपर्यासप्रत्ययकाले ii. 4 In or at the time of 'error-notion', erroneous belief.

—विपर्यासम् iii. 45.

—विपाक— i. 24; iv. 8.

—विपाक— ii. 13, 34; iii. 43, 50, 55; iv. 89.

—विपाकः ii. 13.

विपाकः i. 24; ii. 13; iv. 8 'Cooking'; maturation; ripening; (the result of the process of maturation, viz; consequence, result, fruit, product, fruition. वि + पच्).

विपाककालाभावः ii. 13 Lack of time for maturation; 'absence of maturation-time'.

विपाकप्ररोही ii. 13 (Capable of) 'sprouting into maturation'; putting forth the sprout of maturation.

—विपाकम् i. 19; ii 3, 13; iii. 22; iv. 8.

विपाकम् ii. 34.

—विपाकस्य ii. 5, 13, 34.

विपाकहेतवः iii. 18 Causes of fruition or maturation.

विपाकाभिमुखम् ii. 13 'Facing towards ripening', 'with face turned to fruition'; tending to bear fruit; ready to put forth, or come to, fruit; on the point of, or approaching, fruition.

विपाकारम्भी ii. 13 The commencer, initiator, of fruition.

विपाके ii. 15.

—विप्रकृष्ट— iii. 25 (Distant).

—विप्रकृष्ट— iii. 36.

—विप्रकृष्टस्य i. 49.

विप्रकृष्टे iii. 25 In or on a distant (object). (वि + प्र + कृष् , to draw, drag, plough).

विप्रलीनानाम् ii. 27 Of the hidden, disappeared, merged, absorbed, dissolved; (pl: some editions read प्रविलीनानाम् ; see प्रलयम्).

विप्रसृतम् ii. 15 Extended; (वि + प्र + सृ, to 'slide', move).

—विप्लवा ii. 26 (See अविप्लवा and प्लवते).

विभक्तः i. 42; v. iv. 15 Divided off; separate; (वि + भज्).

विभक्तम् ii. 6.

विभक्तानाम् i. 42.

—विभजन्ते iv. 23.

विभज्य iv. 33 Having distinguished, distributed; 'distributively'; discriminately.

—विभज्य iii. 17.

विभज्यमानाः i. 42 Being separated, distinguished.

—विभाग—ii. 6, 18.

—विभागः iii 17.

विभागः iii. 17 Division.

—विभागाः ii 18.

विभुत्वम् Pervasiveness; omnipresence; all-pervading greatness and glory; (वि + भू to be in a special, impressive, great, glorious manner).

विभुनः iv. 10 Of the omnipresent.

विभूतिपादः iii. 1 The 'foot', 'quarter', section, chapter, of or on 'great beings', excellences, superphysical accomplishments, powers, splendours, glories, perfections.

—विभ्रमः ii. 24.

विमर्दवैचित्र्यात् iii. 13 Because of the wonderfulness of the 'crowding', the mutual stress, crush, squeezing, struggling, wrestling.

—विमल— i. 1 (Stainless).

विमुक्तः iv. 30 Free; liberated.

विमुक्तस्य iv. 31.

—विमुक्तिः ii. 27.

विमुक्तिः ii. 27 Freeing; freedom.

वियुक्तः iii. 13 'Dis-joined'; separated; (masc: वि + युज्).

—वियुक्तः iii. 13.

वियुक्तम iii. 13.

वियोगकारणम् ii. 28 The cause of separation, 'dis-junction'.

—वियोग— ii. 18.

वियोगस्य ii. 23 Of separation, dis-junction.

वियोगान्यत्वधृतयः ii. 28 Disjunction, and hetereity (otherness, change into another form), and 'holding on' (stability, are three of the nine causes).

विरक्तः i. 16; ii. 4; iii. 13 Desireless; 'passionless'; indifferent; 'dis-affected'; 'dispassionate'; (वि + रञ्ज्, to color, to tinge, to 'affect' with attachment).

विरक्तम् i. 2 Detached, satiated, ceased from attachment; (neu:).

विरक्तस्य iv. 29.

विरज्यमानस्य iii. 50 Of the (yogi who is) becoming desireless.

विरागाय iv. 21 For freedom from attachment; for desirelessness.

विरामप्रत्ययः i. 18 'The idea, the thought of cessation from enjoyment'; (or, as Vāchaspati explains it, that extreme vairāgya, desirelessness, which is) the 'cause' of the cessation, the non-being, of the functionings of the mind. (See प्रत्ययः).

विरामप्रत्ययाभ्यासपूर्वः i. 18 Preceded by the practice of the thought of cessation, laya, nothingness; or, by the practice of extreme vairāgya as the cause of extinction, cessation, (of mental activity).

—विरुद्धः ii. 5.

विरुद्धत्वात् i. 24 Because of contradictoriness, opposition.

—विरुद्धा ii. 55.

विरुध्यन्ते ii. 15; iii. 13 Are opposed (to each other); conflict (with each other; वि + रुध्, to obstruct, oppose, besiege, enclose).

विरूपः ii. 20 'Other-formed'; without form; different in form.

विराधात् ii. 15.

—विरोधात् ii. 5; iv. 3.

—विरोधिनः i. 51.

—विरोधिन्यः i. 5.

—विरोधी i. 51.

विलङ्घ्य iii. 6 Jumping across; having skipped over, crossed over.

—विलीय i. 51.

—विवक्षितः iii. 44.

—विवरः iii.51.

विवरम् iv. 22 Hole; hollow; cave; chasm.

—विवर्जनात् ii. 17.

विवर्त्तते iii. 26 Revolves; turns round.

विवर्द्धते ii. 28 Increases; (वृध्, to increase, to grow).

विवर्द्धन्ते ii. 15 Do: (pl:).

विविच्यते ii. 19 Is discriminated, distinguished; (वि + विच्, to divide, separate, discriminate).

विविच्यन्ते ii. 19 Do: (pl:).

विवृद्धिः ii. 28 Increase; expansion.

विवृद्धिकाष्ठाम् ii. 19 The stage or condition of expansion.

—विवेक— iii 55; iv. 27.

विवेकख्यातिः ii. 26 'Discrimination-cognition'; discriminative knowledge; awareness of the distinction between Purusha and Prakṛti, Self and not-Self, God and Nature. (वि, विच्, ख्या, to tell, relate, declare, make known; to know).

विवेकख्यातिः i. 2; ii 26, 28; iv. 29.

विवेकख्यातिरूपः ii. 27 Of the form of do:.

विवेकख्यातेः ii. 28; iv. 29 (Up to, till) discriminative knowledge (arises).

विवेकख्यातेः ii. 28.

—विवेकज—iii. 55.

विवेकजज्ञाननिम्नम् iv. 26 'Low', inclined towards, the knowledge born of discrimination.

विवेकजज्ञानभागिनः iii. 55 Of the (yogi) 'sharing in,' possessing, the knowledge do:.

विवेकजज्ञानात् iii. 53 From the knowledge do:.

विवेकजम् iii. 52, 54 Born of discrimination

विवेकजम् iii. 18, 49, 52.

विवेकजस्य iii 33

विवेकज्ञानावरणीयम् ii. 52 (Karma 'belonging to', 'connected with', the veiling of, i. e,). veiling, barring (the rise of) discriminative knowledge.

विवेकदर्शनाभ्यासेन i. 12 By the perseverent practice of the discriminative vision.

विवेकनिम्नम् iv. 26 Inclined towards discrimination.

विवेकप्रत्ययः iii. 50 The idea, notion, consciousness, awareness, belief, of destination.

विवेकप्रत्ययप्रवाहः ii. 26 The flow, current, stream of discriminative consciousness.

विवेकविषयनिम्ना i. 12 Inclining

towards the region of discrimination.

विवेकस्रोतः i. 12 The stream, current, of discrimination.

विवेकार्थिनः i. 20 Of him who seeks discriminative knowledge.

विवेकिनः ii. 15 Of the discriminator; (विच्, to separate).

विवेकिनः ii. 5, 27.

—विंशति iii. 45.

—विशन्ति ii. 34; iii. 43; iv. 3.

विशारदीकरोति i. 10 'Makes keen, acute, refined, purified'; (शृ, to tear away, destroy; शरत्, the autumn, 'destroys', 'clears away', the dirt, the mud and mire, caused by the rains).

विशारदीभवति iii. 5 Becomes lucid, limpid, pellucid.

—विशिष्ट—i. 4.

विशिष्टः iii 15, 35 Differentiated; distinguished; specialised. (वि + शिष्, to distinguish, to leave a residue behind).

—विशिष्टम् i. 44, 50.

—विशिष्टा ii 20

विशिष्टानाम् ii. 4.

—विशिष्टाम् iv. 22.

विशुद्धः iii. 35 Very pure; (वि + शुध्, to become pure).

विशुद्धिः ii. 52 Purity; purification.

विशेष—ii. 19.

—विशेष—i. 7, 25, 43; ii. 19; iii. 1 , 44, 47; iv. 12, 13.

विशेषः iii. 35.

—विशेषः i. 10, 25, 43; ii. 19; iii. 35, 53.

विशेषः i. 22 Special degree; surpassingness; excel-lence; peculiarity; (see विशिष्टः).

विशेष: i. 22, 35, 49; ii. 15, 51; iv. 24 Special; particular; differential; specific; 'that which marks off from the rest.'

विशेषणापरामृष्टा ii. 20 'Untouched' by specifying or differentiating qualities

विशेषदर्शनबीजम् iv. 25 The germ or seed of special and true vision.

विशेषदर्शिनः iv. 25 Of him who sees the 'minute peculiarity'; of the deep seeker, the profound investigator, who sees the precise differentia and propria; (the yogi who has seen the true nature, the being, of the Self).

विशेषदर्शिनः iv. 25.

विशेषपरिणामः ii. 19 'Specific' transformation.

विशेषप्रतिपत्तौ i. 25 In or on the learning of particulars.

—विशेषस्य ii. 19.

विशेषस्य i. 49.

—विशेषाः ii. 19.

विशेषाः ii. 19; iii. 44, 53 Special, specific, particular forms; specifications; particularisations; concretions; materialisations.

—विशेषाणाम् ii. 19.

विशेषाणाम् ii. 19.

—विशेषात् i. 22, 23, 34.

विशेषान् iii. 13.

विशेषानुग्रहणम् iv. 12 Special favoring or helping. (Some editions read विशेषानुग्रहम्).

विशेषार्थत्वात् i. 49 Because of having a special, particular, concrete object.

विशेषार्थत्वात् i. 49.

विशेषावधारणप्रधाना i. 7 Predominantly cognitive, discriminative, or determinant of the specific, demarcating, distinguishing, differentiating, particular or peculiar characteristic or aspect (of a given object).

विशेषाविशेषलिङ्गमात्रालिङ्गानि ii. 19 (a) Specific, differentiated, particular, concrete (as opposed to abstract), (b) non-specific, generic, abstract, undifferentiated, (c) archetypal, and (d) differenceless, imperishable, homogeneous. (See लिङ्गम् and अलिङ्गम्).

विशेषे iii. 17.

विशेषेण i. 49.

विशेषेभ्यः ii. 19.

—विशेषेभ्यः ii. 19.

—विशेषेषु ii. 19.

विशोका i. 36 'Sorrowless'; serene; tranquil.

विशोका iii. 49.

विश्वभेदसमापन्नम् i. 41 Become transformed to, having 'attained' to, conforming to, the 'diversity of the world'; having taken on, assumed, the form of all sorts of diverse things.

विश्वभेदोपरक्तम् i 41 Tinged with diverse objects, or with the diversity of objects, or with all sorts of things.

विश्वरूपाभासम् i. 41 Appearing as, showing forth, the form of all sorts of objects.

विश्वासोपगतेषु ii. 12 Towards the trusting

—विष— i. 1; ii. 15.

विषमविषधरः i. 1 Bearing the wondrous venom, or the venom of non-equilibrium.

—विषय—i. 11, 15; ii. 51, 54.

—विषय— i. 12, 15, 16; ii. 1; iii. 48.

—विषयः i. 14, 32, 47, 49; ii. 20, 51; iii. 17, 48 (Some editions read **एकबुद्धिविषयम्** in iii. 17).

विषयः i. 43, 45; ii. 20, 50; iii. 16; iv. 14, 18 (वि, specially, सि to bind, fasten, permeate, pervade). Object; range; domain; subject-matter; object of sensuous enjoyment.

—विषयताम् ii. 17, 22.

—**विषयत्वम्** i. 45.

—विषयत्वम् ii. 4, 20.

—विषयत्वात् i. 8; ii. 17, 20; iii. 35.

विषयत्वात् iv. 23 Because of objectivity, objectness, being object.

विषयदोषदर्शिनः i. 15 Of him who sees the defects or evils of sense-enjoyment.

विषयप्राग्भारम् iv. 26 'Heavy-fronted' with, heading or gravitating towards, heavily inclined in the direction of, sense-enjoyment.

—**विषयम्** i. 37; iii. 54.

—विषयम् i. 35, 49; ii. 23; iii. 17, 41; iv. 12.

विषयम् i. 32.

विषयमृगतृष्णया iii. 51 By the mirage, the 'deer-thirst', of sense-objects.

विषयवती i. 35 Having an object; (fem:).

विषयवती i. 35, 36.

विषयवायवः iii. 51 The winds, strong breezes, storms, of sense-objects, sense-attractions.

विषयविशेषः iii. 47, 53 Special or peculiar object.

विषयविषयिनिर्भासम् iv. 23 Showing forth, reflecting, both object and subject.

विषयसम्प्रयोगात्मगर्धः i. 30 Craving of the nature of attraction towards sense-objects; 'greed for con-junc-tion with objects of sense'.

विषयसुखकाले ii. 14 At the time of sensuous pleasure.

विषयसुखम् ii. 15 Sensuous pleasure; the pleasure yielded by sense-objects.

—विषयसुखापेक्षया iii. 18 In comparison with sense-joys, sensuous delights.

—विषयस्य ii. 23.

विषयस्य i. 11; ii. 4.

विषयस्रोतः i. 12 The stream of sense-enjoyments.

—**विषया** i. 44, 49.

—विषया i. 7, 44, 49; iii. 35.

—विषयाः i. 5; iii. 26.

विषयाः iv. 17.

—**विषयाणाम्** i. 33.

विषयाणाम् ii. 30.

—विषयाणि iii. 4.

विषयात्मकम् iv. 23 Of the nature of 'object'.

विषयानालोचितः ii. 51 (?) Without cognisance, reconnoitre, thought, of the range (of the breath, but, instead, by a sudden effort).

विषयानुवासितः ii. 15 Permeated with (craving for) sense-objects.

विषयान्तरम् ii. 28 Another object.

विषयान्तरे ii. 4.

विषयाभावात् i. 3, 43 Because of non-existence of object; for lack of object.

विषयाभासम् iv. 19 Object-showing; object-reflecting.

—विषयायाम् i. 35.

विषयावधारणात् ii. 51 From ideation of objects.

विषयिणा iv. 23 By the subject.

—विषयी—iii. 20 (The subject; the knower or experiencer of an object).

—विषयी—iv. 16.

—विषये i. 15.

विषये ii. 4; iii. 1.

—विषयेण i. 8.

—विषयेभ्यः iii. 51.

—विषयेषु ii. 31.

विसदृशप्रत्ययप्रवाही i. 32 'Streaming with dissimilar cognitions, ideas, thoughts, perceptions'.

—विसर्जनीयाः iii. 17.

—विसहचरः iv. 14.

विहन्यते iv. 33 Is slain, defeated, destroyed. (हन्, to kill).

विहरति iii. 42, 49 Roams; plays; amuses or enjoys oneself; (वि + हृ to take away).

विहाराः iv. 10 Pleasure-places; places of recreation.

विहृत्य iii. 42 Having played about, enjoyed himself.

वीतरागचित्तालम्बनोपरक्तम् i. 37 'Tinged with the support (as object of meditation) of a being with a passionless mind'; filled with the image, the thought, of a being who has risen above all passions.

वीतरागविषयम् i. 37 Having for object the passionless; i e., a being who has transcended human passions.

वीरासनम् ii. 46 (Name of a meditation-posture).

—वीर्य—i. 20 Determined vigour; indomitable and irresistible energy).

—वीर्य—i. 35.

वीर्यम् i. 13, 20; ii. 34 Virile power; energy; semen; vigor; seminal virility.

—वीर्यम् ii. 34.

वीर्यलाभः ii. 38 Gain of energy.

—वीर्यस्य i. 20.

वीर्याक्षेपात् ii. 34 By the breaking down of (the other's) strength.

—वीर्याणि iii, 23.

वृक्षः iii. 17, 44; iv. 14 Tree.

—वृत्तः i. 7; ii. 4; iii. 13.

—वृत्तम् iii. 9, 13; iv. 15.

—वृत्तयः i. 30, 35.

—वृत्तयः ii. 11; iv. 18.

वृत्तयः i. 5 (Pl.; see वृत्तिः). Moods, modes, functionings of the mind.

वृत्तयः i. 5, 11; ii. 11.

—वृत्ति—i. 2; ii 15.

—वृत्ति—i. 1, 18; ii. 5, 20; iv. 9.

—वृत्तिः ii. 50.
—वृत्तिः i. 4, 35; ii. 4, 20; iii. 39; iv. 22.

वृत्तिः i. 10; iii 43 (वृत् to exist; see वर्त्तते); way of existing, (also of earning one's living) modification, state (of mind); function; functioning, activity; operation: working.

वृत्तिः i. 7, 9; iii. 47; iv. 10
वृत्तिभिः i. 5.
—वृत्तिभिः i. 30.
—वृत्तिम् ii. 20; iv. 22.
वृत्तिम् ii. 18.
वृत्तिमात्रेण iii. 1, 43 By mere functioning, activity, stirring.

वृत्तिलाभः iii. 43, 48 Attainment of functioning, operativeness, existence; finding expression.

वृत्तिषु i. 35.

वृत्तिसंस्कारचक्रम् i. 5 'The wheel of mood and seed'; the rotation of germ and manifestation, conduct and tendency, functioning and disposition, habitual practice and acquired character.

वृत्तिसारूप्यम् i. 4 'Same-formedness, uniformity, similarity, identity, with the moods.'

—वृत्तेः i. 41.
—वृत्तेः—i. 17; ii. 19, 20; iv. 22.
वृत्तेन ii. 33.
वृत्त्यंतिशयाः ii. 15; iii. 13 Excesses of moods, or manifestations, functionings.

—वृत्त्या ii. 15.
वृत्त्या iv. 23.
—वृद्धि—ii. 19.
वृन्दारकाः iii. 26 (A race or class of perennially youthful and beautiful gods).

वृश्चिकविषभीतः ii 15 Afraid of the venom (or sting) of the scorpion.

वृषदंशविपाकोदयः iv. 9 'The uprising, coming into manifestation, of the cat-maturation'; reincarnation as a cat.

—वृषदंश—iv. 9.
वेद ii. 17 Knows; (विद्, to know).

—वेदन— iii. 36 (Knowing; but here the word is used in the technical sense of superphysical sense of touch).

—वेदनम् iii. 18, 38.
—वेदनाः iii 26.
—वेदनात् iii. 38.
—वेदनात् iii. 38; iv 19.
वेदनात् iii. 36 From the power or faculty known as vedana; (see—वेदन—).

—वेदनीयः ii. 12 (To be known, inferred).

—वेदनीयः ii. 12, 13.
—वेदनीयत्वात् ii. 34.
—वेदनीयम् ii. 13.
—वेदनीयस्य ii. 13.

वेदयन्ति ii. 13 Make known; declare. (Some editions read वेदयन्ते).

वेदयन्ते ii. 13; iv. 22 (The sages) know, or declare.

—वेदाय iv 21.

वेदितव्यः iii. 13 To be known, borne in mind; (masc:).

वेदितव्यम् i 1; iii. 21 Do: (neu:).

वेदितव्या i. 35 To be known; (fem:).

वेदितव्ये ii. 13 (Two) do: (neu:).

—वेदिनम् iv. 21.

—वेलायाम् ii. 18.

—वेश— iv 13.

—वेशयितुम् iv. 3

वेश्म iii. 34 Palace.

वेष्टितः iii 26 Surrounded.

—वेष्टिताः iii. 26.

वैजयन्तः iii. 26 (The name of the palace of Indra, the king of the gods).

—वैतृष्ण्यम् i. 16 ('Thirstless-ness'; freedom from all desire).

वैतृष्ण्यम् ii 15.

—वैदूर्य— iii. 26 (Lapis lazuli; sometimes used for मरकतं or emerald, and also for इंद्रनीलः or sapphire).

वैदूर्यप्रभानुरागात् iii. 26 Because of being tinged with the lustre of sapphire.

वैनतेयबलः iii. 24 Having the strength of 'the son of Vinatā', Garuda, the king of the birds, in Purāṇa mythos).

वैनतेयबले iii. 24.

वैनाशिकः iv. 24 'Annihilator'; 'nihilist' (in philosophy); denier of the existence of Ātmā and of life apart from the physical body.

वैनाशिकैः iv. 21.

वैरत्यागः ii. 35 Abandonment of hostility.

—वैराग्य— i. 2

वैराग्यम् i. 15 Absence of desire, attachment, passion or craving for the world; detachment; dispassion; surfeit; disgust with, revulsion from, the world. (वि + राग).

वैराग्यम् i. 15, 16, 18.

—वैराग्यात् iii. 50.

वैराग्यात् i. 20.

—वैराग्याभ्याम् i. 12.

—वैराग्याभ्याम् i. 32.

—वैराग्ये iv. 10.

वैराग्येण i. 12.

वैशारद्यम् i. 47 Lucidity. (See विशारदीकरोति).

—वैशारद्यात् i. 36.

—वैशारद्ये i. 47.

वैशारद्ये ii. 26; iii. 49.

—वैश्वरूप्यम् iii. 14.

वैश्वरूप्यम् iii. 17 'Omniformity'; universality.

—वैषम्यम् i. 30 (Inequality;

dissimilarity; differentiation; वि + सम).

वैहायसम् iii. 51 'Spatial; aerial; celestial.

—व्यक्त— i. 16, 44; iii. 14.

—व्यक्तः ii. 4; iv. 9.

व्यक्तम् ii. 5 'Made clear', thrown into relief', 'picked out', 'outlined', 'shown cut', manifested. (वि + अञ्ज्; see अभिव्यक्तिः) .

—व्यक्तम् ii. 5.

व्यक्तसूक्ष्माः iv. 13 Manifest and subtile.

व्यक्तात्मानः iv. 13 Of manifest nature; or 'manifesting their nature'.

—व्यक्तानाम् iii. 50.

व्यक्ताव्यक्तधर्मकेभ्यः i 16 From or with (the guṇas with) manifest and unmanifest qualities or functions; (dis-gusted) with (the guṇas) whether manifesting or not manifesting their properties, i. e , in their manifest as well as subtile form.

—व्यक्तिः iv. 8 (Manifestation).

—व्यक्तिः ii. 23; iii 13, 14, 17; iv. 12.

—व्यक्तिकम् iv 12.

—व्यक्तिकेन iv. 12.

व्यक्तिभिः ii. 19 By manifestations.

व्यक्तिम् iii. 15.

व्यक्तिविशेषापन्नम् iv. 12 Attained to specific manifestation.

व्यक्तेः iii. 13.

व्यक्तेन i. 43.

—व्यक्तौ iii. 13.

व्यक्तौ iii. 13.

—व्यग्रस्य iii. 53 (Of the distracted).

व्यग्रे iv. 16 In the (state of the mind being) distracted; when distracted. (वि, away from, without, + अग्रं, front; not attending to what is in front).

व्यङ्ग्येन iv 12 By the to-be-manifested.

व्यज्यन्ते iv. 8, 9 Are shown forth, made manifest.

—व्यज्यमाना iii. 15.

व्यज्येत iv. 9 Would be manifested.

—व्यञ्जक—i. 11, 43; ii. 4; iii. 13; iv. 9. (The cause of manifestation; that which evokes, stimulates, induces, manifestation).

—व्यञ्जकम् iv. 9.

व्यतिरिक्तः i. 24.

—व्यतिरेकेण iv. 10.

व्यनक्ति iv. 11 Developes; brings out; throws into relief; shows forth; unfolds; precipitates; discovers; discloses. causes; (व्यञ्ज्).

व्यपदिश्यते i. 9, 24 Is qualified, characterised, indicated; is attributed, assigned (as attribute, or deed).

व्यपदिश्यन्ते i. 24 Do: (pl;).

व्यपदिश्येते ii. 18 Do: (dual).

व्यपदेशे i. 9 In characterisation.

—व्यपदेश्य— i. 44; iii. 49.

—व्यपदेश्याः iii 14.

—व्यपरोपणात् ii. 34

व्यभिचरति iii. 17 Strays away; behaves unfaithfully. (वि + अभि + चर्, to move about).

—व्यभिचाराः ii. 31.

—व्यय— ii. 19.

व्यवतिष्ठते i. 5 Stands, rests. (वि + अव + स्था).

—व्यवधि— iii. 53.

व्यवसायव्यवसेयात्मकाः iii. 49 Of the nature of 'determination', ascertainment, and the determinable, the to-be determined, to-be-ascertained. (वि + अव + सो, to put an end to, to finish).

व्यवसायात्मकाः iii. 47 Of the nature of determination; (pl:).

—व्यवसीयेत iii 47.

—व्यवसेय— iii. 49

व्यवस्थितानाम् iii. 49 Of the 'seated', established, existing, manifesting; (pl:).

—व्यवहार— i. 43; iii. 17.

व्यवहारः i. 9 Behavior, conduct; business; convention; mutual intercourse or commerce; (वि + अव + हृ).

—व्यवहारम् ii. 23.

व्यवहारम् i. 32.

व्यवहाराः i. 43.

—व्यवहित— iii. 25.

—व्यवहित— i. 49; iii. 36.

व्यवहितः iv. 9 Screened; hidden; intercepted, interrupted. (वि + अव + धा).

व्यवहितत्वात् iii. 13 Because of being hidden, interrupted, obstructed.

व्यवहितानाम् iv. 9.

—व्यवहितानाम् iv. 9.

व्यवहिते iii. 25.

—व्यवहितेन ii. 17.

व्यवायी ii. 33 Adulterous. (वि + + अव + अय्, to go; 'to go to a person of the other sex').

—व्यसनम् ii. 55.

व्यसनम् ii. 55 Addiction; a habit that 'carries away', 'carries a person off his feet', 'flings him away from the right path', 'misleads', 'leads astray'; (वि + अस्, to throw).

व्यस्यति ii. 55 Flings, carries, whirls, away.

व्याकरणीयः iv. 33 To be 'construed grammatically'; to be expounded in detail; to be put specifically; (वि + आ + कृ).

व्याकरणीयम् iii. 17

व्याक्रियेत iii. 17 Would be interpreted.

व्याख्यातः ii 5, 22 (Has been) explained; (masc:; वि + आ + ख्या; see ख्याति:).

व्याख्यातम् i. 45; ii. 20 Do: (neu:).

व्याख्याता i. 44 Do:; (fem:).

व्याख्याता i. 43, 44.

व्याख्याताः iii. 13 Do:; (pl:).

व्याख्याताः iv. 1.

व्याख्यायिष्यन्ते ii. 19 Will be explained; (pl:).

व्याख्येयाः i. 11; iii. 52 To be explained, to be made known.

व्याधिः i. 30 Illness.

व्याधि— i. 30 Do:.

—व्याधित— ii. 12.

व्याधिप्रभृतयः i. 29 Illness etc.

व्यानः iii. 39 (Name of one of the nervous-vital forces).

—व्यापदम् ii. 5.

व्यापदम् ii. 5 Misfortune, ill-fare, evil 'happening'; (acc:).

—व्यापार— iii. 17; iv. 12.

व्यापारः iii. 13 'Operation'; functioning; activity; business; work. (वि + आ + पृ).

—व्यापारम् iii. 13, 14.

व्यापारमात्रेण ii. 18 Only by their operation.

—व्यापारा iii. 14.

व्यापारान् iii. 14.

व्यापारेण iii. 13.

व्यापी iii. 39 Pervasive; (वि + आप्, to find; 'all-finding').

व्यावृत्तः i. 7 Changed, inverted, reverted, turned round; marked off; (masc:).

—व्यावृत्तिः iii. 44 (Differentiation; demarcation; distinction).

व्युत्थानचित्ते i. 3 In the 'exhibition-mind', the up-risen, 'rampant', active, exhibitive (mood or state of) mind.

व्युत्थानधर्मिणा iii. 10 By (the mind) having the 'exhibition-quality'.

व्युत्थाननिरोधयोः iii. 13 Of exhibition and inhibition, 'getting-up and holding-back', 'going forward and withdrawing', 'letting oneself go and holding oneself in', pro-gress and re-gress, pro-cess and re-cess, advance and restraint.

व्युत्थाननिरोधसंस्कारयोः iii. 9 Of the two tendencies, the exhibitional (wakeful, outgoing) and the inhibitional (indrawing), the processive and the recessive.

व्युत्थाननिरोधसमाधिप्रभवैः i. 51 Together with (the dispositions) born of exhibition, inhibition, and rapport (absorbed meditation, communion).

व्युत्थानम् iii. 13 Exhibition (as opposite of inhibition); wakefulness; 'uprising', 'getting up', 'standing up'; display (as opposite of retirement); activity; patency (as opposite of latency); dynamicity (as opposite of staticity); tenseness; tumescence; impulsiveness; impetus; momentum.

व्युत्थानसंस्काराः iii. 9, 13 Propensities, dispositions, to exhibition; exhibitive proclivities.

व्युत्थानसंस्काराभिभवात् i 50 Because of the overpowering, the defeat, suppression, of the wakeful, exhibitive, out-going, tendency.

व्युत्थानसंस्काराशयम् i. 50 The 'receptacle', 'capsule', 'cyst', 'seed-pod', 'germ', of the tendency to outward activity.

व्युत्थानसंस्कारेण i. 14 By the exhibition-tendency.

व्युत्थाने iii. 37 In or on exhibitiveness, dynamicity; in the state of out-turned-ness; when the mind is in the outward exhibitive mood.

व्युत्थाने i. 4.

व्युत्थितचित्तः ii. 1 One with aroused, wakeful, uprisen, active mind.

व्युत्थितचित्तस्य iii. 37.

व्युत्थितदर्शनानाम् iii. 52 Of those whose vision is 'arisen', outward-turned, extro-spective, (therefore erroneous).

व्यूढम् iii. 26 Organised; marshalled; arranged in order; firmly bound together; (वि+वह्).

—व्यूह— iii. 27, 29 (Organisation; arrangement).

व्यूहम् iii. 27 Organisation; system; place; order; (military) formation (of an army, as in squares, or with wings, etc. वि + ऊह्, to reason, to arrange in an ordered manner).

—व्यूहम् ii. 151 iii. 29.

—व्यूहानाम् iii. 45.

व्यूह्यमानम् ii. 15 Being carried, borne, rushed, whirled along. (The correct reading seems to be व्युह्यमानम्, i. e., वि+उह्यमानम्, passive form of वह्; and it is so printed in the Poona Ānandāshrama edition; but the editions by Bālaram and by the Bombay Government Central Press, print व्यूह्यमानम्, probably by inadvertence).

व्रजन् ii. 32 Going; (व्रज्, to go).

—व्रतम् ii. 31 (See महाव्रतम्).

—व्रतम् ii. 31,

व्रतानि ii. 30, 32 Vows; observances.

श

शक्तः iii. 45 Able; 'might-y'; (शक्, to be able).

—शक्ति—ii. 18; iii. 17, 18, 21.

—शक्तिः ii. 6, 23, iii. 17, 50; iv 22.

शक्तिः iii. 14, 15, 21 Ability; that which 'might do' a thing; 'might'; power; force; energy; potency; potentiality.

शक्तिमात्रप्रतिष्ठानाम् ii. 4 Of those (afflictions, moods) which exist only as potencies.

—शक्त्योः ii. 6, 23.

—शक्त्योः ii. 6. 17.

शक्यः i. 49 Possible; able to be done; (masc:).

शक्यम् ii. 15 Do:; (neu:) .

शङ्कते ii. 18 Doubts; suspects.

—शङ्का iv. 19.

शतम् iii. 13 Hundred.

शतसहस्रायामः iii. 26 A Hundred thousand yojanas in extent. (Some editions read—साहस्र-).

—शतसाहस्रम् iii 26 (Some editions read —सहस्रम्).

शतस्थाने iii. 13 In the place of the hundreds.

—शतेन iv 9.

—शब्द—i. 2; ii. 18; iii. 36.

शब्दः i. 42, 49; iii. 17; iv. 14 Sound; word.

शब्दग्रहणानुमितम् iii. 41 Inferred from sound-apprehension; (some read शब्दग्रहणनिमित्तम्, i. e., the conditional cause of the apprehension of sounds).

शब्दज्ञानमाहात्म्यनिबन्धनः i.9 'Bound up with', dependent on, the greatness or power of 'verbal knowledge', word-perception, knowledge of words.

शब्दज्ञानानुपाती i. 9 Following upon, arising out of, the cognisance or perception of the sound or word; 'pure verbalism'; merely verbal knowledge (an image conjured up by words, without any reality or substance behind it; a concept without a percept).

शब्दज्ञानानुपाती iii. 52.

शब्दतन्मात्रम् i. 45, ii. 19 Sound-in-itself; the 'that-measure', 'that only', 'root-form', of sound. (See तन्मात्रम्).

शब्दतन्मात्रभावेन iv. 14 In the form of pure sound.

शब्दधर्माः i. 42 The properties or functions of word-sounds.

शब्दपृष्ठेन iv. 33 'With', 'by means of', the 'back' of (mere) words; (riding on airy words only, without substance or reality).

शब्दप्रत्यययोः iii. 17 Of the word and the notion (cognition); of the term and the concept.

शब्दभावेन iv. 14 In the form of sound. (Some editions read शब्दतन्मात्रभावेन)

शब्दविषयम् iii. 41 Having sound for object.

शब्दसंवित् i. 35 Consciousness of superphysical subtile sound.

शब्दसङ्केतश्रुतानुमानज्ञानविकल्पस्मृति-परिशुद्धौ i. 43 On the purification (i. e. the clearing away,) of the memory (i e , the associations born) of the conventions of language and of evidential and inferential and hypothetical knowledge; in other words, when the mind has been freed from all pre-conceived notions, biases, pre-judices, arising from the conventional meanings of (catch-) words, from hearsay, from (hasty) inference, and from (mere) imagination and fancy.

शब्दसङ्केतस्मृतिपरिशुद्धौ i. 42 On the clearing away, the 'purification', the 'cor-rec-tion', the righting, of the 'memory', the associations, due to the conventional usage of words.

शब्दसहगतः iii. 17 Accompanying (but not inherently connected with) the word.

शब्दात् i. 7 From word, or sound.

शब्दादयः ii 19; iii. 44; iv. 19 Sound etc.; (pl:).

शब्दादिः iii. 47 Do:; (sing:).

शब्दादिज्ञानम् ii. 55 The cognition of do:.

शब्दादिविषयवत् iv. 18 Like such objects as sounds, etc.

शब्दादिषु ii. 55.

शब्दादिसम्प्रयोगः ii. 55 Contact with, or use and employment of, sound etc.

शब्दादीनाम् iii. 13; iv. 14.

शब्दाद्यन्तर्धानम् iii, 21 Disappearing, 'screening' off, of sounds etc. (अन्तर्+धा).

शब्दानाम् iii. 41.

शब्दार्थः iv. 19 Word-meaning.

शब्दार्थज्ञानविकल्पानुविद्धः i. 42 'Pierced through', penetrated or permeated with, ideas (or hazy notions or doubts regarding words, objects, and cognitions thereof.

शब्दार्थज्ञानविकल्पैः i. 42 By (doubtful and indistinct ideas or) suppositions (fancies, biases) connected with the word, the sense, the cognition; i. e, notions regarding language, thing, and thought.

शब्दार्थप्रत्ययाः iii 17 Word, object, and idea.

शब्दार्थप्रत्ययानाम् iii. 17 Of do:.

शब्दार्थसम्बन्धः i. 27 The relation of word and meaning, sound and sense.

—शब्देन iii. 44 iv. 21.

शब्देन i. 7; iii. 44 By word or sound

शय्यासनस्थः ii. 32 Stretched on a bed or seated on a seat.

—शय्येते iv. 10.

शरणम् ii, 15, 33 Refuge; shelter; place of shelter; house.

—शरीर— iii. 38.

शरीरनिरपेक्षा iii. 43 'Not looking to', independent of, the (physical) body.

शरीरप्रतिष्ठस्य iii. 43 Of the (mind) fixed, seated, in the body.

शरीरम् ii. 28; iii. 44 (शृ, to crumble). 'That which is incessantly crumbling'; the body. (*Manu-smṛti*, i. 17, says that sharīra is so named because it is made up of 'shat', six, things, as chief components; it is the sheath or locus of the mind, manas, and the five sense-organs).

शरीरस्थ ii. 28.

शरीराणाम् ii. 28

शरीरात् iii. 43.

—शरीरात् iii. 38.

शरीरादिक्रियाम् iii. 45 The operation of the body, etc

—शरीरादिसाधनापेक्षम् iv. 10 Looking to, waiting for, dependent on, such means as the body etc.

शरीरान्तरेषु iii. 38 In other bodies.

शरीरपरिणामाकारमात्रम् iv. 10 Of the size and form of the body only.

—शरीरावेशो iii. 38.

शरीरे ii. 5; iii. 38.

शशाङ्कलेखा ii. 5 The line or the curve of the moon; the curving moon; the lunar crescent.

शस्त्रादिनिपातेन ii. 34 By the 'letting fall', the stroke, of weapons, etc.

शाक—iii. 26 (Name of a dvīpa, continent, island).

शान्तः iii. 12 Placid; restful; peaceful; reposeful; unexcited tranquil; calm; (शम् to subside, be extinguished, become peaceful; also to inspect. The shānta quality is connected with sattva, also with the 'past'; as ghora is with rajas and the 'present', and mūdha wit htamas and the 'future')

शान्तम् i. 36; ii. 15.

—शान्तये iv 21.

शान्ताः— iii. 14.

—शान्तिः ii. 15.

शान्तेभ्यः iii. 14

शान्तोदिताऽव्यपदेश्यधर्मत्वेन iii. 49 By being of the nature of the attributes past, present, or future, (the 'subsided', the 'uprisen', the 'unpredicable' or indistinguishable; see शान्तः).

शान्तोदिताऽव्यपदेश्यधर्मानवच्छिन्नेषु i. 44 Amongst or on (abstract concepts) undemarcated, undetermined, unspecified, undefined, by the attributes, viz., past, present, or future, (subsided, uprisen, indistinguishable or unpredicable); i. e. on abstract timeless concepts, unconnected with any concrete embodiments.

शान्तोदिताव्यपदेश्यधर्मानुपाती iii. 14 'Running after or with or through' the subsided, the manifest, and the unmanifest attributes.

शान्तोदितौ iii. 12 Subsided and uprisen; past and present.

शारीरः ii, 15 Bodily, physical.

शारीरेण iv. 10.

—शालि— iii. 50.

शालितण्डुलाः ii 13 Paddy-grains; rice-grains

—शाल्मल— iii. 26 (Name of a dvīpa or continent).

शाश्वतम् iv. 22 Eternal.

शाश्वतवादः ii. 15 The doctrine of (the) eternity (of the Self, Purusha).

शाश्वतिकः i. 24 Eternal

—शासनम् iv. 13.

—शास्त्र— i. 35; ii. 1, 30.

शास्त्रगताः ii. 23 Contained in the (appurtenant) science

—शास्त्रम् ii. 15.

शास्त्रम् i. 1, 24; ii. 15 (शास् to teach; Lat *scire*, to know). Teaching; science.

—शास्त्राणाम् ii. 32.

शास्त्रानुमानाचार्योपदेशोपोद्बलनार्थम् i. 35 For the sake of the development or confirmation of the teachings of Science, of the inferences therefrom, and of the instructions of the Teachers.

शास्त्रानुशासनम् iv. 13 The teaching of (a or the) science.

शास्त्रे ii. 28.

शास्त्रेण i. 33.

शास्त्रोत्कर्षयोः i. 24 Of science (or wisdom) and of glory, elevation, greatness, superiority, supremacy.

—शिखर— ii. 27.

—शिरः iii. 39.

शिरःकपाले iii. 32 In the 'head-shard', 'head-case', skull.

शिलाम् iii. 45 To the rock.

—शिष्या iv. 22.

शीतोष्णादिभिः ii. 48 By cold and heat, etc.

शीतोष्णे ii. 32 Cold and heat.

—शील— ii. 6.

—शीलत्वात् i. 2.

—शीलम् ii. 18; iii 35.

—शीलाः iii. 44, 47.

—शीलानाम् iv. 14.

—शीलेषु iii. 23.

—शुक्राणि iii. 29.

—शुक्ल— iv. 7.

शुक्लः i. 33 White (masc:).

शुक्लकर्मोदयात् ii. 13 By the 'arising', the coming into operation, the becoming active, the 'dawning', of 'white' or good karma, good or happy 'deservingness', desert, merit.

शुक्लकृष्णा iv. 7 'White and black'; good and evil.

शुक्ला iv. 7.

—शुचि— ii. 5.

शुचिख्यातिः ii. 5 The belief, idea, awareness, of purity.

शुचिविपर्यासप्रत्ययः ii. 5 The erroneous notion of pureness.

शुचेः ii. 41 Of the pure (person).

—शुचौ ii. 5.

शुद्धः ii. 20 Pure; purified,

शुद्धः i, 29; iii. 35, 50; iv. 25 (Some editions read विशुद्धः in iii. 35).

शुद्धनिवासाः iii. 26 (One of the highest orders of the gods).

शुद्धमुक्तः i. 51 Pure and emancipated. (Some editions read शुद्धः केवलो मुक्तः).

शुद्धा i. 2.

—शुद्धि— ii. 41, 43.

—शुद्धि— i. 16; ii. 28.

—शुद्धिः ii. 1, 41.

—शुद्धिम् ii. 40; iii. 57.

शुद्धिसाम्ये iii. 55 On equality of purity; in case of equal purity.

शुद्धिसारूप्यम् iii. 55 'Same-formness', uniformity, of purity.

—शुद्धे ii. 28.

शुध्यशुध्योः iv. 3 Of purity and impurity.

शुष्के iii. 22 In dry (straw, grass, dead wood).

शुष्येत् iii. 22 May dry up.

—शून्यः i. 18.

—शून्यम् iii. 3.

—शून्यम् ii. 55.

शून्यम् iii. 3, 13; iv. 10 Empty.

—शून्या i. 43.

—शून्या i. 15, 44.

—शून्यानाम् iv. 34.

—शून्यायाम् i. 43.

—शृङ्गवन्तः iii. 26.

शृङ्गाणि iii. 26 Peaks; horns.

शृणोति iii. 22 Hears; (श्रु, to hear).

—शेरते iv. 8, 28.

—शेष— iii. 49.

—शेषः i. 18.

—शेषः ii. 41, 47.

—शेषम् iii. 9.

शेषासु iii. 13 In the remaining; (fem:; pl:).

—शैथिल्य—ii. 47 Laxity; (laxness; looseness).

—शैथिल्यम् iii. 38.

—शैथिल्यात् iii. 38.

—शैलाः iii. 26.

—शैल— iii. 26.

शैलस्थः i. 47 Seated on a mountain.

शोचतः i. 47 To the sorrowing, grieving.

शोचति ii. 5 Sorrows, grieves.

—शोच्यः i. 47.

शौचसन्तोषतपःस्वाध्यायेश्वरप्रणिधानानि ii. 32 Purity of body, contentment of mind, asceticism, study of spiritual sciences, self-surrender to God.

—शौचत्वात् ii. 5.

शौचम् ii. 32, 40 Purity; cleanliness.

शौचस्थैर्यात् ii. 41 Stability, establishment, steadiness, confirmation, of purity.

शौचात् ii. 40 From purity.

—श्यामः iii. 26 (Blue; dark).

—श्यामाक— iv. 3.

श्रद्दधानस्य i. 20 Of the trusting, the believing; (श्रत्, truth + धा, to do, to hold).

श्रद्धया i. 14 By faith.

श्रद्धा— i. 35.

श्रद्धादि iv. 10 Faith etc.

श्रद्धावीर्यस्मृतिसमाधिप्रज्ञापूर्वकः i. 20 Preceded by i. (cheerful, resolute, earnest) faith, ii. zealous energy, iii. retrospective and introspective memory, iv. attentive composure and collectedness, v. (discriminative) consciousness.

—श्रद्धीयते i. 35 (Some editions read श्रद्धीयते).

—श्रद्धेय— i. 7.

श्रद्धेयवचनाः iv. 14 Possessed of 'credible speech', (pl:); trustworthy; (i. e. persons whose words would be worthy of respectful credence).

श्रवण— ii. 33 (Hearing).

—श्रवणम् iii 36.

—श्रवणानाम् iii. 41.

—श्रवणेन iv. 25.

—श्रावण— iii. 36 (See प्रातिभ).

श्रावणात् iii. 36 From the 'auditory'.

श्रुतम् i. 49; ii. 30 (श्रु, to hear). The 'heard'; 'revealed'; scripture; revelation; testimony generally.

श्रुतानुमानज्ञानविकल्पशून्यायाम् i. 43 When (the intelligence is) 'empty', 'void of', freed from, the imaginations, associations, arising out of testimonial and inferential knowledge.

श्रुतानुमानप्रज्ञाभ्याम् i. 49 From or than the 'testimonial' and the 'inferential' consciousness.

श्रुतानुमानयोः i 43 Of testimony and inference.

श्रुतानुमानविषयः i. 49 Object of do:.

श्रुतानुमानज्ञानसहभूतम् i. 43 'Born with', accompanying, knowledge derived from testimony and inference.

श्रुतानुमाने i. 43 Testimony and inference.

—श्रुतित्वम् iii. 41.

श्रुतेः ii. 23 From 'revelation', or oral testimony.

श्रूयते iii 18 Is heard.

श्रूयमाणैः iii 17 By the (letters) being heard

श्रेयसः ii 55 From the good.

श्रेयसी iv 33 Excellent (fem:).

श्रोतुः i. 7 Of the hearer.

श्रोतृभिः iii. 17 By the hearers.

श्रोत्रचक्षुषी iii 51 Ear and eye.

श्रोत्रत्वक्चक्षुर्जिह्वाघ्राणानि ii. 19 Ear, skin, eye, tongue, and nose.

श्रोत्रम् iii. 41 The ear.

श्रोत्रम् iii 17; iv. 14.

श्रोत्राकाशयोः iii. 41 Of ear and ākāsha, space (or ether)

—श्रोत्राणाम् iii. 41.

श्रोत्रादिना ii. 18 By the ear etc.

श्रोत्रियः iii. 17 Student of, or versed in, scripture

श्लथयति i. 1 'Slides' away; relaxes, loosens.

श्लिष्टपर्वा i. 16 Close-jointed.

—श्लेष्माणः iii. 29
—श्लोकः iii. 26 (Verse).
श्ववृत्तेन ii. 34 With the conduct of the dog.
श्वा ii. 34 Dog.
—श्वास— i. 31.
श्वासः ii. 49 Inspiration, in-breathing.
श्वासपूर्वकः ii. 50 Preceded by inspiration.
श्वासप्रश्वासयोः ii. 49 Of in breathing and out-breathing, inspiration and expiration.
श्वासप्रश्वासयोः ii. 51.
—श्वासप्रश्वासाः i. 31.
श्वासप्रश्वासैः ii. 50.
श्वेतः iii. 17, 26 'White'. (Possibly the earlier form of the English word was 'shwite').
श्वेतते iii. 17 Shines as white; whitens.

—ष—

षट् ii. 19; iii. 26 Six.
षडरम् iv. 11 Six-spoked; having six spokes.
षडविशेषरूपाः iv. 13 Of the form of the undifferentiated six.
षण्डकः ii. 24 Barren, sterile; eunuch. (Some editions read पण्डकः).
षण्डकोपाख्यानेन ii. 24 By or with the story of the sexless, the eunuch. (Some editions read पण्डको—).
षष्ठः ii. 19 Sixth.
षोडशकः ii. 19 Sixteenth; (masc.)
षोडशीम् ii. 42 To the do; (fem:).

—स—

सः i. 14, 26 He.
सः i. 1; ii. 2; iii. 11; iv. 3 etc.
—संयमः iii. 28, 31.
संयमः iii. 4 (A technical word meaning concentration, contemplation, and absorbed raptness, all three together ; meditation; restraint. (सं + यम्, to regulate).
संयमः ii. 30; iii. 4, 5, 6, 16, 18, 23.
संयमम् iii. 6, 26, 27, 28, 29, 32.
संयमस्य iii. 5, 6, 16.
—संयमस्य iii. 41.
—संयमात् iii. 16, 17, 21, 22, 35, 41, 42, 44, 47.
संयमात् iii. 26, 52.
संयमात् iii. 16, 19, 21, 24, 30, 34.
संयमाभावात् iii. 23 Because of, from, absence of meditation.
संयुक्तः ii. 23 Combined, joined.
—संयोग— ii. 17.
संयोगः ii. 17, 23 (सं + युज्, to join). Junction; combination.
संयोगः ii. 15, 17, 22, 23; iv. 19.
संयोगनिमित्तम् ii. 23 The cause of, or caused by, conjunction.
संयोगविभागधर्माणः ii. 18 Having

the properties of conjunction and disjunction, combination and separation.

संयोगस्य ii. 15.

संयोगस्वरूपाभिधित्सया ii. 23 By or with the wish to declare the form or nature of the combination.

संयोगाख्यम् ii. 25 That which is named conjunction.

—संयोगात् ii. 22.

संयोगात् ii. 23.

संयोगाभावः ii. 23 Absence of conjunction.

संयोगे ii. 23.

—संयोगे iv. 19.

—संवित् iii. 34.

—संवित् i. 35, 36; iii. 36.

संवित् i. 17 (सं + विद्, to 'wit', to know). Consciousness, awareness.

—संवेगः i. 21 (Speed; rapidity; intensity).

—संवेगानाम् i. 21.

—संवेगेन ii. 12.

—संवेदनम् iv. 22.

—संवेदनम् iii. 39.

—संवेदनात् iii. 39; iv. 19.

—संवेदिनम् iv. 21.

—संवेदी i. 7; ii. 17, 20.

—संशय— i. 30.

संशयः i. 30 (सं + शी, to sleep; that which sleeps, or goes together, with its opposite, in an inseparable pair); doubt; alternation.

संशयम् i. 35.

संशुष्येत् iii. 22 Might or would dry up.

—संश्रयाणाम् iv. 11.

—संसर्गः ii. 40.

संसर्गात् iii. 13 Because of mergence, assimilation, absorption, "together-produced-ness"; (such close association with, clinging to, its cause as amounts to disappearance in it).

संसारः ii. 15; iv. 10 (सं + सृ, to move); 'procession'; trasmigration; the world-process.

संसारचक्रम् iv. 11 The wheel of the world-process.

संसारनिबन्धनम् ii. 52 Binding to the world-process.

संसारप्राग्भारा i. 12 Heading towards world-activity; 'heavy-fronted' towards worldliness.

संसारबीजक्षयम् ii. 32 The decay of the seed-germ of (the tendency to) 'procession.'

संसारस्य iv. 33.

संसारहेतुः ii. 15 The cause of the world-process; the cause of 'procession', of births and rebirths.

संसाराग्नेः iii. 51 Of the 'fire of the world', i. e. the misery of the procession of birth and rebirth.

संसाराङ्गारेषु ii. 33; iii. 51 In the burning embers, the fires, of the world-life.

संसारिणः i. 25 The 'moving', revolving, wandering, reincarnating, evolving, worldly (jīvas).

—संसृज्यमानाः ii. 19.

संसृज्येत ii. 40 May contact; may come into contact.

संसृष्टम् i. 2; ii. 19 (सं+सृज्, to create; to emanate; to throw forth). Integrated, aggregated, evolved or emanated, together with; born together, mixed up, associated, colored or tinged, with; attached to; latent; potential in.

संसृष्टाः ii. 19.

संसृष्टानि ii. 19.

—संस्कार— i. 50; ii. 15; iv. 9.

—संस्कार— i. 19, 51; ii. 5, 15, 23; iii. 10.

—संस्कारः iv. 28.

संस्कारः i. 50 (सं+कृ, to do). 'Well-doing'; 'con-secra-tion'; refinement; purification; sacrament; impression; education, refining, polishing; stamping with a tendency; tendency; disposition; potentiality; aptitude; inclination; faculty; bent; stamp; acquired character; propensity; disposition.

संस्कारः i. 51; iii. 10.

संस्कारदुःखता ii. 15 The pain (–ful–) ness of (i. e., due to, the creation, the setting up of) tendencies.

संस्कारबीजक्षयात् iv. 29 By decay, consumption, of the 'seeds' (germs, 'cell-vehicles') of impressions and tendencies.

संस्कारम् i. 11.

—संस्कारयोः iii. 9; iv. 9.

संस्कारशेषः i. 18 Remnant of tendency; remaining as mere tendency.

संस्कारशेषम् iii. 9 'Tendency-remaindered'; having only the tendency left; left as nothing else than a mere tendency.

संस्कारसाक्षात्करणात् iii. 18 By 'vision' of tendency; from, because of, by means of, observation, (in meditation) of the (hidden) tendency (of one's own or another's mind).

संस्कारसाक्षात्क्रियायै iii. 18 For do:.

— संस्काराः iii. 9, 13, 15; iv. 9.

संस्काराः i 5, 50, 51; ii. 13; iii. 18; iv. 9.

संस्काराणाम् i 51.

—संस्कारात् iii. 10.

संस्कारात् iii. 10.

संस्कारातिशयः i. 50 Excessive impressing; great consecration; excellence, surpassingness, of the re-fining, the culturing.

(Some editions read संस्काराशयः).

संस्कारान् i. 51.

संस्कारान्यथात्वम् iii. 9 The 'otherwiseness', transformation, change, of implanted tendency.

संस्काराशयः i. 50 The 'receptacle', 'gland', 'capsule', 'cell-reservoir', germ, of the tendency.

—संस्काराशयः ii. 15.

संस्कारेण iii. 10.

संस्कारेभ्यः iv. 27.

संस्कारेभ्यः iv. 9.

संस्कारैः i. 5, 51.

संस्कारोपगम् i. 2 Approximating towards, tending to become, leading on to, resulting in, a propensity.

—संस्कृता iv. 9.

—संस्कृताः iii. 18.

संस्थानम् iii. 13 Placing; organising; arrangement; position; connection; con-stitu-tion; construction; formation; form; structure.

—संस्थानम् ii. 46; iii. 26.

संस्थानविशेषः i. 43 Peculiar 'placing', organising, arrangement, structure.

—संस्पृश्य iii. 17.

संहत (or त्य) कारिणा iv. 24 By the co-operating, co-working; by (a thing) which acts in conjunction (with another).

संहत्यकारित्वात् iv. 24 Because of co-operativeness; by reason of acting (only) in collaboration (with another); because of interdependently joint causation.

संहत्यकारित्वात् ii. 20.

—संहननत्वानि iii. 46.

—संहृत— iii. 17.

—संहार— iii. 17.

सकृत्प्रयत्नात् ii. 50 By or from a single unique or sudden effort.

सकृदारब्धः ii. 51 Begun once, or once for all, or suddenly.

—सक्तः ii. 13.

सक्तिः ii. 55 Attachment, addiction. (सञ्ज्, to cling, adhere, embrace).

—सङ्करः iv. 21.

—सङ्करः iii 13.

सङ्करः iii. 17 Mixture, con-fusion, adulteration. (सं+ कृ)

सङ्करः ii. 13.

सङ्करगन्धः iv. 15 'Distant smell, flavor, savor', i. e. 'touch', taint, trace, of mixture, adulteration, alloy, confusion, mistakability for each other.

सङ्कल्पः iii. 45 'Will-imagination'; mental picture; determination, resolution, resolve; formation of clear and definite picture in the mind; (सं, सम्यक्, well, clearly, क्लृप्, कल्प्, to form, to image).

—सङ्कल्पता iii. 45.

सङ्कल्पसिद्धाः iii. 26 Perfected in imaginative-will, in resolve.

सङ्कल्पसिद्धिः iv. 1 Accomplishment, perfection, of determination, of will-and-imagination, of the power of the will (so that whatever is determinately imagined, becomes realised, materialised).

सङ्कल्पान् iii. 45.

सङ्कल्पानुविधायिन्यः iii. 44 Obedient to will-and-imagination; following, acting or shaping according to, the resolve.

—सङ्कीर्णयोः iii. 35 (सं + कॄ to scatter; scattering together, mixing up).

—सङ्कीर्णम् i. 43.

सङ्कीर्णा i. 42 Mixed; con-fused; alloyed; adulterated; crowded; also narrow, tight.

सङ्कीर्णा iii 17.

—सङ्केत— i. 43.

सङ्केतः i. 49.

सङ्केतः i. 27; iii. 17 (An, or a, mutual,) understanding; agreement; convention; wish; design; intention; 'sign'; mark; technicality.

सङ्केतकृतम् i 27 Made or created by convention or agreement.

सङ्केतबुद्धितः iii. 17 Because of convention-mind, of an understanding or convention, a fixed association.

सङ्केते iii. 17.

—सङ्केतेन iii. 17.

सङ्केतेन i. 27.

सङ्केत्यते iii. 17 Is indicated, signified.

सङ्कोचम् ii. 50 To shrinking, contracting.

सङ्कोचविकासि iv. 10 Contracting and expanding; contractive and expansive; shrinking and swelling.

सङ्कोचविकासिनी iv. 10 Do:; (fem:).

—सङ्क्रमः i. 16 (Transference).

—सङ्क्रमा ii. 20; iv. 22.

—सङ्क्रमायाः iv. 22.

—सङ्क्रान्तये i. 7; ii 30.

—सङ्क्रान्ता ii. 20.

सङ्ख्यापरिदृष्टः ii. 50 Calculated by or in numbers.

—सङ्ख्याने iv. 29.

—सङ्ख्याभिः ii. 50.

—सङ्ख्याभिः ii. 51.

सङ्ख्याभिः ii. 50 By numbers.

—सङ्ख्येय— iv. 24.

—सङ्ख्येयस्य ii. 13.

—सङ्ख्येया ii. 34.

—सङ्ग— ii. 30.

—सङ्गः iii. 39; iv. 21 (Attachment).

सङ्गच्छन्ते iv. 21 (They) go together with; go in accord with; fit in with.

सङ्गदोषान् iii. 51 The demerits, evil consequences, faults,

defects, of addiction and attachment.

सङ्गस्मयाकरणम् iii. 51 'Not making', avoidance, of attachment and egoism or conceit. (सञ्ज्, to 'sink' into, to become attached, and स्मि, to 'smile' with self-satisfaction).

सङ्गृहीतत्वात् iv. 11. Because of being bound up with, grasped together by.

सङ्गृहीताः iv. 11 Collected; connected together; clasped; accompanied.

सङ्ग्रहश्लोकः iii. 26 Summarising verse.

सङ्घः iii. 44 An organised assemblage; (सं+हन्, to strike; 'struck together', 'welded together').

सङ्घातः iii. 44 Collection; 'striking together'; organism.

सचन्द्रतारका ii. 5 With moon and stars.

सचित्तानि iv. 4 'With minds'.

—संज्ञा i. 15.

—संज्ञा i. 15; iii. 13.

संज्ञा i. 48 (सं+ज्ञा, to know). Consciousness; sentience; that by which a thing is known, a name; designation.

संज्ञादिविशेषप्रतिपत्तिः i. 25 The learning of the specific properties, name, etc.

—संज्ञाभिः i. 8.

—संज्ञायाम् ii. 26; iii. 49.

संज्ञासंज्ञिनः iii. 26 (Name of a race of gods).

सतः iv. 12 Of the existent.

—सतत्त्वम् ii. 5 (Of the same 'that-ness', essence, nature, quality).

सताम् ii. 4 Of the existing, the real, the good and true; (pl.).

—सत्ता— ii. 19.

—सत्ता iv. 25.

सत्ताम् iii. 17 To being or existence.

सत्तामात्रस्य ii. 19 Of (the Mahat-taṭṭva, possessed of) mere being or existence.

सत्तामात्रे ii. 19.

सति ii. 13, 49 (In the condition of) there being.

सति i. 3, 5, 30, 32; ii. 4, 27; iii. 13, 21.

—सत्कार— i. 14 ('Well-making', 'good-regarding', honoring, faith, reverence).

सत्कारवान् i. 14 Honored; honoring; treated respectfully.

—सत्त्व— i. 24; ii. 17 iii. 35; iv. 34.

सत्त्वः iv. 21 A living being.

सत्त्वगुणात्मिका i. 2 Composed of, of the nature of, the attribute or aspect (called) Saṭṭva.

सत्त्वपुरुषयोः iii. 35, 55 Of Saṭṭva and Puruṣha.

सत्त्वपुरुषान्यताख्यातिः ii. 2 The consciousness or awareness of the 'otherness', hetereity, difference, non-identity, of Saṭṭva and Purusha. (Some editions read **सत्त्वपुरुषान्यतामात्रख्यातिः**).

सत्त्वपुरुषान्यताख्यातिमात्रप्रवाहिणः iv. 27 Flowing, streaming, with only do:. (Some editions read—**प्रवाहारोहिणः**).

सत्त्वपुरुषान्यताख्यातिमात्रम् i. 2 (Consisting) only (of) the consciousness or awareness of non-identity of Saṭṭva (i. e. Prakṛṭi, in even its finest subtlest form) and Purusha, the Self, the Spirit.

सत्त्वपुरुषान्यताख्यातिमात्ररूपप्रतिष्ठस्य iii. 49 Of one established in the form of do:.

सत्त्वपुरुषान्यताख्यातिमात्रस्य iii 49 Of (the yogī, or the mind, the soul, consisting) only (of) the consciousness or awareness of the non-identity of Saṭṭva and Purusha; of the soul whose whole being has been resolved into mere awareness of 'the otherness of the Self than the not-Self'; ("I-am-Not-This").

सत्त्वपुरुषान्यताप्रत्ययः ii. 26 The consciousness, idea, belief, of the non-identity of Saṭṭva and Purusha.

सत्त्वपुरुषान्यताप्रत्ययेन iii. 35.

—**सत्त्वम्** i. 2. 36; iii. 35; iv. 31.

सत्त्वम् ii. 5, 17, 18, 52; iv. 21 (**विद्यमानत्वम्**) Existence (as cognisable, through cognisability); goodness; harmony; energy; fortitude; stamina; a living creature; the Saṭṭva-guṇa, the principle of cognition. (See **गुणाः**).

सत्त्वमात्रम् iv. 21 Only Saṭṭva.

सत्त्वशुद्धिः ii. 41 Purity of Saṭṭva.

सत्त्वशुद्धिद्वारेण iii. 55 By the 'door-way', by means, of the purification, the refinement, of Saṭṭva.

सत्त्वशुद्धिम् iii. 51.

सत्त्वशुद्धिसौमनस्यैकाग्र्येन्द्रियजयात्मदर्शनयोग्यत्वानि ii. 41 Purity and clearness of intelligence, cheerful-mindedness, one-pointed-ness, control of the senses, and fitness for vision of the Self.

—**सत्त्वस्य** i. 47; ii. 41; iii. 18, 43, 47, 49.

सत्त्वस्य ii. 26; iii. 35, 50; iv. 21.

सत्त्वात् iii. 35.

सत्त्वानाम् iv. 19.

सत्त्वे ii. 17.

—**सत्त्वे** i. 24.

—**सत्त्वेन** iii. 18.

—**सत्य**— ii. 30.

सत्यः ii. 11 'Existent'; having been; (fem:, pl: of सती).

सत्यप्रतिष्ठायाम् ii. 36 On confirmation of truthfulness; on unshakeable fixity in the virtue of truthfulness.

सत्यम् i. 45, 48; ii. 4, 30 True; truth.

सत्यमहाभास्वराः iii. 26 (A race of very high gods).

सत्यलोकः iii. 26 (The name of the 'seventh heaven', a superphysical subtile world or plane).

सत्यलोके iii. 26.

सत्यसङ्कल्पता iii. 45 'True-willedness'; the state of one whose will always takes effect 'truly', irresistibly, indefeasibly.

सत्याभाः iii. 26 (A race of the highest orders of gods).

—सत्याम् iv. 25

सत्याम् ii. 6; iii. 13, 15 (Loc: sing: of सती, being; fem:).

सत्सु ii. 13 (Loc: pl: of सत्).

सदा iv. 18 Always; ever; perpetually.

सदा i. 24; ii. 20; iv. 34.

सदाज्ञातत्वम् iv. 18 The state of being always 'known', ever cognised.

सदाज्ञातविषयत्वम् ii. 20 Condition of unbroken, constant, awareness of objects.

—सदृशः iii. 12.

सदृशः iii 2 Similar. (स, same, similar, together with, दृश्, to see; 'similar-seeming').

सदृशप्रत्ययप्रवाही i. 32 Streaming similar cognitions; flowing with a flow of similar ideas.

सदृशप्रत्ययप्रवाहेण i. 32 By or because of a continuous stream of similar cognitions, ideas, awarenesses

सदृशम् iv. 9.

—सद्भावः iii. 14.

—सद्भावाः ii 18; iii. 15.

सद्भूतम् i. 1, 35 Good and real; having real existence as well as excellence.

सद्यः ii. 12 'Suddenly'; at once; immediately.

सद्विषयेण i. 8 By (a cognition) which has something real for object; (is not concerned with unrealities, emptinesses).

—सधर्मकम् iv. 17.

सनिमित्तः i. 24 With reason; having a cause; well proven.

सनिमित्तम्—ii. 25.

—सन्तानस्य ii. 5.

—सन्ताप—iii. 18.

सन्ति i. 24; iii. 29, 52 (अस्, to be). Are. (Some editions omit the word in iii. 29).

—सन्तोष— ii. 32.

सन्तोषः ii 32 Contentment; (सं + तुष्, to be satisfied, pleased).

सन्तोषसुखम् iii. 18 The joy of contentment.

सन्तोषात् ii. 42 From or by contentment.

—सन्दधाति iv. 21.

—सन्नम् ii. 19.

—सन्निधानाः ii. 18.

सन्निधिमात्रोपकारि i. 4; ii. 17 Helping, doing good, benefitting, supporting, by mere proximity, mere juxtaposition.

सन्निधिमात्रोपकारिणः ii. 18 Do: (pl:). (सं + नि + धा).

—सन्निधौ ii. 35.

सन्निविष्टाः iii. 26 Placed; deposited; studded; (सं + नि + विश्, to enter).

सन्निवेशविशेषमात्रम् iv. 13 Only peculiarity of position or arrangement.

सन्निहितसाधनात् ii. 32 Than the 'nearest means', the most easily available necessaries.

—संन्यासः ii. 1.

—संन्यासात् iv. 7.

संन्यासिनाम् iv. 7 Of the renouncers.

सपत्नः ii. 5 'Co-spouse'; 'a rival spouse'; an enemy.

सपरिहारः ii. 13 'With a counteractor'; 'neutralised'; 'counterbalanced'; neutralisable; remediable.

सप्त iii. 15, 26, 29 Seven.

सप्तद्वीपा iii. 26 Seven-isled; having seven isles or continents.

सप्तधा ii. 27 Sevenfold.

सप्तप्रकारा ii 27 Of seven kinds.

सप्तविंशति ii. 34 Twenty-seven.

सप्तविधा iii. 51 Sevenfold; of seven kinds.

सप्तविधाम् ii. 27.

सप्रत्यवमर्षः ii. 13 'With endurance'; endurable; tolerable. (प्रति + अव + मृष्, to endure. This is different from प्रत्यवमर्शः, q. v.).

सबीजः i. 46 'Seedful'; seeded; 'with seed'; having an object; objective.

—सभा iii. 26 (Assembly; assembly-hall).

समः ii. 19 Equal; 'same'.

समनन्तरः iii. 14, 15 Next without 'inter'-val; next after; next in succession; (सम्, well, together; अन्, not; अन्तरम्, 'inter'-val).

समनन्तरत्वम् iii. 15 Immediacy.

समनन्तरा iii. 14.

समनन्तरेण iv. 21.

समन्ततः ii. 15; iii. 22 On all sides.

समन्वागतः iii. 13, 14 Accompanied; following; coming with and after. (सम्, with, or well, अनु, after, आ-गम्, to come).

—समन्वागतौ iv. 12.

—समन्वितानाम् iii. 44.

समम् iii. 39; iv. 3 Evenly: evenness; same; similar; of the same level.

—समय— ii. 31 (सम्, with, ई, to go).

समयावच्छिन्ना ii. 31 'Cut off', delimited, conditioned by conditions, reservations; defined by 'mutual agreement or understanding', or by 'terms'.

—समये iv. 20 ('That which goes').

—समये i. 11.

समये iv. 12 In or at the time.

समयेन iii. 52 By time.

—समयैः ii. 31.

—समर्थः ii. 23.

समर्थः ii. 38; iii. 18 Able, competent; 'having the same meaning, intention, will'; 'equal (to the task)'; 'equal in power'; 'ad-equate'.

—समर्थम् ii. 23; iv. 31.

समर्थम् i. 25, 35; iv. 12.

—समर्थाः ii. 13; iv. 28.

—समर्थानि iii. 50.

समसंस्थानम् ii. 46 "Even-seat"; (the name of a yoga-posture).

समस्तेन्द्रियवृत्तिः iii. 39 Functioning in or pervading all the organs.

समादित्सते ii. 30 (सम् + आ + दा). Wishes to take up.

—समाधयः ii. 29.

—समाधयः i. 35.

समाधयः i. 17 (See समाधिः).

—समाधि— i. 20; iv. 1.

—समाधि— i. 51; iii. 4, 7, 16.

समाधिः i. 46, 51; iii. 3; iv. 29 (सम्, well + आ, on all sides + धा, to 'do', hold, maintain). 'Holding' and maintaining the mind steady; 'collectedness' of mind; absorbedness; absorption; raptness; rapt-ure; rapport; entranced attention; meditation; concentration; contemplation; fixedness; communion; trance; ecstasy. (As समाधानं) explanation; reconciliation; solution and satisfaction of doubts; co-ordination; justification.

समाधिः i. 1, 2, 11, 17, 18, 20, 23, 50; ii. 19; iii. 3, 23.

समाधिचित्तम् iii. 12 The 'absorption-mind; the absorbed, rapt, profoundly attentive mind; the mind which is tending towards absorption.

—समाधिजम् i. 43.

समाधिजम् iii. 38, 55 Born of, resulting from, produced by, raptness.

समाधिजा i. 50.

—समाधिजाः iv. 1.

समाधिजान् i. 51.

—समाधिना ii. 27.

समाधिपरिणामः iii. 11 Having raptness as consequence; resulting in absorption; or, the result of raptness.

समाधिपादः i. 1 The name of the

first chapter, 'foot', 'quarter', relating to Samādhi.

समाधिप्रज्ञा i. 50; iii. 5 'Absorption-consciousness'; the condition or state of 'sublime intelligence or consciousness' during samādhi. (Some editions read **समाधिजा प्रज्ञा**; see **प्रज्ञा**).

समाधिप्रज्ञानिर्ग्राह्यः i. 49 Apprehensible by the do:.

समाधिप्रज्ञाप्रतिलम्भे i. 50 On the gain of do:.

समाधिप्रज्ञाप्रभवः i. 50 Of the (propensity) born of do:.

समाधिप्रज्ञायाः iii. 5.

समाधिप्रज्ञायाम् i. 35, 42, 43, 44; iv. 23.

समाधिप्रज्ञाविरोधी i. 51 Hostile to do:.

समाधिप्रज्ञास्वरूपम् i 44 The true form of the rapt consciousness.

समाधिप्रतिपक्षाः i. 32 Opponents of, hostile to, raptness.

समाधिप्रतिलम्भे i. 30 On the gain of samādhi.

समाधिफलम् i. 21, 22, 23 Fruit of do:.

समाधिबलात् iii. 38 By the power of do:.

समाधिभावनार्थः ii. 2 Having for purpose, the realisation of do:.

—समाधिभिः ii. 12.

समाधिभूमेः i. 30 Of the 'stage' of do:.

समाधिभ्रेषात् iii. 12 Because of, or from, the breaking up of do:.

समाधिम् ii. 2; iii. 51.

समाधिलाभः i. 21, 22, 23 Achievement of do:.

समाधिसाधनानाम् i. 30 Of the means, 'accomplishers', 'securers', 'achievers', helpers of do:.

समाधिसिद्धिः ii. 45 The successful accomplishment of samādhi.

समाधीयते i. 20, 32; iii, 11 Is 'collected', brought together, gathered up, brought into rapport, brought to attention, fixed; reconciled, explained, solved (as a contradiction, a dilemma, an antinomy, is solved).

समाधीयमानम् i. 32 Being collected, synthesised, co-ordinated, justified, explained.

समाधेः i. 47; iii. 7.

समाधेयः iv. 14 Is to be 'gathered', understood, explained, found.

—समाधौ iii. 9.

समाधौ iii. 37 In samādhi, rapt or absorbed meditation.

समाधौ i. 10

—समान— iv. 14.

समानः ii. 23; iii. 39; iv. 8 'Same-like'; of the 'same measure', 'similar'; equal; (also the name of one of the vital currents or nerve-forces).

समानकालम् iii. 14 At the same

time; simultaneously; synchronously.

समानजयात् iii. 40 By conquest of the current of vital force named samāna.

—समानम् i. 24.

समानम् ii. 13.

समानसत्त्वोपनिबन्धने iii. 35 Equally inseparably bound up with the sattva-guṇa.

समाना ii. 9.

समापत्तयः i. 46.

—समापत्ति— ii. 47.

—समापत्तिः i. 41 (Some editions read समापत्तिः as a separate word, not compounded with the preceding words).

समापत्तिः i. 42 (Some editions omit this word). 'A coming to pass'; 'a be-falling', happening, occurrence; developement; eventuation; denouement; outcome, effect, result; issue; event; consummation. (सम + आ + पद्, to go, to move, to happen; cf. सम्पत्तिः, good fortune, wealth; आपत्तिः, misfortune; विपत्तिः, calamity, destruction; निष्पत्तिः, fulfilment, etc.).

समापत्तिः i. 41, 42, 43, 44.

—समापत्तिम् iii. 42.

—समापत्तेः iii. 42.

—समापत्तेः i. 43.

—समापन्नम् i. 41.

समापन्नम् i. 36; ii. 47 (सम् + आ + पद्); come to pass, happened, accomplished, finished; come to a denouement, a final development; consummated.

समापन्नस्य i. 42.

समाप्ताधिकारा ii. 2 That whose function, business, work, office, duty, is over, finished, completed, discharged.

—समाप्तिः iv. 32. (सम् + आप्, to find, to gain; completion, finishing).

—समाप्तिः ii. 18; iii. 54; iv. 33.

—समाप्तिम् iv. 28.

—समाप्तौ iv. 34.

समारूढः i. 42 (सम् + आ + रुह्, to mount). 'Mounted on', 'ascended to'; entered into; accomplished in.

—समाहारः iii. 52.

समाहितचित्तस्य i. 20, 31, 48; ii. 1; iii. 12, 37 Of him whose mind is collected, absorbed in meditation.

—समुच्चय— i. 25; ii. 34 (सम् + उत्, up + चि, to gather. A gathering up; bringing together).

समुदाचरति ii. 4 (सम् + उत् + आ + चर्, to move); up-rises; breaks out; operates; behaves; moves forth; comes forth; is active.

समुदाचरन्ति ii. 4 Do: (pl:).

समुदाचारः iii. 13 Conduct; activity; way of existence.

—समुदाचारात् iii. 13.

समुदायः iii 44 'A coming together'; a group. (सम् + उत् + आ + ई or अय्).

—समुदायस्य ii. 15

समुद्रम् iv. 10 To the ocean.

समुद्राः iii. 26 Oceans.

समुपजातवीर्यस्य i. 20 Of him who has developed, or in whom has been born or grown, seminal energy, vital 'virility' and vigor.

समूलकाषम् iv. 30 'With destruction of root'; with e-radication; rad cal extermination.

समूलघातम् iv. 30 Do:.

समूहः iii. 44, 47 Store; collection; gathering; crowd. (सम् + ऊह् , to guess, to infer, to bring together in mind).

संमूहस्य iii. 44.

—सम्पत् iii. 45, 46 (Wealth; riches; perfection; excellence. See समापत्तिः).

—सम्पत्त्या i. 28.

—सम्पदम् ii. 5.

सम्पदम् ii. 5 To wel-fare, weal-th.

सम्पद्यते i. 28; ii. 13, 26; iii. 17 iv. 31 Becomes; happens; comes about; is fulfilled; eventuates; becomes accomplished, achieved; arises; developes; grows into. (See समापत्तिः).

—सम्पद्यमानम् iii. 13.

—सम्पद्येत iii. 52.

सम्पश्यता iii. 18 By the (person) beholding.

सम्पादयति iii. 16 Brings about; causes to happen; produces. (सम् + पद्; caus:).

सम्पादयेत् i. 34 May or should secure.

सम्पादितः i. 14 Gathered, performed, accomplished; (masc.).

सम्पिण्डितम् iii. 22 Folded up, lumped up, gathered up into a ball, rolled up.

—सम्पिपादयिषया i. 13.

सम्प्रजानीते i. 36 Knows.

सम्प्रज्ञातः i. 17 (सम् + प्र + ज्ञा; सम्प्रज्ञायते किञ्चित् यस्मिन् सः). That in which something is known; conscious of some object; objective (as distinguished from अ-सम्प्रज्ञात, i. e , purely in-turned and subjective, 'un-conscious' of any object other than Self).

सम्प्रज्ञातः i. 1, 2, 11, 17.

सम्प्रज्ञातस्य iii. 7.

सम्प्रज्ञायते i. 2 Is known.

सम्प्रतिपत्तिनित्यतया i. 27 By the continuity or permanance of the mutual understanding, i.e , agreement (or convention or custom of accepting and using a certain word-sound in a certain sense, for a certain thing).

सम्प्रतिपत्त्या iii. 17 By acceptance, acquiescence. (सम् + प्रति + पद्).

सम्प्रबोधे i. 10 In or on waking up.

—सम्प्रयोग— i. 30.

—**सम्प्रयोगः** ii. 44 (Meeting, intercourse, converse, communion).

—सम्प्रयोगे ii. 54; iii. 21.

—सम्प्रयोगे i. 15.

सम्प्रसादः i, 20 Placidity; lucidity; cheerfulness; (something more positive than 'peace'; as a silvered looking-glass is something more than pure, transparent, glass; see प्रसादः).

—सम्बद्धम् iv. 23.

—सम्बध्य iv. 17.

—सम्बध्यते iv. 15.

सम्बध्यमानम् iv. 16 Being 'bound up', 'tied up', connected together.

—सम्बन्ध— ii, 27.

—सम्बन्धः i. 24, 27; ii. 5; iii. 42; iv. 6.

सम्बन्धः i. 7, 24, 27; iii. 42 Connection; relation; 'binding together'; (सम् + बन्ध्, to 'bind').

सम्बन्धसंयमात् iii. 41 By meditation on (the) relation or connection (between two things).

—सम्बन्धात् iii. 17; iv. 34.

सम्बन्धात् iv. 16.

—सम्बोधः ii. 39 (Knowledge).

सम्भवः iii. 13; iv. 12 Birth; coming into being; possibility.

सम्भवति ii. 13, 15; iv. 8 Becomes possible. (सम् + भू, to be).

सम्भवन्त्यः iv. 12 Becoming; (fem:; pl:).

—सम्भवम् ii. 28, 34.

—सम्भावितः ii 9.

सम्भाव्यते i. 24 Is regarded as possible; is possible or inferrible.

—सम्भिन्न— ii. 18 (Mixed up).

सम्भेदम् ii. 1 Breaking-up; attenuation; abolition. (Ordinarily, भिद्, to break, joined with the prefix सम्, means the very opposite, viz., to attach; but here संभेदः means attenuation, breaking up).

—सम्भोग— i. 33.

सम्मुखीभावः ii. 4 'Face-to-face'-ness; inclination towards; facing towards.

सम्मुखीभावे ii. 4.

सम्मुखीभूते ii. 4. In (the state of an object) being 'before the face', being in front.

सम्मूर्च्छितः ii. 13 'Fainted together'; welded together; mixed up; amalgamated; compounded; precipitated together.

सम्यग्ज्ञानम् i. 43 'Well', true, right, 'knowledge'.

सम्यग्ज्ञानस्य ii. 28

सम्यग्दर्शनम् ii. 15 'Well-seeing'; right knowledge; wisdom; the vision of the Truth.

सम्यग्दर्शनापेक्षम् iv. 15 Because of, basing on, looking to, dependent on, relying on, true vision or right knowledge.

सम्यगदर्शिनः iv. 23 The 'true-seeing'; the seers of the truth.

सरूपः ii. 20 'Same-formed'.

—सर्ग – iii. 26.

सर्गस्य i. 26 Of emanation, creation, evolution, manifestation. (सृज्, to 'surge' out, to emanate, to throw forth).

—सर्गाः iii. 37.

—सर्गात् iii. 13.

—सर्गादिषु i. 26.

सर्गान्तरेषु i. 27 In other creations, worlds, systems.

सर्पः iii. 31 'Serpent'

—सर्पिः— iii. 26 (Liquid clarified butter)

—सर्व— ii 45; iii. 16.

सर्वः i. 32; ii. 5; iv. 33 All; (masc:, sing:).

सर्वकर्मार्पणम् ii. 32 Offering up of all acts; assigning of all acts (to another, here God; feeling that whatever the aspirant does is done by Him, or for Him).

सर्वकारकाणाम् iii. 17 Of all conjugational forms; of all 'act-causers'.

सर्वकार्यकरणसमर्थम् ii. 23 Capable of doing all deeds.

सर्वक्रियाणाम् ii, 1 Of all actions.

सर्वक्लेशानाम् iv. 11 Of all the primal sins, miseries, afflictions.

सर्वचित्तानाम् iv. 5 Of all minds

सर्वज्ञः i. 25; iii. 49 'All-knower'; omniscient.

सर्वज्ञबीजम् i. 25 The seed of the omniscient; the omniscient seed; the principle of omniscience.

सर्वज्ञबीजस्य i. 25.

सर्वज्ञातृत्वम् iii. 49 All-knowingness.

सर्वतः i. 2, 32, 44; ii. 13, 50 From or on all sides.

सर्वतन्मात्राणि iii. 44 All ṭanmātras, things-in-themselves.

सर्वतोगतिः iii. 44 Going every where; all-reaching.

सर्वथा iv. 29 In all ways.

सर्वथा i. 44; ii. 30, 31.

सर्वथाविषयम् iii. 54 Having for object of knowledge 'all ways', methods, manners, laws whatsoever; pertaining to all objects whatsoever, past, present, and future; omnisciently cognising all the contents and all the methods of all the world-process, in all time and all space.

सर्वदा ii. 30 Always; ever.

सर्वदिक्स्थानि ii. 37 Existing in all quarters.

सर्वदुःखक्षयकारणम् ii. 15 The cause of the destruction of all pain.

सर्वधर्मात्मकेषु i. 44 In or on (abstract concepts) having (the seed of) the nature of all (particular) attributes.

सर्वधर्मानुपातिनः ii. 19 (The three guṇa-s) 'accompanying', running through, all 'functions.'

सर्वधर्मानुपातिषु i. 44 In do:.

सर्वनिरोधात् i. 51 By inhibition of all.

सर्वपदेषु iii 17 In all (complete) words.

सर्वपुरुषसाधारणः iv. 16 Common to all 'persons.'

सर्वपुरुषाणाम् ii. 23 Of all purushas, persons, egos.

सर्वप्रकृतिविकारवशित्वम् iii. 48 Control over all the transformations of Nature or Matter.

सर्वप्राणिनाम् ii. 35 Of all living beings, breathing creatures.

सर्वप्राणिषु i. 33 Amongst all do:.

सर्वबोध्यबोधसमर्थः ii. 23 Capable of cognising, perceiving, knowing, understanding, comprehending, being aware of, all that is cognisable.

सर्वभावाधिष्ठातृत्वम् iii. 49 Being the supreme ruler of all states or forms of existence; supremacy over all states or things.

सर्वभावान् ii. 18 All conditions of being, forms of existence.

सर्वभूतरुतज्ञानम् iii. 17 Knowledge of the (meaning of the) cries, voices, languages, of all beings, all creatures

सर्वभूतहितम् ii 30 The good of all beings.

सर्वभूतानाम् ii. 30 Of all beings

सर्वभूताभयप्रदानेन ii. 33 By the 'gift of freedom from fear' to all beings, i. e, by complete harmlessness.

सर्वभूतोपकारार्थम् ii. 30 For the good of all beings.

सर्वभूमिषु ii. 31 In all 'grounds', stages, states, conditions planes; towards all objects.

सर्वम् ii. 15; iii. 33 All; (neu:, sing:).

सर्वम् i. 32, 35, 43; ii. 5, 45: iii. 14, 18, 22, 26, 33; iv. 13, 21, 24.

सर्वरत्नोपस्थानम् ii. 37 'Attendance', 'near-standing', coming-up, self-presentation, accrual, of all gems, precious things.

सर्वरूपाः ii. 15 Of all forms

सर्वरूपाकारनिर्भासम् iv. 23 Reflecting or showing out all forms.

सर्वलक्षणयोगात् iii. 13 Because of conjunction with, admixture of, all characteristics. (Some editions read –लक्षणायोगात्, whih seems incorrect).

सर्ववित् iii. 17 All-knower.

सर्वविषयम् iii. 54 'Having-all-objects'; cognising all objects at once.

सर्वविषयेषु ii. 31 With regard to all objects.

सर्वत्रवृत्तिप्रत्ययस्तमये i. 18 In the condition when all mental activities have "set", subsided, dis-appeared.

सर्ववृत्तिनिरोधे i. 1 On the inhibition of all mental functionings.

सर्वशब्दाग्रहणात् i. 2 Because of the non-use of the word 'all'.

सर्वश्रोत्राणाम् iii. 41 Of all ears.

सर्वस्य i. 32; ii. 9, 14, 15; iii. 13; iv. 10 Of all; (masc:, sing:).

सर्वाः i. 11; iv. 11 All; (fem:, plu:).

सर्वात्मकम् iii. 14 All-natured; all-comprehensive; (neu:).

सर्वात्मनां iii. 49. Of the all-natured.

सर्वात्मानः iii. 49 All-natured; all-en-souling; (pl:).

सर्वान् i. 47; iii. 13.

सर्वानुकूलम् iii. 18 All-helpful; all-favoring.

सर्वाभिधानशक्तिपरिवृत्ताः iii. 17 "Turned away" from, deprived of, all-denoting potency.

सर्वाभिधानशक्तिप्रचितः iii. 17 Determined by, or filled with, the potency of denoting all things whatsoever.

सर्वार्थता iii. 11 'All-objectness'; many-pointedness; distractedness.

सर्वार्थतायाः iii. 11

सर्वार्थतैकाग्रतयोः iii 11 Of all-pointedness and one-pointedness; of distractedness and concentratedness, distraction and concentration.

सर्वार्थम् ii. 19; iv. 23 'For the sake of all'; 'going to all things'; all-including; all-apprehending.

सर्वार्थाध्यवसायकत्वात् ii. 20 Because of determinate cognisance of all matters.

सर्वावरणमलापेतस्य iv. 31 'Of the (knowledge) which has gone beyond, transcended, all veiling foulness'; of pure, stainless, un-erring (knowledge).

सर्वे i. 17; ii. 4, 15, 17; iii. 26; iv. 14 All; (masc:, pl:).

सर्वेषाम् ii. 28; iii. 41.

सर्वेषु ii. 4; iii. 26, 51.

सर्वैः iv. 31.

सर्षपराशिकल्पाः iii. 26 Like heaps of mustard-grains.

—सलिल— iii. 26.

सविचारः i. 17,46 'Reflectional', 'reflective'; 'thought-accompanied'; (samādhi, 'absorption', 'absorbed meditation', of the nature of) abstract-thinking.

सविचारध्यानसुखाः iii. 26 Rejoicing in the discriminative contemplation of subtle or abstract objects; enjoying abstract, reflective, thought-ful meditation.

सविचारा i. 44 'With cogitation'

(on subtle or abstract matters). (see वितर्क...रूपानुगमात्).

सचित्रशैलावतंसाः iii. 26 'With-wonderful-hill-ornaments'; adorned with grand mountains and mountain-scenery.

सवितर्कः i. 17, 46 (See वितर्का... नुगमात्). Biassed, prejudiced, emotion-tinged, con-fused meditation concerned with external sensuous objects.

सवितर्कध्यानसुखाः iii. 26 Rejoicing in the 'mixed', 'emotion-tinged', contemplation of concrete objects.

सवितर्का i. 42 (See सवितर्कः).

सवितर्का i. 42, 44.

सविपाकस्य ii. 5 Of (the seed of karma) with its developments, maturation, fruition.

सव्यापाराः iii. 14 'With operation' actively functioning.

—सह— iv. 14, 15.

सह i. 27, 30, 51; ii. 10, 15, 23; iii. 13, 44, 52 Together with.

सहकारिवर्णान्तरप्रतियोगित्वात् iii. 17 By delimiting or restricting connection with other co-operating letter-sounds.

सहक्षणभेदात् ii. 53 By separateness, distinction of the accompanying, the co-efficient, the concomitant moment of time.

—सहगतः iii. 17.

—सहनम् ii. 32.

—सहन्ते iv. 11, 32.

सहभुवोः iii. 52 Of the two 'together-becoming', i. e. of (two things) which are born together, are simultaneous.

सहभूतं i. 43 Accompanying; 'born or existing with.'

—सहस्र— iii. 26.

—सहस्राणि iii. 26.

सा i. 20; ii. 4; iii. 15; iv. 7 etc. 'She.'

साक्षात्करणम् iii. 18, 52 'Sighting'; direct cognising.

—साक्षात्करणात् iii. 18.

साक्षात्करणात् iii, 18, 19 Because of, by, from do:.

साक्षात्कर्त्तव्यम् iii. 26 Should be directly seen. (Some editions read –करणीयम्).

साक्षात्कुर्वतः iii. 51 Of one who is cognising directly.

साक्षात्कृतम् ii. 27 Perceived directly.

साक्षात्क्रियमाणम् iii. 16 Being 'fronted', 'faced', 'sighted'; being brought before the senses, perceived, directly cognised.

—साक्षात्क्रियायै iii. 18.

—साक्षिणि ii. 18.

साङ्ख्यपक्षे iv. 15 In the Sāṅkhya doctrine, theory, view; on the 'side', 'wing', of the Sāṅkhya.

साङ्ख्ययोगादयः iv. 21 Sāṅkhya and Yoga doctrines etc.

सातिशयत्वात् i. 25 Because of 'exceedability', of being relative to things which are comparatively larger and smaller; because of being comparative.

—साधन— i. 13; ii. 15; iii. 51; iv. 7, 10.

साधनत्रयम् iii. 8 Triad of means, (i. e., contemplation, concentration, absorption).

साधननिर्देशः ii. 55 The pointing out, enunciation, enumeration, of the means.

साधनपादः ii. 1 The 'foot', quarter, section, part, chapter, on the 'means'; (the name of the 2nd section of the work).

साधनम् ii. 28 That which accomplishes; means of achieving or accomplishing (something). (साध्, to accomplish).

—साधनस्य iii. 16.

—साधना iii. 17.

—साधनात् ii. 32.

—साधनानाम् i. 30.

—साधनानि ii. 15.

साधनानि ii. 28; iii. 1, 4 Means; (pl:).

—साधनाय i. 18.

—साधने ii. 7, 8.

साधनेभ्यः iii. 7.

साधयति iii. 43 Accomplishes, brings about, causes to be achieved. (Some editions read साधयन्ति, pl:).

साधारणः i. 43 Common; general; ordinary; current; universal.

साधारणत्वम् iv. 15 Commonness.

—साधारणत्वात् ii. 22.

साधारणम् iv. 15.

साधारणविषयम् ii. 23 'Common-factored'; possessed of a common feature or factor.

साधिकारम् i. 50; iv. 11 Having a function; possessed of a specific functional operativeness or activity; functioning; active; 'officious', holding a definite 'office'; inspired by a specific momentum; restless; unreposing; full of 'right-and-duty'.

साधिकारा ii. 24.

साधिकारे i. 19.

—साध्या iv. 7.

सानन्दः i. 17 'With-bliss'; blissful; accompanied with 'enjoyment'.

—सान्तपन—ii. 32 (The name of a particular ascetic practice).

—सामर्थ्यम् ii. 4.

—सामर्थ्याः ii. 18.

—सामर्थ्यात् i. 35; ii. 17 (By or because of ability, capacity, adequacy; see समर्थः).

—सामान्यम् iii. 44.

सामान्यम् i. 32 Common; similar; general; abstract; universal; 'equalness'; sameness'.

सामान्यमात्रग्रहणाकारम् iii. 47 Of the form of only a general notion; of the apprehension of only the general.

सामान्यमात्रम् iv. 24 All or only the general.

सामान्यमात्रोपसंहारे i. 25 In a general conclusion (or induction) only.

सामान्यविशेषसमुदायः iii. 44 A conglomerate of genera and propria.

सामान्यविशेषात्मनः i. 7 Of the genero-specific; of that which is both abstract and concrete, one as well as many, general as well as singular; (psycho-physical, spirituo-material); of that which has both general and special, common and proper, features, has 'similarity in diversity'.

सामान्यविशेषात्मा iii. 14, 44, 47.

सामान्यविषयम् i. 49 Having only the 'general' for 'object'.

सामान्यस्य iii. 44, 47.

सामान्यानि ii. 15; iii. 13.

सामान्यावधारणप्रधाना i. 7 Predominantly determinant or cognisant of the common or generic feature or quality; chiefly of the nature of or concerned with general notions.

सामान्येन i. 49; iii. 13, 14 By way of generalisation (induction-deduction); 'generally speaking'.

साम्प्रतिकस्य ii. 13 Of the present (birth).

साम्यातिशयविनिर्मुक्तम् i. 24 Free of, beyond, possibility of being equalled or excelled.

—साम्ये iii. 55; iv. 15.

—सारूप्यम् iii. 55.

—सारूप्यात् iii. 17.

—सारूप्ये iii. 53.

—सारूप्येण iv. 23.

सार्वभौमः i. 1 Belonging, appertaining, extending, common, to, pervasive of, all 'grounds', stages, modes (of the mind).

सार्वभौमाः ii. 31 Do: ; (pl:).

सालम्बनः i. 18 'With-rest'; leaning on'; having an object; objective; tied to or inclusive of, referring to, some object; (masc:).

सालम्बनम् iii. 20.

सालम्बनाः i. 17.

सास्नादिमन्तम् iii. 17 To the dewlap-possessing; to (the animal) possessing a dewlap, (i. e., a cow) etc.

साहङ्काराणि iii. 47 With or including egoism.

—साहस्राणि iii. 26.

—साहस्रं iii. 26.

—साहस्र— iii. 26.

सितविमलतनुः i. 1 Of the white and stainless body.

—सिद्ध— iii 44, 47.

सिद्धः i. 26; ii 38 Accomplished; perfected; (masc:; सिध्, to go, to command, to suc-'ceed', to be accomplished, to be finished and effected completely).

सिद्धदर्शनम् iii. 32 Vision of perfected beings.

सिद्धम् ii 20; iv. 9, 12 (Neu:).

सिद्धयः iii. 37; iv. 1 (Super-physical) accomplishments; perfections; extra-ordinary powers; occult powers.

सिद्धयः ii. 39; iii. 48; iv 6.

सिद्धवत् iii. 17 As if, or as one, accomplished; also, as real, fixed, achieved, certain, perfected, proved, established

—सिद्धस्य iii. 45

सिद्धा ii. 28.

—सिद्धाः iii 26.

सिद्धाः ii. 44; iii. 51 'Accomplished' or 'perfected' beings; adepts.

सिद्धान् iii. 22.

सिद्धानाम् iii. 32, 45.

—सिद्धि— ii. 30.

—सिद्धिः ii. 43, 45.

सिद्धिः ii. 28; iii. 49 (Sing: of सिद्धयः).

सिद्धिभिः ii. 46.

सिद्धिसूचकम् ii 35 Indicative, prognosticative, of accomplishment.

सिद्धौ i. 24

सिद्ध्यति ii. 1, 47 Becomes accomplished; accrues. (सिध्, '*cedere*', to go; see सिद्धः).

—सीमा— iii. 26.

सुकृतानि ii. 13 'Well-doings'; good or virtuous deeds; well-done, virtuous, meritorious, doings.

—सुख— ii. 5, 42.

—सुख— ii. 14, 15; iii, 18.

सुखख्यातिः ii. 5 Belief or consciousness of pleasure or pleasantness or pleasurableness.

सुखख्यातिम् ii. 5.

सुखचित्तम् iv. 24 The 'pleasure-mind'; the pleasure-ward mind; the mind tinged with the feeling or tone of pleasure.

सुखज्ञानम् iv. 15 Knowledge of pleasure.

सुखत्वे ii. 28 In pleasurableness.

सुखदुःखपुण्यापुण्यविषयाणाम् i. 33 Of (mental moods) having for objects joy, sorrow, merit, and sin, (or, the joyful, the sorrowful, the virtuous, and the sinful), respectively.

सुखदुःखमोहाः i. 11 Pleasure, pain, and perplexity.

सुखदुःखमोहात्मिकाः i. 11 Of the nature, character, or tone of, or ensouled or inspired by, pleasure, pain, and perplexed dullness, or dull indifference, or confused ignorance.

सुखदुःखयोः iii. 18 Of pleasure and pain.

सुखदुःखशून्यम् ii. 55 Devoid of do:.

सुखदुःखे iv. 11 Pleasure and pain.

सुखप्राप्तौ ii. 34 On obtaining pleasure.

सुखफलाः ii. 14 'Pleasure-fruited'; fruiting, resulting, in pleasure; pleasure-producing; (pl:).

—सुखम् ii. 46.

—सुखम् ii. 15,42; iii. 18.

सुखम् i. 10; ii. 15, 42; iii. 18; iv. 11 Pleasure; pleasantly.

सुखसंस्काराशयः ii. 15 'Pleasure-tendency-germ'; innate disposition created by experience of pleasure

सुखसम्भोगापन्नेषु i. 33 Amongst those who have found pleasant enjoyment.

सुखसाधनानि ii. 15 'Accomplishers', means, bringers about, of pleasure.

—सुखस्य ii. 42.

सुखस्य ii. 15, 28.

—सुखाः iii 26.

सुखात् iv. 11.

सुखादिवत् iv. 15 Like pleasure, etc.

सुखानुभवः ii. 15 Experience of pleasure.

सुखानुभवात् ii. 15.

सुखानुशयी ii. 7 'Sleeping with', hiding in, going with, accompanying, resulting from, produced by, pleasure.

सुखानुशयी i. 11

सुखानुस्मृतिपूर्वः ii. 7 Preceded by remembrance of pleasure

सुखाभिज्ञस्य ii. 7 Of one who knows, feels, recognises, pleasure.

सुखार्थम् iv. 24 For the sake of pleasure.

सुखार्थी ii. 15 Desirous of, seeking, wanting pleasure.

सुखावस्थायाम् ii. 15 In the state of pleasure.

सुखितेषु iii. 23 In, on, towards the happy.

सुखे ii. 7, 15.

—सुतल— iii. 26.

सुतुच्छकम् iv. 13 Very trivial; sordid; to be ignored.

सुदर्शनम् iii 26 (Name of the capital of heaven).

सुधर्मा iii. 26 (Name of the assembly hall of the gods).

सुप्रतिष्ठितसंस्थानम् iii. 26 Firmly fixed in (its) place; well-established; well-jointed; with a firmly articulated organisation; strongly con'stitu'-ted and in-'stitu'-ted.

सुभोगी i. 1 Of the excellent body; or having fine bodily enjoyments.

सुमानसम् iii. 26 (Name of an elysian garden).

सुमेरुः iii. 26 (Name of a mountain); the axis of the Earth; the North Pole; the gold-mountain.

सुमेरोः iii 26.

—सुरा— iii. 26 (Alcohol).

सुवर्णकारः ii. 28 Gold-smith; 'gold-maker'. (Su-varṇa, is, literally, 'good-color'; the

English word 'sovereign', for the gold coin, is perhaps the same as this).

सुवर्णभाजनस्य iii. 13 Of a golden vessel.

सुवर्णस्य ii. 28 Of gold.

सुवर्णान्यथात्वम् iii. 13 'Otherwise-ness' of gold; change of gold into some other substance.

सुश्रद्धीयते i. 35 Is well believed in. (Some editions read श्रद्धीयते).

सुसूक्ष्मविषयम् i. 35 Very subtle subject-matter. (Some editions read सूक्ष्मविषयम्).

सुस्थितम्मन्यतया iii. 51 By belief, over-confidence, overweening conceit, of (his own) firm-fixed-ness, thorough 'steadi'-ness.

—सूः iv. 28.

—सूक्ष्म— iii. 44.

—सूक्ष्म—i. 41, 49.

—सूक्ष्मः ii. 50.

सूक्ष्मः i. 17. 45; ii. 11 Small; subtile; fine; (masc:).

—सूक्ष्मः ii. 51.

सूक्ष्मम् i. 43, 45.

सूक्ष्मरूपम् iii. 44 Subtile form.

सूक्ष्मविषयत्वम् i. 45 The state of having the subtile for object.

सूक्ष्मविषयम् i. 35 Having the subtile for object.

सूक्ष्मविषया i. 44 Do:; (fem:).

सूक्ष्मव्यवहितविप्रकृष्टज्ञानम् iii. 25 Knowledge of the subtle, the hidden, the distant.

सूक्ष्मव्यवहितविप्रकृष्टस्य i. 49 Of the subtile, the hidden, the distant.

सूक्ष्मव्यवहितविप्रकृष्टातीतानागतज्ञानम् iii. 36 Knowledge of the subtle, the screened or concealed, the distant, the 'bygone' or past, the 'not-come' or future.

सूक्ष्मस्थूलेन ii. 18 By subtile and dense or gross.

सूक्ष्मा ii. 2.

—सूक्ष्माः iv. 13.

सूक्ष्माः ii. 10.

सूक्ष्माः ii. 11.

—सूक्ष्माणाम् i. 43.

सूक्ष्मीकृताः ii. 11 Made subtle; sublimated; transformed into the subtile; subtilised,

सूक्ष्मे i. 40, 46; iii. 25.

सूक्ष्मेषु i. 35.

—सूचकम् ii. 35.

सूत्रम् i. 2, 4; ii. 23 'Thread'; aphorism; theory; principle; outline; plan. (सूच् , to 'suggest', to reveal, hint, indicate; also सूत्र् , to tie, bind, 'sew' together; that which suggests and binds together many meanings and much meaning in a few words).

सूत्रान्तरेषु ii. 33 In other aphorisms.

सूत्रेण i. 43.

सूर्यद्वारे iii. 26 On the gateway of

the sun; (the sushumnā-nerve, or the brahma-randhra ?).

सूर्यप्रचारात् iii. 26 By or from the motion of the sun

सूर्ये iii 26 In or on the sun.

सूर्येन्दुग्रहमणिप्रभारूपाकारेण i. 36 By or in the form of the luminosity of the sun, moon, planets, gems.

—सृज्य— iv. 14.

—सृज्यमानाः ii. 19.

—सृज्येत ii. 40.

—सृष्टम् ii. 19.

—सृष्टाः ii. 19.

—सृष्टानि ii. 19.

—सेव्यम् ii. 1.

सोपक्रमम् iii. 22 "With initiative', 'with active steps': actively helped and supported; energetically operative. (See निरुपक्रमम्)

सोपक्रमम् iii. 22.

सोपाश्रयम् ii. 46 Supported by apparatus, by some mechanical means or external object.

सौक्ष्म्यम् i. 45; iii. 13 Subtleness; subtilty.

सौक्ष्म्यात् iii 13.

—सौमनस्य— ii. 41.

सौमनस्यम् ii. 41 'Good-mindedness'; cheerfulness; placidity of temper; lucid-mindedness.

स्कंधान् iv 21 Sheaths, stems, 'trunks' (of trees).

स्कंधानाम् iv. 21.

—स्तम्भ— ii. 50.

—स्तम्भे iii. 21.

स्तुतिदानाभिवादनादि iv. 10 Praise, presents or alms-giving, and obeisance, etc.

—स्तेय— ii. 30.

स्तेयम् ii. 30 Theft.

—स्त्यान—i. 30.

स्त्यानम् i 10, 30 Dried up, shrunken, sapless; cheerless; worried; repetitive, echoing; wandering; scattered; confused; jumbled; hollow. (स्त्यै, to be heaped up; also, to be scattered).

स्त्रियः i. 15 (Pl: of स्त्री).

स्त्रियाम् ii. 4; iii. 13.

स्त्री iii. 13 Woman.

स्त्रीप्रत्ययस्य ii. 28 Of the (one) idea of (a) woman.

स्त्रीषु ii. 4

—स्थातुम् iv. 32.

स्थातुम् iv. 11 To 'stand' or 'stay'.

—स्थानम् iii. 26; iv. 34.

स्थानात् ii. 5 From the place (of origin).

स्थानासने ii. 32 Standing and sitting.

स्थानिनः iii. 51 'Place-holders'; local (gods).

—स्थाने ii. 24; iii. 13.

स्थानैः iii. 51 With places, offices; with authority or control over places.

स्थान्युपनिमंत्रणे iii. 51 On being

invited by the 'local' authority, the super-physical entity in charge of the world, plane, tract.

—स्थापयंति ii. 3.

—स्थापितम् iii. 17.

—स्थापितः iii. 17.

—स्थाप्य iii. 17.

स्थावराणाम् iii. 14 Of the 'standing, staying', unmoving; of the immovable.

स्थावरेषु iii. 14.

स्थास्यति i. 9 Will stand or stay. (स्था, to 'stand' or 'stay').

स्थितः i. 9, 27; iii. 14 Standing; staying; established; fixed.

—स्थित—iii. 26.

स्थितम् i. 27.

—स्थितम् iv. 14.

स्थितस्य i. 41.

स्थिताः iii. 26.

—स्थिताः iv. 12, 16.

स्थितानाम् ii. 11.

स्थितिः i. 13 'Steadi'-ness; 'staid'-ness, staying power; 'stand'ing; 'status'; fixity; firmness; establishment; 'estab'lished condition; 'state'; the 'stable' 'steady' desire which con'sti'-tutes the 'staying' power that fixes and 'estab'lishes the mind in one course, makes it cling firmly to one object; desire; inertia; tamas; 'stead'-fastness.

—स्थिति— ii. 18.

—स्थिति— i. 2, 51; ii. 15, 28; iii. 44, 47; iv. 14.

—स्थितिकम् i. 39.

स्थितिकारणम् ii. 28 Cause of steadiness.

स्थितिनिबंधनी i. 35 'Binder', tier, establisher, of fixity; helpful to steadiness of concentration.

स्थितिनिबन्धनी i. 36.

स्थितिपदम् i. 33, 36, 37, 38, 39, 40 The level, condition, 'state', 'stage', of 'steadi'ness.

स्थितिप्रवाहः i. 47 Flow or continuity of steadiness and fixity.

स्थितिम् i. 34.

स्थितिवैशारद्यात् i. 36 By clearness, keenness, lucidity, of fixity.

स्थितिशीलम् ii. 18 Inclined in the direction of, disposed towards, having the character and nature of, steadiness.

स्थितिसंस्कारक्षये ii. 23 On the decay, attenuation, consuming away, of the propensity to rest, to be 'steady'.

स्थितिहेतवः i. 51 Causes of steadiness.

स्थितौ i. 13 For 'steady' fixedness.

स्थितौ i. 35.

स्थित्या ii. 23; iv. 33.

स्थिरपदः iii. 5 Firm-footed; firm-based; firmly grounded.

स्थिरपदम् iii. 31.

स्थिरसुखम् ii. 46 Steady and easy or comfortable.

स्थूलः i. 17; ii. 11 'Thick', 'stolid', 'solid'; dense; gross; large.

स्थूलरूपसमापन्नम् i. 41 'Accomplished' into gross or dense form; (that which has) assumed, taken on, put on, a gross form.

स्थूलरूपाभासम् i. 41 Showing out a dense or gross form.

स्थूलशब्देन iii. 44 By the word 'sṭhūla'.

स्थूलाः ii. 11.

स्थूलालम्बनोपरक्तम् i. 41 Tinged with a gross 'support', a gross object.

स्थूले i. 40, 46.

—स्थूलेन ii. 18.

स्थैर्यम् iii. 31 'Steadi'ness; motionlessness.

—स्थैर्यात् ii. 41.

—स्थैर्ये ii. 39.

—स्नायु—iii. 29 ('Sinew'; tendon; muscle).

स्निग्धाः iii. 45 Smooth; fluid; liquid; lubricant; oily; (also, loving, affectionate).

स्नेहः iii. 44 Lubricity; oil; liquidity; fluidity.

स्नेहौष्ण्यप्रणामित्वावकाशदानानि iv. 14 Moisture, heat, bendingness, (i. e., the property of making other things bend) and 'space-making' (i. e. giving or making room).

—स्पंद— iv. 11.

—स्पंदते ii. 15.

स्पंदमानाः ii. 3 Vibrating; surging; heaving; struggling; energising; 'sput-'tering.

—स्पर्श—ii. 19; iii. 36.

स्पर्शतन्मात्रम् i. 45; ii. 19 The root-matter of touch; tact-in-itself.

स्पर्शवान् i. 43 Tangible; possessed of touch or tangibility, the quality of tact; palpable.

स्पर्शसंवित् i. 35 Consciousness of touch; tactile sensation.

स्पर्शेन ii. 15.

—स्पृश्य iii. 17.

स्पृशति iii. 45 Touches. (स्पृश्, to touch).

स्पृशामि i. 32 I touch.

—स्पृहा ii. 30 ('Aspiring'; desiring too high, too much, or wrongly)

स्फटिकः i. 41 Crystal; marble.

—स्फटिक— iii. 26.

स्फटिकमणिकल्पम् iv. 23 Like the crystal gem.

स्फुटप्रज्ञालोकः i. 47 Clear light of knowledge.

—स्मय—iii. 51.

स्मयम् iii. 51 'Smile' of self-complacence; conceit; self-confidence; arrogance; also, the 'smile' of wonder. (स्मि, to 'smile'; स्मील्, to wink).

स्मयात् iii. 51.
स्मरणम् iii. 14 Remembering. (स्मृ, to remember, to 'memor'ise).
स्मरति i. 11 Remembers.
—स्मर्तव्या i. 11.
स्मर्ता i. 32 Recollector.
स्मृतम् ii. 28 Remembered.
स्मृतयः i. 10, 11; iv. 21 Memories.
—स्मृतयः i. 6.
स्मृतिः i. 11 Memory.
स्मृतिः i. 11.
—स्मृति— i. 20.
—स्मृति— i. 35, 43; ii. 7, 8; iii. 14; iv. 10.
स्मृतिक्लेशहेतवः iii. 18 Causes of memory and causes of misery (i e., klésha, wretched, miserable, pain-bringing, irrational, male-scient, wrong-knowing 'desire', a-vidyā, etc.).
स्मृतिपरिशुद्धौ i. 43 On the clearing up of the memory; (the freeing of it from biassing associations, and making it precise and exact).
स्मृतिम् i. 11.
स्मृतिसंकरः iv 21 Confusion, inter-mixture, adulteration, of memories.
स्मृतिसंस्कारयोः iv. 9 Of memory and of implanted or induced tendency or 'acquired or stamped character'.
स्मृतिहेतवः ii. 13 Causes of memory; or caused by memory.
—स्मृतीनाम् i. 11.
स्मृत्यात्मकः iii. 17 Of the nature of memory.
स्मृत्युपस्थाने i. 20 On the coming up, the arising, of memory.
स्यंदमानाः ii. 3 Flowing, streaming; operating; functioning. (Some editions read स्पंदमानाः).
स्यात् iv. 16 Would be; may be; might be.
स्यात् i. 7, 30, 43; ii. 1, 30; iii. 13; iv. 19.
स्युः i. 10; ii. 35; iv. 14, 18 Do:; (pl:).
—स्रोतः i 12; ii. 3, 15 (Torrent, 'stream', flow, current).
—स्रोतसा ii. 15.
स्वः iii. 26 Heaven.
स्वकम् ii. 12 Own.
स्वकर्मोपहृतम् ii. 15 Brought up by one's own karma.
स्वकर्मोपार्जितदुःखवेदनाः iii. 26 Experiencing the pains earned by one's own deeds.
स्वकरणसंवेद्यः i. 35 Cognisable by one's own 'instrument' of knowledge, sense-organ.
स्वकारणे ii. 27 In (their) own cause.
स्वकार्यात् i. 50. From (its) own work or effect.
स्वक्षणे ii. 16 In (its) own moment.

स्वगुणैः iii. 51 By (your) own virtues, high qualifications.

स्वचित्तस्य ii. 23; iii. 38 Of (one's) own mind.

स्वचित्तेन ii. 23.

स्वच्छः i. 47; iii. 26 Very clear or pure. (सु + अच्छः).

स्वतन्त्रः iv. 16 Self-dependent; self-willed; self-reliant; self-'organised'. (See तन्त्रम्).

स्वतन्त्रम् ii. 17.

स्वदेशक्षणानुभवभिन्ने iii. 53 (The two myrobolan fruits) distinguished by the experience of the moment plus place or position or location of each.

स्वदेहे iii. 22 In (one's) own body

स्वपररूपावधारणम् iv. 20 Cognisance, clear ideation, notion, of one's own and another's form or nature.

स्वप्नज्ञानालम्बनम् i. 38 (See next word).

स्वप्ननिद्राज्ञानालम्बनम् i. 38 Resting or depending on, directed to, the knowledge or experience occurring in the condition of dream or slumber.

स्वप्नविषयोपमम् iv. 14 Like the stuff of dreams.

स्वप्नादौ iv. 14 In dream, etc.

स्वप्ने i. 11 In sleep or dream.

स्वप्नोपमेभ्यः iii. 51 To the dream-like.

स्वप्रतिष्ठम् iv. 15 Self-established; self-'standing'; self-upheld; self-based; self-maintained.

स्वप्रतिष्ठाः iii. 26.

स्वप्रतिभोत्थम् iii. 54 Arising out of one's own intuition; born of one's own insight. (See प्रातिभम्; प्रति + भा, to shine out, to appear in a flash).

स्वबुद्धिप्रचारप्रतिसंवेदनात् iv. 19 By recognition, awareness, consciousness, of the movement of one's own intelligence; (i. e., by Apperception).

स्वबुद्धिसंवेदनम् iv. 22 Apperception of one's own intelligence.

स्वबुद्धेः iv. 19 Of (one's) own intelligence.

स्वबोधसङ्क्रान्तये i. 7; ii 30 For the transmission of one's own knowledge (to another).

—स्वभावः iv. 12.

—स्वभाव— ii. 40; iii. 44.

—स्वभावकम् iv. 16.

स्वभावभिन्नाः i. 32 Different in 'own-being' or nature; distinguished, divided, differentiated, by (their respective) natures.

स्वभावम् iv. 25 'Own-being,; (one's) own (characteristic way of) existence; essential or fundamental nature. (स्व + भू, to be).

स्वम् i. 4, 43; ii. 17, 40; iv. 2, 3 Own; one's own; the owned property; (one's) own Self.

स्वमाहात्म्येन iv. 14 By (its) own greatness.

स्वयम् iv 3, 23 Of 'own-self'; itself; themselves; one-self; by oneself.

स्वरसनिरुद्धम् iv. 21 Inhibited by its own 'taste', 'juice', 'humour', inclination, wish, instinct.

स्वरसवाही ii. 9 'Flowing by or according to its own taste, own humour'; flowing, streaming, welling up, of itself, naturally; self-maintaining; self-persisting.

—स्वरूपः iii. 52.

—स्वरूप— iii. 44, 47.

—स्वरूप— i. 41, 43; ii. 6, 18, 28; iii. 13, 15; iv. 23.

स्वरूपतः iv. 12 From, by, or of, its 'own-form'; specifically; by nature.

स्वरूपतः iv. 12.

—स्वरूपत्वात् iv. 17.

स्वरूपदर्शनम् i, 29; iii. 44 Vision of 'own-form', of the exact and true form or essence; the seeing, recognition, vision, of the Self.

स्वरूपप्रतिलम्भे ii. 6 On gain or recovery of the true own-form or nature.

स्वरूपप्रतिष्ठः i. 51; ii. 25 Self-established; established in its 'own-form' or nature.

स्वरूपप्रतिष्ठम् i. 2.

स्वरूपप्रतिष्ठा i. 3; iii. 50 Do:; (fem:).

स्वरूपप्रतिष्ठा iv. 34 Do:; (masc:)

स्वरूपभेदावधारणार्थम् ii. 19 For the sake of discrimination of the separate forms or natures (of the guṇas).

स्वरूपम् i. 9; ii. 15, 18, 21, 29; iii. 44; iv. 16 Own-form; essential and fundamental nature or character.

—स्वरूपम् i. 43, 44; ii. 18, 21; iv. 14, 19, 21.

स्वरूपमात्रज्योतिः ii. 27 'With the light of its own form'; lighted by its own form; self-luminous.

स्वरूपमात्रप्रतिष्ठेषु iv. 33 In (regard to souls) abiding or existing in their own pure nature (as mere consciousness, without any particular accretions).

स्वरूपमात्रे iv. 19 In mere pure 'own-form', ('thing-in-and-by-itself').

स्वरूपव्यक्तिः iv. 12 Manifestation of nature, of 'own-form'.

स्वरूपशब्देन iii. 44 By the word 'sva-rūpa'.

स्वरूपशून्यम् iii. 3 Devoid of 'own-form'; free of all self-reference, all self-consciousness.

स्वरूपशून्या i. 43 Do:; (fem:).

स्वरूपशून्या i. 44.

स्वरूपहानात् ii. 19, 21 By loss of 'own-form'; by loss of characteristic, specific, distinctive, nature.

—स्वरूपाः iii. 17.

—स्वरूपा i. 41, 43.

—स्वरूपानुकारः ii. 54 Imitating, functioning, according to one's 'own-form'; pursuing, one's own nature or natural bent.

स्वरूपाभिव्यक्तौ iii. 13 On or in manifestation of 'own-form', inner essential nature.

—स्वरूपायाः iv. 22.

स्वरूपावधारणम् ii. 18 Ascertainment of 'own-form' or peculiar nature.

स्वरूपावधारणार्थम् ii. 20 For the sake of do:.

स्वरूपास्तिता iv. 33 Existence of 'own-form'.

स्वरूपे i. 3 In 'own-form' or (fundamental nature or character.

स्वरूपेण i. 44; ii. 39; iii. 3, 13; iv. 12.

—स्वरूपेण ii 17; iii. 50.

स्वरूपोपलब्धिः ii. 23 Gain of, recovery of, recognition of, 'own-natnre'.

स्वरूपोपलब्धिहेतुः ii. 23 The means or cause of realisation of do:.

स्वर्गम् ii. 36; iii. 22 Heaven, elysium, paradise.

स्वर्गवैदेह्यप्रकृतिलयत्वप्राप्तौ i. 15 On the attainment of heaven, or of the condition of the 'bodiless gods', or of that of beings who are dissolved in and identified with the Root-principle of Matter or Mother-nature.

स्वर्गे ii. 13.

स्वर्लोकः iii. 26 The 'Svar'-world; the mental plane; the heaven-world.

स्वल्पः ii 13 Very small; very little.

स्वल्पप्रतिपक्षाः ii. 11 'Little-enemied'; meeting with feeble resistance; needing to make but small hostile effort to conquer (their opponents); or, (being of the nature of) weak enemies; offering feeble opposition.

स्वविषयसंप्रयोगाभावे ii. 54 In the absence of contact with their (appropriate) objects.

स्वविषयाऽसंप्रयोगे ii. 54 On 'non-contact' with 'own-objects'; in the absence of conjunction or meeting with their appropriate objects.

स्वव्यंजकांजनः i. 11 ;43 'Manifester of its own cause'; the developer, manifester, thrower into relief, of that which manifests, developes it, throws it into relief; or, showing forth, bringing out, making inferrible, that which has brought it forth in manifestation (as the father procreates the son, but the son, being born, makes the man a father at all, creates his paternity; reproducing its producer in turn (as seed and plant and seed etc.); or, disctinctively tinged, marked, stamped, characterised, by the special circumstances or conditions (as distinguished from the essential cause) which have immediately stimulated its birth and growth, (as the differences and peculiarities of soil, climate, weather, temperature, etc, give peculiar qualities to the products from the same kind of essential cause, viz., seed; as the same pair of parents give birth to children with more or less different faces, figures, temperaments, owing to the different moods or conditions in which the several conceptions have taken place and the gestations been carried on and completed; so that the peculiarities of the subsidiary causes are manifested by, and can be inferred from, the peculiarities of the seed-products or children); bearing on it the marks of its manifesting cause.

स्वव्यंजकांजनस्य iii. 13.

स्वव्यंजकांजनाभिव्यक्तः iv. 9 Manifested by do:.

स्वव्यंजकांजनेन ii. 4.

स्वव्यापारम् iii. 13, 14 'Own-operation', 'own-business; characteristic function.

स्वव्यापारोपारूढम् iv. 12 Engaged in, 'mounted on', riding on', its peculiar or appropriate activity or functioning.

स्वशब्देन iv. 21 By the word sva.

स्वशरीरात् iii. 38 From (one's) own body.

स्वसा iii. 13 'Sister'.

स्वसामान्यं iii. 44 'Own-common' (characteristic); i. e., the specific property 'common' to all its own variations; the generic attribute of each, (as 'shape' of all pieces of solid earth, 'liquidity' of all sorts of fluid water, etc.).

स्वसंज्ञाभिः i. 8 By their own designations.

स्वसंस्कारमात्रोपयो (or भो) गेन i. 19 With (a chitta or mind) which has to do with only its own 'tendency' or tendencies; or, which enjoys or utilises for enjoyment, only the feel of its own propensities or dispositions (and not any concrete manifestation of them; as a person indulging in conscious fanciful reverie may 'enjoy himself').

स्वसंस्कारविपाकम् i 19 The maturation, the ripening, into fruit, the exercise or fulfilment, of one's ingrained disposition

स्वस्ति iii 51 'It is well'; 'may it be well' (with you); 'fare-well'.

स्वस्तिकम् ii. 46 (Name of a posture of meditation).

स्वस्तिमती iii. 53 'Having the svasṭikā-mark'; or, auspicious, gentle, affectionate.

स्वस्थः ii. 132 'Self-seated'; self-con-tent; self-contained; healthy.

स्वस्मिन् ii. 23 In one-self.

स्वस्याम् i. 51 In its own.

स्वस्वामिशक्त्योः ii. 23 Of the 'powers' or faculties of the 'owned' and the 'owner', i. e. Prakṛṭi and Purusha.

स्वाङ्गजुगुप्सा ii. 40 Disgust with one's own limbs, i. e., body.

स्वाङ्गे ii. 40 In one's own body.

स्वात्मप्रतिष्ठम् iv. 19 Established in one's own Self; supported by one's own Self.

स्वात्मभूतम् ii. 23 Become one's own Self, one's own essential nature.

स्वात्मभूतयोः iii. 11 Do: ; (dual).

स्वात्मावलम्बनम् iii. 35 Dependent on itself.

स्वात्मानुभवापह्नवः i. 32 Flouting, ignoring, repudiating, traversing, of one's own self-experience, self-consciousness.

—स्वाद— iii. 36.

—स्वादु iii. 26.

स्वाध्यायः ii. 1, 32 (स्व + अधि + ई, to go; to go to one-self). Self-study; the study which leads to knowledge of the Self; study in general.

—स्वाध्याय— ii. 1, 32.

—स्वाध्याय— iv. 7.

स्वाध्यायम् i. 28.

स्वाध्याययोगसम्पत्त्या i. 28 By the 'wealth', the 'fullness', the 'perfection', of study and of yoga-practice.

स्वाध्यायशीलस्य ii. 44 Of him who is devoted to study.

स्वाध्यायात् ii. 44.

स्वाध्यायात् i. 28.

स्वानुभवग्राह्यः i. 32 Apprehensible in or by (one's) own-experience.

स्वाभाविकम् iv. 10 Self-natured; natural; (neuter).

स्वाभाविकी iv. 10, 25 Do: ; (fem:).

—स्वाभाव्यम् iii. 13.

स्वाभासम् iv. 19 Self-showing; self-lighted, self-luminous. (स्व + आ + भास्, to shine).

स्वाभासानि iv. 19.

स्वाभिः iii. 17 By one's own.

—स्वामि— ii. 23.

स्वामिनः i. 4; ii. 17, 23 (See स्वामी)

स्वामिनम् iii. 49; iv. 21.

स्वामिनि i. 24; ii. 18.

स्वामी ii. 23, 33 The owner, proprietor, possessor.

स्वार्थः ii. 20 For the sake of self; 'one's-own-interest'.

स्वार्थम् iv. 24 For 'self-sake'; for one-self.

स्वार्थसंयमात् iii. 35 By meditation on (the fact that the Self is) for Self (only, and not for another; that all things are means to the Self, are desired for the sake of the Self; while the Self is its own end, is end-to-it-Self. Cf: आत्मनस्तु कामाय सर्वं प्रियं भवति । *Bṛhad Upan:*)

—स्वित् ii. 39; iv. 25 (A particle expressive of surprise and enquiry).

स्वीकरणम् ii. 30 Appropriation; acceptance.

स्वीकरिष्यामि ii. 33 I will appropriate and make my own.

स्वेच्छया ii. 55 By own-wish; of one's own accord.

स्वेन ii. 23; iv. 12 By its own.

— ह —

—हत— iii. 26.

हताः iv. 30 Slain; defeated; suppressed. (हन्, to kill).

—हत्य— iv. 24.

हनिष्यामि ii. 31, 33 I will slay.

—हन्ति iv. 11.

—हन्यते iv. 33.

हरिवर्षम् iii. 26 (The Purāṇic name of a country or continent).

—हरेत् iv. 24

—हर्ष— iv. 25.

हस्तिनिषदनम् ii. 46 ('Elephant-seat'; elephant-posture', the name of a yogic posture of meditation).

हस्तिबलादीनि iii. 24 The strength of the elephant, etc.

हस्तिबले iii. 24 In or on the elephant's strength.

हातव्याः ii. 11 To be abolished, abandoned, avoided. (हा, to go, to move, to abandon).

हातव्ये ii. 15.

हातुः ii. 15 Of the avoider.

हानम् ii. 25; iv. 28 Avoidance; abolition; casting off; destruction; cure; remedy.

हानम् ii. 15, 25, 27.

हानस्य ii. 26.

हाने ii. 15.

हानोपायः ii. 26 The means of abolition; means of avoidance; way of cure; remedy.

हानोपायः ii. 15, 27, 28.

—हार्याः iv. 9.

हावगर्भाभ्याम् ii. 5 With (eyes), 'pregnant with coquetry.'

हि i. 2; ii. 2; iii. 6; iv. 3 etc. Verily; indeed; in sooth; in truth; in fact; as a fact; as a matter of fact.

हिंसकः ii. 34 Slayer; injurer,

—हिंसा— ii 30.

हिंसा ii. 31, 34 Slaying; slaughter; violence; malevolence. (हिंस्, to kill).

हिंसाकृतः ii. 15 'Done by slaughter'; produced, created, caused, by murder, by killing.

हिंसादयः ii. 35 (Thoughts, intentions, of) killing, etc.; malevolence, etc.

हिंसादयः ii. 33.

हिंसानिदानेभ्यः ii. 30 From the 'causes of slaughter'; i. e., from actions which cause destruction of life.

हिंसायाः ii 34.

—हित— iv. 9.

—हितम् ii. 30; iv. 22.

हित्वा ii. 12; iii. 13 Having abondoned. (हा, to cast off).

हिनस्ति ii. 43 Slays; destroys. (हिंस्, to slay).

—हिम— iii. 26 (Snow).

हिरण्यम् iii. 26 'Golden'; (name of a country).

हीयन्ते iii. 9 (They) weaken; diminish; decay. (हा, to go, to move; to abandon).

—हृत— iii. 17.

—हृदय— iii. 39.

हृदयपुण्डरीके i. 36; iii. 1 In the 'heart-lotus', the cardiac plexus.

हृदये iii. 34 In the 'heart'. (Gr. *phren*).

—हेतवः i. 51; ii. 13, 27; iii. 18.

—हेतु— ii. 17.

—हेतुः ii. 17, 23.

—हेतुः ii. 15, 17.

हेतुः ii. 24; iii. 15 Cause; reason; motive; occasion.

हेतुः i. 4, 45; ii. 19; iii. 53; iv. 3, 11, 15.

—हेतुकाः i. 5; ii. 14.

—हेतुत्वात् ii. 14.

—हेतुत्वात् i. 50; ii. 13.

हेतुफलाश्रयालम्बनैः iv. 11 By cause, effect, substratum and object or 'locus' (i. e., error, pain, mind, and pleasant-painful objects).

हेतुवादः ii. 15 The doctrine of origination by a cause.

—हेतोः ii. 17.

हेतोः ii. 34. (Some editions read the sentence, in which this word occurs, with ii. 35).

—हेम— iii. 26.

—हेमकूट— iii. 26 (Name of a 'mountain-of-gold'; Cf. The south American Andes, 'mountains of gold or copper', from the old Peruvian word *anta*, copper).

हेयकारणम् ii 25 The cause of what is to be avoided.

हेयताम् ii. 16 (To) avoidability.

हेयपक्षे ii. 16; iii. 18, 50 On the side of, in the class or category of, the to-be-shunned.

हेयम् ii. 16 To-be-avoided.
हेयम् ii. 15, 17, 25, 27.
हेयः ii. 15.
हेयहेतवः ii. 27.
हेयहेतुः ii. 17 Cause or source of the to-be-avoided.
हेयहेतुः ii. 15, 17.
—हेयाः ii 10, 11.
हेयाः ii. 35.
हेयोपादेयशून्याः i. 15 Empty, devoid, free, of (the thought of any object as) to-be-avoided or to-be grasped at or sought after; i. e., free of all dislikes and likes, free from all desires.
—ह्नुवते iv. 15 (or 16), 21.
ह्लादः i. 17 Joy.
ह्लादपरितापफलाः ii 14 'Fruiting joy and sorrow'; having joy and sorrow as consequences, as resultant fruit.

॥ इति ॥

ॐ

SOME OPINIONS ON THE WORKS OF DR. BHAGAVAN DAS.

THE SCIENCE OF THE EMOTIONS. (3rd edn., 1924; translations, of the earlier editions, of 1900 and 1908, have appeared in Dutch, French, Spanish, Norwegian; an epitome, of the 3rd enlarged edn, has been published by Miss K. Browning, M. A). "Has for the first time introduced order into this confused region of consciousness"; Annie Besant; she has repeatedly referred to the work in her own books, and gave lectures on it in Britain, U. S. A., India, shortly after the first edition was published. "One of the most original and suggestive publications"; *The Indian Review*, Madras. "The correspondence and transmutation of the emotions, and the method of practical application..come as a revelation"; Ernest Wood. The late Shri P. T. Srinivasa Iyengar, then Principal of the Vizagapatam College, published a summary of it in a series of instalments, in the *Theosophist*. G. Coster refers to it in her book, *Yoga and Western Psychology* (pub: by the Oxford University Press, London, 1934), and includes it in "the selection of readable books" given at the end of it.

THE SCIENCE OF PEACE (1st edn., 1904; 2nd., 1921). "Metaphysical questions expounded with rare acumen and felicity"; Annie Besant. "The gifted author of *The Science of Peace*"; Edward Carpenter in his book, *The Drama of Love and Death*. "The view that is here indicated seems to approximate rather closely to the views that have been more or less definitely suggested by some of the Oriental philosophers. See, for instance, *The Science of Peace*, by Bhagavan Das"; Professor J. S. Mackenzie, L.L.d., Litt. D., Co-editor of *International Journal of Ethics*, in the *Theosophist* for May, 1913.

THE SCIENCE OF SOCIAL ORGANISATION, OR THE LAWS OF MANU. (1st edn., 1910; 2nd, Vol. I, 1932, Vol. II, 1935; Vol. III, in preparation). "A work of the highest excellence and value...Has the indefinable quality of distinction"; the late Professor E. A, Wodehouse, M. A., (Oxon). "A revelation of the scientific principles which underlie our old social organisation"; the late Maha-maho-padhyaya Pandit Aditya Ram Bhattacharya, M.A., Professor of Samskrt, Muir College, Allahabad, later, Vice-Principal, Central Hindu College, Benares. "Simply grand"; the late Rai Bahadur Lala Baijnath, ex-Judge. "Amongst the most illuminative contributions to the study and understanding of the all-important subject it treats of"; Dr. Sir S. Subramania Iyer, ex-Chief Justice of the Madras High Court. "A rare combination of deep learning and felicitous phrasing"; Annie Besant. "I also owe a debt of gratitude to many Indian writers; in particular I would mention the writings of Bhagavan Das, whose book, *The Science of Social Organisation or the Laws of Manu*, I have used extensively in the introductory chapters"; E. J. Urwick, Preface to *The Message of Plato.* "The most interesting exposition of the Indian caste system with which I am acquainted is that which has been supplied by Bhagavan Das in his two writings on *The Science of Social Organisation,* and *Social Reconstruction*"; Prof. J. S. Mackenzie, in his *Fundamental Problems of Life* (*1928*). *The Vedic Magazine,* the monthly organ of the Gurukula, Kangri, published a series of articles summarising the work. Mrs. Adams Beck, in her *Story of Oriental Philosophy* (1930) transcribes and quotes extensively, and with high appreciation, from this work; "Bhagavan Das has written a remarkable book on *The Laws of Manu*..This is a passage of extraordinary beauty and insight.." etc. So also Lala Lajpat Rai in his *Unhappy India.* The monthly *Prabuddha Bharata,* of Calcutta, organ of the Rama-Krishna Mission, in its issue for August, 1933, says, at the beginning of a eulogistic review, "This is a marvellous book." *The Modern Review* of Calcutta published a very appreciative review. Dr. G. H. Mees, in his books, *Dharma and Society* (1935), and *The Human Family and India* (1938), quotes repeatedly from this work, and, expounds the same main ideas, ably and freshly, with variations here and there.

THE SCIENCE OF THE SACRED WORD, OR THE PRANAVA-VADA OF GARGYAYANA, 3 vols. "This unique treatise...The author's elucidations of the many statements in the text surpass in value his work which gave to the world two highly important works, *The Science of the Emotions* and *The Science of Peace*"; Dr. Sir Subramania Iyer, ex-Chief Justice of the Madras High Court; he published a synopsis of the work in a series of instalments in the *Theosophist.*

THE SCIENCE OF RELIGION, OR SANATANA VAIDIKA DHARMA. "Worthy of careful study by the younger generation of Hindus"; Sir Goorod Dass Bannerjee, ex-Judge of the Calcutta High Court. "I have again read it with great profit and pleasure, with admiration for the learning, earnestness of spirit, and elevated enthusiasm of the author ...The presentation of the principles is very attractive to the English-educated mind"; Sir P.S. Sivaswamy Aiyer, ex-Executive Councillor of the Madras Government, and ex-Vice-Chancellor of the Madras and the Hindu Universities. "Has given me much pleasure...Ancient learning formally presented in a way intelligible and attractive to modern modes of thinking"; Sir John G. Woodroffe, (then) Judge of the Calcutta High Court, author of many publications on Tantra Shastra, *Serpent-Power, Shakti and Shakta,* etc., and co-editor of many Tantra Texts. "...An original production..laying down lines of thought which are extremely suggestive and full of independent interest...offering new points of view from which to survey world-problems"; Shri Satish Chandra Mukerji, M. A., B. L., ex-Editor of the *Dawn*, Calcutta. "A production of striking excellence..The fine poetic language is as noteworthy as the profound learning, the clear analysis, the vigorous logic, and the broad humanity of the book.. I am astonished at the felicity of expression and beautiful turn of phrasing in some places"; Prof. P. Seshadri, M. A., (then) of the Central Hindu College, Benares. "I have read your articles and book with interest and deep respect. They remind me strongly of Ruskin's views on social and national organisation..I feel deep sympathy with the purpose which you and Ruskin had in view in your writings"; Sir Michael E. Sadler, (1918), Vice-Chancellor of the University of Manchester, ex-President of the Calcutta University Commission.

ANCIENT VS. MODERN SCIENTIFIC SOCIALISM. "Full of useful suggestions...Every politically minded Indian should read it..The author is an acute observer of events and has logical acumen of the very first order..This strange (for India is asked to go back to the time of Manu) and brilliant thesis (brilliant for it seems to be proved that what Communism and Fascism are trying to establish had long ago been more successfully established by Manu;" review in the *Forward* of Calcutta, dated 28-1-1935. "The subject matter is one of profound interest....The Great Indian Lawgiver Manu has given us the plan of individual and social life with its planned education, planned family life, planned economy, planned defence-sanitation-judication, and planned religion-recreation-art. But how many of our economists know any thing about Manu and his comprehensive plan of life ?......The little book deserves to be widely circulated and read"; the *Hindustan Times*, Delhi, dated 25-3-1935. "The Indian reformer is taunted as superficial, and a reconstruction is demanded, which will be thorough and at the same time suited to the tradition and the special needs of India. Few attempts have been made to meet this demand; but among them, the solutions offered by Dr. Bhagavan Das merit honorable mention. A life...has been devoted by him to the analytical and historical study of Indian problems. His known mastery of Eastern and Western thought has enabled him to offer singularly fresh interpretations of the old Indian Social Organisation and of its adaptability to modern requirements. His views demand the attention due to great erudition, acute reasoning, and knowledge of the world... He claims that the Hindu Scheme offers the middle course between individualism and socialism and alone reconciles conflicting claims. Each system which is criticised is described in the words of its latest exponents, the results of its working are given on the observations of competent critics, and the theory is judged by its practice.. A suggestive work, animated by the spirit of real altruism;" review, in the *Hindu* of Madras, dated 20-11-1934, by R. B. Prof. K. V. Rangaswami Iyengar, M. A., (for some years Director of Public Instruction, Travancore, and then, for some years, Principal of the Central Hindu College of the Benares Hindu University); "In this rebirth of Indian civilisation, the student and scholar concerned with the science of sociology comes across solutions, hoary with age and sanctified by centuries of vogue, which the superficial critic often either does not see, or seeing dismisses as fantastic. The venerable Dr. Bhagavan Das, better known by his unadorned name for his wide culture and saintly simplicity, has discharged a noble duty by addressing himself to the task of inviting public attention to the principles of ancient scientific socialism in comparison with those of its modern counterpart. In this study he shows up the contrast between a socialism that is based upon a materialist interpretation of history and a spirituo-materealistic interpretation thereof, between one that fosters class war and one that promotes class co-operation, between one, again, that stands for equality and one that stands for equitability. In other words, the contrast is between dictatorship, on the one hand, and a balanced distribution of power in society, so as to reconcile individual speciality with social solidarity, between a wholesale break with the past and a healthy preservation of tradition which makes the past live in the present and the present herald the future. In this system of ancient socialism, religion, family, and property are not abolished but are purified, by a control of priestcraft, financial jugglery, and individual selfishness. This is the argument of Bhagavan Das' thesis, and he pours into his work such a volume of learning, knowlege, and wisdom that it is impossible to cull out from this ocean of culture samples of its waters to prove to an ignorant, superstitious, and perverted world their true life-giving character. Yet we have to taste a few drops of this eternal spring, and satisfy our doubting minds that we have in our culture and in our institutions a 'well and truly laid' foundation of a social system which applies, on a large scale, to society as a whole, the simple ideal of the joint family........."; Dr. B. Pattabhi Sitaramayya, in the *Triveni* of Madras, for Oct, 1936, art: "Indian Socialism re-discovered". Mr. Jo. Henri Buchi, of London, discussed the book, in two articles, entitled, "Manu, Marx, and Engels", in the *Hindustan Times* (Delhi) in Aug-Sep., 1935.

THE ESSENTIAL UNITY OF ALL RELIGIONS. This book has grown out of a paper read at the first All-Asia Education Conference, held in Benares, in December, 1930. The first section dwells on the world's 'Need for Scientific Religion'. and explains the three aspects of Religion. The second, expounds the Way of Knowledge. The third treats of the Way of Devotion. The fourth lays out the Way of Works. The fifth deals with 'the One Way to Peace on earth and Good-will among men'. The sixth discusses the relation, to the subject, of 'Education and the Educationist'. The seventh forms the 'Conclusion'.

Over 450 passages, from the Scriptures and Sacred Books of eleven living religions have been quoted, mostly in the original, transcribed into roman script with translations in English, and have been arranged in parallels, in appropriate sections and sub-sections, in the elucidative setting of exposition and comment. They prove how identical are the teachings of all the living religions, not only on all essential points, but even on many of those of secondary inportance. There is no copyright in the book.

Shri Rabindranath Tagore, in a letter to the author writes: "Your work on Universal Religion has a profound significance for suffering humanity to-day torn by sectarian bias, bigotry, and general apathy for the abiding verities of life. It was greatly needed to reveal the fundamental plane of unity where the human mind meets in its diverse realisations, and to manifest the kinship of the great founders of religions who in different ages and countries have come with the message of the divine spirit of man. I am deeply grateful to you for your book."

"The book is full of aphorisms which delight us by their clear insight and ruthless pruning away of unessentials. Dr. Bhagavan Das makes a moving plea to us to enjoy rather the search for agreements than the usual critical search for differences. He emphasizes those agreements and builds them into a working philosophy and scheme of education"; *The Theosophist* (Madras) for April, 1933.

Sir S. Radhakrishnan, the most brilliant exponent of Indian Philosophy to the west today, wrote "..I shall certainly ask my students to read *The Essential Unity of all Religions*...I really believe that a book like this should be made accessible to all interested in the religious future of our country".

"When the first All-Asia Educational Conference met at Benares in December, 1930, Dr. Bhagavan Das delivered a magnificent address on *The Essential Unity of All Religions*...now revised, enlarged, and published in book form..Anything from the pen of Dr. Bhagavan Das is worth perusing, because not only do we find his deep learning in every page of his writings but his sincerity and devotion to service of fellowmen pervade the whole of them...."; *The Leader* (Allahabad), dated 9-6-1933.

"I have read and re-read with great interest *The Essential Unity of All Religions* by Dr. Bhagavan Das...It is a remarkable contribution to a more reasonable and intelligent method of arriving at the truth and unity of religious ideals. The marshalling of thoughts as well as the quotations cited..show wide range of study and patient research. The quotations of numerous texts..are very apt and exact, while the parallel passages cited, to illustrate the similarity of ideas of the Reformers and Founders of different systems of religion, are unique and remarkable for their forceful elucidation. The fascinating pages of the book tend to arrest the attention at every turn and clearly bring out the important fact that the religious minds of all ages revolve in the same spiritual grooves.. that the essence of all religions *is* the same, that there is hardly any conflict in their ideals, and that rancour and discord of sects and sectarianism are mainly due to misunderstanding and lack of appreciation of one another's views. To the student of religious history, who desires to solve the problem of religious conflict and to understand in a rational manner the origin and development of religion itself, this unique book will be especially useful. It should be widely read and included in the curriculum of colleges...The Universities of India will do well if they recommend and prescribe such books for higher study"; Maulvi Wahid Husain (Advocate, High Court. Calcutta; Law Examiner, and ex-Extension Lecturer, Calcutta University; Secretary, Bengal Presidency Muhammadan Educational Conference).

"An opportune contribution on the subject. The author writes with a thorough knowledge of the principles of different religious scriptures. His knowledge of our Vedanta Philosophy is unique...He is just the person to have undertaken the task of bringing home to all, the fundamental unity of all religions. He has shown that the fundamentals of all religions are one and the same...A book like this was greatly needed at present when our unfortunate country is torn asunder by bigotry and communalism. I hope it will be included in the curriculum of our Colleges"; Acharya Dr. Sir P. C. Ray.

"Has appeared at the right psychological moment, when the several religions are being made the ground for dissensions of all sorts, on the one hand, and, on the other, the minds of our young men are being weaned from all Religion on the ground that *that* is the sole obstacle in the path of our political advancement. A perusal of the book will show that no religion sanctions in any way the animosities that have cropped up and are cropping up in our country, but that, on the contrary, all religions provide the same reasons for universal brotherliness and good will. The animosities have their root solely in motives which are superficial, sordid, often immoral; they are due, not to religion but to ir-religion. The book deserves to be placed in the hands of every young man, and also to be brought to the notice of all those elder persons who are wishing and working for the true welfare of the younger generations. The scholarly manner in which the main ideas have been presented makes the book fit for serious study in our Universities and Colleges. It will bring spiritual profit and pleasure to any person of intellectual tastes who will keep a copy by him, and dips, now and then, into the collections of fine parallel texts from the scriptures of the several religions, arranged amidst interweaving and systematising exposition"; Maha-maho-padhyaya Dr. Ganga Nath Jha, M. A., D. Litt., Vice-Chancellor for nine years of the University of Allahabad.

"This small book of less than 300 pages, cannot be adequately praised. It is an inspired psychic plea for the unity of all religions. It is almost poetic in its expression like a Sufi song, which, while expressing deep philosophical truths has the capacity of taking the reader unawares by Beauty and giving some rare touch of the soul's inner rapture. In a very clear, simple, lucid style the author discloses to us the real aims, objects, and the Ideal of all our various conflicting religious strivings, and finally convinces the reader of their ultimate essential unity. The work is done with admirable care and masterliness and is replete with apt and carefully chosen quotations from almost all the scriptures of the world, and the sayings of many great religious masters and poets. There is hardly a page which does not contain a rare and inspiring quotation, and there are pages after pages where one softly glides on from quotation to quotation of rarest charm and beauty as well as of greatest spiritual wisdom. From the beginning to the end, the book is delightful, captivating, inspiring. The author performs his work so well and is so successful in it that one can safely say that after reading it even the most obstinate sceptic is bound to modify his views and get a broad vision of Truth ...There will be many who will be inspired and guided by this book and will find their way greatly cleared and illumined. Religion is something very intricate and complex...This little book points the straight way with an unerring finger and is a very good guide to an individual wanderer as well as for the masses, and specially for India it will be of great help and use to dispel the dark clouds of superstition and ignorance that are floating over the atmosphere today...It is an extremely difficult task to apply the philosophical terms of one religion to another, for there are intricacies of thoughts and conceptions that differ greatly in their inner sense; but the accuracy with which it is done in this book is striking and extremely praiseworthy. The passages selected from various scriptures are appropriate and correct and its quotations do supply very instructive material for a comparative study of religions;" Syed Ibrahim Dara, profound scholar of Islamic mysticism and also of Indian philosophies, religions, and yoga, in the *Triveni*, of Madras, for May-June, 1933. in a letter to Dr. Bhagavan Das, Syed Dara wrote that "Shri Aurobindo Ghosh" (in whose Ashrama at Pondicherry he was then studying) "considers it a good book."

"Dr. Bhagavan Das has rendered a public service in bringing out such a useful and informing work...In these days of communal conflict and aggressive self-assertion it is a solace to be able to turn to a volume which attempts to prove that religion has its roots in Unity and not Strife...Every student ought to have the chance of going through this book to help him to realise that his own particular religion is but one aspect of a great harmonious whole and that the well-being of the individual as also of the race lies in trying to get at this Fundamental Unity...With his keen spiritual perception, brilliant intellect, and wealth of scholarship, Dr. Bhagavan Das was pre-eminently fitted for the task...which he has accomplished with such remarkable success;" Dr. G. N. Chakravarti, M.A., LL.B., D. Sc, D. Litt., Vice-Chancellor, for six years, of the Lucknow University.

"I read some extracts from your address on *The Essential Unity of All Religions* and found them extremely interesting and instructive. I am now glad to learn that you have expanded your address into a book, and have no doubt that the book will be welcome as a real contribution to the religious thought of our country"; Dr. Sir Mohammad Iqbal, M. A, Ph. D., Bar-at-Law, of Lahore, the most famous Urdu poet of the time.

CONCORDANCE-DICTIONARY TO THE YOGA-SUTRA-BHASHYA. "An important and instructive glossary-index"; M.M. Dr. Ganga Nath Jha, M.A, D. Litt. "Not only a concordance but a very full dictionary also;...bears ample evidence of the author's well-known masterly capacity of going deep into the meanings of words and vast comparative knowledge of eastern and western lore..Simply indispensable by every one who wishes to study the Yoga-Bhashya with the wish to judge the meanings of words and phrases independently.. Even more indispensable to one who wishes to study the Samskrt text through the medium of the English language and in comparison with convesponding ideas of western psychology and philosophy:" Dr. Mangal Deva Shastri, M.A., D. Phil. (Oxon.), Principal, Goverment Samskrt College, Benares.

THE MANAGER, INDIAN BOOK SHOP, BENARES CITY.